They're Playing Our Song

Max Wilk

NEW YORK ZOETROPE

1986

They're Playing Our Song

New York Zoetrope
838 Broadway
New York, NY 10003

© *1973, 1986 Max Wilk*
All rights reserved. Published 1973.
Revised edition 1986.
Printed in the United States of America
90 89 88 87 86 5 4 3 2 1

Library of Congress Cataloging in Publication Number:
86-42926

ISBN 0-918432-79-0

They're Playing Our Song *was set in Caledonia by Crane Typesetting Services. The book was printed and bound by the Maple-Vail Book Manufacturing Group at their York, PA plant.*

The author wishes to thank the following music publishers for special permission to reprint portions of the lyrics of these songs:
BARTON MUSIC CORP.: "High Hopes" and "Time After Time"

CHAPPELL & CO., INC.: "I Wish I Were in Love Again." Copyright © 1937 by Chappell & Co., Inc. Copyright renewed. Used by permission of Chappell & Co., Inc.

"Bewitched." Copyright © 1941 by Chappell & Co., Inc. Copyright renewed. Reprinted by permission of Chappell & Co., Inc.

"The Eagle and Me." Copyright © 1944 by Chappell & Co., Inc. Reprinted by permission of Chappell & Co., Inc.

"How Are Things in Glocca Morra?" Copyright © 1946 by Chappell & Co., Inc. Reprinted by permission of Chappell & Co., Inc.

"Zip." Copyright © 1951 by Chappell & Co., Inc. Reprinted by permission of Chappell & Co., Inc.

FAMOUS MUSIC PUBLISHING COMPANIES: "Louise" by Leo Robin and Richard A. Whiting. Copyright © 1929 by Famous Music Corporation. Copyright renewed 1956 by Famous Music Corporation.

"Beyond the Blue Horizon" by Leo Robin, Richard A. Whiting and W. Franke Harling. Copyright © 1930 by Famous Music Corporation. Copyright renewed 1957 by Famous Music Corporation.

"Thanks for the Memory" by Leo Robin and Ralph Rainger. Copyright © 1937 by Paramount Music Corporation. Copyright renewed 1964 by Paramount Music Corporation.

"Says My Heart" by Frank Loesser and Burton Lane. Copyright © 1938 by Famous Music Corporation. Copyright renewed 1965 by Famous Music Corporation.

"I Said No" by Frank Loesser and Jule Styne. Copyright © 1941 by Paramount Music Corporation. Copyright renewed 1968 by Paramount Music Corporation.

FRANK MUSIC CORP. (*Music and lyrics by Frank Loesser*): "Adelaide's Lament" (From: *Guys and Dolls*). © 1950 Frank Music Corp. Used by permission.

"Fugue for Tin Horns" (From: *Guys and Dolls*). © 1950 Frank Music Corp. Used by permission.

"Guys and Dolls" (From: *Guys and Dolls*). © 1950 Frank Music Corp. Used by permission.

"I'll Know" (From: *Guys and Dolls*). © 1950 Frank Music Corp. Used by permission.

"The Oldest Established" (From: *Guys and Dolls*). © 1950 Frank Music Corp. Used by permission.

"Paris Original" (From: *How to Succeed in Business Without Really Trying*). © 1961 Frank Music Corp. Used by permission.

T. B. HARMS COMPANY: "All the Things You Are," "Ol' Man River," and "Why Do I Love You"

On My Way to the Theatre, by Hy Kraft (The Macmillan Company)
The Elegant Auctioneers, by Wesley Towner (Hill & Wang)
The Story of Irving Berlin, by Alexander Woollcott (G. P. Putnam's Sons)

Gracious thanks are extended to the ASCAP Archives and Michael Kerker for numerous photographs, to the BMI Archives for the photograph of Jerry Bock & Sheldon Harnick, and to the collection of Toby Garson for the photograph of Bert Kalmar & Harry Ruby.

To **Irving Caesar,** *who got me started, and to*

the late **Robert Emmett Dolan,** *who kept me on key*

Author's Note

A FTER THE many months spent on this work, one is left with a sense of accomplishment, but also a certain measure of frustration. The *ASCAP Biographical Dictionary* of 1966, which lists that organization's members and their songs, runs 814 pages. Broadcast Music, Inc., represents another phalanx of active members.

No matter how much one would wish it to be all-inclusive, this collection of oral histories is far from definitive. Space, time, and physical effort have arbitrarily dictated its cast of characters and their vast contributions to the area of half a century's history.

Before angry critics and single-minded partisans descend on me, demanding to know why Mr. X has received longer shrift than Mr. Y, and where is the in-depth study of Mr. Z—a final word.

Those who don't appear on these pages are men whose biographies or personal stories already exist on library shelves. There are others, such as Duke Ellington, Arthur Schwartz and his witty partner, Howard Dietz, who are known to be writing their own books. Cheers, gentlemen. There are far too many of your fellows whose wisdom and experience are lost to us, primarily because no one thought to start them writing it all down. Let's hope that, from now on, American songwriters will cast off their somewhat anonymous existence.

Mr. Abe Burrows, a demon etymologist, has picked me up on that particular word. "Anonymous?" he complained. "I don't think it's right to call them that! Just remember, they *did it*, man!"

But hadn't far too many of those talented creators been reduced by time to an ignominious silence, mere printed names atop pages of yellowing sheet music?

"Maybe," agreed Abe, "but let's face it, nobody can have a better reward than to have somebody, years after, singing his song!"

When an author completes a work of fiction, he has usually no one to thank except his loving wife (for having kept the house quiet during moments of creative stress), his publisher (for the underwriting), and his faithful typist.

But with an assemblage of personal reminiscences such as this book, a great many more obligations are incurred. Having spent the past eighteen-odd months recording and writing down this collection of profiles of American songwriters, I have a long list of debits against my personal account. Herewith I would like to try and settle them. Or at least to let my creditors know I am aware of the obligations.

First off, to those who are no longer present, but whose accounts are long-standing . . .

To my father, the late Jacob Wilk, who had the foresight to leave Minneapolis and come to New York and take up a career in show business. Thus, when other youths of my tender pre-teens were involved in Saturday games, I was gorging myself in free seats at Saturday matinees in New York, developing a massive taste for the American musical comedies of the 1920s and '30s—a vice that continues to this day. For having constantly encouraged me in this pursuit rather than insisting that I play baseball, I will always owe my father my heartfelt thanks.

To the late Lee Shubert, who, remarkably, provided me with a pass to his local theatre in New Haven, Connecticut, for the entire four years of my stay at Yale, 1937–1941, where I matriculated in musical comedies by Rodgers and Hart, Schwartz and Dietz, Cole Porter, Irving Berlin, *et al.*, again, thanks.

To my late friend and employer Leland Hayward, master agent, theatrical producer, and raconteur, whose original notion it was to have me do a magazine article about Irving Caesar, the lyricist of *No, No, Nanette,* and who took it upon himself to sell said article, sight unseen, to Clay Felker at *New York* magazine, thank you.

And to the late Robert Emmett Dolan, who was not only a skillful and wise teacher, a constant source of ideas, as well as an open-handed donor of his time, his experience, and his considerable store of anecdota about Broadway and Hollywood (Bobby worked on both coasts for four decades, as musical director, composer, film producer, and author), the mere word *thanks* seems inadequate . . . especially since he's no longer around to take his bow in person.

Wherever these gentlemen have gone, I hope it's a paradise where every tryout is a winner and every song an immediate hit.

And now for some of those who have assisted in the mammoth task of getting me to the printer on time (well, only six months late).

P. G. Wodehouse, who took time out from a busy schedule involving his ninetieth birthday and a new novel to write his reminiscences of the late Jerome Kern and their joyful collaboration on the Princess Theatre musicals. Who could ask for a more stimulating pen pal? Thank you, sir.

To Abel Green, Ye Ed of *Variety,* who opened up his newspaper files to this wandering quondam stringer, and who was generous with his advice, counsel, and recollections. Sans Abel and *Variety,* one would be steering through show biz like some tourist trying to fight his way in and out of the Paris Métro without a Frenchman. Thanks!

To Joshua Logan, Renaissance man of the theatre, who cheerfully shared his recollections of the various shows with which he was associated, thank you, sir. And the same gratitude must be shown to Larry Adler, virtuoso of the mouth organ; to Robert Russell Bennett, the dean of American musical arrangers and a composer in his own right; to William Hammerstein, son of the late, great Oscar, who gladly spent many hours discussing the personal life of his father; to Margaret Whiting, daughter of the late Dick, who illuminated the work of her father; to Bernard Herrmann, composer of the scores of *Citizen Kane* and *Psycho*, who was especially helpful on the subject of Vincent Youmans; to John Fearnley, the director, for background information on Rodgers and Hammerstein; and to Edward Eliscu, for encouragement and for directing me to others . . . Thanks.

Richard Lewine, who with Alfred Simon compiled the valuable *Encyclopedia of Theatre Music* (a new edition of which is due soon), deserves special thanks for long and friendly assistance. To anyone interested in our pop music, the Lewine-Simon book is as vital as a scuba outfit to a diver.

Mrs. Pat Englund Lefferts helped me a great deal to amass tapes; if you can't get there to do the interview yourself, I recommend highly this attractive, witty actress. Walter Wager, a successful author, as well as editor of *ASCAP Today*, the bulletin of that society, has helped with photographs, and with certain extracts from interviews of his own, published in that mazagine. I am indebted to the *Dramatists Guild Quarterly* for use of material originally published in its pages.

Buddy Robbins, of Chappell, Inc., who is the son of the late, great music publisher Jack Robbins, has been truly helpful with the ever complicated problem of clearing away certain copyright restrictions on quotations of lyrics printed herein, as have many other music firms. Knowing full well how difficult they might have made it, I appreciate their cooperation.

Producers Cy Feuer and Ernie Martin, composer Burton Lane, and the jovial Abe Burrows have all contributed their reminiscences of the late Frank Loesser with lavish enthusiasm. Lee Adams, Harold Rome, Sheldon Harnick and Jerry Bock, Saul Chaplin and Jay Gorney, lyricists and composers all gainfully employed, have taken valuable time off from their professional labors to indulge this author's curiosity and often naïve questioning. Far too many of their contributions have, alas, not reached the printed page because of time and space limitations, but they all have my deepest gratitude.

And to return to my opening thesis, this is not fiction—ergo, not a one-man job. To Miss Pat Irving, who has miraculously brought a certain amount of order out of the 220,000-odd words of material, the author's awe-struck thanks. To Miss Louise Stein, who cheerfully transcribed some sixty-odd tape cassettes onto manuscript paper, likewise. And to Mrs. Barbara Wilk, the author's wife, who did manage to keep the house quiet for all these months without complaint, a low bow.

Now, to all those people whom I've seen and talked with and whose personal reminiscences and herein set down, one small confession. It's been a positive pleasure to be with you all—a dream assignment for anyone who's been humming and whistling your works for all these years. How could it be anything but joyful to chat with Ira Gershwin? To have Harold Arlen relate how he broke into songwriting? (He still insists it was purely accidental.) To have Leo Robin report on the very first stirrings of the film musical, back in 1929 at Paramount, when he supplied lyrics to the young Maurice Chevalier? To schmooze with Harry Ruby about his hilarious collaboration with the late Bert Kalmar? To spend hours with the venerable Harry Warren, who started the tidal wave of Hollywood musicals when he and the late Al Dubin sat out in sun-baked Burbank and turned out the score for *42nd Street*? To listen to Johnny Mercer reminisce, to talk with Richard Rodgers, and to travel backward in time to the early origins of Messrs. Berlin, Kern, Youmans, Hammerstein, Larry Hart, and the rest? I can only hope that they all give my readers as much pleasure as they have given to me.

But actual credit for the origin of this book does not rest with me. The initial spark was ignited by an energetic gentleman named Irving Caesar, lyricist, scholar, raconteur, enthusiastic performer of his own considerable body of work ("Tea for Two," "Sometimes I'm Happy," "Swanee," "I Want to Be Happy," *et al.*), and a very good friend. Mr. Caesar, the subject of that first interview in *New York* magazine, it was who got me in here, so to speak, on yet another pass.

So, to paraphase the great Brahms, if there's anybody else I've forgotten . . . I thank you.

Westport, Connecticut
New York
London

Author's Note:
November 1986

In a very specific sense, this book and the oral histories which are its spine have become a time capsule, circa 1971–1972. Now, sixteen years later, rather than deal with the question of tenses, i.e. "he said" rather than "he says" in the myriad quotations from those who have since left us, I have made a conscious decision to retain the original form. Their words still pertain here, even if the talents who originally spoke them are, alas, not.

Contents

They're Playing Our Song

Preface

It's fifteen years since this book was first published, and far too many of the talented people it celebrates have left us. But not their work. American musical comedy, the popular song, our jazz and our blues—they're all an origination of a purely American culture.

I must confess I feel sorry for the songwriters who are working today. Not that there aren't a lot of wonderful new talents around, but they're going to have it a whole lot tougher than my contemporaries. At one time, the songwriter had control of the ballgame, so to speak. When he wrote a song, he took it to his publisher; then that worthy took it and bet his own money on it. He published the song, put it out in front of the people, and worked to get it on records, or pushed to have it performed by leading stars in cabarets, or on vaudeville, or on radio and TV.

That, alas, is a gone era. Nowadays, the publisher doesn't control anything. Everything is in the hands of the performing and recording artists. Most artists have their own publishing companies, and their own crew of writers—that is, whenever they don't write their own songs. As for the publisher (those few who are left), chances are he's owned by a conglomerate, and when you're controlled by such a massive structure, it's what that organization wants done which counts. And conglomerates know only one thing—they want big name stars, with big name hits . . . all the way.

None of the stars of my day, the Doris Days, the Sinatras and the Streisands, started as big names. When they began, they were unknown. But individuals —not conglomerates—recognized their talents, and nurtured them into stardom. The same went for us songwriters; publishers nurtured us, too. Today, there's nobody around to discover talent and nurse it along, and to take chances with it. It's a conglomerate world.

There are many books—too many—written about show biz, theatre, movies, and performers. But most of them are written by well-meaning people who are on the outside, forever looking in. Since they really don't know, they make a lot of it up. Too much of it.

Max Wilk's book has to do with the opinions, ideas, and the philosophies of most of America's greatest songwriters. Read it because it's authentic. He didn't make it up. He sat with us all and listened, and asked us the right questions. He knew which ones to ask because he's been around the business all his life. He was, so to speak, to the manner born; he's written and produced, and he's been there with us. When you find it all laid out by him on the printed pages, know that it was not done by a johnny-come-lately outsider assembling old newspaper clippings. Max knows us, warts and all, and when you've read the book, you'll know us too. If you missed reading *They're Playing Our Song* in its first (long out-of-print) edition, I urge you to grab the book. If you want to be a songwriter—and it always seems everyone who can strum or hum does, you owe it to yourself to learn how the successful ones of my era accomplished it.

If you ask me about the future, I have to be bullish about the work of all my songwriting friends of what I am certain has to be called a golden age. Fifty years from now, you'll still be hearing Kern and Rodgers, Berlin and Sondheim, and Cole Porter. Believe me, I've seen proof of the stamina and longevity of my own work. Just in the past couple of years, I've had two big hits, Linda Ronstadt doing "Guess I'll Hang My Tears Out To Dry," and Barry Manilow with "I've Heard That Song Before"—both forty-year-old songs!

And it's heartwarming to know that right now, here in 1986, when we've come through rock-and-roll, and punk rock, and hard rock, and bubble-gum music, and whatever other noise you hear being toted down the street by kids with boom-boxes, or by cowboys with their car-stereos playing full blast in traffic, I could go last night to the Kool Jazz Festival and hear my own "Time After Time" being played by great jazz musicians for umpteen lovely choruses!

Tomorrow night they'll be playing Gershwin, or Lerner & Loewe, or songs by Arthur Schwartz, perhaps Harold Arlen, Burke and Van Heusen, always more Berlin, and professor, could you give us some Robin and Rainger, or Warren and Dubin, Gordon and Revel, or Johnny Mercer, or Kalmar and Ruby, or even more

June 1986   Jule Styne

Introduction

E ARLY IN the fall of 1970, a revival of *No, No, Nanette* opened in Boston and was immediately the surprise hit of the season. Ruby Keeler and Patsy Kelly, Bobby Van and Helen Gallagher, tap dancing, music and lyrics by Vincent Youmans, Otto Harbach, and Irving Caesar—the critics and the audiences adored it all. Faithfully transported to the stage, this 1924 musical comedy, re-created with style, affection, and respect, was the talk of Boston. (And the utter confusion of Broadway, where nobody had expected anything from its revival.)

When I first heard about *Nanette* from Lester Osterman, who had booked it for his 46th Street Theatre, I called on Irving Caesar at his Brill Building office on 49th Street, where he has been for more than forty years, to congratulate him on the good news from Boston.

Irving is a short, effusive man in his early seventies, gifted with total recall, a deep fund of anecdotes, and a solid sense of social responsibility. He is also a major American songwriter. He stretched out on his Barcalounger and puffed on one of his ever-present cigars. "You know why *Nanette* works today?" he demanded. "It's the Big Pendulum—*taste*—and, friend, when that starts to swing . . . Here it comes, swinging back from all the rock music and the strobe lights and raggedy kids and the nudity. Here's a show where the old man takes his wife and up on the stage there's music and pretty people and tap dancing, and he's sitting there telling himself, '*This* is one those damn kids of ours are going to see—and they'll enjoy it or else!' " Caesar beamed. "This is camp backlash!

"This whole revival is like a show libretto," continued Caesar. "*Nanette* and me—the whole thing was always crazy!"

Young Irving was standing outside the old Friars Club, on 48th Street, one balmy spring evening in 1924. "Waiting for the afternoon poker game to start. I was a kid, but I was doing all right. Songs in the *Greenwich Village Follies*, and I'd had 'Swanee' with my friend George Gershwin, so I had plenty of money for cards and horses. Then Otto Harbach came along. Wanted to know what I was doing. I couldn't tell him I was waiting for a card game, so I let him walk me over to the theatre where Harry Frazee had *Nanette* in rehearsal. 'You know, Irving, maybe you could give us a couple of extra lyrics,' Otto said. 'Vincent Youmans and I are running dry and we could use a little help.'

"Vincent and I went home that night and in about ten minutes I wrote 'You Can Dance with Any Girl at All'—I can write very fast when it hits me. Sometimes lousy, sure, but always fast. What the hell, Gershwin and I wrote 'Swanee' in about eleven minutes flat!

"Then, the next night, we wrote 'Too Many Rings Around Rosie.' Working with Youmans was like with Gershwin. There was inspiration in just being around the guy. Little by little, I supplanted all the lyrics except for a couple of Harbach's.

"Now comes the crazy part. We open in Detroit. Disaster. The show dies. Five thousand the first week. Four thousand the second. Harry Frazee, who probably never drew a sober breath in his life but was a hell of a producer, didn't get upset. Why should he? He never looked at the show. But he knew how to produce. He got hold of me and Youmans and said, 'You guys write me a big hit for the second act by tomorrow, or I'm sending for McCarthy and Tierney.' They were hot—they'd just written *Kid Boots*—so we didn't want them to take over. I got hold of Youmans, and we met the next morning in the dining room of the Statler, where they had a piano on the bandstand. The waiters were setting the tables for a Rotarian luncheon. We're up there, working away against time—Detroit's a town where people eat early. Would you believe it, we had 'I Want to Be Happy' in ten, eleven minutes, and we started playing it up there, and, so help me, the waiters were all singing it with us. Even those first Rotarians who came in early joined in, before they ate their lunch!"

That song helped, but not enough. "Frazee was a gambler with guts. He whipped us all. Frank Mandel, Harbach, Youmans, and me, never gave up pushing us to make the show better. We opened in Chicago. Terrible notices. Business rotten. Frazee never quit. Sam Harris, who owned the theatre, let us stay there. We kept on rehearsing, changing, fixing."

And what about the eventual show-stopper? From what cockeyed set of circumstances did "Tea for Two" spring?

"Hell," says Irving, "that one is even crazier. We had it before we even went out of New York! I lived in an apartment up on 54th. Gertie Lawrence and Bea Lillie had a little maisonette down the street. They'd just arrived in town in *Charlot's Revue* and they were the belles of the town. Gave parties every night. You'd see every blueblood there, hanging around the showgirls.

Vince played piano so beautifully, was talented, charming, and I had a song in their show, so Gertie always invited us. She'd run down the street, stand under my window, and whistle up. That meant the party was starting.

"Well, one night I was lying down, taking a little nap before the party, and Youmans came into my apartment and started shaking me. He had a tune he wanted set. 'Aw, Vince,' I mumbled, 'not now, I'm half asleep—tomorrow.' But he went to the piano and started it—dee, da *dum*, dee da *dum*, dee da *dum*, and me, I'm like a fire horse, I get up, I'm half awake, he plays it a couple of times and I say, 'Okay, here's a dummy lyric: tomorrow I'll write the real one. *"Picture you upon my knee, with tea for two and two for tea, and me for you and you for me alone."* That's lousy, but it'll do.' 'Keep going, keep going!' he yells, and I went on, still half asleep, so help me, and groggy. I don't know where the words were coming from. Subconscious, I guess. Anyway, in about eight minutes it was done, finished!

"It went in in Chicago, after that lousy opening. We kept on working, and after a couple of weeks, would you believe it, we got the critics back in? We got raves! We stayed in Chicago for *three years!* We had four companies playing all over the country before we ever opened it in New York!"

Eventually, we began to discuss the deep cloud of anonymity which has descended upon songwriters in the past decade or so. In times past, a more receptive public had treated its balladeers as celebrities. In fact, audiences flocked to night clubs and vaudeville theatres whenever popular composers appeared.*

"With the material we had, how could we be bad?" said Irving. "You know, there never was a songwriter who ever played vaudeville who wasn't a hit! And we could do it again today, believe me." (A fact which he was to prove in his one-man recital at the YMHA on 92nd Street in New York, and in several appearances on the David Frost TV show.)

I asked him why there was such rapport between audiences and song-writers.

"We make contact!" said Irving, between furious puffs of his cigar. "I'm a lyric-writer, correct? What is a real lyric-writer? He's a fellow who can't help singing, and he sings through his words. A poet or a versifier—they must be satisfied to write their words down. That's all. But a lyricist—he's a *minstrel!* Think how this whole business of popular songs came about—through the old-time minstrel shows. The fellows who sang in those shows needed more songs to sing, and if they could write 'em, they wrote 'em for themselves, and if they could write fast enough, instead of going on the road for ten dollars a week and living in those terrible boardinghouses in small one-horse towns, they learned that they could *sell* their songs—for ten dollars or fifteen—and it saved them from going out on the road! So some of the earliest writers of popular songs in this country were those guys who wanted to stay home!

"Now take me. I'm an inarticulate composer. Believe me, if I could write music instead of lyrics, I'd be glad to, because it's much easier. Why, composers,

---

* I later mentioned this broad generality to William McCaffrey, who began his career as office boy in the executive offices of the massive B. F. Keith circuit and ended up booking the showcase Palace, on Broadway. "Absolutely correct," said he. "Song-writers' acts were known as 'And-then-I-wrotes,' and the audiences loved them. Sang and hummed along with the man up there on the stage. It was early Mitch Miller."

even the great ones, ought to get down on their knees every day and say, 'Thank God I'm a composer—it's so easy. I can write a tune every hour of the day or night, but thank God I don't have to write the words!' Look at the statistics! For every lyric-writer there are thirty composers, at least! Now, when I tell you I'm inarticulate, I mean most of the time I'm hovering over the piano with my collaborator, helping him get the right melodic line. Just remember this fact— when you write a song in ten or twenty minutes, nobody knows who did what to whom!"

Ten or twenty minutes?

"It's happened," said Irving. "An idea hits you—you both take off. You know all this stuff about how songs are written? Well, kid, if you're a born songwriter, you just *know* how to do it. It's *instinct*. Go ask a tightrope walker how he walks that tightrope. He says, 'Well, when I think I'm going too much to the left, I go to the right, et cetera.' And he walks his tightrope and he makes a helluva living."

When was he first infected with the songwriting virus?

"Oh, a long time ago. I was a kid, and somebody took me into the Minor's Burlesque Theatre, on the Bowery, near Houston or Stanton Street. A very famous place. Harry Minor was a great producer of burlesque; he also owned Minor's Drugstore. This would be about 1909 or 1910. Anyway, there was Irving Berlin, and I heard him up there singing 'Alexander's Ragtime Band.' See, that's how you sold a song in those days; you got up and sang'em to the people. So if I'm a songwriter today, it's because of Irving Berlin.

"The next time I can remember getting a thrill was when I saw Harry Von Tilzer, at Hammerstein's Victoria—a music hall. I can see him before me right now, in his striped pants and cutaway coat (in those days it was called a Prince Albert). Ah, he looked so smart and dapper; he had a little grayish hair, and he was singing all his own songs, huge hits of the day: 'Wait Till the Sun Shines, Nelly,' 'I Want a Girl Just Like the Girl Who Married Dear Old Dad,' 'She's Only a Bird in a Gilded Cage.'

"That's when I decided I wanted to be like those guys, standing up on the stage and singing your own song, and getting such a great audience response— all the people in the theatre humming along with you, letting you know they like your stuff."

All the great people who've written the music and lyrics that my generation grew up with for the past forty or fifty years—why doesn't anybody want to listen to *them?*

Irving shrugged, and stared out his office window at the skyline of the city. After a moment he spoke softly. "Time is very cruel," he said. "Nobody pays any attention. Turn on your radio—what do you hear? Music? No. *Noise!*" His voice began to rise along with his temper. "There's a whole new generation out there that've never heard of us. Why? Because they've been brainwashed. Yes, you heard me right, brainwashed! The people who have taken over this so-called music business—the jukeboxes, the record business, the mass communications media, radio, TV—they have it tied up tight, and they're peddling junk. It's easy—you keep good stuff off the air long enough and fill the kids' ears with junk, something quick and noisy, twenty-four hours a day, then what do you expect the formative minds will prefer? Read Pavlov! We're raising a generation of zombies!

"And it's a damned shame," he went on, "when you consider that the popular song of the past half-century had the largest impact on American culture of any so-called art form. Why, for God's sake, the popular song *is* American culture! A universal language, we exported it all over the world. Our jazz, our dances, they loved it everywhere! Ballads, fox-trots, one-steps, everything—we made the world sing and dance. But today our own kids haven't a clue."

Wouldn't they tell you they created their own art form?

"*I* tell you, they've been brainwashed," Irving said.

I went away from Irving Caesar's Brill Building office that afternoon feeling depressed. I walked up Broadway, past the busy record shops with amplified noise braying from speakers above their open doors.

Irving had claimed that the success of *Nanette* was indicative of a change in public taste—that the pendulum was swinging back toward melody. But was it? Or was the success of *Nanette* just an isolated fluke, an outpouring of nostalgic worship for the good old days by middle-aged types like yours truly, who've grown up with American popular music as a sort of second language?

I stepped inside a record shop. Outside, the store window featured the latest hits on LPs and tape cassettes. Down the street, the film version of *Fiddler on the Roof* was playing, but this store was featuring the latest recordings of Cat Stevens, Chicago, Sly and the Family Stone, Joe Cocker, Frank Zappa and the Mothers of Invention. The "groups," the purveyors of "youth-oriented" music, were all over the place.

Show tunes? In a small bin, about eighteen inches deep.

Jazz? In the same segregated area.

Pop singers *à la* Sinatra, Dean Martin, Ella Fitzgerald, Barbra Streisand, and Steve and Eydie? Also tucked away in a small pocket of their own.

Sheet music? Forget it. Thirty, forty years ago it was part of our lives, available on racks in every music store, or at your local Woolworth's, where the pianist would cheerfully "demonstrate" the latest songs for you before you plunked down your quarter and took one home.

A few days later I talked with the late Robert Emmett Dolan, who was a composer, conductor, and film producer of musicals for more than four decades. "In terms of harmonics, I don't feel that we've simply stood still," he observed. "As opposed to the 1930s or '40s, when songwriters like Gershwin and Kern and Rodgers and Arlen were using harmonics, I actually think we've retrogressed. Those days were much richer musically. Remember how often the word 'lush' was applied to our popular music? One of the things I've said to my own son Casey, who's seventeen and very much into this hard-rock thing, is, 'I listen to it, but I get no surprises.' I've heard records galore today where, literally, the guitarists will play one chord, from beginning to end. They'll keep on doing variations on that one chord, but it's the same chord all the way through."

A few weeks later, when I came to discuss this phenomenon with Harold Arlen, he said ruefully, "Nobody wants harmony. This is a percussive era."

I am the father of two young men, and in the past few years, whether I wanted to or not, I've been exposed to a good deal of what they considered "current." And, believe it or not, this middle-aged Social Democrat has discovered quite a few current talents to whom he responds. I was a Beatle fan from the first yeh-yeh-yeh. I am impressed by Bob Dylan, enjoy Simon and Garfunkel, respond to Joan Baez and Judy Collins, rock with Carole King, and find the classic blues form well served by Taj Mahal, B. B. King, and quite a few others. Burt Bacharach and Jim Webb are writing first-rate songs, and so is the less well-known Randy Newman, and if you dug Bessie Smith, how can you not respond to the late Janis Joplin?

I may not be completely turned on, but I will not stand accused of refusing to tune in.

Conversely, I am not a mindless idolator of everything that's gone on before. I refuse to serve as the Clarence Darrow of kitsch and try to make some sort of case for the "cultural value" of most of what's been pounded into our ears for the past half-century by tone-deaf publishers, greedy jobbers, and all those hack songwriters who've been trying to turn a fast buck. Perhaps *you* enjoy such exhibits as Roy Acuff and his Smoky Mountain Boys singing "I've Got Pins and Needles in My Heart," but *I* pass. If your psyche was touched by "There's a Star-Spangled Banner Waving Somewhere," good for you. Mine was not, and I can also do without most songs about Dixie, Texas, sweethearts named Ida, Charmaine, Marie, Sue, old farm homes, old gangs, buddies, pals, rivers, lakes, and hometowns. (Of course they were popular hits. Wasn't it H. L. Mencken who postulated, "Nobody ever went broke underestimating American public taste"?)

But there is still one basic rule that applies even to current pop music. Only two or three percent of what's written and recorded "makes it." Ninety-seven percent of all the music and lyrics that are being recorded in eight-track stereo today will be forgotten by this time next year. Two, three percent get a response from the listeners and make the Top Fifty on the charts, or scale the heights of the Top Ten. The rest, as they always have, disappear into limbo.

What propels those chosen hit songs up to the Himalayan heights of mass success? I only wish I could tell you. I'd be rich and so would you. The best approximation I've been able to unearth is that something indefinable in the music or the lyric manages to pluck at a nerve inside the listener. Somehow, it *induces a response.* When enough of those nerves respond, people remember the song, and the chances are good that they'll make it into a success.

Some songwriters have pounded away at the piano all their lives and come up with a lot of songs but no hits. Some have hit it once—one song that remains in the public memory bank. When I was young, the entire country was suddenly delighted with a nonsense ditty called "The Music Goes Round and Round." I leave it to other researchers to unearth what became of its authors, Mike Riley and Eddie Farley. Years later an obscure country-music fiddler named Al Dexter burst into success with a lament called "Pistol Packing Mama." To the best of my knowledge, he never repeated it . . . nor did the authors of "Yes, We Have No Bananas" or "The Hut-Sut Song."

But other songwriters have a long list of "standards"—successful songs that became lasting hits. People listened to their music, responded to it, hummed it. Sang the lyrics in the street, in the shower, or into some lady's ear. Songwriters who have consistently turned out successes must certainly have something to communicate about the creative process of songwriting.

I went to search for the literature on the subject. Surely, I thought, there must exist a decent number of books in which songwriters such as Irving Berlin or Jerome Kern or their contemporaries—those who have consistently plucked at that public nerve—have discussed the subject.

The library shelves I checked were disappointing.

True, there are a few biographies in which one can read the early life history of Mr. Berlin, Rodgers and Hammerstein, Hoagy Carmichael, and certain others. Cole Porter is the subject of a definitive book, only lately published and long overdue. The Gershwins have been discussed in *The Gershwin Years*. But from that point on, unless you wish to include those lushly produced and decorated "songbooks" which publishers are wont to put out from time to time, usually at Christmas, that's about it.* If you really want to know something about most American songwriters and lyricists, and you haven't access to *Variety's* bound anniversary issues, where rich personal reminiscences are often published, you're about to enter a peculiar zone of silence.

Songwriters are semi-anonymous.

Eventually, I went to discuss the changes in the American pop music scene with Abel Green, the editor of *Variety*, who has been reporting and interpreting show business all his life and must be considered a major authority. I queried him on the anonymity of songwriters.

"Yes, it's true, and I don't know how to explain it," said Mr. Green. "Everybody in this country is involved with music. I used to have a gag that, out of a population of a hundred million Americans, there were a hundred million potential songwriters. When the new census figures came out, I rewrote the gag—now it's *two* hundred million . . .

"Hell, there are more stories about songs and songwriters," he continued, "than about any other branch of show business! I've heard them all my life. Whenever you get a songwriter to talk, he's damned interesting."

"No question," I said. "Maybe I'm prejudiced, but very few songwriters I've ever met have been dull."

"You know something?" mused Mr. Green. "I think songwriters have the greatest obituaries in the world. When a songwriter dies, the minute you read the list of the songs he wrote, you start to identify with him. All those titles, they strike nerves inside of you. It's like Noel Coward said in one of his plays —the remarkable power of cheap music. People read the obit and they respond, 'Oh, my God, he wrote *that*. I remember the first time I heard that song, I was at a dance with a girl . . . ' To remember what each one of his songs did to you is like running through the chapters of your own autobiography."

"A damn shame that reaction sets in only after he shows up on the obit page," I said.

"Well, I can think of one way to avoid that," said Mr. Green. "The woods are still full of healthy songwriters and lyricists. Go talk to them *now*."

If, as Irving Caesar remarked at the very first stirrings of this venture, there's a pendulum of public taste and there are signs that it's beginning to swing away from dissonance and amplified noise back toward melody and harmony and a graceful turn of phrase—well, is it too much to hope that this book may serve to give that pendulum a solid push?

A-one, a-two—and let's take it from the top.

---

* There are two superb exceptions to my thesis about the anonymity of songwriters: Ira Gershwin's *Lyrics on Several Occasions* and Oscar Hammerstein's slim volume *Lyrics*, both of which are excellent representations of the wit, the thoughtfulness, and the assembled wisdom of their authors.

'All the Things You Are'

(Jerome Kern)

YOU CAN'T say anyone's bringing Kern back; it seems that his music has
always been there.

For our elders, there were his early operettas, lovely concoctions that
culminated with those elegant little Princess Theatre shows from 1915 on. For
our parents, there were his later Broadway operettas, the joyous *Sally*, and
Sunny, and then *Show Boat*. Came the '30s and he was turning out *The Cat
and the Fiddle*, *Roberta*, *Music in the Air*, and *Very Warm for May*. And for
us—and now for our own kids, thanks to TV and those film-revival houses—
there's his remarkably fruitful Hollywood period, when he supplied all those
rich scores for Fred and Ginger, for Gene and Rita, and for Irene Dunne, at
the behest of producers who rarely realized how fortunate they were to have
his services.

Songwriters and lyricists and musicians rarely agree on anything, least of
all on someone else's music, but mention any melody of Jerome Kern's and its
potential for posterity—and the argument's over. It was always so. "Kern,"
George Gershwin wrote in a letter to Isaac Goldberg, "was the first composer
who made me conscious that popular music was of inferior quality, and that

musical-comedy music was made of better material. I followed Kern's work and studied each song that he composed. I paid him the tribute of frank imitation, and many things that I wrote at this time [1916] sounded as though Kern had written them himself." Richard Rodgers says, "Kern had his musical roots in the fertile Middle European and English school of operetta-writing, and amalgamated it with everything that was fresh in the American scene to give us something wonderfully new and clear in music-writing." Kern and Irving Berlin maintained a staunch mutual-admiration society. And whenever any of Kern's lyricists—Hammerstein, Harbach, Ira Gershwin, Dorothy Fields, E. Y. Harburg, Johnny Mercer, Leo Robin, or P. G. Wodehouse—discusses his music, it falls into a special category.

The years have flashed past so quickly since that sad day in November 1945 when Kern collapsed and died, in cruel anonymity, on a Manhattan street. To listen to his music gives no indication of the sort of man he was. But to those who knew Kern, who worked with him, were exposed to his strong personality—querulous, iron-willed, assertive—the man himself remains, like his music, very much *there*.

Here, then, a few recollections . . .

From Edward Laska (as told to *Variety*), who collaborated on Kern's first song hit, in 1905, when the young composer was twenty years old:

> It was in 1905 . . . that I was in the midst of writing a musical comedy with the late George McManus, Sam Lehman and Willard Holcomb, based on Mac's first two comic strips, *The Jolly Girls* and *Panhandle Pete*.
>
> . . . I had already achieved a year's experience and a little success in writing and getting songs published . . . and at the Harms rendezvous [T. B. Harms & Co., then headed by Max Dreyfus] I often chatted with a kid who was an aspiring composer . . . he wished he could try me out sometime with some of my lyrics. New composers have great difficulty in getting lyricists to work with them, and in my case I was a double difficulty, for I usually wrote both the words and the music myself. . . .
>
> However, I liked the kid—I say "kid" although he was really only one year younger than I, but at that period of life one year is an enormous difference. I decided to do some songs with him and waited for the right opportunity or idea to come up. . . .
>
> It came suddenly. . . . I had written two songs for a musical comedy that had just opened in Albany, under the management of Frank L. Perley. The show was called *The Girl and the Bandit,* and "My Sweet Little Caraboo," an Indian song of the type that was the rage at that time, turned out to be the hit of the show. . . . I visited Mr. Perley to see if there was something new he needed, for songs are often taken out during those tryout weeks. "Yes," he said. "Write me a duet for Joe Myron and——" I can't even recall the name of the actress, but she was even larger than Joe Myron, and he weighed at least 290.
>
> . . . I got to the Harms building and there was my young friend, as usual, with a straw hat on, of which the top was knocked out, and

a long black cigar in his mouth, being cold-smoked—I don't think I ever saw him really smoke one, but it seemed to inspire him, as he ground out melody after melody without ever bothering to jot them down. He seemed to have an unfathomable well of them. . . . "Jerry," I said . . . "we've got to do a song," and then I gave him the title "How'd You Like to Spoon with Me?" and just its rough rhythm. At once, as though it were a song he had known all his life, he improvised a tune that fit it exactly. "Swell," I said. "Now toss me a verse," and again, in just as long as it takes to play it, he gave me a melody for a fitting verse. At once I wrote what we call a dummy lyric. . . . Jerry was elated and we went over it a few times, when George McManus arrived and I sang the rough dummy lyric to him as Jerry played. "Very good," said Mac, little foreseeing that he was commenting on what was to be the very first song hit of one of America's top composers of musical comedy, and we should not overlook the fact that McManus, too, was yet to achieve his greatest success, *Bringing Up Father*.

The next afternoon I appeared with the completed lyric, and we rehearsed ourselves, Jerry to play and I to sing.

Over to Perley we sped, and when several attractive but later-arriving females were ushered in to him ahead of us, Jerry got sore and wouldn't take it. "Come on, Ed, we'll go to Hayman," so we told the receptionist that we'd be back later, and off we went to Alf Hayman, who was Charles Frohman's general manager, atop the old Empire Theatre.

Hayman liked the song but wanted me to change the word "spoon," as it was entirely unknown in England, and if I would fix it he would have Edna May sing it there. She was then the American sensation of England, as the Salvation Army lass in the famous *Belle of New York*.

Out on the street we discussed the situation, and Jerry agreed that it would kill the song to eliminate the main title word "spoon," and I suggested we go over to the Shuberts.

The Shuberts were then just starting as producers and had one show on and another in rehearsal. Their office was atop the Lyric Theatre on 42nd Street, which had been built for them by the socialite composer Reginald De Koven, especially famous for his "Oh, Promise Me."

Sam Shubert, the leading one of the three brothers, came out to see us, and up chirped Jerry, "We are protégés of Reginald De Koven and have a song for you to hear." I nearly collapsed at hearing who we were, and Shubert, impressed with our connection, led us to an adjoining room with a piano. Jerry played and I sang. All the brothers and several of their managers present were enthusiastic, and at once agreed to feature the song in their then-rehearsing show, *The Earl and the Girl*, to star Eddie Foy, at the Casino Theatre.

Out in the street, we kids, nineteen and twenty respectively, slapped each other on the back and I think we gleefully went into an apothecary's to have a couple of ice-cream sodas. We hardly could realize that we were to have the featured song of this forthcoming Casino Theatre production. . . .

The show . . . opened in Chicago in about two weeks. Jerry went

out, and a wire to me told of the song's enormous hit. It swept the
entire country and then on to England, and all the rest of the English-
singing world, and despite Alf Hayman's skepticism about the word
"spoon," it then became a well-known term throughout Great Britain
and the song was a stupendous hit. . . . In fact, I received a charming
letter from Jerry's widow in response to my condolence when he
passed . . . in which she told me how she met Jerry when she was
seventeen, and when he mentioned that he had composed "How'd You
Like to Spoon with Me?" she thought he was jesting, for since her
childhood she had known it and always thought it was an old English
song. . . . Sweetly, she added that the little song had been a great part
of the beginning of their thirty-five-year romance. . . .

"How'd You Like to Spoon with Me?" was introduced in the
London *Gaieties*, and it led to Kern doing songs for Charles Frohman's
English importations in New York. . . . From this writing of several
songs only for an English production, he gradually got to do a complete
score to the lyrics of an English author he had encouraged to come here
to America, and who has remained here intermittently since then, P.
G. Wodehouse.

. . . Kern's early idol was the late Leslie Stuart, the English author
of the famous *Floradora* . . . And it might be interesting to note that
Kern was the cornerstone of the music-publishing empire of the Dreyfus
brothers, Max and Louis [Chappell, *et al.*], and it was greatly due to
Kern's enormous success that, like the Pied Piper of Hamlin, composers
followed him to Max Dreyfus for great advice and guidance. . . .

. . . Little did we know that day when we wrote "How'd You Like
to Spoon with Me?" that it was the beginning of a great composer's
career. . . .

Edward Laska died three years after he wrote this, but P. G. Wodehouse
is very much still with us, and so are his recollections of his good friend and
collaborator. He writes:

Yes, it certainly was fun doing the princess shows.* We were
all reasonably young and very confident that we were on the verge
of big things . . . though our first effort, *Have a Heart*, had only been
one of those Henry W. Savage things—not much on Broadway but
five years on the road, like most of Savage's. The great thing was that
Guy [Bolton] and Jerry had put them in right with *Very Good, Eddie*,
so we assumed that the next one, *Oh Boy!*, was bound to be a success.
There's nothing that bucks you up like having a manager who just
signs the contract and tells you to go ahead and doesn't make any
suggestions or criticisms. And *Oh Boy!* turned out to be a smash,
though we were dubious about it on the preliminary road tour—

* Kern was then thirty. After contributing songs to European imports, he had
written "They Didn't Believe Me" for *The Girl from Utah*, with Michael Rourke. He
had become friends with Guy Bolton, a librettist from England. The two men were asked
by F. Ray Comstock to supply a show for his tiny 299-seat Princess Theatre in 1915. The
first Princess show was *Nobody Home*. The second, a huge success was called *Very Good,
Eddie*, from which came the lilting song "Babes in the Wood."

especially when I overheard a lady in Schenectady say disgustedly
as she came out, "I do like a show with some *jokes* in it."

My part in the Princess productions was always fun because
Jerry was such a perfect composer to work with. I had met him in
London in 1906 when I had a job at three pounds a week writing
encore verses for Seymour Hicks and Ellaline Terriss (who died not
long ago, aged 100). One day Hicks said that Frohman had brought
over a young American composer who he said was promising, and he
introduced me to Jerry, who looked about fifteen. He had down two
or three songs, including a terrific tune to which I wrote a lyric called
"Mister Chamberlain." The lyric wasn't much, but the music was
irresistible and it always got at least six encores, which kept me busy
writing encore verses. Years later I met Jerry again at the opening
of *Very Good, Eddie,* which I had gone to as the dramatic critic of
Vanity Fair. We fell on each other's necks and he insisted on my
doing the lyrics for the next Princess show.

Our collaboration was conducted mostly over the telephone, as
I was living in Great Neck and he in Bronxville. I would go to bed
all set for a refreshing sleep, and at about three in the morning the
phone would wake me, and it would be Jerry, who had just got a
great tune. He played it to me over the phone and I took down a
dummy.

Jerry hated to turn in at night. I remember once I was staying
at his place and mentioned that I had taken a house in Bellport. This
was at about two A.M. "Let's go and take a look at it," said Jerry.
"What, now?" "Of course." So we set out, arriving at about five, and
I was fully occupied on the return journey with prodding Jerry in the
ribs, he having dozed off at the wheel.

What I loved in Jerry was his indomitable spirit. It was before
my time, but I was told that in his struggling days he had managed
to sell a song to one of the Charles Dillingham shows. He attended
an orchestra rehearsal and frowned a dark frown. "Is that the way
you're going to play my song?" he asked. He was assured that it was.
He immediately collected all the orchestra parts and walked out with
them. And that was at a point in his career when he would have given
his eye teeth to have a song in a Dillingham show. He was a perfec-
tionist, and was prepared to starve in the gutter rather than have his
stuff done wrong.

Nothing could have been more pleasant than my relations with
Jerry. Not a cross word, as they say. But I am told that after *Show
Boat* he became a little difficult and had a good deal to say to his
lyricists about their defects. He also changed from the rollicking spirit
of the Princess days into what you might call The Music Master. I
never saw that side of him. To me he has always been the Jerry of
Oh Boy! and *Oh, Lady! Lady!* and the dozen other shows we did
together.

Perhaps the most famous of all of the Wodehouse-Kern collaborations will
remain the delicately shaped torch song "My Bill," which was written in 1918
but was dropped from *Oh, Lady! Lady!* Three years later, in 1921, it was tried

again in Marilyn Miller's starring show *Sally.* Again it was dropped. Finally, in
a revised version, it came to rest, happily and permanently, in *Show Boat.*
Wodehouse adds:

> What a strange history that song had! I wrote it for Vivienne
> Segal to sing in *Oh, Lady!* and we cut it out as too slow. And I think
> we were right. (Jerry must have thought so, or the cut would never
> have been made, because he and Guy and I were a pretty haughty
> trio by that time and would merely have said, "Oh, yeah?" if the
> management had suggested it.) It was certainly a bit of luck for it
> that it was not done in *Oh, Lady!* Vivienne would have sung it beau-
> tifully, but the atmosphere would have been all wrong for it, *Oh,
> Lady!* being a rapid farce. It was probably Jerry who suggested cutting
> it, for in addition to all his gifts as a composer he was a wonderful
> showman with an instinct for what was right and what wasn't, and he
> would never have hesitated to jettison his best melody if he thought
> the song did not fit.
>
> I never can remember if I wrote the lyric and he set it or the
> other way around. The way we usually worked was that he wrote the
> melody and I put words to it, except in the case of comic trios like
> "Bongo on the Congo" and "Sir Galahad," where the words came
> first.

Kern lived and worked for many years in Bronxville, New York, where,
in addition to creating the music for Broadway successes such as *Sally, Sunny,
Show Boat, Sweet Adeline,* and *Roberta,* he indulged in what was to become
his major passion, the collecting of rare books. Wesley Towner writes, in *The
Elegant Auctioneers:*

> He could not pass a bookstore. A small, amicable, quiet man, with
> tremendous stores of nervous energy, Kern wore horn-rimmed glasses,
> smoked constantly, poured forth hundreds of facile tunes with the
> radio blaring in his ears, and modestly called himself a dull fellow
> with a little talent and lots of luck. In a chronic state of collectomania,
> he amassed in his Bronxville, New York house, a superlative library
> of rare first editions, manuscripts, and autograph letters. . . . He was
> a prudent buyer. An insomniac with a prodigious memory, the Mel-
> ody King, though not much of a reader, nightly pored over old vol-
> umes and acquired an impressive knowledge of collecting points and
> technicalities. His first editions were among the finest extant, many
> of them unique in that they contained notes or autographed senti-
> ments by the authors. . . . Nor was he, for all the immensity of his
> earnings, an easy mark for the price-gouging dealer. "What, three
> hundred dollars for a book!" he would exclaim affably. "That's a lot
> of money to me."
>
> It was perhaps the chase that intrigued Kern most. For once
> in possession of his enviable cache, he decided to sell. His books
> were a source of worry, he said. But he also may have had a pre-
> monition. Luck had dogged him all his life. He had hit the jackpot
> with almost everything he wrote; he had missed embarking on the
> *Lusitania,* and probable death on her ill-fated voyage, because an

alarm clock unaccountably stopped and failed to wake him up. Now, in the closing months of 1928, when Wall Street still portended sky-high profits, some instinct told him to cash in not only his books but also his stocks at their inflated value. . . .

The auction of Kern's books remains one of the landmark sales in the history of American auction houses. He consigned 1,482 items to the Anderson Galleries, a collection that he had spent nearly half a million dollars acquiring. The ensuing sale was held over ten sessions.

When all the chips were down, and the tenth session ended, the dogged players had heaped into the pot $1,729,462 for Kern's half-million dollars' worth of books. . . .
. . . Kern paused in the composition of his newest operetta to send Mitchell Kennerley and his staff a gracious telegram of congratulation and appreciation for their "wonderful conduct of the auction." The next day he went out and bought a book, the first of a new collection that would be sold for his estate by the Parke-Bernet, though for no such astounding figure, far off in 1962.

"I worked with Kern perhaps more than any other composer," says Robert Russell Bennett, the great arranger-conductor. "I went down to Palm Beach and lived on his boat with him once before he went out to Hollywood with a show. First thing he ever did in Hollywood, way back, 1930. A thing called *Men in the Sky*. And it came out and died a horrible death. One of the few pictures in those days that simply didn't pay its way. I worked with him on that. He came back with one number that started out: *'Pat's going to have some luck, Pat's going to have some luck today.'* It didn't get into the show that it was for, but he liked the little 6/8 tune, took it out, and the next show, he brought it out again and said, 'Here's an old friend of yours.' And he was trying it out, and it didn't go in *that* show. So the next time it came up I said, 'Well, maybe you can use Pat in *this* show.' And he laughed and said, 'Poor old man, we'll never see him again.'

"Which is a quote from Ivor Novello, who was a very cute wit in London. I remember once when we were walking past Stone's restaurant on Panton Street in London—Ivor Novello, Kern, and Vivian Ellis, I think—and Novello turned to me and said, 'I say, shall we lapidize?' 'What do you mean, old boy?' I asked. And he said, 'Turn into Stone's!'

"Anyway, the 'Pat' line came from Novello. One time they all went to the theatre, and Novello sat in the box with Kern where they'd been given seats to see this performance. And an actor came on in the first act, and as he made an exit Ivor said, 'Poor old man, we'll never see him again.' And Kern said, 'Oh, Ivor, what are you talking about? He comes back in the second act—it's a very important part.' So Novello says, 'We're not going to see him again because we're jolly well getting out of here!' That's what Jerry was referring to, about his own little song.

"You just wouldn't know where to start in talking about Kern. He's an absolutely fantastic character. It was a different stunt every day. He'd wake up and say, 'How'm I going to shock them *today*?' Kern used to say to me, 'Anybody that dislikes Beethoven—that's all right with me. I have no use for him.' Kern didn't think that statement was silly.

"And he came up to me on the boat one time—we used to travel by sea all the time, going back and forth from shows in Europe. And he comes across the dining saloon and he stood at my table and put this little head of his to one side, and he said, 'They can say all they want to, but Brahms is just a big pile of gymnastics, with a lot of material under it that even Lou——[a current pop songwriter] wouldn't write!'

"I said, 'Jerry, you might as well go back and eat, because you don't have to listen to Brahms unless you want to, and *I* have to listen to Lou—all the time.' Which meant I also had to listen to Jerome Kern!"

"I used to go up to Bronxville and visit a good deal," says Irving Caesar. "Jerry lived there, and so did his good friend and publisher, Max Dreyfus. Jerry had great charm. Most fine piano players have that, you know. And he was very clever about certain things. He'd never say anything against another composer; he had a devilish way of getting *you* to do that. We'd be sitting at the table; some show had recently opened, and Jerry would start to praise it lavishly. '*Never* have I heard such great music!' he'd say. '*Never* have I heard such magnificent lyrics!' And he'd carry on in that fashion until the rest of us would jump in and say, 'Oh, stop it—you know that stuff is perfectly awful!' And he'd sit there beaming. Absolutely devilish, that ploy of his."

Kern made several trips to California in the early days of the sound films, with varying success, but it wasn't until 1934 that he accepted a lucrative contract and made a permanent move to Beverly Hills. He very much enjoyed living in California; within a few short blocks of his comfortable home were many of his New York friends and fellow composers.

There he wrote with Oscar Hammerstein, and later with Dorothy Fields, Ira Gershwin, and Leo Robin. He became very close friends with Harry Warren; the two composers enjoyed each other's company hugely.

"Jerry was quite a character," says Warren. "He loved fun, he loved jokes. He was a great worker. He had a guy named Charlie Miller, meek little chap, who was his sort of musical amanuensis, you know. He'd call Charlie up in the middle of the night, and say, 'Charlie, *listen.*' He had a phone near the piano, and he'd play a melody and wake poor Charlie up every night. And finally, one night, I don't know what happened, he played something, and when he got to the release, poor Charlie finally got brave, and he said, 'Jerry, I don't like it.' And Jerry said, 'Why?' Charlie said, 'Well, it doesn't sound like *Kern.*' He waited for the roof to fall in, but all Kern said was, 'I guess maybe you're right, Charlie.'

"He loved camaraderie, he loved fun. Max Dreyfus used to call him a brain-picker, you know. You couldn't tell Jerry anything without him going into full details. 'Wait a minute,' he'd say. 'Just start at the beginning, let's hear it, word by word.' Even in a restaurant he'd call the *maître d'*—we used to go to dinner with him and Mrs. Kern—and he'd pick up the menu and he would see something he didn't know. Now, he'd been all over the world, Europe and lots of places, but he'd see a dish that he'd probably never heard of, so he'd call the *maître d'* over. 'What is this?' 'Oh, well,' says the *maître d'*, 'this is some sort of—' Jerry says, 'Wait a minute, start slowly. Tell me what it *is.*' And he'd tell him, you see. And Jerry says, 'How do you cook it?' 'Well, you cook it in the —' He says, 'Now wait a minute—step by step, please.' The whole recipe, step by step!

"Quite a man. He had another gag he used to do. He'd say, 'Come on over tomorrow night.' Harold Arlen, myself, and a whole gang of composers. And he would say, 'Let's play capitals of the U.S.' Who would win? Him, you know. He'd cram up on them in the afternoon! Whatever game he was going to play that night, he'd start preparing in the afternoon.''

"I got along very well with him," says Ira Gershwin. "He liked me. But I wasn't used to working with anyone like that, you know. We started first on *Cover Girl*. He would say, 'Here'—and hand me tunes. He'd say, 'We have to use this,' and he played me a sixteen-bar schottische. Rather monotonous. I said, 'Very nice, Jerry, but I'll have to find a spot for it, you know.' And every time we'd keep on working—we worked a long time on that thing—every time he'd say, 'Have you done that schottische yet?' And I'd say, 'No, I'm waiting for a spot.'*

"Finally, at the very end we had to write a title song, and I said, 'Jerry, I think I can find that!' It was that schottische! And that was the last thing I wrote in the picture—the thing he had given me so many months back to write up!

"Oh, he was a brilliant man. No question about his ability and talent. But he was a strange man. One day he said to me—he lived right around the corner here in Beverly Hills—'I'm surprised your brother used actual automobile horns in *American in Paris*, realistic things like that.' Couple of years later he writes 'The Last Time I Saw Paris,' using auto horns! And I hadn't thought about it at the time, but when he did that show with Oscar Hammerstein about Vienna, *Music in the Air*, he was very proud that they'd gotten the actual effect of the chandeliers in the wind, the tinkling of the chandeliers. So he was *for* realism . . . that way.

"You know, I remember when radio came in, Kern saying, 'I'm not going to let *my* songs be played!' Actually, it wasn't that he didn't want them broadcast; he was greatly annoyed by some of the versions of his songs on the air, whether live or recorded. What he hoped for was to be able in some way to make sure that he could negate any recording that would not do justice to his work . . . but of course this was an impossibility. With more and more record companies popping up and with so many various recordings of any hit song, it was wholly impractical for any creator to control the manner in which his work was presented.

"Do you realize that Kern once had four shows in one year? My brother George rehearsed one of them, I think—*Love of Mike* or *Rockabye Baby*, one of those. He was the pianist. Of course, Kern could work very fast. I remember for one show he locked Mike Rourke up in a room at the Hotel Astor. Mike Rourke wrote under the name of 'Herbert Reynolds.' An old Irishman, he'd been a newspaperman in Ireland. Kern wouldn't let him out! He would shove the lead sheets to him under the door . . . and in two weeks he had the whole score done. Kern would give Rourke the tunes first, and he'd say, 'This fits such and such.' That's how he could turn out that many shows in a year.

"But when Kern said something rather arbitrary," adds Gershwin, "I just always shrugged my shoulders."

"When I was a young kid," says Margaret Whiting, one of the two talented daughters of Richard Whiting, the composer, "my father, if he were working on

* Meanwhile Gershwin and Kern were writing "Put Me to the Test," "Sure Thing," "Long Ago and Far Away," and "Who's Complaining?"

a score or something else and couldn't get out to the golf course to play a game, would go to a little pitch-and-putt course which was right below our house, Comstock Avenue at Beverly Glen. And I'd go over with him, and we'd always bump into Harry Warren and Jerome Kern, Harold Arlen and Johnny Mercer, sometimes Arthur Schwartz, and they'd all practice their golf swings. They'd talk about different songs, and then afterwards they'd take me over to their houses, and that is how I came to hear so many film scores before they were even published.

"I remember Kern calling me up one day after my father passed away, and he said, 'Your father said you were the greatest judge of songs in the business, and I want you to come over.' In other words, what he'd used to do with my father, he now wanted to do with me—use our opinions. He played me several songs; one was 'I'm Old Fashioned,' another was 'Dearly Beloved.'

"He said, 'Well, what do you think?' I was so nervous. You see, my father was my father, and I knew that he was great, but he was my father. I could say, 'I don't like that song' to my father . . . but how could you say *that* to Jerome Kern? I almost died.

"Luckily enough, it happened that these were two of Kern's greatest songs, so I said, 'Well, what can you say about perfection?' I found one little thing that I thought could be changed. Kern said, 'Well, that's very good advice, Margaret. I'll consider that.' "

"I was completely in awe of Kern from the minute we got together," says Leo Robin, "and it cramped my style a little bit, He was a very nervous, impatient man, very erudite—I remember once I used the word 'encyclopediac' in referring to a man we knew, and Kern said, 'Encyclope*dic*.' He was that kind of a person.

"A very cultured musician, too; he knew music and he knew orchestration. What can you say about Kern? When we did the picture *Centennial Summer* he said to me, 'Look, we're going to do this picture with straight actors—there's not one singer in the picture. I've never done that before.' So he took a big gamble on the project. After we got started, he used to call me up every day, bugging me—'You got anything yet?' I wanted so much to please him and to measure up to his high standards that I don't think I did my best work in that picture. But I had one song that Kern liked very much—'In Love in Vain.' He used to play it at parties."

Harry Warren recalls: "I was sitting with him out at Metro one day when they were making a picture of his life story—you know, *Look for the Silver Lining*. We were out on the stage, and they were recording. They played the verse to one of Jerry's songs. I don't remember exactly what happened, but they didn't get into the verse the way it had been written, and Jerry was so upset. He couldn't understand why they did that. So he called Roger Edens, the arranger, over and asked who'd done it and why, and you know all those studio bastards were all the same. He said, 'Well, Mr. Kern, we had to do that for some reason that's technical,' which is a lot of crap to me, you know, because I'd been in the picture business before this, thirty years. They'd made a change, and that was that."

"You know the funny thing about Kern," says Robert Russell Bennett, "he was terribly affectionate when there was a show coming up, and then I never heard from him until the next show was due. And we were very good friends; in fact, on the road, when we'd go out with shows, we'd eat together, play bridge together. And then the show would open in New York. Kern might as well not exist. I might as well not exist. Never heard a word from him. Then, maybe in one or two years, I'd get a note or a little letter, and I'd say to my wife, 'Oh-oh, another show coming up.' The letter would say nothing about the show, but then I knew I was going to get a phone call soon and he'd say, 'How're you fixed for such-and-such dates?'

"You know he died twice? They brought him to life after the first time he had a stroke. His heart had actually stopped beating, and yet the doctors out in California were actually able to revive him and get him going again. So he spent about eight years more, as he referred to it, on borrowed time. That was when he wrote so many of those beautiful things like 'Long Ago and Far Away.' Then he collapsed here on the street in New York, and they took the body over to Welfare Island. Nobody knew who he was. Finally his friends located the body and went out and rescued it from a burial in Potter's Field.

"I went to the funeral, and Oscar Hammerstein got up and did one of his beautiful eulogies, just a lovely thing. He said, 'Let's have no tears, because Jerry wasn't a man to shed tears over, nor was he a man to shed tears himself.' And Oscar read this thing, and at the end he almost broke down himself. It was insane! The lovely things he said about Kern, what a darling man and all that, and I found tears coming down my cheeks. What for? There'd never been any great affection between us. We were just excellent collaborators, in a certain way.

"So much talent! When you hear a thing like 'They Didn't Believe Me,' or some of the other tunes like 'All the Things You Are,' you forgive him anything."

'Three Little Words'

(Kalmar and Ruby)

H E S T A N D S ramrod-erect on a Beverly Hills street, seventy-seven years after his birth on the Lower East Side. ("In two tenement rooms," he once remarked, "which I got out of as soon as possible.") His bushy crop of gray hair crowns his prominent hooked nose and sharp eyes. ("Woollcott was fond of calling me 'the corrupt Abe Lincoln,' and my partner, Bert Kalmar, always referred to me as 'Hook-and-Eyes.' ") His sense of humor and lunatic wit have enraptured a huge collection of friends for more than half a century. His latest lyric runs:

> *I'll go without a murmur when*
> *The Good Lord sends for me.*
> *But if I had my life to live over again,*
> *I'd leave town immediately.*

Harry Ruby's passionate love of baseball is famous. As one dedicated fan once put it, "Harry doesn't want to write the nation's hits, he wants to hit its homers!"*

* There is a story of a lunchtime discussion at the Metro commissary between Joseph L. Mankiewicz and Ruby wherein Mankiewicz put Ruby to the supreme test.

If the songwriting team of Kalmar and Ruby had written only "Hooray for Captain Spaulding," which has become Groucho Marx's theme song, that alone should have sufficed to make them immortal. But the record book on Harry Ruby and his late partner shows that they batted over .400 for more than three decades. Before they migrated to California in 1930, they wrote a cluster of hit Broadway scores; their successes include "All Alone Monday," "Thinking of You," "Who's Sorry Now?" "I Wanna Be Loved by You," and "Nevertheless," not to forget "Three Little Words." For their own amusement (and later the public's) they poured out many comedy songs, most of which Groucho will be delighted to render for you—"Show Me a Rose," "Today, Father, Is Father's Day," and "A Doctor Is a Man's Best Friend," to cite but a few.

Kalmar died in 1947, but the fabled Mr. Ruby is still one of Beverly Hills' leading citizens, a lunchtime regular at Nate and Al's Delicatessen, a popular guest on TV talk shows, a devoted baseball fan, and a tireless sidewalk watcher. "Whenever I see loose change on the ground, I pick it up," he explains. "In the past few years I've found over $300 this way, which I then give to charity. Of course, my friend Groucho maintains that the money I'm always picking up is what's falling out of my own pockets!"

One particularly bright California afternoon last summer Harry Ruby sat down at a luncheon table, ordered a corned-beef sandwich on seeded rye, and began reminiscing about his songwriting career with equal helpings of philosophy and wry humor.

How had he decided on a career in songwriting?

"The urge to write, or whatever you call it—the *talent*," said Ruby, "has always baffled me. I don't believe in heredity—or maybe I do to a certain extent. I've got a big nose, my mother had a big nose. But I do believe in a thing called atavism, which means traits inherited from remote ancestry. Otherwise, how can you explain Irving Berlin? He came from Russia when he was seven, and he was brought up on the Lower East Side. He had brothers and sisters who had no talent, nothing. Same with me. I'm the only one in the whole family who had any talent for music. It must be a trait inherited from remote ancestors. Three generations back, maybe four. I believe in that, and a lot of scientists do. Otherwise, if this thing is based on heredity, why wasn't *everybody* in my family or Berlin's family musical? My sister studied, my brother studied, they all took piano lessons. Nothing!

"In the days when I was growing up on the Lower East Side, you've got to remember that all the families around us were poor. But *they had pianos.* Waters, I think they were called; you could buy one for a hundred dollars and pay it off on time payments. They'd hoist it up to the apartment on a rope. I lived on the same block as the Gershwins—Eldridge Street—that's how the piano came into their house.

"These people, who had barely enough to eat and pay the rent—for some

"Let's assume you're driving along a mountain road, high up," he hypothesized. "You see a precipitous cliff with a sheer six-hundred-foot drop. Two men are hanging there, desperate. One of them is Joe DiMaggio, the other is your father. You have time to save only one of them. Which one do you save?"

"Are you kidding?" replied Ruby instantly. "My father never hit over .218 in his life!"

reason they wanted their children to *learn* something. Everybody got lessons, in the hope that it would lead to something. You see, it was a struggle; my father was raising a family of six kids, but he wanted his children to be something so they wouldn't have to go through what *he* went through. What did he want them to be? A doctor or a lawyer. That would give them a position, prestige. Me?" Ruby chuckles. "Well, you know that old joke, they had to burn down the school to get him out? Well, I was left back so many times that they were going to move the school out of the neighborhood!

"My father—he was a lovely man—wanted me to be a doctor or a lawyer. I said I didn't want to be either of those. 'So what do you want to be, a bum?' My uncle said, 'Who knows what's better for you than your own father?' I said, 'I don't know how to explain this, but I do not want to be a doctor or a lawyer.' What did I want to be? he asks. I didn't know, but I guess I wanted something connected with show business. I was probably already stage-struck. But I couldn't tell them I wanted to be a songwriter; I was still too young to know that. And as far as saying I wanted to be a baseball player, which I've always wanted to be, that would be even worse!" Ruby chortles. " 'A baseball player? A bum he wants to be.'

"The trouble with most questions that are put to songwriters," Ruby says, "is the answers need a lot of explaining." To wit, the following answer from the *Dramatists Guild Quarterly:*

> Once, on a TV show, I was asked, "Harry, of all the songs you have written, is there one you are sorry you wrote?" Said I, "Yes, there is one song I am sorry I wrote and that song is 'Three Little Words.' " They thought I was kidding, but I wasn't. In order to explain, I had to tell the following story.
>
> Way back in the year 1931, Bert Kalmar and I wrote "Three Little Words" for a movie made by RKO. I cannot remember how many records have been made of the song. It was used as a title of at least three albums. And it has sold quite a lot of copies through the years.
>
> That same year, I received a wire from the one-and-only Walter Johnson, then manager of the Washington Senators, inviting me to play in an exhibition game with the Senators against the Baltimore Orioles. What did I do? I did what any sensible man would do. The very next day I reported, spike shoes, sweatshirt, sliding pads and all, to Walter Johnson at Griffith Park in Washington, D.C.
>
> Well, the afternoon of the day I reported, in the seventh inning of the ball game, Al Schacht, the Senators' third-base coach, announced over the loudspeaker, "Harry Ruby now playing second base for Buddy Meyer." Here was the big moment of my life. It was like a dream come true.
>
> As I took my place at second, I could hardly believe it. There was Joe Judge at first, Ossie Bluege at third, Joe Cronin playing short, and Harry Ruby at second: the million-dollar infield. As I stood there beaming and pounding my fist into the pocket of my glove, all I could think of was making a double play. My life would be complete if I could see my name in the box score the following day making a double play.

Just before the inning got under way, the following came over the loudspeaker: "Harry Ruby is the writer of that song 'Three Little Words.' " It was Al Schacht again. Then, using a baseball bat as a baton, Al led the fans, nine thousand of them, in singing the song.

Right then and there, I went to pieces. I wanted them to think I was a real baseball player. Having been told by Al Schacht that I was a songwriter, they must have thought I was some kind of a clown or something. Now they couldn't possibly take me seriously. What I called Schacht under my breath I cannot repeat here.

The inning started. The first Oriole up hit a single. The next man up hit a grounder to Ossie Bluege. Ossie was about to throw to me at second, when he saw that I wasn't there. I hadn't covered the bag to complete the double play. I was glued to the spot, telling Al Schacht what I thought of him. It was one of the easiest double-play set-ups that ever was. Joe Cronin, seeing that I was not going to cover, dashed over to second, but not in time to make the double play. He got only one man out.

The next day the following banner line appeared in the sports section of the Washington *Post:* SONGWRITER MISSES DOUBLE PLAY.

And that, folks, is why I am sorry I wrote "Three Little Words."

"Bert Kalmar was a headliner in vaudeville with his wife," continues Ruby. "He always wanted to be a magician, but in vaudeville he and his wife did a dance act. He got $1,000 a week, which was darn good money. He also wrote songs, he'd had a couple of big hits, and then he went into the publishing business with a guy named Puck—Kalmar & Puck.

"I got a job there as a song-plugger. I was getting $25 a week. Bert was making his $1,000 a week in vaudeville. I guess you know what happened—if you watch the Late Show, you can see the picture *Three Little Words* which Jack Cummings made of our life story. Fred Astaire played Bert, and Red Skelton played me. Quite an improvement—for me, that is.

"Well, anyway, here's how it went. Bert and his wife got together a big new act. He spent almost $11,000 on scenery and costumes; it was a beautiful act. They opened in Washington. President Wilson was there—he loved vaudeville, you know. Coming offstage—this scene is in the picture—Bert hit something backstage and hurt his leg. He couldn't go on, and they had to cancel the act. He couldn't dance.

"He came back to New York and he was broke. By that time I was working for Watterson, Berlin and Snyder, and since I knew him from working at his own firm, he asked me if I'd ask Watterson if he'd take him on as a songwriter.

"Watterson said sure, he'd be glad to have Bert, but he could only give him a $60-a-week drawing account. I went back and told this to Bert, and he said, 'I'll take it!'

"The first song Bert wrote there was with Edgar Leslie and it was called 'Oh, What a Pal Was Mary.' The first statement on it was $90,000! Sold two million copies.

"Then we started writing together. One day the phone rang and it was a vaudeville booker calling up to offer Bert a firm booking on the Keith circuit—$1,000 a week. 'Wonderful,' I said. 'I turned it down,' he said, 'turned it down cold.' 'You turned down $1,000 a week, and you're getting a $60-a-week drawing account here?' I said. 'You're crazy!' 'Harry,' he said, 'I am through. From now on, I am a songwriter.' Then he grinned and said, 'But I have to tell you, it's a kick—turning down $1,000 a week . . .'"

"They were a marvelous pair," recalls Robert Russell Bennett. "I remember one day they were waiting in Grand Central Station for a train to go up to Westchester, and I said, 'Oh, Bert, I just remembered. I owe you a quarter.' I handed him the quarter. He said, 'What do you owe me this for?' I told him I'd owed it to him for a couple of weeks, and tried to remind him when I'd borrowed it. Bert said, 'Aw, forget it, you don't owe me any quarter!' So Harry came up to me, very confidentially, and he said, 'Do you know that's how Bert has made his pile—refusing quarters? After a while—*it adds up!*'

"And Harry once really put me down. I said to him, 'You know, the trouble with all of you popular songwriters is that you get an eight-bar phrase and you have to plug it all afternoon. You write a strain like "Some Enchanted Evening," and then you say a few bars later, "All right, now in case you didn't hear it, you dumb clucks out there, 'Some Enchanted Evening,' here it is again." And then a little bit later you say, "All right, I know you've forgotten it by now, so you say 'Some Enchanted Evening' *again*." 'But,' I said, 'you take a thing like "La Donna è Mobile" from *Rigoletto*—listen to Verdi, he never goes back, never returns to the original statement; keeps on going, always something new!' And Harry quieted me down right away; he said, 'Well, there've been popular songs like that. Have you ever listened to "School Days," by Gus Edwards?' And he was so right!"

"Of course, everybody knows about us," says Ruby, "the two songwriters who always wanted to be something else. When Jack Cummings decided to make our story into a movie, he went into Louis B. Mayer and he said, 'This is gonna be a good musical, because for once we're gonna do a story about songwriters that has a *story!*' And when Mayer asked him what story he had in mind, he said, 'It's a natural—two successful songwriters. One schmuck wants to be a magician and pull rabbits out of a hat; the other one would rather play professional baseball than eat!'

"And it was true. Once we had an appointment to go to meet a producer for a Broadway show—I think it was Charles Dillingham. Very important man, wanted us to do a whole score—a big job for us. Bert said, 'I'll be there a day later.' 'Why?' 'Harry, I gotta take care of something. But I'll be there, I promise.' He didn't show up to meet Dillingham or sign contracts for three days! I was furious. When he finally showed up, he couldn't understand why I was sore. 'Where were you?' 'Look,' he said, 'there was a big convention in Chicago, magicians came from all over the world—Australia, London. I couldn't miss it!'

"And listen to *this*. We were living up in New Rochelle. I was in a semi-pro game, playing second base. The game is going on, and suddenly we hear horses' hooves. Turn around, we see a *horse* coming through center field. *Kalmar is riding!* I'm furious. I take my baseball seriously, and here's my partner being funny about it, riding through the diamond on a horse! Everybody's looking. The game stops. He rides up to me and says, 'Hi, Harry.' I said, 'Hi.' He says, 'Sign this.' I said, 'Sign *what?*' He tells me it's a contract to do a show for Florenz Ziegfeld. Puts the contract on the side of the horse, gives me the pen, I sign the contract, he takes it back and then says, 'Go ahead, Harry—have a nice game!' And rides off the field . . . Oh, we were crazy, but we had fun.

"Bert loved animals. Even when he was a headliner in vaudeville, he'd always traveled with a monkey. Later on, when he and I moved out to California to work in pictures, he bought himself a ranch out in the Valley, had all sorts of animals. Horses, dogs, a big monkey named Brutus, a parrot. 'Animals love me,' he used to say. 'I got a way with animals.' The parrot bit him, the monkey bit him, but he insisted he had a way with animals! Eight-acre place in Encino, full of animals. I wish Bert had hung on to those eight acres—he'd have been rich. But one day he decided it was too large a place, so he sold it and moved to Beverly Hills, into a smaller place. Couldn't bring the animals with him, so he sold them too, to the man who bought the ranch.

"But Bert loved Brutus, the monkey. One day he's in Beverly Hills, and he says to his wife, 'I miss Brutus. The rest of 'em I don't much care about, but I really miss Brutus.' And she says, 'Why don't you go out and visit him?' And Bert says, 'I think I will.'

"Now, you have to know that things weren't so good with any of us about that time. Musicals weren't so popular out in Hollywood in the late '30s, Bert's not working, I'm not working, Bert's son is looking for work and not finding anything, and his daughter, a beautiful girl, is also looking for a way to get started. Nobody in the family can get a job—including me.

"Bert goes out to Encino and rings the bell. 'Remember me?' Sure, the guy remembers him. 'I hate to bother you, but I just thought I'd drop in and visit with my old friend Brutus, the monkey,' Bert says. 'Is that all right?'

" 'Oh, he's not here,' says the guy.

" 'What's the matter, is he sick or something?' Bert asks.

" 'Oh, no, he's in a picture!' says the guy. 'He got a job at one of the studios, and he's over there today shooting his scenes!'

"Bert comes back to our office laughing. The only one in the whole crowd who was working was Brutus, the monkey! 'I don't know about you and me,' he said, 'but *Brutus* is doing fine!' "

Having finished his energy-building corned beef on rye, Mr. Ruby waves cheerfully, and walks out of the restaurant, a Beverly Hills boulevardier ready to stroll back home. There's a baseball game on TV this afternoon, and he doesn't want to be late for the opening pitch.

Hooray for Captain Spaulding . . . and hooray for Kalmar and Ruby.

'Tea for Two'

(Vincent Youmans)

VINCENT YOUMANS' career, his success on Broadway, even, alas, his life
span flashed by at top speed. He was to die young, only forty-seven, in
1946. His creative years were to be equally brief. His first song was published
in 1920, after he'd served a World War I hitch in the Navy. One of his biggest
hits, "Hallelujah!," was written while he wore Navy blue, but did not find a
place in a Broadway show until 1927, when it electrified audiences at *Hit the
Deck*. Youmans' last published works were the songs he contributed to the film
Flying Down to Rio in 1933, only thirteen years later.

But in that brief period young Youmans wrote music for ten other shows.
He had his first production, *Two Little Girls in Blue*, in 1921, when he was a
mere twenty-three. (His lyricist, Ira Gershwin, who was still writing as "Arthur
Francis," was twenty-four.)

These days audiences flock to *No, No, Nanette*, and Mr. Youmans is enjoying a justified renaissance. His other shows may be temporarily forgotten,
but his music has a remarkable strength. You may not remember the book of
Wildflower or *Hit the Deck* or *Great Day*, but the Youmans songs that enlivened
them have lasted. Measured against the output of his contemporaries—say, the

work of his good friend George Gershwin, or of Berlin and Kern and others who were writing in the 1920s—the volume of Youmans' published catalogue is slender indeed. In the *ASCAP Biographical Dictionary* the list of his titles runs to a mere forty-odd. But assess him in terms of quality, and Youmans moves right up to front rank. It's not only the excitement of his "Hallelujah!" and "Great Day" and "Drums in My Heart," nor is it the score for *Nanette* or that deceptively gentle melodic strength he demonstrated in "Without a Song," "Time on My Hands," "More Than You Know," and "Sometimes I'm Happy." Rather, it is Youmans' steady ability to make a melodic statement that evokes an instant response from the listener. His songs are not only popular, they seem to be permanent. Examine the one film score he wrote, in 1933, for RKO—the first Fred Astaire–Ginger Rogers musical, *Flying Down to Rio*. Despite the surrealistic madness of rows of chorus girls dancing thousands of feet above South America, clutching ropes on the wing of a huge flying boat, you cannot fault Youmans' music. The picture may be a "camp" hoot today, but there's absolutely nothing antiquated about Youmans' title song, or "The Carioca," or that lovely tango "Orchids in the Moonlight."

If Youmans' music had that strength, unfortunately he himself did not. Tuberculosis sapped his vitality; after 1932 the years he had left were filled with a downhill physical struggle. But he continued to write. When he died, he left behind a stack of unpublished manuscripts in a trunk.

Edward Eliscu, a trim, graying man who wrote the lyrics for the *Great Day* and *Flying Down to Rio* scores, can still call back memories of his talented friend.

"In the early days I took to hanging around Harms, the music publishers, picking up assignments on Broadway shows. At that time, the late '20s, Harms was a marketplace. A Broadway producer would come in with a property—he would have a musical-comedy libretto and he'd raised the money to produce it. He'd come into Harms and say, 'I need a composer and a lyricist to do the score for this show.' And then Max Dreyfus, the boss, would *assign* the proper team or the proper individual.

"One of my fans was an agent named Dick LaMarr, who later became agent for Alan Lerner and Frederick Loewe. Once my lyrics began to be talked about, he called me one day and said, in his excitable way, 'Listen, kid, I've got a great thing for you! I want you to meet me at three at Vincent Youmans' house!'

"This was a big surprise for me. I mean, I knew Youmans was a great composer; I knew all the things from *Wildflower*, *Nanette*, and *Hit the Deck*, and I had the greatest respect for his work. The possibility that I might work with him was just astounding.

"LaMarr brought me up there and introduced me. After a while I got to know Vincent very well. He was not a very warm person. Extremely talented, but he always seemed somewhat defensive. What that was due to, I don't know . . . it was like a person who feels there's something lacking in his background. You know, there are some people who've never been to college and they never get over it. It certainly wasn't Youmans' social position—his family were Youmans the hatters, and he wasn't a poor boy. It was more an intellectual self-consciousness. One day he and I were having a discussion about something and he remarked that someone had been very ve*hee*ment. And then I realized that he had read, but hadn't spoken, or listened. . . .

"After a bit, that afternoon, Oscar Hammerstein came in. A large, craggy-faced man, a wonderful character. He was working on two shows at the time, and he had committed himself to do this one—a third—with Youmans. It was to be called *Rainbow* [1928]. Apparently, he and Youmans had decided that if they could find an acceptable substitute writer for the lyrics, Oscar could relinquish that part of the job. So Oscar sat on the couch and I stood four feet away from him, without any music, singing and reciting my 'repertoire.'

"Fortunately, Hammerstein was a very kind-hearted and sympathetic person, and he had confidence in the stuff I'd done, so he decided to engage me. It was a bonanza! Suddenly, I was to be the collaborator of Vincent Youmans, Oscar Hammerstein, and Laurence Stallings! On a big Broadway show—one that was going into rehearsal in three weeks! All the work had to be done instantly, so I picked up where Oscar had left off, and I worked very hard to get the score finished.

"The very first day of rehearsals, a man walked down the aisle and asked me if I were Edward Eliscu, and when I said yes, he presented me with a paper. A subpoena, or a restraining order, or whatever, served on me at the instigation of Max Dreyfus!

"It seems that sometime in the past, from some previous show I'd done at Harms, I owed an advance of $57; and because of that advance, which hadn't been repaid, I was to be prevented from working on this show!

"Youmans said, 'You never told me you were tied to Harms!' I told him I wasn't—but apparently my contract on that show had provided that I couldn't work on any *other* show unless the advance was completely repaid.

"So I ran up to Harms instantly. I was kept waiting, as you can well imagine, and finally I was ushered into the august presence. Dreyfus was a rather small man. I pleaded with him. 'Look,' I said, 'this is an opportunity for *you*. I haven't been worth anything to you up till now. If *Rainbow* is any good, I'll be worth that much more to you!* Let me do the show; I'll give you back the $57!'

"Well, it wasn't the $57. *This* was the crux of the matter: Youmans had been with Harms for eight years. Without notifying Max Dreyfus, without consulting him or saying anything, Youmans had decided that he was going to publish on his own, and when *Rainbow* came up, he made the condition that he was to be his own publisher. So I'd become the innocent victim of Dreyfus' wrath, justifiable or not, and nothing could budge Dreyfus from that position! So far as publishable numbers were concerned, I was taken out of *Rainbow*. The rest of my things—openings, or endings, or ensemble numbers and choruses—they remained, but that was all.

"I guess I must have repaid Dreyfus the $57, because there was no problem when I went to work with Youmans on his next show, in 1929—*Great Day*.† And then, later, when I was out in California and he came out to do *Flying Down to Rio*, I worked on that with him.

"Youmans was a great composer, but the public doesn't really know him because he never publicized himself. He never was a public party-figure, like so many other composers. Very often people sing songs. without ever knowing who was the author—although, actually, it's the lyricist who suffers more from this anonymity. Everyone knows that Hoagy Carmichael wrote 'Stardust,' but I

---

* Unfortunately, the show proved to be a flop. After thirty performances, it closed.

† Eliscu wrote the lyrics of "Without a Song," "Great Day," and "More Than You Know" with Billy Rose.

defy you to find one person out of twenty who knows that Mitchell Parrish wrote the lyric.

"Vincent always looked like a hayseed, if I can use that old-time expression. In the summer he wore a stiff straw hat; his clothes weren't fashionable. He certainly looked anything but a Broadway songwriter; he didn't talk like one, he didn't act like one.

"But he loved people. He loved night life. At midnight his life would begin. Midnight—Ring Lardner, or Joe Kennedy long before he became an ambassador, people like that would troop into his apartment. Even when he worked, he liked to work at night, and he would keep poor little Max Steiner* up all night working on orchestration. Max would be half blind, with his bad eyes and sheer exhaustion.

"Max had to be there because when Youmans composed, he would play the bass chords and whistle the melody. He was a very good and strong whistler. He'd had a good musical education—he'd gotten it in the church. His music had some kind of leaning to a Spanish strain; I don't know where that came from. Just as Kern leaned toward the German and the Austrian, and Gershwin's toward the black idiom, the Spanish was Youmans'.

"He wasn't jazz-oriented, but he had tremendous vitality and drive in his music, and I think a melodic gift unequaled by anybody. People say that Kern had a great melodic gift; I think that's so, but I think that Youmans was unequaled for a sustained line of melody. It's like a theme that works out to a perfectly correct, and yet *unexpected,* conclusion.

"The score that he and Billy Rose and I wrote for *Great Day* was, I think, a magnificent one, but it wasn't popular when it first came out. The show was a failure, and the songs didn't get a proper play until after a long time. 'More Than You Know' became a hit only after Benny Goodman made a record and popularized it.

"Youmans was a person who could not be influenced. I've worked with composers who are willing to do anything you want, and it makes you nervous. They're too accommodating, and you very often have to restrain them from ruining their own melodic line by making a smooth transition, say, merely to accommodate the odd syllable in your lyric. But Youmans changed his melodies only once, so far as I know. That was when we were doing *Great Day* out of town, with a wonderful singer named Marion Harris—she sang 'More Than You Know.' The ending of that song, as he had written it, was a nice, beautiful, original ending. But Marion Harris, being a pop singer of those times, wanted to end it with a very corny, wavering climax. When she did, it was so effective that Youmans let her keep it that way . . . and that was the only time I ever remember his doing that.

"When he first played me 'Without a Song,' he said, 'Of course, I haven't finished the verse.' I said, 'But this is complete in itself'—it's a long song, I think it's sixty-four bars—'why do you need a verse?' 'No, gotta have a verse, gotta have a verse,' he kept saying. But we never got around to it, and eventually we went into rehearsal, and he accepted 'Without a Song' without a verse. But otherwise, the way Vincent saw and heard his things, that was the way they had to be transcribed.

---

* The same late great Max Steiner whose film scores in the '40s for such films as *Casablanca* and *The Treasure of the Sierra Madre* earned him Academy Awards.

"His downfall, if you can call it that, was because he neglected his health. He had no self-discipline about his body. Stayed up all hours, drank, with total disregard of any rules of health."

"I first came across Youmans in the early '30s," says Bernard Herrmann, the composer and conductor (*Citizen Kane, Jane Eyre, Psycho*). "Hans Spialek, the great arranger up at Harms, told me that Youmans was looking for someone to write some ballet music for *Take a Chance*. So I got to know Youmans. He had sort of sketched out the ballet, but I had to put it all together for him and orchestrate it. His way of working was altogether unique. He would sit by the hour at the piano and play a vamp—

> *Um ta da da, de-dah*
> *Um ta da da, de-dah—*

he'd play that for hours and hours. And then he'd start to whistle. When he liked what he'd whistled as a melody, he'd call for Dr. Albert Sirmay to come over. Sirmay was a great orchestrator who was connected with Harms, and old Sirmay would come and write down the whistling part. Youmans was a great intuitive composer; he had music *in* him, but not at his fingertips. He could only whistle, and play the vamp for himself.

"I once went with Youmans to a concert where they played Debussy's *Iberia*, and he became very upset when he heard it. He said, 'I hear music like that inside myself, but I can't get it out.' Perhaps that was one of the reasons he drank a lot. I think he was troubled by his own inadequacy all the time. He was Irish, and he was much taken by that melancholia of the Irish, as well as the good spirits.

"There was no pretense about him. Never went after publicity. When I knew him, he had only one mania—he loved driving beautiful cars. Cars like Isotta-Fraschinis, Duesenbergs. He had a big Stutz convertible, and this was in the midst of the Depression, too.

"Youmans may have been the most gifted of all the composers of his time, but he was the most inarticulate. His fast music has a flair that none of the others had, excepting maybe Gershwin. None of the others were capable of writing a tune like 'Rise and Shine' or 'Flying Down to Rio' or 'Hallelujah!'—that was a great rhythmic gift. But Gershwin was a sophisticated musician. Look at the way he developed his talents with *Porgy and Bess*. Youmans couldn't develop that way—he didn't have the equipment that George had."

"I was just a young struggling songwriter," says Burton Lane (*Finian's Rainbow, On a Clear Day You Can See Forever*), "and I'd been sent out to California with Harold Adamson, who was then writing lyrics with me. Youmans was living at the Garden of Allah, writing a picture for RKO which turned out to be *Flying Down to Rio*. We'd met him in New York. In fact, we'd auditioned some songs for him—by then he had his own publishing company—so in California we saw Youmans socially on a couple of nights. I'd written a new tune, which I'd played for him, and he liked it very much.

"One night, at a Hollywood party, I was in one room and he was at the piano in another room, and suddenly I heard what sounded very familiar to me—except it was Youmans playing it! It's my tune and he's whistling it! I went into the room. People were gathered around the piano, and somebody said, 'Jesus, doesn't Youmans write gorgeous tunes? This is his new one!'

"Youmans finished playing it, and then he looked up, shook his head, and quietly said, 'This is Burt's tune.'

"Never mind how beautifully he played it—I can't forget that gesture he made."

From 1932 until his death in 1946, Youmans was absent from the Broadway scene. His songs were being played and sung, there were stage and film versions of *No, No, Nanette,* but he had withdrawn from active work. His health was bad, and progressively worsened. Unable to write for Broadway, Youmans kept very busy studying. In New Orleans he studied composition and counterpoint with Ferdinand Dunkley at the Loyola School of Music. While there, Youmans was introduced to a young writer, Ray Samuel, who remembers him well after a quarter of a century.

"He was a tired, thin little man then," says Samuel, "very nervous, who somewhat resembled Fred Astaire or Hoagy Carmichael. He had been sweated out for his alcoholism, and was only drinking ale. That was all he'd take, wherever we went.

"Perhaps earlier he wasn't a great piano player, but Professor Guy Bernard, who was also at Loyola with Dunkley, says he saw and heard Youmans play as well as anybody. He remembers vividly that when Youmans came and played his songs for the other students, he played 'The Carioca' and at one point he would use his entire forearm for the bass accompaniment. Bernard said it was great!

"Youmans used to drop into my little office at the Hotel Roosevelt, where I worked, and when I'd get to a pleasant stopping place, we would get into my convertible and go out for long drives around New Orleans. He liked the lake front, and we'd get out there and sit on the sea wall and talk. I wish I could remember all or even some of the interesting things he said back then, but the one that stands out in my recall is his statement that he had lots of beautiful music to write but didn't feel the world was ready for it now. 'Now,' of course, was the very late '30s, when we knew that the war in Europe was imminent.

"Incidentally, the man he was studying with, Professor Dunkley, was a giant in the music world down here. Indestructible. On his eightieth birthday he gave an organ recital in Temple Sinai.

"Youmans made several trips down here to study with Dunkley. The last one was during the war. One night I arranged with the band that was appearing in the Blue Room at the Roosevelt to do an evening of Youmans tunes. It was advertised in the papers, and people crowded in to hear all those songs, and it was a big success. Youmans sat in a corner, drinking ale, occasionally smiling at what he heard. But he wouldn't be introduced to the crowd. He stayed off in the shadows and listened."

'I'm in the Mood for Love'

(Dorothy Fields)

YOU NEVER ASK a lady her age. But if your parents grew up singing such songs of the '20s as "I Can't Give You Anything But Love" or "On the Sunny Side of the Street" and *your* kids are wriggling to "Hey, Big Spender!" and if you know that Dorothy Fields is responsible for the lyrics to those songs (as well as a truckload of other hits in between), then the subject of her age can be dropped and we can concentrate on her amazing career.

"When I was born," she says, "my family was spending the summer down at the Jersey shore. I must have arrived ahead of time, because I've always heard how Lee Shubert and Willie Collier, the actor, who were both good friends of my father, Lew Fields, ran through the streets looking for a doctor or a midwife."

Perhaps that last word dates Miss Fields' entrance into the world, but nothing else about her is passé. She's an attractive woman, so soft-spoken and essentially female (her maid apologized on the phone that Miss Fields couldn't answer—she was having a pedicure) that it's almost impossible to realize that this charming lady has been a successful survivor in an essentially masculine jungle, the music business, for more than forty years.

And it's not only as a top-flight lyricist that she's left her indelible imprint on our popular culture of the past forty-odd years. Dorothy Fields and her late brother Herbert fashioned the books of *Something for the Boys, Let's Face It, Up in Central Park, Mexican Hayride,* and wrote another one called *Annie Get Your Gun* which still stands as the textbook of musical comedy—that is, what to do right in two acts if you're planning to have yourself a smash-hit show.

Her roster of songwriting collaborators sparkles with talents: Messrs. Jerome Kern, Sigmund Romberg, Harold Arlen, Arthur Schwartz, Burton Lane, Jimmy McHugh, Morton Gould, Harry Warren. ("Wait a second," she cautioned, "I'm sure you left some others out. Albert Hague, J. Fred Coots, and what about Cy Coleman? He and I are writing a show right *now*.")

How did she manage to write successfully with so many complex and disparate men? ("I just remembered, I also wrote lyrics to a melody by Fritz Kreisler, 'Stars in My Eyes.' ") One lady lyricist, a dozen gentlemen composers. Is there some magic formula she might divulge?

"I don't know," she says. "In my case, I guess it just evolved."

In a milieu where every fourth word is "greatest" and every second word is some grammatical form of "I/me," the lady's laconic understatement is refreshing.

We sit in her large and beautiful apartment on Central Park West in that old building, the Beresford, which houses such a large population of successful songwriters that it should perhaps be renamed the Brill Building North.

Had she always wished to be a lyricist?

"I didn't really know what I wanted to do," she said. "Pop, of course, was a famous producer,* and he didn't want any of us in the theatre. So out of four, three of us ended up there—Joe, Herbert, and myself! I was married very early; my first husband was a doctor who's now dead. I taught school, and I was a lab technician. But I'd written a few poems that had been published in Frank Adams' famous column, 'The Conning Tower,' in the old *World*. I was introduced to a songwriter named J. Fred Coots, and the two of us began writing songs.† We wrote a few bad ones, and, boy, if you've ever heard bad lyrics, they were the ones. We went around to all the publishers, and the response I got was, 'Well, if you're so great, why doesn't your father do something for you?' Which of course militates against you, if you know what I mean.

"Coots introduced me to Jimmy McHugh, and Jimmy, who was professional manager of Mills Publishing Company, introduced me to Irving Mills. McHugh had already written songs like 'What's Become of Hinky Dinky Parley Vous?' and 'When My Sugar Walks Down the Street,' and he took a slightly dim view of my talent, but he introduced me to Mills all the same. Mills Music was the kind of firm that when Valentino died, the next day they had a song out, 'There's a New Star in Heaven Since Valentino Passed Away.' When Caruso died, the next day there was 'A Songbird in Heaven Named Caruso.' Now, at this time a lady named Ruth Elder was going to fly the Atlantic. So Mills says, 'She's going to fly today and we have to have a song. I'll help you out. I'll give you fifty dollars to do this if you can do it by tomorrow. I'll even give you a title—"Our American Girl." The two lines of verse you have to use are, You took a notion

---

* Lew Fields, partner to Joe Weber in one of the great dialect-comedy acts of American show business, later turned to successful production.

† J. Fred Coots has written such hits (with others) as "Love Letters in the Sand," "Why?," "You Go to My Head," and "Santa Claus Is Coming to Town."

to fly across the ocean.' I said, 'Mr. Mills, you don't take a *notion* to fly across the ocean!' Well, anyhow, Ruth Elder never made it, so the song was never published. Then McHugh said, 'Would you like to do some songs for the Cotton Club in Harlem?' And I said, 'I would write for the Westchester Kennel Club. I don't care what it is!' So we did a few shows there. Three, I think, before Harold Arlen and Ted Koehler came in.

"We didn't have any hits. And the curious thing about the Cotton Club was that they had their openings on Sunday nights so that all the stars could come. Big celebrity nights. The night that our show, our first, was to open, they also had Duke Ellington and his orchestra—first time he appeared in New York. We'd rehearsed with a woman—let's not mention her name. We'd rehearsed her in some nice songs. Opening night, Walter Winchell was there because he was a good friend of my father's. Huge family table—my mother, my father, my first husband, Joe and his wife, and Herbert. And she came out after intermission and she sang three of the dirtiest songs you ever heard in your life. 'Easy Rider'* was mild compared to these songs. My father looked at me and asked, 'Did you write these lyrics?' And I was green. I said, 'Of course I didn't.' So Winchell said, 'You'd better do something about it, Lew.' So Pop went to the owner, a man named Block—he was partners with a gangster named Owney Madden. He said, 'If you don't make an announcement that my daughter Dorothy didn't write those lyrics, I'm going to punch you right on the floor.' So they made an announcement: 'These lyrics of Miss Blank were *not* written by Dorothy Fields. The music was *not* written by Jimmy McHugh.' That was my first experience in theatre.

"And the second was with a man named Harry Delmar, who had a show called *Delmar's Revels.* He asked us to do a song about a poor little Brooklyn boy, who was Bert Lahr, and a poor little girl named Patsy Kelly. They're sitting practically in rags on a cellar step. The song we wrote was 'I Can't Give You Anything But Love.' Well, they did one verse and one quick chorus, and the curtains parted and there were the girls of the chorus, practically nude, dressed as rubies, diamonds, opals, amethysts, sapphires, everything! Next day Delmar said, 'This is a lousy song. Take it and get out of my theatre.' "

She smiles. "Rude beginnings. R-u-e-d . . .

"Then Lew Leslie hired us to do a show called *Blackbirds of 1928.* First, we'd written songs for a show of his in a club called Les Ambassadeurs, on 57th Street, where we had Roger Wolfe Kahn—he was Otto Kahn's son—and his orchestra, and a lovely lady named Adelaide Hall, who sang. We tried again with that song. Horrible reviews for *Blackbirds.* Panned. Everybody loathed it. Gilbert Gabriel, who later became a close friend of mine, wrote, 'And then there was a sickly, puerile song called "I Can't Give You Anything But Love." ' " So we waived royalties and the show limped along until Leslie got the idea to do midnight shows on Thursdays. And that became the rage of New York. Everybody went to *Blackbirds* on Thursday midnights. Woollcott re-reviewed it, Gabriel, everybody re-reviewed it, and it ran for two years! Ran in Paris, ran in Chicago, everywhere. And that 'sickly, puerile song' became an enormous hit. Sold over three million copies."

There were other big hits with McHugh—"Exactly Like You," "On the Sunny Side of the Street," "Diga Diga Doo"—and an entire show for Florenz

---

* "Easy Rider" is a blues song made famous by Bessie Smith.

Ziegfield with Paul Whiteman and Maurice Chevalier. Then the team went to Hollywood, where they worked on early musicals. What was McHugh like as a collaborator?

"Very facile. Taught me a lot. I sat beside him at the piano and wrote as he composed."

In the early '30s Fields and McHugh had "Don't Blame Me," "Dinner at Eight," "The Cuban Love Song," and, from a 1935 musical called *Every Night at Eight,* one of their biggest hits, "I'm in the Mood for Love."

Then came her collaboration with Jerome Kern.

"It's a curious thing how I started to work with Kern. Of course, he knew my father and he knew my brothers, everybody in the family. He was a little older than I. And I was with RKO. Pandro Berman was producing *Roberta,* and he asked me if I'd take a couple of days off and work on it. He said, 'We have a curiously uneven melody of Jerome Kern's that he's given us to add to the score; it needs a lyric. It has to be sung by Irene Dunne, who comes down the steps all in ermine for a fashion show, and it can be a love song.' So I wrote 'Lovely to Look At,' which absolutely astounded Mr. Berman. And he had the nerve to shoot this whole sequence without Jerry okaying the lyric! But Jerry loved it. And when he signed with RKO to do a picture with Lily Pons, *I Dream Too Much,* he said, 'I'd like to work with Dorothy Fields.' That's how we got to be such good friends.

"I always found Jerry easy to work with. We'd sit down at the piano together—first at the Beverly-Wilshire Hotel, before he built the house on Whittier Drive. He always had next to him on the piano a basket of pencils and a little bust of Wagner. He didn't play the piano very well—not a great pianist like Arthur Schwartz, or Harold Arlen, or Cy Coleman, who play beautifully. He'd play something he'd written, and if there was an expression on your face that showed you didn't care for it—he'd react very quickly to what you thought—he'd turn this little statuette around facing away and say, 'Wagner doesn't like it.' "

When Wagner did like it, his approbation resulted in some immortal Kern-Fields works. There was not only the score for *I Dream Too Much,* but the Astaire-and-Rogers hit musical *Swing Time;* firmly imbedded in that sound track were such lovelies as "A Fine Romance," "Pick Yourself Up," and "Bojangles of Harlem."

"I remember the day at the Beverly-Wilshire Hotel we were just planning *Swing Time.* We had to get a number for Fred Astaire. We couldn't get Jerry to write down a number that he could do. Jerry went to the bathroom, and Fred took me aside and said, 'My God, can we ever get a tune that I can *dance* to? Syncopated?' And the two of us sat with Jerry, and Fred hoofed all over the room and gave him ideas . . . and finally Jerry came up with a very good tune, 'Bojangles of Harlem.' "

And "The Way You Look Tonight," which won the Academy Award in 1936 for best film song. "The first time Jerry played that melody for me, I went out and started to cry," she says. "The release absolutely killed me. I couldn't stop, it was so beautiful.

"Oh, it was a lovely collaboration. Don't let anybody tell you Jerry was unhappy in Hollywood; he loved it out there. He made an excellent living and he did a lot of good work. And he was never difficult . . . except perhaps once," she muses. "This is the only time he ever let *me* have it. When George Gershwin bought a Cord. Remember the Cord car? It was beautiful.

"We went down to Palm Springs. George started to teach me how to play golf down there. I fell in love with his car, and he said, 'Well, why don't you get one too?' So I went out and bought a Cord. I always used very blue pencils to write with, and I had the car painted that bright blue color. I used to drive Jerry to the studio every day, because he didn't drive. And I drove up in my brand-new bright blue Cord, very proud, to pick Jerry up. There he was, waiting for me. But he became very incensed, the only time he ever lit into me. He said, 'I won't drive with you in that vulgar, repulsive car!' Do you believe I had to take it back and have it painted black?"

A martinet to others, a sharp-tongued man possessed of sharp opinions, Kern obviously enjoyed working with Miss Fields, and the feeling remained mutual. The two wrote another film, *The Joy of Living*, and were originally slated to do the score for *Annie Get Your Gun*. Kern's death ended a joyful collaboration.

"Jerry was wonderful, just wonderful," she murmurs. "He was always obsessed by hats. Had all sorts of them—jockey caps, captains' caps, all sorts of funny hats, just like Ed Wynn. One day we were all going to the races at Santa Anita, Jerry and his wife, Eva, me, and Sigmund Romberg—Rommie, the oom-pah-pah boy. He'd been here almost forty years, but he always garbled the language so. Ockie Hammerstein called them Rommie-isms. We drove up to the Kerns', and on this day Jerry came out wearing a checkered cap. Rommie took a look at him and said, 'Jerry, you look like a race-horse trout!' "

A few years later she collaborated with Romberg on the score of the Broadway show *Up in Central Park*, for which she and her brother Herbert also contributed a libretto.

"Oh, those Rommie-isms were classic. He had a rehearsal pianist once, a very nice girl, but he insulted her so much. Finally, he blew up one day at rehearsal and yelled, 'The trouble with you, Miss, is you haven't got enough shows behind your belt!' "

Miss Fields departed Beverly Hills in 1939 to write the score, with Arthur Schwartz, of a Broadway musical that satirized Hollywood filmmaking, *Stars in Your Eyes*. The stars of this joyfully mad venture were Ethel Merman and Jimmy Durante, and anyone who was a witness to the sights and sounds of Merman and Durante dueting the Schwartz-Fields ditty "It's All Yours," with Miss Merman aping Jimmy's inimitable strutaway—complete with hilarious jokes, head-wagging, and hot-cha-cha ("he actually *taught* her how to do him")—was party to a titanic display of talent, a perfect meld of material and performers.

Later on, Miss Fields worked with Arthur Schwartz on the scores for *By the Beautiful Sea*—for which she also did the book with brother Herbert—and *A Tree Grows in Brooklyn*. Both shows starred Shirley Booth, and they were, again, happy collaborations. Among their songs are such lovely works as "I'll Buy You a Star" and "Make the Man Love Me." And the echoes of Miss Booth singing "Look Who's Dancing" should inspire a producer to bring the joys of *A Tree Grows in Brooklyn* back to the stage; its nostalgia quotient was probably a few years ahead of its time.

Collaborating with Mr. Schwartz? "It's never been anything but a pleasure. Arthur's very easy to work with, and we're close friends," she says.

But Miss Fields' long career seems top-heavy with pleasant working relationships. Harry Warren, with whom she worked at Metro in the '40s on a film called *Texas Carnival*, is another good friend. "We did a couple of songs together. We'd work at the Beverly Hills Hotel, where I had a bungalow. You know, Harry has carried on for years about how anonymous he is. With him, it's always some sort of a mass plot on the part of the world to keep his name hidden. Harry always says, 'If anybody gets the smallest billing, I get it!' I remember one day we were on our way to the studio to play our songs, and he said, 'Now remember, Dorothy, when we get to the Metro lot, you walk three Oscars behind me'—because I had only one."

That talent for pleasant yet professional working relationships also extended into the more complex and demanding field of musical-comedy librettos. Dorothy and Herbert Fields wrote a string of smash-hit books for Cole Porter: *Let's Face It*, *Something for the Boys*, and *Mexican Hayride*.

Some of the Fields talent has to have been inherited. Lew Fields, their father, was a tremendous comedy star with Joe Weber. It was in Weber and Fields' "Dutch" act that "Who was that lady I saw you with last night? That was no lady, that was my wife!" first began to convulse audiences. "Growing up, we knew all the jokes. Everybody in the family contributed to a collection, picking them up wherever we heard them, writing them down in a big black ledger. After my father broke with Joe Weber, he became a producer and did musical shows of his own. He discovered Vernon Castle; he brought Blossom Seeley to New York from San Francisco. In 1911 he had five separate hits going!

"We lived in an atmosphere of comedy—jokes, blackout lines, funny routines. My father assigned me to keep his scrapbooks. At first I was interested in reading only his rave notices, but when I began to grow up, I got more interested in reading what the critics were saying about whether the *play* was good or not. And I began to be impressed by what made a good book—how, even if you had a great comic star like my father, you needed to have a sensible story, a plot that developed, with a beginning, a middle, and an end that would tie everything together. What I learned then still applies, all these years later. If you don't have a story that will hold the audience, you won't have a successful show. And as for the songs that go into that book, they have got to *move* the plot forward. I don't care how good a song is—if it holds back the story line, stalls the plot, your audience will reject it."

What about Cole Porter? What was it like working with him?

"Wonderful," she says promptly. "Herbert and I never had any set pattern with Cole. He didn't care too much about the book. He came to some rehearsals. But generally he just wrote songs, and he'd rewrite them, and then Herbert and I would have to fit them.

"Oh, I loved Cole. He and Herbie had worked together so many times before—they'd done *Fifty Million Frenchmen* and *The New Yorkers*, *Panama Hattie* and *DuBarry Was a Lady*—and they were very close friends. So I learned to disregard the way Cole ignored the book. I got used to it. Lots of times he'd read something in a scene we'd written and he'd say, 'Oh, you two people are so talented!' And then he'd cop a couple of lines of dialogue from that scene and put them into his lyrics. He'd say, 'Oh, you don't need this—you'll write something else, I'm sure you will.'

"I remember whenever we'd get to Boston to try out one of our shows with him, we loved to go out into the theatre lobby on Saturday afternoons when all the Back Bay dowagers would come to the matinee. I think it was during the tryout of *Let's Face It*, which starred Danny Kaye. Cole and Herbie and I were standing and listening to all the stuff those old biddies were talking about. And right next to us was a very aristocratic old dame. She said, 'I don't know *how* these actors think up all those funny things to say!' Cole was delighted with her remark. He nudged us, and he said, 'You see? You Fieldses want to write *book*?' "

Did she ever find it difficult to retire as a lyricist and bequeath that spot to Mr. Porter?

"Oh, honey, let me tell you, it's great," she says fervently. "The book is always the toughest thing to do; one doesn't need the added responsibility of doing the lyrics, I can assure you."

She managed the same shift most successfully in 1946 when Irving Berlin wrote both music and lyrics to the Fields' book for *Annie Get Your Gun*. On the American musical-comedy scene *Annie Get Your Gun* almost instantly assumed classic status. It's been filmed, done as a TV special, played all over the world. ("When it opened in London, the producer made records of the opening night and sent them to us. It's remarkable. Four sides of nothing but applause and cheers. And on closing night, that British audience wouldn't let the cast go, they loved them so.") And just a couple of seasons back *Annie* was revived in Lincoln Center, with Ethel Merman in her original part.

The last book that the Fields team wrote was *By the Beautiful Sea* in 1954. By now the lady was back at her lyricist's station. In fact, her post-*Annie* period was an extremely busy one. Not only was she busy on Broadway but she was also constantly involved in films—some with Arthur Schwartz and Harry Warren, another with Harold Arlen. In 1959 she returned to Broadway and worked with Albert Hague on *Redhead*, a starring vehicle for Gwen Verdon. That won the Tony Award for the best musical comedy of the year.

Hadn't there ever been one of those creative "dry spells"?

"Oh, honey," she says, "of course. They can happen to anybody. I just seem to manage to write my way out of them. I remember working with Fritz Kreisler, back in the '30s, when we were doing a picture at Columbia for Grace Moore, called *The King Steps Out*. Fritz says to me, 'You know, Dorothy, darling, for months, months, *months*, nothing comes out. Nothing. Break my heart, and break my head, and break the piano . . . ' And that was Fritz Kreisler! I don't care who you are, you hit those patches. Ockie Hammerstein, Irving, we've all gone through them."

The word "through" is the key word. Hammerstein also observed that the professional writer does not wait for inspiration to strike. To that, Miss Fields would add her own footnote; she keeps a book, one in which she records ideas, titles, lines for future reference, random thoughts. And she has a further piece of pragmatic advice: songwriters must not become married to one particular song. "You keep on writing. If the one you've written doesn't work, you write another."

She has a schedule worked out for audience acceptance as well. "You do a song in a show. Give it four performances. Monday, Tuesday, Wednesday— matinee and evening. If it hasn't clicked with the audience by then, take it out."

A rather ruthless timetable, isn't it?

"Sure it is," she concedes. "But remember, when I'm working on songs, I'm still a book-writer. I'm not out to write popular song hits, though I've written songs that have *become* popular; I'm writing a song to fit a spot in the show. To fit a character, to express something about him or her . . . to move that story line forward. You can't fool that audience out there. They'll always tell you whether a song is right or not." She shakes her head reminiscently. "And they're not polite about it, either."

Her work defies easy classification. The score of *Redhead* was essentially British in flavor, the show having been set in the Victorian period, against the background of Madame Tussaud's wax museum. A few years later, when Neil

Simon adapted Fellini's *Nights of Cabiria* into *Sweet Charity*, she and Cy Coleman created a score completely contemporary in its style. That show's music and lyrics were very close to the hard-rock idiom of the mid-'60s. How did she accommodate herself to that style? The one which Harold Arlen somewhat gloomily refers to as "a percussive era'?

"Well, you must stay *au courant,*" she says. "I don't pull myself into a shell like a turtle and withdraw. I go to the theatre, I listen to what's being played, I get a *feel* of what's around. And don't forget, my collaborator, Cy Coleman, is a very contemporary sort of guy."

Then what happens is a sort of osmotic process? Composer feeding lyricist, and vice versa?

She nods. "And you have to keep thinking of the situation in the play. Sometimes that gives you an idea for a lyric. Other times the sheer pressure of knowing that you need something will draw it out of you. I remember once during the tryout of *Charity* in Philadelphia we knew we needed another song for Gwen Verdon, and we wrote her 'I'm a Brass Band.' We wrote that in one morning. Here's what happened. I was living at the Barclay and Cy was at the Warwick. I went over to work with him, and I had the title in my head. I had the first line for it—*'I'm a brass band, I'm a harpsichord'* . . . We called Bobby Fosse, our director, who lived at the Warwick too. He came up and said, 'Fine, do it.' I wrote the lyric and Cy wrote the music, almost simultaneously. We've done that several times. I write very fast," she adds.

"But when we got to Detroit, we had a song called 'Raincheck' that was done in the garage scene. And it really was a stinker. We said, 'Oh, we can't keep this.' Not only did *we* say it, Fosse, everybody said it. So we wrote Saturday afternoon and part of Sunday, and we got 'The Rhythm of Life,' which was great for the show."

Sweet Charity was also remarkable for having in its score "Hey, Big Spender," which proved to be a show-stopper and went on to become a popular song hit, with attendant record sales and TV and radio plugs. And, as anyone around Broadway will be very sad to tell you, these days you don't hardly get those any more. A Broadway musical show may run to capacity houses for one or two seasons, but song hits from its score are harder to come by today than a parking space along 45th Street. So if Miss Fields was able to make contact with the record buyers of the '60s, something she started doing back in 1926, she has to be doing something right.

Perhaps the underlying element of Dorothy Fields' remarkable span of activity is embodied in the title of one of her own numbers, a song she wrote with Arthur Schwartz for Ethel Merman to chant in *Stars in Your Eyes* back in 1939. She called it "A Lady Needs a Change." Here, in her fifth decade of creativity, she's abiding by her own words, living a life compounded of various parts: loving parenthood, domesticity, auditions, conferences, Long Island summer retreats, rewrite sessions, theatre-going, socializing, public service (she's long been involved in work for the Girl Scouts and for the Federation of Jewish Philanthropies), more rewrites . . . and pedicures.

And she's already off on a new tack. She and Cy Coleman have made a musical version of William Gibson's hit play *Two for the Seesaw*. "Which is very much in the contemporary idiom of the '70s—not at all hard rock," she says, 'because that period's already over. Now there's a whole new sound. We're very lucky, Cy and I. Work fast when the ideas flow. We wrote the title song for *Seesaw* in three hours."

And if, because of some as yet unforeseen set of circumstances, *Seesaw* flounders—Broadway being the chanciest, costliest creative crap game ever devised—what then?

"I'll start another one, what else?" she quips instantly.

Which is something you learned early, and never forgot, if you were Lew Fields' daughter.

'Bewitched, Bothered, and Bewildered'

(Lorenz Hart)

L ONG AGO, in 1934, the D'Oyly Carte Opera Company of London's Savoy
Theatre crossed the Atlantic and took up temporary residence at the Martin
Beck Theatre on 45th Street, there to perform a season of Gilbert-and-Sullivan
light opera. My father, a dedicated Savoyard buff, led me to a succession of
Saturday matinees.

One afternoon, during the intermission, he introduced me to Larry Hart,
a diminutive black-haired gentleman. No pomposity about him: everyone—
actors, musicians, even acquaintances of a moment's duration—called him Larry.

What did Larry Hart do for a living?

He was a lyricist, my father explained later. A man who wrote the words
to the music of a gentleman named Richard Rodgers.

"He writes pretty good stuff of his own," I complained to my father. "What's
he doing *here* every week, listening to W. S. Gilbert's?"

"Homework," said my father. "You could say he was taking a refresher
course."

I had no idea what he meant by that remark until some years later, at a
summer-stock playhouse in Cohasset, Massachusetts, when I listened to Larry

Hart talk. He was erudite, witty, charming; his head was crammed with fact and fancy, reflecting the remarkable scope of his learning. To sing or to read his lyrics is to encounter an endless succession of exotic references, gracefully turned into rhyme. As the afternoon wore on, he had quite a few drinks and his speech became somewhat slurred. But Larry's mind never went under the influence.

I reminded him then of his steady attendance at those D'Oyly Carte Saturday matinees, and of my father's explanation for his presence there at the Martin Beck.

"Your old man was absolutely right!" said Larry. "I *was* there to study! Old man Gilbert was the greatest lyricist who ever turned a rhyme!"

Hart was born in 1895, descended on his father's side from Heinrich Heine. He was a voracious reader with an early-developed taste for the theatre. He went to Columbia (the alma mater of many others who went into show business, including Rodgers and Hammerstein) but left to work for the Shuberts.

A remarkable, mercurial man, Larry Hart.

"He was always skipping and bouncing," Oscar Hammerstein once recalled. "In all the time I knew him, I never saw him walk slowly. I never saw his face in repose. I never heard him chuckle quietly. He laughed loudly and easily at other people's jokes, and at his own, too. His large eyes danced and his head would wag. He was alert and dynamic."

Recalling their first meeting, Mr. Rodgers said, "He was violent on the subject of rhyming in songs, feeling that the public was capable of understanding better things than the current monosyllabic juxtaposition of 'slush' and 'mush.' It made great good sense, and I was enchanted by this little man and his ideas. I left Hart's house having acquired in one afternoon a career, a partner, a best friend, and a source of permanent irritation."

The first Rodgers-and-Hart song, written before Rodgers was even a student at Columbia, was "Any Old Place with You," which Lew Fields added to the score of a musical in which he was appearing on Broadway, *A Lonely Romeo.*

Rodgers wrote about their friendship and collaboration for the *Dramatists Guild Quarterly:*

> In many ways, a song-writing partnership is like a marriage. Apart from just liking each other, a lyricist and a composer should be able to spend long periods of time together—around the clock if need be—without getting on each other's nerves. Their goals, outlooks, and basic philosophies should be similar. They should have strong convictions, but no man should ever insist that his way alone is the right way. A member of a team should even be so in tune with his partner's work habits that he must be almost able to anticipate the other's next move. In short, the men should work together in such close harmony that the song they create is accepted as a spontaneous emotional expression emanating from a single source, with both words and music mutually dependent in achieving the desired effect.
>
> I've been lucky. During most of my career I've had only two partners. Lorenz Hart and I worked together for twenty-five years; Oscar Hammerstein II and I were partners for over eighteen. Each man was totally different in appearance, work habits, personality, and

practically anything else you can think of. Yet each was a genius at his own craft, and each, during our association, was the closest friend I had.

I met Oscar before I met Larry. I was twelve and he was nineteen when my older brother Mortimer, a fraternity brother of Oscar's, took me backstage to meet him after a performance of a Columbia Varsity Show. Oscar played the comic lead in the production, and meeting this worldly college junior was pretty heady stuff for a stagestruck kid.

I met Larry about four years later. I was still in high school at the time, but I had already begun writing songs for amateur shows, and I was determined even then to make composing my life's work. Although I had written the words to some of my songs, I was anxious to team up with a full-fledged lyricist. A mutual friend, Philip Leavitt, was the matchmaker who introduced us one Sunday afternoon at Larry's house. I liked what Larry had written, and apparently he liked my music. But most important, we found in each other the kind of person we had been looking for in a partner—our ideas and aims were so much alike that we just sensed that this was it. From that day on, until I wrote *Oklahoma!* with Oscar, the team of Rodgers and Hart was an almost exclusive partnership.

Larry Hart, as almost anyone will agree, was a genius at lyric construction, at rhyming, at finding the offbeat way of expressing himself. He had a somewhat sardonic view of the world that can be found occasionally in his love songs and in his satirical numbers. But Larry was also a kind, gentle, generous little guy, and these traits too may be found in some of his memorable lyrics. Working with him, however, did present problems, since he had to be literally trapped into putting pen on paper—and then only after hearing a melody that stimulated him.

The great thing about Larry was that he was always growing—creatively, if not physically. He was fascinated by the various techniques of rhyming, such as polysyllabic rhymes, interior rhymes, masculine and feminine rhymes, and the trick of rhyming one word with only part of another. Who else could have come up with the line, *"Beans could get no keener re-/Ception in a beanery,"* as he did in "Mountain Greenery"?* Or *"Hear me holler/I choose a/Sweet Lolla-/Paloosa/In thee"* in "Thou Swell"? Or *"I'm wild again/Beguiled again/A whimpering, simpering child again,"* in "Bewitched"?

Yet Larry could also write simply and poetically. "My Heart Stood Still,"† for example, expressed so movingly the power of *"that unfelt clasp of hand,"* and did it in a refrain consisting almost entirely

---

* From the second edition of *The Garrick Gaieties*, which the team wrote in 1926.
    † The story has been often told of how "My Heart Stood Still" came into being. The two young collaborators were in Paris in 1926, riding in a Paris taxi with two girls. The cab skittered into a truck, and one of the girls blurted out, "Oh! My heart stood still!" From the floor of the taxicab, where the collision had thrown him, his hat jammed over his eyes, diminutive Larry Hart is supposed to have said promptly, "Hey, Dick, there's a good title for a song!"

of monosyllables. Larry was intrigued by almost every facet of human emotion. In "Where or When" he dared take up the psychic phenomenon of a person convinced that he has known someone before, even though the two people are meeting for the first time. As the years went on, there was an increasingly rueful quality in some of Larry's lyrics that gave them a very personal connotation. I am referring to such plaints as "Nobody's Heart Belongs to Me" (from *By Jupiter*), with its feigned indifference to love, and "Spring Is Here," a confession of one whose attitude about the season is colored by his feeling of being unloved. It should not be overlooked, however, that Larry was also attracted to the simple life. Remember his paean to rustic charms in "There's a Small Hotel,"* or to *"our blue room far away upstairs."* Or his attitude in "My Romance," in which he dismissed as unnecessary all the conventional romantic props when two people find themselves really in love.

Eventually Rodgers and Hart were to form a working partnership with Herbert Fields, the son of the great Lew. Dorothy Fields, later a collaborator with her brother Herbert, grew up with the young triumvirate in her home. "Upstairs on the top floor of the house on 90th Street they were all working hard on musical shows," she recalled. "After Columbia Varsity Shows they had formed a combination. Herb was to do the book—and he was obsessed with the necessity of a strong book (as I was to be later), Dick the music, and Lorenz the lyrics. They had bright, fresh, wonderful ideas, but no one gave them an ear—least of all the famous actor-producer [Fields père] sitting downstairs in his library on the second floor.

"Fields, Rodgers, and Hart peddled their wares to diverse producers who fixed a baleful eye upon brother Herbert and said, 'If you guys are as good as you think you are, how come your father, Mr. Fields, isn't interested in producing your show?' "

Lew Fields came from an earlier era in which musical comedy meant what it said—a certain amount of music and a double helping of laughs. A coherent libretto? A book show? Miss Fields said, "Pop would say, 'What book? In a musical, give them gags, blackouts, belly laughs, great performers, and great performances: that's what they've come for. They don't come to a musical comedy for a story.' But he changed, and when Pop changed, he changed all the way.

---

* Students of the craft of lyric-writing should refer to Hart's "dummy" lyric for "Small Hotel"—that is, the one he wrote before he did the actual song. It went:

> *There's a girl next door*
> *Who's an awful bore,*
> *It really makes you sore*
> *To see her.*
> *a. . . .*
> *b. . . .*
> *c. . . .*
> *d. . . .*
> *By and by, perhaps she'll die,*
> *Perhaps she'll croak this summer;*
> *Her old man's a plumber,*
> *She's much dumber.*

Herb, Dick, and Larry had to come through with two enormously successful *Garrick Gaieties* produced by the Theatre Guild, and then a charming play, *Dearest Enemy*, before Pop began to believe that the kids had something there."

The first edition of *The Garrick Gaieties* was scheduled to have only two performances, on a Sunday in May 1925. Its ostensible purpose was to give the young talent of the Theatre Guild a showcase, and also to raise money to purchase tapestries for the theatre on 52nd Street that the Guild was building. What the show actually did was to launch Rodgers and Hart into a songwriting orbit that was to last until Hart's death in 1943.

Years later, so the story goes, Rodgers and Hart attended a performance at the Guild Theatre. Rodgers nudged Hart and pointed at the tapestries that decorated the walls. "We're responsible for those," he murmured. Hart shook his head. "They're responsible for *us*," he said.

Out of the score of that first revue came "Manhattan" and "Romantic You and Sentimental Me." That fall, in *Dearest Enemy*, the young team had another hit, "Here in My Arms." And there followed the show which Lew Fields produced, *The Girl Friend*.

"It had a lively story and a stunning score," remembers Dorothy Fields. "And those boys [Rodgers, Hart, and Fields] were really hell on 'book.' During rehearsals Pop dusted off the old ledger and came up with some blockbusters, but the boys wouldn't accept one joke. Nothing went into that show that didn't go along with the story!"

More than four decades later the strength of their score survives remarkably well. One of the show's hits was "Blue Room," and another, the catchy and carefree "The Girl Friend."

"Only one thing remained constant in Larry's approach to his job," Dick Rodgers was to remark. "He hated doing it and loved when it was done. I saw him write a sparkling stanza to 'The Girl Friend' in a hot, smelly rehearsal hall, with chorus girls pounding out jazz time and principals shouting out their lines. In half an hour he fashioned something with so many interior rhymes, so many tricky phrases, and so many healthy chuckles in it, that I just couldn't believe he had written it in one evening."

Under the beneficent production auspices of Lew Fields, the Herbert Fields–Rodgers–Hart partnership was to evolve three more successful musicals: *Peggy-Ann*, with its wistful ballad, "Where's That Rainbow?," *A Connecticut Yankee*, and *Present Arms*.

The pleasures of the score of *A Connecticut Yankee* cannot be put into words; such works were meant to be listened to, hummed and sung. What is there to say about "Thou Swell" that Larry Hart has not already set down in his gay, intricate lyric? "I Feel at Home with You," "On a Desert Island with Thee," "My Heart Stood Still"—the eye reads the titles, the brain evokes the strains of the music happily melded with the words, everything floods back into the mind, and if you're a Rodgers-and-Hart fan, how can you help but sing?

In *Present Arms* was "You Took Advantage of Me." In *Spring Is Here*, "With a Song in My Heart." In another show of the same period, *Heads Up*, there was the beautiful torch song "A Ship Without a Sail." A couple of years later, in *America's Sweetheart*, there were two deft love songs called "I've Got Five Dollars" and "We'll Be the Same," in which Hart maintained, *"There may be thirteen months in the year/Nations may disappear/Hi-ho, we'll be here and we'll be the same."*

Although neither of the two men enjoyed their Hollywood experiences, they did some remarkably advanced work for the early cinema musicals. They wrote a sparkling score for Maurice Chevalier and Jeanette MacDonald in the film *Love Me Tonight*, providing "Mimi," "Lover,"* and a title song. But some of their most inventive work was done for a film that was far from successful, an original musical called *Hallelujah, I'm a Bum*, which starred Al Jolson.

Back on their home ground, Broadway, they did the score for *Jumbo* and serenaded the audience with "Little Girl Blue," "The Most Beautiful Girl in the World," and "My Romance." Then came *On Your Toes*, with "There's a Small Hotel," "It's Got to Be Love," and a song whose title seems to express a great deal about Larry Hart's attitude toward life, "Glad to Be Unhappy."

The man who wrote all these brilliant lyrics—who could range from the beautiful ballad "Falling in Love with Love" (from *The Boys from Syracuse*)† to the sardonic ripostes of "The Lady Is a Tramp" (*Babes in Arms*), who could craft all those acid-edged rhymes that mark the score of *Pal Joey* and then write a paean to his beloved, "Wait Till You See Her" (*By Jupiter*)— was far from a simple personality. In his work he never ceased to seek out new and more inventive ways to express himself. Back in 1938 *Time* magazine's theatre critic wrote, "As Rodgers and Hart see it, what was killing musicomedy was its sameness, its tameness, its eternal rhyming of June with moon. They decided it was not enough to be just good at the job; they had to be constantly different also. The one possible formula was, *Don't have a formula;* the one rule for success, *Don't follow it up.*"

But evidently the success of Hart's work wasn't enough. "He needed laughter the way some men need praise," commented David Ewen in his biography of Rodgers. "A carefully timed wisecrack, a well-told joke, a neatly turned pun, a skillfully perpetrated prank—these were the meat and drink of his soul."

The success of the Rodgers-and-Hart collaboration—and it was remarkably constant during the late 1930s and early 1940s—never seemed to answer Hart's emotional needs. His humor, which bubbled out into brilliant rhyme, covered a deep-seated unhappiness. "Larry was a night person," says a friend who knew him well. "He never seemed to have any place to go. He'd hang around Louie Bergin's tavern on 45th Street, where actors and show people always congregated after the show, stay there until closing time, buying everybody drinks, paying no attention to what it cost. All he wanted to do was to talk. He'd haul out a big wad of bills and spend it without a second thought. And remember, back in those days his weekly royalties would be considered a huge sum even by today's standards." Once Hart told Ted Fetter, another talented lyricist, "I can't believe I make so much money—it's completely disproportionate for the work I do to earn it."

* Hart later wrote a set of lyrics for "Lover" that was to turn it into one of the team's most enduring songs.

† "Larry was drinking heavily," wrote George Abbott, the producer-director of that show, "and would be absent for two or three days at a time during the preparation of the show. This didn't bother me because he was quick as lightning when he was there. If we needed a new verse, he'd pick up a pencil and paper, fidget himself into the next room for a few minutes and then come back with what we needed. I remember that this was how he wrote the verse for 'Falling in Love with Love'; he scratched it on the back of an old piece of paper while Dick [Rodgers] and I talked about something else." (From Abbott's autobiography, *Mister Abbott*.)

Robert Russell Bennett recalls another occasion: "We were having supper after the theatre one time in London. Simpson's Restaurant, I think it was. I was talking to Larry about writing lyrics, and I mentioned one of his ballads, and I asked him, 'Larry, what inspired you to write such a lovely lyric?' And Larry said, 'Oh, Russ, when I write the lyric, the only time I'm inspired . . . pencil in my hand and a piece of paper in front of me,' he said, '*that's* the inspiration.'"

Such self-effacing statements are astonishing when one contemplates the scope of his work; it represents a dazzling display of virtuosity. Think of the cynical boy-girl duet "I Wish I Were in Love Again," in which he penned "*When love congeals/The air reveals/The faint aroma of performing seals.*" Listen to the dazzling score of *The Boys from Syracuse*, in which the first eight or nine minutes of intricate Shakespearian exposition is brilliantly distilled for the audience in Hart's rhymes and Rodgers' music. Treat yourself to all those lightly mocking works in which he contemplated the various aspects of love—"This Can't Be Love," "I Didn't Know What Time It Was," "My Romance," "Love Never Went to College." And should your taste run to social comment, listen to his words for songs like "Too Good for the Average Man," and the song in which the pseudo-intellectual stripteaser in *Pal Joey* ruminates on the intellectual world while removing her clothes, "Zip." ("*Zip! Walter Lippmann wasn't brilliant today/Lip! Will Saroyan ever write a great play?/Zip! I was reading Schopenhauer last night/Zip! And I think that Schopenhauer was right.*")

Toward the end of his life Hart was increasingly depressed and moody. The score for *By Jupiter* in 1942 was brilliant, but his propensity for work was diminishing. Perhaps his sense of loneliness is somewhat prophetically expressed in his own lyric, written for the very last show he worked on, a revival of *A Connecticut Yankee* in 1943. His partner, Dick Rodgers, was already discussing a collaboration with Oscar Hammerstein on a musical version of Lynn Riggs' *Green Grow the Lilacs*. It was a project Hart had turned down. He didn't feel it was his sort of show; Oklahoma and the Southwestern scene weren't his turf. They would be better served by Hammerstein, whose outlook was different. Where Hart saw the irony, the sharp contradictions of life, Hammerstein saw the optimistic side. But Hart did contribute to the *Connecticut Yankee* revival. He wrote a magnificent song for Vivienne Segal to sing—"To Keep My Love Alive"—in which the lady described in a superb procession of couplets how she had done away with many of her past lovers, medieval-style. And then he wrote a gentle ballad called "Can't You Do a Friend a Favor?"in which he penned a verse, the words of which may embody his final self-analysis:

> You can count your friends on the fingers of your hand,
> If you're lucky, you have two.

On the opening night of *A Connecticut Yankee*, Hart stood up throughout the performance in the back of the theatre, and when the curtain fell—the revival was again a success—he wandered out into the cold November night. Two days later he was found unconscious, with pneumonia, in a hotel room. He died three days after, at the age of forty-eight.

But Larry Hart would have been the first to object to finishing any discussion of his career on such a downbeat note. Since his stage works invariably finished with a joyful strain, he would undoubtedly prefer us to chortle over an incident that took place when *On Your Toes* was running on Broadway.

In the first act of the show, which starred Ray Bolger as a vaudeville hoofer who took up ballet, there was an opulent ballet spoof, staged by George Balanchine, called "The Princess Zenobia," complete with slaves, harem trappings, and broadly satirized echoes of the Far East. At a given point in the ballet, the chorus boys, dressed as Nubian slaves, made a tumultuous entrance to Rodgers' music.

Larry Hart's agent, a legendary Broadway character named "Doc" Bender, spent many evenings hanging around backstage, chatting and passing jokes back and forth with the chorus boys.

Dick Rodgers, who was (and is) a stickler for keeping up the level of a show's performance after opening night, noticed that on successive evenings the entrance of the Nubian slaves was happening later and later, to a point where it disrupted the entire number. Upon investigating, Rodgers discovered that "Doc" Bender's presence backstage was responsible. Irritated, Rodgers called his partner to complain. "It's up to you to see to it that Bender stays away, at least until after the curtain comes down!" he instructed.

Without hesitating, Hart ad-libbed (to the tune of "There's a Small Hotel," the hit song from the team's score):

> *Looking through the window, you*
> *Can see six slaves and Bender.*
> *Bender's on the ender—*
> *Lucky Bender.*

It's a safe guess that old W. S. Gilbert would have laughed.

'The Sound of Music'

(Richard Rodgers)

WE ARE SITTING in the main office of Williamson Music, Inc. It is a large room, tastefully furnished with antiques, and its windows look down on Madison Avenue and 57th Street. This might be the board room of a major American corporation, except that such corporate GHQs rarely house the company's major assets; they're usually tucked away in downtown vaults. Not here. Across an antique desk sits Williamson Music's corporate cornerstone, Richard Rodgers. Over there in the corner is the company's entire stock of machinery —one grand piano.

In truth, Rodgers does resemble a chairman of the board. He wears banker's gray suits, discreet button-down shirts, and soberly striped ties. But when he sits down at the grand piano and begins to play, that corporate image vanishes. Rodgers has lately celebrated his seventieth birthday, but none of his mental processes has slowed down one beat. His mind is brisk, sharply tuned, and as agile as his fingers.

He has been writing major song hits for a long time now. Somewhere in the world tonight there will be a performance of his and Oscar Hammerstein's *Oklahoma!* or *Carousel* or *South Pacific. The King and I* is a regular at Jones

Beach during the summer. In the movie theatres their film *The Sound of Music* has long since become the top-grossing musical of Hollywood's history. The most superfluous question one could ask Mr. Rodgers is that old chestnut, Which comes first, the music or the lyrics?, because he's functioned both ways. When he wrote hit songs with Larry Hart, the words usually came after the tune; with Hammerstein the process was reversed. One thing remained constant—the vast number of popular hits he had with both.

Is he not the logical man to answer a far more basic question: What is it that makes a song a popular success? What is the secret ingredient that plucks at a mass nerve, that makes some sort of electrical contact with the listener? And why is it that composers like Rodgers or Kern or Berlin can make that electrical contact with their audience quite regularly, while others can go through their whole lives and never connect more than once or twice, if at all?

"I don't think this is a very esoteric situation," he said. "It is quite simple. If you have any integrity, you start out by writing what you like. A tune that you finally settle for is your tune—and you like it, otherwise you wouldn't have written it. Or, having written it, you'd tear it up. But you say to yourself, this is the tune that ought to go in this particular spot, whether as a popular song, or part of a play, or a motion picture, or TV. You are writing for yourself. Now, if your taste is lucky enough to be a common denominator, and coincides with the tastes of the public, you have got it made. If it isn't, if it doesn't coincide, then you are that fellow you were just talking about who never makes it, or makes it very infrequently . . . so infrequently that he isn't anybody.

"Say you have thirty-two bars that the composer really likes *himself*. Then he gives it to the public. If the public likes it, that's the only criterion that one has to go by. It doesn't mean anything necessarily if *I* like it, either. *But* if I write enough songs that the public also likes, then I have established what you call that electrical contact, over a broad spectrum."

Once he has established that contact with the audience, does he have the feeling that it diminishes, or does it stay steady?

"You begin all over again, every time you do a piece of work," he said. "The next one may establish no contact whatsoever, but that doesn't put you out of the business."

In other words, those creative juices that have been sustaining him from the days of *The Garrick Gaieties* back in the '20s are still flowing reliably every day?

Rodgers shrugged. "Not necessarily. They may not flow until next week, or next month. But you keep looking for new projects . . . and doing what you enjoy."

John Fearnley, who was closely associated with Rodgers and Hammerstein while that team was writing successful shows and even producing the works of others (*Annie Get Your Gun, The Happy Time*, and others), once recalled a production meeting during the preparation of *South Pacific*. It was at a time when Rodgers was suffering from severe back trouble, and he was lying on the floor, resting against a pillow. Mr. Hammerstein entered the room, bringing the first lyric he'd written for their new show; Rodgers, lying supine, read his partner's lyric and, after a few moments' thought, said, "I can hear the beginning of the show." He got up from the floor and went over to his piano. "When the overture starts, you'll hear these notes," he said, and played the first three notes of "Bali Ha'i." The rest of the song followed very rapidly.

A rather extraordinary demonstration of the interaction between the two creative men. "Except that very little of the story happened that way," said Mr. Rodgers. "What John left out was that Oscar and I had known for months that we were going to do a song called 'Bali Ha'i,' and something must have been going around in my head about it without the lyric actually being written. But I knew that I had a certain approach to the way the music should *sound* in describing this exotic island with the two peaks rising from it. We were at Josh Logan's apartment, and at lunch Oscar did take the typewritten piece out of his pocket and hand it to me, the lyric to the song. And I went into the next room and I wrote. The melody took me very little time because I *knew* so much about it already. And I had his lyric to build on. That may account for the speed."

But hasn't it always been legendary, that rapid "shorthand" between the two men—Hammerstein handing Rodgers a new lyric he'd sweated over for days, and Rodgers quickly supplying the required tune?

"Only if I knew what it was about in advance," said Rodgers. "I knew that *Oklahoma!* was going to open with the cowboy coming onstage, singing a song about what a beautiful day it was. I knew it had to be in 3/4 time. I knew it had to have a certain taste . . . long before I ever saw the lyric. Now, all these preconditioning items can force you into a certain groove."

A groove which produces "Oh, What a Beautiful Morning" can hardly be faulted.

"It was flying around subconsciously, I'm sure," he remarked.

"When we started to do *Oklahoma!* Oscar meant to be helpful. I'd never been to Oklahoma. And I certainly wasn't in the Southwest in 1906; I was only four years old at the time. So he sent me a book about the subject. And I opened it up, took one look at it, and then closed it and never opened it again. The only thing I could do was what any self-respecting artist would do. I put on music paper *my idea* of how Oklahoma sounded in 1906. The way Indian Territory sounded at the beginning of the century. Did it again in *The King and I*. I certainly hadn't been to Siam before I wrote that. But I wanted to express my feeling about the way Siam sounded."

The same thing with *Carousel?*

"Sure," he said, 'but that's a little closer to home. I expected that a fellow who'd lived in Connecticut as long as 1 have could make sounds like New England."

Mr. Rodgers' description of how he never opened the book on Oklahoma again has an uncanny parallel to Mr. Hammerstein's own remarks on the writing of lyrics. In his book *Lyrics*, written in 1949, Hammerstein said, "A rhyming dictionary is of little use and may, in fact, be a handicap when one is writing a song. . . . If you would achieve the rhyming grace and facility of W. S. Gilbert or Lorenz Hart, my advice would be never to open a rhyming dictionary. Don't even own one."

So, in a sense, the work patterns of Hammerstein and Rodgers did have that inherent parallel?

"Absolutely," said Mr. Rodgers. "Once you have learned the rules, you then have the need to break them. Unless you're like a song publisher I used to know many, many years ago, who said there was only one way to write a popular hit and that was to begin writing the chorus, the refrain of the song, on the *first* note of the bar, with the *first* note of the diatonic scale and *with* a *major* chord. In other words, the first note of the song couldn't be the second note of the tune. And he insisted you couldn't start with a musical rest; it had to be dominant, from the beginning, the first note! And furthermore, he insisted that it had to be a *major* chord in the key of C—and that chord *had* to be C, E, and G! Now, think of the limitations *he* already had imposed on you. If you were trying to say something, it was an impossible situation. That had to be the most inhibiting thing you could possibly think of to lay on a songwriter."

It sounds like those iron rules Hollywood producers used to hand down about what makes a good picture. All those old formulae—story has to be upbeat, boy has to meet girl, then lose girl, then get girl . . .

A grimace crossed Mr. Rodgers' face when the subject of Hollywood surfaced. He obviously had few pleasant thoughts on the subject of the so-called "golden era" of the mid-1930s, when so many New York composers and lyricists became resident in the Hollywood canyons, writing for the seven film factories which were churning out musical films.

"One of their pet procedures," he recalled, "was to assign four or five different songwriters to the same spot in the same picture, and then to take the song they liked the best. So you found yourself working in competition with other writers. They did it to Larry Hart and to me, to everybody, even to Jerry Kern—and if they would do that to *Kern*, for God's sake . . ." He shook his head sadly. "This was sheer suicide for a composer."

And yet, the early film work of Rodgers and Hart, especially for *Love Me Tonight*, was remarkably innovative and lasting ("Isn't It Romantic?," "Mimi," "Love Me Tonight," "Lover").

"All of that depended on the director. In *Love Me Tonight* it was Mamoulian. At that time he was God at Paramount. Whatever he wanted to do, he did. He believed in Larry and me, and we believed in him and got along beautifully," said Rodgers. "So we were able to do something new and, fortunately, successful. In those days they used to plant the camera in front of the boy and the girl and start to grind, and they'd sing, and that was it. But in *Love Me Tonight* we took numbers all over the place. It was the first time that musical sound track was cut—dialogue and music interspersed. As a matter of fact, in the opening song, 'Isn't It Romantic?,' we went from Chevalier's tailor shop in Paris to Jeanette MacDonald's castle, far away. Various people or groups sang the song, passed it along, so she heard it on the balcony of her castle and learned it, and picked it up. We established a romantic contact between two people who not only had never met but were in different parts of France. All done through the use of the music, sound track cutting, and so forth. But only because Mamoulian believed in this technique."

I mentioned *Hallelujah, I'm a Bum*, which Rodgers and Hart wrote for Al Jolson in 1933, a motion picture years ahead of its time in the use of rhyming couplets instead of spoken dialogue.* Among the joys of this almost-forgotten film was a chorus of Central Park hoboes, led by Jolson, strolling through the green and singing "Hallelujah, I'm a Bum;" a haunting love ballad, "You Are Too Beautiful;" and a delightful scene in which a postcard from the hero is delivered to the leading lady. As she reads it, we hear Jolson's voice, off screen, *singing* the contents of the message in rhyme: "*Dear June, I got to Cleveland okay, the weather's fine . . .*" and so on.

"It has a certain number of partisans who remember it," said Rodgers.

---

* Hart was quoted at the time as saying, "The dramatic action, the flow of photography, and the humor and pathos of the characters will be inherent in the music. We wrote lyrics and music especially for the camera."

"Once in a while it shows up on the Late Show or plays downtown at the little Elgin Theatre. We just went down to see it a couple of weeks ago." He smiles at the recollection. "We did all sorts of things that had never been done before. But, again, they were totally dependent on having a director who was sympathetic. In that case, Lewis Milestone.

"But that picture and *Love Me Tonight* and, many years later, the one I did with Oscar, *State Fair* [from which score came such musical jewels as "It Might as Well Be Spring"] were the only three experiences I ever had with California that were enjoyable. They made many good moving-picture versions of stage shows of ours, but these are the only *original* ones for film that worked well. And that's hardly a career," he added sardonically.

"The most terrible lies have been all those Hollywood musicals which purport to be the life story of people like Gershwin, or Porter, or Kern. They give no insight whatsoever into the working patterns of the men they're supposedly about." Rodgers shrugged. "They did it to Larry and me." (He was referring to *Words and Music*, in which Metro-Goldwyn-Mayer somewhat improbably cast Tom Drake as Rodgers and Mickey Rooney as Hart.) "The only good thing about that picture was that they had Janet Leigh play my wife. And I found *that* highly acceptable." He grinned.

It is well-known that Rodgers never went back to see the second act of *Hair*. Is it true that he doesn't like the music or lyrics that are being written for the theatre today?

"It's true," he admitted. "There's only one current score that I have real respect for—this is my own opinion, not necessarily the public's—and that is *Company*. I know I was very much affected by that score." (*Company* was written by Stephen Sondheim, who a few years ago collaborated with Mr. Rodgers on the score of *Do I Hear a Waltz?*)

What about popular music?

"There I'm left high and dry," said Rodgers ruefully. "With a few exceptions. Burt Bacharach is one, and Jim Webb is another. I think these two are extremely musical and original. I think they are great. But the hard-rock stuff . . . I don't pretend to understand."

Twenty years ago the late Howard Lindsay, playwright, director, and producer, took it upon himself to chair an organization called the New Dramatists Committee. Its function was to encourage and sustain tyro playwrights. The group was a no-nonsense operation, dedicated not to theory but to pragmatic learning about the theatre (something which anyone on Broadway will tell you is extremely hard to come by).

One evening Lindsay brought his friends Rodgers and Hammerstein into a cluttered room above the Hudson Theatre where they held still for several hours of question-and-answer. It was the fall of 1951, and the state of the theatre—especially the musical theatre—seemed particularly parlous. In the course of the evening a question was asked of Hammerstein: "Where do you think the new songwriters and lyricists and book writers are going to come from if they don't ever get a chance to be heard?"

"Well," said Hammerstein, "I've been around a long time now, and the only thing I can tell you is that it always looks this way—dark and depressing. But somewhere, somebody new always crops up. It may be in a new form, or he may write in a new way—you never can be sure exactly how—but sooner or later a new guy shows up and he comes through. Does that help answer your question?"

"I'd almost forgotten that," admitted Rodgers when reminded of that evening. "But obviously Oscar, as usual, made a lot of sense."

True enough. For since those dark days of 1951 the Broadway theatre has seen the emergence, in the musical field, of such exciting new talents as Steve Sondheim, Jerry Bock and Sheldon Harnick (*Fiddler on the Roof*), Kander and Ebb (*Cabaret*), and Galt MacDermott (*Two Gentlemen of Verona*).

"No, I don't believe that the theatre is dead at all," he said. "If *No, No, Nanette* can happen, then a new work can happen. Who would have thought that the biggest hit in town would be a forty-year-old musical show? If the public will accept that, they will accept something that is new, I am sure of it. It just has to be good *of its kind*. The public is amazingly flexible."

Then the whole secret is to keep writing. That's what Hammerstein really meant, isn't it?

"Oh, sure," said Rodgers. "And I think you have to stick to it, and if what you write doesn't become popular, then you are not going to do well in the music-writing industry. But if what *you* have to say coincides with what the *public* wants to hear—then you are in pretty good shape."

We were back again at that indefinable something which vaults across the space from the composer's keyboard into the public ear and causes some intuitive response. That secret ingredient. Can it ever be defined?

Perhaps not. But, whatever it is, Rodgers' music has always contained more than a fair share of it, ever since those days back in 1925 when he was setting Larry Hart's couplets to the melodies of "Manhattan" and "Mountain Greenery," through all those years of Rodgers-and-Hart shows, then to the succession of hits he wrote with Oscar Hammerstein—and even now, after *No Strings*, for which he did both music and lyrics, and *Do I Hear a Waltz?* with Sondheim, right up to *Two by Two*.

"The only way I can define it," said Robert Russell Bennett, who has been orchestrating for Rodgers for many years, "is that down deep somewhere in that soul of his there must be a warm, beautiful thing . . . to come out with all these melodies."

"It's funny," said Rodgers, half to himself. "I remember wanting to quit at the age of twenty-two. I felt I was getting old!"

He stood up and glanced at his watch; we'd been talking for more than an hour. The man who supervises the operations of Williamson Music and of all the other operations allied with such a large commercial enterprise clearly had other things to do besides answer metaphysical questions about talent. Questions which over the past half-century he'd discussed many times, and yet over which, like his late partner Hammerstein, he showed no impatience on this busy spring afternoon.

"I hope these questions haven't bored you," I said.

"They're very good, very valid questions. I hope the *answers* were all right."

Now that there isn't, for the first time in years, a Richard Rodgers musical score playing in a Broadway theatre, there was one more question for him, and one for which we all hope there's an answer (to borrow a Rodgers-and-Hart title) "Soon":

What, Mr. Rodgers, is your next?

'This Was a Real Nice Clambake'

(Oscar Hammerstein II)

WHEN Oscar Hammerstein II wrote his first produced play in 1919, he was twenty-four years old. The play, *The Light,* was tried out in New Haven, Connecticut. "After the first act Dad knew he had a flop," recalls his son, William. "In fact, later he always referred to it as 'The Light That Failed.' Well, he left the Shubert Theatre during the first intermission and went for a walk around the Yale campus. He wasn't just going out for a depressed ramble; what he was doing was thinking what he would write for his *next* play."

That sturdy resilience of young Oscar's, the commingling of determination and forward motion, was to sustain him well for his next forty years as author, lyricist, and producer. But if he were still here to discuss his behavior in New Haven all those years ago, Hammerstein would probably dismiss it with a pragmatic, "Well, what else should a writer do, if he's really a writer?"

For that is what Oscar Hammerstein was—a pro. From his earliest days on Broadway—writing books for operettas during the '20s, setting lyrics to the music of Jerome Kern, Sigmund Romberg, Vincent Youmans, and Rudolph Friml—young Oscar always demonstrated that his talent was only one facet of his work, and that his meticulous application of it was what made the difference between the amateur and the pro. It is a lesson that appears to be lost on the current crop of slapdash songwriters, but they would do well to ponder it. *Show Boat*, which Hammerstein wrote with Kern in 1927, is running to packed houses in London as this is written, forty-six years after the fact. True, *Jesus Christ Superstar* is also having its run; but forty-five years from now, will they be reviving that? It's a cinch that *Show Boat* will still be playing somewhere. "We certainly wouldn't consider it a revival," sniffed a prominent London theatrical manager. "We've always had a production of it around here. And we also had Hammerstein's *Desert Song* doing quite nicely here in the West End, three years back."

If his earlier work demonstrated staying power, then Mr. Hammerstein's later years proved to be truly vintage ones. In the seventeen years of his collaboration with Richard Rodgers, the two men wrote and produced a series of musical shows that for verve, innovation, and sheer imaginative entertainment are truly something wonderful—*Oklahoma!*, *Carousel*, *South Pacific*, *The King and I*, *The Sound of Music*. It was Cole Porter who, when asked to name the most profound changes in the musical-comedy field of *his* past forty years, replied simply, "Rodgers and Hammerstein."

"Ockie," as his friends always fondly called him, was more than a gifted author and lyricist. As Rodgers was to write in 1967, "His view of life was positive. He was a joiner, a leader, a man willing to do battle for whatever causes he believed in. He was not naïve. He knew full well that man is not all good and that nature is not all good; yet it was his sincere belief that someone had to keep reminding people of the vast amount of good things that there are in the world."

In Hollywood, in the early 1930s, Hammerstein was among the first of the creative people living and working in that often frightened and mute community to take a positive stand against Nazism, both in Europe and here. Producers didn't relish having songwriters take stands on political issues; that didn't stop Hammerstein for a minute. During World War II he worked long and hard at various jobs designed to hasten V-J Day, and when the peace came, he dedicated himself to the idealistic cause of World Federalism.

Was there work to be done at the Dramatists Guild? Did neophyte television writers need help in forming a guild of their own? Oscar was always available, and never as a figurehead but as a worker, an adviser, a negotiator. A man with manifold pressures on him as a producer and writer, he was lavish with his valuable time.

Stephen Sondheim provides the most tangible evidence of Hammerstein's consideration for others: "I first got into lyric-writing because when I was a child we moved to Pennsylvania, and among my mother's friends were the Hammerstein family. Oscar Hammerstein gradually got me interested in the theatre, and I suppose most of it happened one fateful or memorable afternoon. He had urged me to write a musical for my school. With two classmates, I wrote a musical called *By George*. I thought it was pretty terrific, so I asked Oscar to read it—and I was arrogant enough to say to him, 'Will you read it as if it were just a musical that crossed your desk as a producer? Pretend you don't know me.' He said okay and I went home that night with visions of being the first fifteen-year-old to have a show on Broadway. I knew he was going to love it.

"Oscar came over the next day and said, 'Now, you really want me to treat this as if it were by somebody I don't know?' and I said, 'Yes, please,' and he said, 'Well, in that case, it's the worst thing I ever read in my life.' He must have seen my lower lip tremble, and he followed up with, 'I didn't say it wasn't talented, I said it was terrible, and if you want to know why it's terrible, I'll tell you.' He started with the first stage direction and went all the way through the show for a whole afternoon, really treating it seriously. It was a seminar on the piece as though it were *Long Day's Journey into Night.* Detail by detail, he told me how to structure songs, how to build them with a beginning and a development and an ending, according to his principles. I found out many years later that there are other ways to write songs, but he taught me, according to his own principles, how to introduce character, what relates a song to character, and so on. It was four hours of the most *packed* information. I dare say, at the risk of hyperbole, that I learned in that afternoon more than most people learn about songwriting in a lifetime. . . . He saw how interested I was in writing shows, so he outlined a course of study for me which I followed over the next six years, right through college."

Such altruistic advice and counsel is not often available to a beginner; but generosity was always present in Hammerstein. No matter how much success he achieved, he retained a sense of perspective about his own gifts. One of the most lasting Hammerstein legends deals with the advertisement he took in *Variety* after the wildly successful opening of *Oklahoma!* in 1943. Remember, if you will, it was a season in which his version of Bizet's opera, called *Carmen Jones,* was also selling out. In the annual holiday issue of *Variety,* in which successful show-business talents customarily trumpet their achievements to the rest of the fraternity, Hammerstein's ad was modest, succinct, and made a very adroit point. In a quarter-page, his text read:

HOLIDAYGREETINGS
OSCAR HAMMERSTEIN II
author of
SUNNY RIVER
(Six weeks at the St. James Theatre, New York)
VERY WARM FOR MAY
(Seven weeks at the Alvin Theatre, New York)
THREE SISTERS
(Six weeks at the Drury Lane, London)
BALL AT THE SAVOY
(Five weeks at the Drury Lane, London)
FREE FOR ALL
(Three weeks at the Manhattan Theatre, New York)
I'VE DONE IT BEFORE AND I CAN DO IT AGAIN.

"That ad," says William Hammerstein, "really expressed the way he felt, his sense of proportion. He was always afraid of reaching a stage of accomplishment where people expected too much from him . . . that he wouldn't be able to deliver."

There was hard-earned reason behind Hammerstein's modesty. By the time he came to collaborate with Rodgers on *Oklahoma!* he was almost forty-eight years old, and behind him was a theatrical career that had produced equal parts of success and failure. In fact, Hammerstein's story gives the lie to Scott Fitzgerald's observation that "there are no second acts in American lives." Hammerstein's life followed the classic theatrical pattern of a well-made play: early success, adversity in the second act, and a triumphant third act with a smash finale.

The beginnings were as traditional as any show-biz story. If Oscar Hammerstein II wasn't exactly born in a trunk, there was theatre all around his early youth. His grandfather and namesake was a hugely successful producer who brought Victor Herbert's *Naughty Marietta* to the New York Theatre. Young Oscar's father was William Hammerstein, who managed the Victoria Music Hall. How could any young man with such a background be anything but stage-struck? "He could quote all the old vaudeville acts from memory, verbatim, all his life," says his son.

Hammerstein's family sent him off to Columbia, and then to Columbia Law School, but he left there to go to work in the professional theatre. His uncle, Arthur Hammerstein, gave him a job as stage manager for a trio of Rudolph Friml musical operettas—*You're in Love, Sometime,* and *Tumble Inn.* (Later Hammerstein was to provide lyrics for *Rose-Marie,* written by the same Friml, that astonishing gentleman who when past ninety years of age still composed music each and every day.)

After that initial debacle with his own play, Hammerstein wrote book and lyrics for his first musical show, *Always You,* with composer Herbert Stothart. It was 1920, and he was then twenty-five. Again at the suggestion of his uncle, he went to work with Otto Harbach on a show called *Tickle Me.* In the next few years Hammerstein and Harbach were to write *Wildflower, Rose-Marie, Sunny,* and *The Desert Song* together.

"Like most young writers," he confessed years later, "I had a great eagerness to get words down on paper. He [Harbach] taught me to think a long time before actually writing. He taught me never to stop work on anything if you can think of one small improvement to make."

Young Hammerstein developed rapidly into one of the most sought-after lyricists in the busy Broadway theatre of the 1920s. "Sigmund Romberg got me into the habit of working hard," he wrote. "In our first collaboration, *The Desert Song,* I used to visit him. I remember one day bringing up a finished lyric to him. He played it over and said, 'It fits.' Then he turned to me and asked me, 'What else have you got?' I said that I didn't have anything more, but I would go away and set another melody. He persuaded me to stay right there and write it while he was working on something else. He put me in another room with a pad and pencil. Afraid to come out empty-handed, I finished another refrain that afternoon. I have written many plays and pictures with Rommy and his highest praise has always been the same. 'It fits.' Disappointed at first at such limited approval, I learned later that what he meant was not merely that the words fitted the notes, but that they matched the spirit of his music and that he thought they were fine."

But it was with Jerome Kern that Hammerstein reached the absolute high-water mark of his early success. In 1927, when he was only thirty-two years old, he wrote the lyrics and the adaptation of Edna Ferber's *Show Boat.* In that score are such indestructible works as "Can't Help Lovin' Dat Man," "Make Believe," "Why Do I Love You?," and, of course, "Ol' Man River."

It was during the preparation of that superb score that Hammerstein perpetrated a mild practical joke on his somewhat humorless collaborator, Kern. It was Kern's working practice to write a melody, then hand it over to his current lyricist, and send his collaborator off to provide the words. One day he gave Hammerstein a lyrical ballad. The following day Hammerstein turned up at Kern's studio and, without a word, handed Kern a piece of paper on which was written:

> Cupid knows the way,
> He's the naked boy
> Who can make you sway
> To love's own joy;
> When he shoots his little ar-row,
> He can thrill you to the mar-row . . .

Kern read through this mawkish set of rhymes with mounting dismay and horror. He was about to lose his temper when, with no change of expression, Hammerstein handed over a second set of lyrics, which read:

> Why do I love you?
> Why do you love me?
> Why should there be two
> Happy as we?
> Can you see the why or wherefore
> I should be the one you care for?

For once, so the legend goes, Mr. Kern was completely taken by surprise.

As to the origin of the classic "Ol' Man River," an interesting sidelight on how it came into being comes from Teddy Holmes, the general manager of Chappell, Ltd., the London firm which published the score of *Show Boat*. "I remember discussing that song with Oscar Hammerstein when the show was first produced here in London some years back," he said. "Oscar said that during the preparation stages he felt a need for a unifying song, one that would express the feel of the Mississippi River, to tie the libretto together, so to speak. He discussed it with Jerry Kern, and Kern told him that he had too much else to do; at that particular moment he simply couldn't contemplate writing another song. Now, as you know, if you listen to the score, there is that fast-paced banjo music that introduces the show boat *Cotton Blossom* in the first act; very bright and gay it is, too. Oscar said he went back to Kern later and said, 'Why don't you take that banjo music, which you've already written, and merely *slow down* the tempo?' Kern took the suggestion and did exactly that—and there emerged that powerful theme for 'Ol' Man River.' Listen to that banjo music and you'll hear the 'River' strain imbedded in it. It was simply that Hammerstein *heard* it before Kern did."*

"Kern would play pieces for me," says Robert Russell Bennett, who worked

---

* William Hammerstein adds, "Some years later Mike Wallace interviewed my father on TV and asked him if he wrote 'Ol' Man River' as a protest song. 'No,' replied my father, 'I wrote it because we needed it for a spot in the first act.' He went on to explain that he conceived it as a sort of cord to hold together that whole sprawling story. Remember, no one up to that time had ever tried to spread such an expanse of epic drama, covering such a span of time, over the musical stage, and it had to be held together somehow. He felt that the one constant element was the river, and that's what he wrote about."

closely with the two men, "and I'd say, 'Is that the verse or the chorus?' And Jerry used to die because I couldn't tell which was which. One day he showed me this thing, and I put out a piano part to it. This one didn't fall into the same category—that kind of piece Kern wrote that confused me—but it was a meandering sort of thing. It didn't go much of anywhere when you just took the tune by itself. But the minute you got Oscar's words to it—*Tote dat barge, lift dat bale, git a little drunk an' you land in jail**—you had a real poet."

A classic show-business story grew up about that same song. Mrs. Kern and Mrs. Hammerstein arrived at a party, and their hostess began to introduce them to her friends. "This is Mrs. Jerome Kern," she announced. "Her husband wrote 'Old Man River.' " "Not true," said Mrs. Hammerstein promptly. "Mrs. Kern's husband wrote *dum-dum-dee-dah, da dum-dum-dee-dah. My* husband wrote '*Ol' man river, dat ol' man river!*' "

Years later Hammerstein wrote about Kern and their collaboration. "During my several collaborations with Jerry, I was surprised at first to find him deeply concerned about details which I thought did not matter much when there were so many important problems to solve in connection with writing and producing a play. He proved to me, eventually, that while people may not take any particular notice of any one small effect, the over-all result of finickiness like his produces a polish which an audience appreciates."

That "polish" in his own work was what Hammerstein sought throughout his career. Writing lyrics was hard, often agonizing work. His name for that work was "woodshedding." Hour after hour he would stand at his desk, agonizing over the choice of the exact word, the perfect choice for the thought he wished to communicate. "Even when the songs were completed, they might not satisfy him," says his son. "Take that final couplet of 'All the Things You Are,' from *Very Warm for May*, a song which everyone else considered near-perfect. Not Oscar. That next to last line—*'To know that moment divine'*—he wanted to change the word 'divine.' It always bothered him."

After the success of *Show Boat* there was *The New Moon* with Romberg, *Rainbow* with Vincent Youmans, and, with Kern, *Sweet Adeline*, a vehicle for Helen Morgan.

Hammerstein went out to Hollywood in 1930 to work with Sigmund Romberg on a film called *Viennese Nights*. In the very first years of the musical film, producers transferred stage productions directly to the screen with little, if any, adaptation to the film medium. *Viennese Nights* wasn't very good, and Hammerstein went back to New York to do another show with Kern, *The Cat and the Fiddle*. There were beautiful songs in the score—"The Night Was Made for Love," "Try to Forget"—and a Parisian background, but the show wasn't as big a commercial success as the Kern tunes were to be. A year later the two men wrote *Music in the Air*, again with a European background. And again it was full of melodic treats—"I've Told Ev'ry Little Star," "The Song Is You," and others.

Hammerstein returned to Hollywood and spent most of his middle years

---

* "I can never hear those words without feeling a fierce twinge of embarrassment," insisted Richard Bissell, a licensed Mississippi River pilot. "To 'tote' is to pick something up and carry it. A 'barge' is a large non-self-propelled boat used usually for the marine transport of bulk cargoes. Nobody in the long history of the Mississippi including Mike Fink, has ever picked up and carried a barge."

there. The Broadway theatre in the '30s was shrinking in size; there were also changes in the public's tastes. For the price of a $2.20 ticket, the audiences there were beginning to demand more fact and less fantasy than before the Depression years. The era of the lush, opulent operetta was past; people who sought sweet escape from the daily, dreary realities of unemployment and soup kitchens and of stockbrokers leaping out of skyscraper windows were finding it for twenty-five cents in their neighborhood movie palaces.

"Everyone in those days was seduced by Hollywood," comments Hammerstein's son. "They went out there to make money. Oh, some of them may have had noble thoughts about the art of the film, but I don't think in the early '30s it had reached that point yet. As everyone else did, my father succumbed to a big salary. Jerry Kern went out first, and that may also have had a lot to do with it; they were always very close, not only in their work but socially."

In 1934 the two men worked on a film version of their own *Sweet Adeline*. The picture was only a mild success; in the light of the new Busby Berkeley spectacles, it seemed a bit old-fashioned. "Perhaps he wouldn't agree with this," says his son, "but I don't think Dad ever felt comfortable in the movie medium. He understood the stage—he had a fantastic instinct for timing, for climactic construction of a play, how to deal with a live audience, how to fashion an entertainment for the people sitting in a legitimate theatre. But I don't think he ever really grasped the movie as a *form*."

But if Hammerstein's Hollywood years were far from his most creative, the life he led there was *gemütlich* enough. Money was no problem; his ASCAP royalties were more than enough for him to live on. The town was full of his contemporaries—Kern, Romberg, the Gershwins, Dorothy Fields, and actors, writers, wits, other displaced persons from New York, all of them attracted by those steady studio paychecks. It was the era of the swimming pool, Sundays by the tennis court, and smogless sun. One left the studio office and got home with plenty of time for a couple of sets.

And on weekends there were parties, and meetings of the Butterworth Athletic Club, named for the comedian Charles Butterworth, and consisting of such old friends as playwright Marc Connelly, songwriter Harry Ruby, and writer Charles Lederer. The members of the BAC met for drinks and tennis and for practical jokes.

There was nothing solemn about Hammerstein; he loved laughs as much as any of his friends did. "My voice had just changed," recalls William. "My mother and father were due at dinner at Harry Ruby's house one night, and my father suggested that I call up Harry after they'd left and I could impersonate him. I was to say, 'Harry, this is Oscar. Can't make it tonight. That's all.' Very brusque. And then I was to hang up. Well, I got my timing mixed up and called a few minutes too late. Ruby picked up the phone; I delivered my father's dialogue, and then he said, 'Not coming over, Oscar? That's funny, because I can see you walking in my door!'"

Hammerstein and Lederer once fell into a mock feud, which they carried on for many months. When they met at parties, they would speak only through an intermediary. So successful was their performance that many people took their *contretemps* to be absolutely serious. "Then my father went off to London, to attend to some production over there, and he sent Lederer a cable which was the most cliché expression he could think of. It read: DEAR CHARLES ENGLAND IS ONE BIG BEAUTIFUL GARDEN. Charlie never acknowledged that cable. But about two years later he went to London, and one day my father received a cable from him which read: YES ISN'T IT."

Kern and Hammerstein did produce one film score which earned them high marks. In *High, Wide and Handsome* were such hit songs as the title number, "Can I Forget You?," and "The Folks Who Live on the Hill." (The film was directed by Rouben Mamoulian, the same talented film-maker who was responsible for the earlier innovative Rodgers-and-Hart picture *Love Me To-night*.) There were other pictures, less successful but often containing some work by Hammerstein that has lasted. From something called *The Night Is Young* there is "When I Grow Too Old to Dream," set to Romberg's music; and from another long-forgotten musical, starring Grace Moore, there is "I'll Take Romance," with music by Ben Oakland.

But creatively it was a semi-dry period. "He had nothing to worry about," says his son. "Nothing—except if you were him. Money didn't satisfy him. He worried about what was happening to *him*. With all his capacity for enjoying life, it simply wasn't sufficient."

In 1939 Max Gordon brought Kern and Hammerstein back to New York to do the musical show *Very Warm for May*. But despite a score which contains "All the Things You Are" and several other beautiful works, Hammerstein's book faltered badly. (Broadway wags referred to it as "Very Cold for Max.") And to add to his misfortunes, in the 1930's Hammerstein then had a couple of quick failures in London at the Drury Lane.

Again, from Robert Russell Bennett: "Oscar was a man who should have been a poet and never was because he had to write lyrics all his life. I think he was my closest and dearest friend in show business, all his years. One time when we were living in Paris, my wife and I, he and his wife came to see us. Oscar had had nothing but failures for quite some time, it seemed. At this dinner he said, 'Dorothy and I are going to live in a little place here in France and she's going to cook and take care of the household, and I'm going to write poetry.'

"And I told him then, 'Nothing on earth could ever make me happier than to hear that, because you have poetry in you—you have *great* poems in you. But if you always stay in show business, where I've been, it'll never come out.' He said, 'Well, it's going to come out now. This is it.' Then, a little bit later, along came *Carmen Jones* and then *Oklahoma!* and that was the end of Oscar as a poet. After that, he didn't care much about writing a great poem any longer. He was satisfied to write those lyrics, which he made into works of art. But they have it all . . . they all sound as if it's a poet trying to talk. It just *burst* out of him all the time!"

It may have been the fond memory of that evening with the Bennetts in Paris before the war that sparked Hammerstein to write one of his most poetic lyrics, to a melody of Kern's, in 1941. The German Panzer divisions had occupied Paris, and Hammerstein wrote a song that expressed his dismay; "The Last Time I Saw Paris" was sentimental to a degree that caused tears. That the song would win the Academy Award for the best film song of that year (Metro had used it in *Lady Be Good*) was inevitable. Hammerstein had touched nerve ends with his writing; the song affected everyone. Even if you'd never been to Paris, you had to share his feelings.

His so-called "dry period" was over. Almost from that point on, audiences never ceased understanding exactly how Oscar Hammerstein felt. His lyrics told them, and the people responded. But to him it was never poetry, nor even poetic.

"Any professional author will scoff at the implication that he spends his time hoping and waiting for a magic spark to start him off," he wrote in his book *Lyrics*. "There are few accidents of this kind in writing. A sudden beam of moonlight, or a thrush you have just heard, or a girl you have just kissed, or a beautiful view through your study window is seldom the source of an urge to put words on paper. Such pleasant experiences are likely to obstruct and delay a writer's work. . . . Nobody waits to be inspired."

He spent the next stage of his career—that triumphant third act with Richard Rodgers—back in the East, working mostly at his farm in Doylestown, Pennsylvania. There in his study was the captain's desk which his friend Kern had given him, and at it, not seated but standing, he worked. Slowly, carefully, painstakingly. The dialogue for librettos he dictated into a machine; a secretary transcribed it, and then he revised. Lyrics were always done in longhand. What eventually was brought to Richard Rodgers to be set to music was always the result of hours of labor.

Even such a rollicking song as "This Was a Real Nice Clambake" (from *Carousel*), which the team adapted from Ferenc Molnár's *Liliom*, involved long sessions of revision. Meticulous to the smallest detail, Hammerstein instructed his daughter to go to the local library and research all the recipes that were available for cooking clams and lobsters early-American style. (The background of *Liliom* had been changed from Europe to nineteenth-century New England.) The resultant meal, as the chorus of well-fed New Englanders lyrically describes it onstage, is not only a musical delight but an authentic recipe. For seafood lovers, it's almost as good as a shore dinner.

His love songs are simple, clear, and uncomplicated. His attitude toward the female is perhaps idealized and highly irritating for Women's Lib crusaders. "All his love songs are somewhat akin to 'Something Wonderful,' in which the woman in *The King and I* reveals herself as being completely dedicated to her man," commented William Hammerstein, "or in 'What's the Use of Wond'rin?,' where the girl says, *'He's your fella, and you love him, that's all there is to that.'* Those attitudes may have been shaped by his own early years. His own mother died when he was twelve; to him she was the ideal, perfect. Most of his love songs come out of his feeling for her, I think."

Stephen Sondheim insists that "Oscar was able to write about dreams and grass and stars because he *believed* in them." And Richard Rodgers, who was his sole collaborator from *Oklahoma!* on, corroborates that analysis: "As far as his work with me was concerned, Oscar always wrote about the things that affected him deeply. What was truly remarkable was his never-ending ability to find new ways of revealing how he felt about three interrelated themes—nature, music, and love. In 'Oh, What a Beautiful Morning,' the first song we wrote together for *Oklahoma!*, Oscar described an idyllic summer day on a farm when 'all the sounds of the earth are like music.' In 'It's a Grand Night for Singing'* he revealed that the things most likely to induce people to sing are a warm, moonlit, starry night and the first thrill of falling in love. In 'You Are Never Away' he compared a girl with 'the song that I sing,' 'the rainbow I chase,' 'a

---

* Written for the musical version of *State Fair,* done as a film by 20th Century-Fox.

morning in spring,' and 'the star in the lace of a wild willow tree.' In 'Younger Than Springtime' another girl is 'warmer than the winds of June' and 'sweeter than music.' In our last collaboration, *The Sound of Music*, just about everything Oscar felt about nature and music and love was summed up in the title song.

"Oscar believed that all too often people overlooked the wonders to be found in the simple pleasures of life. We even wrote two songs, 'A Hundred Million Miracles' and 'My Favorite Things,' in which Oscar enumerated some of them."

Hammerstein never closed his eyes to the uglier side of life, however. One of his songs for *South Pacific* says it all about race prejudice. The young American officer who has fallen in love with a native girl is well aware of the color bars he will encounter when he sings "You've Got to Be Taught." (*"You've got to be taught to hate and fear . . . It's got to be drummed in your dear little ear/You've got to be carefully taught."*)

Not only did he write on the subject; he participated. When author Pearl Buck opened her Welcome House, an adoption agency in Doylestown dedicated to placing infants of mixed racial backgrounds, the human backwash of the Korean War, in responsible homes, it was with Hammerstein's considerable and constant assistance. And he was not afraid to stand up and allow himself to be counted. Playwright Hy Kraft, who was called before the House Un-American Activities Committee some twenty years ago and was an uncooperative witness, corroborates this in his book *On My Way to the Theatre*:

> There's a heart-warming P.S. to this Washington absurdity. There were two messages waiting for me in New York . . . one from Dorothy and Oscar Hammerstein. It wasn't a message; it was a command to appear at dinner. After dinner Oscar had to catch *The King and I*, the current Rodgers-and-Hammerstein hit; he insisted that we meet later at Sardi's. I was apprehensive about the Sardi's visit. I knew that by the time we got to Sardi's the final editions of the afternoon papers (we had more than one in 1952) and the bulldogs of the *Times* and the *Trib* would carry the review of my out-of-town performance, and I didn't want to frighten those frightened people in show biz. In those days of McCarthy, *Red Channels*, Hedda Hopper, Pegler, Sokolsky, to be seen with an unfriendly witness was just one step away from the unemployment-insurance line. And in Sardi's, yet! Of course, no committee or columnist could pull the rug from under Oscar's standing in show biz, but the gesture of hosting a Fifth Amendment friend was a defiant commitment that raised plenty of eyebrows. And I might add that a number of my colleagues who acknowledged me that night in Oscar's corroborative company turned away in years to come. . . . Oscar inscribed my copy of *South Pacific*, "For Hy. And why not? Oscar." Every once in a while I read his lyric "You've Got to Be Taught to Hate." The man who wrote that was my friend. I liked the world a lot better when he lived in it.

Oscar Hammerstein's initial collaboration with Richard Rodgers, in 1943, confounded most of the Broadway sages. Nobody expected *Away We Go* (the original title of their adaptation of Lynn Riggs' *Green Grow the Lilacs*) to be successful, least of all the audience that went up to New Haven. It is now a theatrical legend how, after the first-act curtain came down, various backers of the Theatre Guild's production, to be retitled *Oklahoma!*, stood around the Shubert Theatre lobby, frantically selling off "pieces" of their investments.

But after that opening night, almost a quarter-century since his first disaster with *The Light*, Hammerstein did not go for a walk and start planning his next. This show would survive all the skeptics, the nay-sayers, and the disbelievers. Certainly there were changes to be made, but he believed in his and Rodgers' work. Away went *Oklahoma!* to Boston, where it caught on, and then on to New York and thundering success. Those faint-hearted ex-backers in the New Haven intermission lost thousands of dollars of eventual profit through their lack of faith; the buyers of their "pieces," even the smallest ones, became rich.

The two men were not only successful in creating their own works, but their partnership extended to the production of shows by others. As Dorothy Fields, who wrote the libretto of *Annie Get Your Gun* with her brother Herbert, points out, Hammerstein's theatrical sense was quick to recognize the basic merit of casting Ethel Merman as Annie Oakley. He and Rodgers agreed that the logical choice for a composer would be someone else; they looked forward with keen pleasure to the prospect of bringing Hammerstein's old friend and collaborator Jerome Kern back to the Broadway scene. Kern's abrupt passing was a crushing personal blow to Hammerstein. Happily for audiences ever since, Irving Berlin agreed to take on the score.

The smashing success of *Annie Get Your Gun* seems all the more remarkable if one considers that Hammerstein, Rodgers, and Dorothy Fields were all top-ranking songwriters. Nowhere in the preparation of the show did any professional jealousy surface. "Both Dick and Oscar were marvelous producers," says John Fearnley. "It was their continual ability to edit, to advise, to listen and then say, 'No, that's not quite right for this spot'—to counsel the other creative people without ever being in competition—that kept everything on the tracks."

Hammerstein's collaboration with Rodgers produced only two shows which could be considered less than absolute smash hits. *Pipe Dream*, based on John Steinbeck's book *Sweet Thursday*, was a simple, joyful story about Steinbeck's waterfront neighbors in his early days in California. It ran for a full season, but, despite a good score, it did not have the lasting qualities of *South Pacific* or the mass appeal of *The Sound of Music*. Nor was *Me and Juliet* vintage Rodgers-and-Hammerstein.

But their *Allegro*, which came earlier, in 1947, was a unique work. Reexamined a quarter-century later in the light of the current theatre, that show seems far ahead of its time. It is simply the musical biography of a young man, his birth, his childhood, and his arrival at what used to be referred to as man's estate. "It was written out of his own heart and experience," says his son. "He tried to say everything he'd learned about life. He had always been tremendously intrigued by his own childhood."

There is a great deal of musical-comedy trail-breaking in *Allegro*. "I've Seen It Happen Before," sung by the young man's grandmother, deals with the universals of growing up. "One Foot, Other Foot" dramatizes the small triumph of the boy's learning to walk in the wilderness of his own backyard. In the second act there is a sardonic comedy trio, "Money Isn't Everything," and an impatient, rejected sweetheart's sad complaint, "The Gentleman Is a Dope."

After the show closed, Hammerstein told an interviewer, "I wanted to write a large, universal story, and I think I overestimated the psychological ability of the audience to identify with the leading character." But the years since *Allegro* was first produced have been more than kind to that work. Much of what Hammerstein wrote two decades ago has a definite kinship with the sort of free and open expression today's songwriters are putting forward. Contemporary lyricists have long since left behind love and Dixie and moonlight bays; they deal now with war and peace, political subjects, leaving home—self-expression on a much more honest level. "As a matter of fact," says Hammerstein's son, "if my father were alive today, he would be trying very hard to understand the new writers, and to find out what they had in mind. People like Randy Newman and Dylan and Nilsson; he'd be listening to them carefully. He always understood that things inevitably changed. He welcomed that."

Oscar Hammerstein II died in 1960.

At the conclusion of the thoughtful, pragmatic notes to his own volume *Lyrics*, written ten years before, he had said, "I am discontented with what I have written here. I have not said nearly all I would like to say about lyrics and the plays for which I write them. 'I could go on and on,' but I don't dare. I feel the self-consciousness of a man who is madly in love with a girl and wants to talk about her but has already imposed too long on his friends' time and politeness. If I have been long-winded, please forgive my extravagances and indulge my blind infatuation. I'm in love with a wonderful theatre."

"He probably would have written more, had he lived," says William. "He had a great deal more to communicate. It's sad that so much that's been written about him makes him sound so somber. He wasn't that way at all; he enjoyed laughter and jokes as well as anybody I've ever known. Some of the stories he told us about his early youth in show business, the vaudeville days and all the rest of it, were hilarious.

"I remember back in 1950 I got after him to work on a sort of autobiography. I knew he was a man of strict routine; every day he would have breakfast and go into his study and start to work. He had enormous self-discipline. So I thought of a way to do it. I went out to California that year to work at Paramount, and before I left I said to him, 'Look, I want you to write me a letter each week. Every week, pick one day, set aside an hour, write it in longhand or dictate it into your machine, but do that letter. Make it the story of your life, from the start when you were a kid hanging around your father's vaudeville theatre, and then how you got into theatricals at Columbia, and why you left school. Do it as a narrative. And I'll keep those letters, I'll put them all away in a file, and when you're all finished, they can be edited or whatever, but there'll be a book, a complete libretto, about *you*.

"Dad was about fifty-five at the time, and after all those years of Broadway and Hollywood—he'd worked with absolutely everybody—he had such a lot to tell. Well, he was agreeable, and he wrote those letters to me for about three months. I have them put away. Then he went into rehearsal with a new show, *The King and I*, and he begged off writing any more letters for a while. He said he had too much else to do during the rehearsals and the tryout and the opening. I told him he was excused until the show opened, but after that he'd have to start again.

"Well, somehow or other, he always kept putting it off. Other shows, that big television special for Ford in 1953, the other things he did, always something, right up till *The Sound of Music*. No more letters.

"Then, in 1960, the night he died—he was a very healthy guy, and it had to be something like cancer to put him down—we were all sitting in his study in the house in Bucks County. I wandered over to his old stand-up captain's desk, and there, on the top of it, I saw a sheet of yellow work paper. I don't know when he'd written it; it must have been in the last few weeks. It said: 'Dear Bill, A few years ago, you were after me to write you those letters, and I'm sorry now that I didn't continue with it . . .'"

So are we all.

'Of Thee I Sing, Baby'

(Ira Gershwin)

IRA GERSHWIN, an amiable, highly literate gentleman, resides in Beverly Hills, California, and has been known to a wide circle of his friends for many years as Permanent President of the Nice Guys Association.

"Let me give you an idea what sort of person Ira is," says Larry Adler, the master of the mouth organ. "When Paul Draper and I were starting out on our first concert tour—I was to play, and he to dance—I was living out in California, about three blocks away from Ira. The day I was to leave by train to meet Paul in Denver for our first engagement, I was pretty nervous, as you can imagine. The doorbell rang; it was Ira. He handed me a package. In it was some formal dresswear. Shirts, collars, bow ties, studs, waistcoats. He said, 'Larry, these belonged to George. You and he wore the same sizes, so I thought they might bring you some luck tonight.' The guy is some sort of an angel."

Eudora Welty has written that humorist S. J. Perelman must be considered one of our national treasures. Surely, the same applies to Ira Gershwin. Since 1918 his words have been sweeping the country. The title of his own first published lyric proved to be descriptive of his whole *oeuvre*—"The Real American Folk Song."

In 1921, using the pseudonym "Arthur Francis," he wrote his first Broadway show, *Two Little Girls in Blue,* with Vincent Youmans. Then came all the marvelous classics that he wrote with his brother George. But since George's passing in 1937, Ira has proved remarkably adaptable to the talents of a phalanx of other fine composers. With Kurt Weill he did the score for *Lady in the Dark;* and ever since things have always looked up when he's written with Harold Arlen, Jerome Kern, Burton Lane, Arthur Schwartz, and Harry Warren.

In his book, *Lyrics on Several Occasions,* he has stated, "Anyone may turn up with a hit song, as evidenced by any number of one-hit writers. . . . A career of lyric-writing isn't one that anyone can easily muscle in on; . . . if the lyricist who lasts isn't a W. S. Gilbert he is at least literate and conscientious; . . . even when his words at times sound like something off the cuff, lots of hard work and experience have made them so. And I do believe that generally I am speaking not only for myself but for—in any order you like—Porter, Fields, Berlin, Mercer, Lerner, Loesser, Dietz, Wodehouse, Comden and Green, Hammerstein, Hart, Harburg, and two or three others whose work I respect."

Gershwin includes in his book the following wisdom: "*A Small Summing Up.* Given a fondness for music, a feeling for rhyme, a sense of whimsy and humor, an eye for the balanced sentence, an ear for the current phrase, and the ability to imagine oneself a performer trying to put over the number in progress—given all this, I still would say it takes four or five years collaborating with knowledgeable composers to become a well-rounded lyricist. I could be wrong about the time element—no doubt there have been lyricists who knew their business from the start—but time and experiment and experience help."

The gallantry he demonstrates toward his fellow lyricists in these quotations is typical of Mr. Gershwin's lack of competitive spirit. In a dog-eat-dog business, his specialty is handing out laurel wreaths. "Ira," said one of his closest friends, "is defter with words than anyone I know—and he hasn't got a bad one for anybody."

For the past several decades he and Mrs. Gershwin have been living in a large, sunny Beverly Hills home, where the living-room walls are graced with brother George's excellent paintings. There are several more recent works by younger sister Frances Godowsky, another artist of sensitivity and talent.

Ira's shelves are stacked with an extensive library of recondite reference books—words have always fascinated him—and there are also vast stores of phonograph records. "Hundreds and hundreds of them in there," he says, beaming behind a small, fragrant cigar. "Most of them I've never gotten around to playing."

Nattily attired in a sports jacket with an ascot knotted at his throat, Mr. Gershwin glances somewhat nervously at the small tape-recorder on the table which is recording him sans obvious microphone. "Is that thing taking every word down?" he inquires. And when informed that it is, he shakes his head in amazement. "I'm still back to where I want to wind the Victrola," he sighs. "I am just not mechan-*ic*-ally inclined. You know who used to say that? Maurice Abravanel—he was our conductor for *Lady in the Dark.* Now he conducts the Utah Symphony. Kurt Weill and I were with him one night and Kurt asked, 'How was the show you saw last night?' Abravanel said, 'Artis-*tic*-ally not too bad, but mechan-*ic*-ally not so good.'"

He shrugs. "But you can't fight progress, can you? Especially phonograph records. They really changed the music business, Expanded the field so much. Especially with Decca, when Jack Kapp brought them out three for a dollar. I remember, during the war, out here we had a little man who supplied us with bedsheets and so on—not black market or anything. He just knew where to get them. Nice little Jewish man who only wanted to help the war effort by entertaining the troops. He'd find an empty store and say, 'We'll put in a checkerboard, get a phonograph—keep the soldiers happy.' He set up five or six of those places. One day he was opening up a place out in Westwood, and he called me up. 'Mr. Gershwin,' he said, 'I got hold of a Victrola, but I have no records. Could you spare some?' I figured it was much easier to do it another way, so I told him, 'Look, I'll give you $25. Go to a store in town here, you'll get seventy-five records.' Three-for-a-dollar Deccas—that meant 150 sides. So later he called me up and said, 'I'm very happy, you've made it nice for the soldiers, and you've made me very happy too. I got the seventy-five records.' I asked him, 'By the way, any Gershwin songs?' He said, 'Nope.' "

Inevitably, the conversation turns to the state of the American musical-comedy theatre, and to how it has changed since the days in the 1920s when George and Ira Gershwin were turning out successes at a rapid-fire pace.

"Funny," says Mr. G, "I was thinking at four o'clock this morning about the finances of *Of Thee I Sing*, which cost $88,000. Of course, that was during the Depression. Imagine, though, putting on a Broadway musical for that; they only needed $50,000 cash. Herb Waters, the scenery man, would wait for his $38,000—he trusted you.

"We were up in Boston trying out, and George Kaufman said, 'You ought to have a piece of the show.' I said, 'I have no money.' He said, 'Well, look, there's still five percent open that we can let you have.' In those days, if you put in $10,000 and the producer had $10,000, you got the same piece as he did. There was nothing like today, when fifty percent goes to the backer after the production cost is recouped, and then the management keeps fifty percent of the profits. So I borrowed $2,500 from my brother George, and I got five percent of *Of Thee I Sing*. I was able to pay George back in a few months because I eventually got $11,000 from my little $2,500 investment!"

He shakes his head. "Today . . . well, you can lose $700,000–$800,000 in one night, if the reviews aren't good.

"Funny thing about Kaufman," he says. "It's very funny, considering he did so many musicals—he hated music, you know. I remember standing at a performance of *Of Thee I Sing*. My brother George and I and Kaufman. Kaufman turned to George and said, 'How do you account for the success of this thing?' And my brother said, 'George, you don't like to be sentimental. You hate love, and so forth. But the people *believe* that the President of the United States, even though he's going to be impeached, is *not* going to give up the girl he loves.' But Kaufman could not understand that. He was very cynical about those things. But, God knows, he was a clever craftsman."

Gershwin has been inactive since 1954, when he and Harold Arlen wrote the score for the remake of *A Star Is Born*. He may have retired from active songwriting, but he keeps up a lively correspondence with his good friends. His pen pal of longest standing is P. G. Wodehouse. "He writes me all the time," says Gershwin, between puffs of his cigar. "In most of the letters he says, 'Oh, when can we get together? When do you come to New York?' Because I haven't *seen* Plum in thirty years. Marvelous fellow. Wonderful lyricist, in the English tradition of W. S. Gilbert. Gilbert was the greatest, no question of that. If he were alive today, he'd be doing good musical-comedy songs. More, of course, in the modern fashion, rather than just versifying.

"You know, Wodehouse and Guy Bolton sent me a copy of their book *Bring On the Girls* some time back, and it started me thinking about them. So many of the things that were left out of that profile *The New Yorker* ran about Plum. For instance, Bolton once told me that Wodehouse and he were working in London on some show. Wodehouse lived on the third floor of the house, and there was an empty lot next door. And Wodehouse would write a letter to Bolton and throw it out of the window. He'd stamp it, of course, and throw it out—knowing that some passing taxi-driver would see it and then deliver it! Bolton would call up, maybe an hour later, and he'd say, 'That's fast delivery!'

"Plum once told my wife, 'You know, I can never live in a house or an apartment which is higher than the second or third floor; I like a walk-up. If there's an elevator, you get into it and the elevator boy says, "Nice day, isn't it?" You don't know what to say to him, do you?' And he meant it! He is very shy.

"I remember we went up to Boston for a show we were opening called *Rosalie*. My brother and I and Plum had written it. Jack Donahue and Marilyn Miller were the stars. For that type of a show, I guess it was pretty good.* Anyway, opening night in Boston, I couldn't see a thing, because I'm only five foot six and all these college boys standing in the back were so tall. Wodehouse is about six foot three. In the first act we were way overlong, and the first act wasn't over until 10:40. Then came the intermission, and at 10:50 the second act started. I'm standing there, trying to listen. I can't *see* anything, but I can hear; Plum is right next to me and I'm trying to catch a view of the stage. I feel a tap on my shoulder. I whispered, 'What is it?' And Plum has reached into his back pocket, where he always kept his dollar Ingersoll, and he says, 'Ira, it's eleven o'clock. I must toddle off to bed.' *Opening night!*

"The next day I asked him, 'On opening night, why did you have to toddle off to bed?' He said, 'Oh, I have to get up early at six o'clock because I like to browse along the bookstalls on the Charles River!'

"He is quite a character. He wrote me a while back after some Broadway show had just opened and closed overnight and lost $600,000, and he said, 'Can you imagine this? How could you put on a show today when it needs that sort of financing?' In the days when Wodehouse and Bolton and Kern would do their musicals at the Princess Theatre, I would imagine the entire cost wasn't more than $30,000 or $40,000."

The '20s, when the partnership of George and Ira Gershwin flourished so remarkably, was a boom period, not only for the Harding-Coolidge economy but for the American musical comedy.

"Do you realize, the night we opened *Oh, Kay!* [November 1926] there were eleven other shows opening? I think four of them were musicals. We had 240-odd shows opening that year—and about the same number in 1927!" Which would account for the number and variety of young composers and lyricists who emerged: Hammerstein, De Sylva, Brown and Henderson, Arlen, Harburg, Rodgers and Hart, Vernon Duke. "Of course, right up until the Depression, and even a little bit after, there were so many more opportunities for people to get started."

Does Gershwin subscribe to Harry Ruby's theory that the proliferation of

---

* The modesty factor again. Mr. G's "pretty good" refers to such songs of his as "Oh Gee! Oh Joy!" and "How Long Has This Been Going On?"

talents (the Gershwins, Irving Berlin, Irving Caesar, Ruby, Harburg) which emerged from the Lower East Side was due to the presence of a piano in the living room of newly arrived immigrant families?

"That could be it," he muses. "I know the piano was very important in our lives. The great thing in those days was this. Say a girl was working in a department store; she could go and buy sheet music. It only cost ten cents. Later on it cost more, but you could still buy half a dozen songs for a dollar or so and have the gang around the piano on Saturday nights, and they would be singing all the songs.

"You know, we got a piano for me. I was supposed to take lessons—my aunt gave me a few at her house. I got as far as page thirty in the lesson book. We lived on Second Avenue, and when the piano came in through the window—they hoisted it up—my brother George sat right down and *he* played it! I was amazed. It turned out he had a friend around the corner on Seventh Street who had a pianola at his house, and George would study things on it. He played with perfect harmonics, and with that wonderful left hand of his. So that business of having a piano around must be true . . .

"Of course, today there's so much distraction, with the radio and the TV, that the best you can do is to learn to strum a guitar, because nobody has the time for basics . . . unless you want to be a concert pianist or something."

Then Gershwin hasn't any further comment about the state of modern popular music?

"Oh, I give no thought to it," he admits. "When you have this influx of country music and that sort of thing, I'm just not interested. Today it's all protesters. Kids protesting against parents, and so forth. And they make a fortune, these protesters. My God, the money they can make!

"The other night a friend called me up, and he said, 'Can you imagine if your brother George were alive today?' You know, George was very attractive and smart-looking, had great authority. And he said, 'If he were alive today, what *he* would make—compared to Bacharach, or Mancini, or any of these men?'

"So I thought that over, and I said, 'No, he wouldn't make as much, because he would want to write things for the symphony, which would take so much time.' But George would do very well, I'm sure."*

Ira Gershwin keeps busy these days annotating Gershwin material for the

---

* "I was with George almost from the beginning of his career in one way or another," reports Robert Russell Bennett. "More or less contemporaries, although I'm older than he. He was six years younger than I. But anyway, I kind of raised him from a pup, as far as his orchestra and that sort of thing went. There was another man named Bill Daley, who's long since dead, who used to sit right down with George and actually taught George a lot more than George could ever learn from any kind of teacher. Because George was not talented as a student. He could not study. Max Dreyfus, who died a few years ago, was George's publisher. Ran Chappell's. A marvelous man. Very ambitious for George, as we all were. He sent George down to Artur Bodanzky, who was then conductor-in-chief for the Metropolitan Opera, so George could read scores and study classical, serious music. Bodanzky took him for six months. Then, one night, they were playing pinochle, Bodanzky and Max. 'Artur,' asked Dreyfus, 'how's my protégé getting along?' And Artur says, 'Max, you know even *studying* requires a certain talent.'

"But you get plenty of examples like that. Abraham Lincoln read just the Bible and Shakespeare and became one of the wisest men in the world. As far as I know, Jesus Christ wasn't a very big student either. George just came in here with that marvelous message for us, and we're all very grateful for it."

Library of Congress, which, considering the worldwide popularity of George's work, must be a full-time job. He has encountered some strange translations along the way. "Especially the Russians," he says. "You know, after the production of *Porgy and Bess* that toured Russia, they published George's *Rhapsody in Blue* and a folio of *Songs by Gershwin*. A varied selection, about eight or ten songs . . . things like 'The Man I Love' and four or five from *Porgy and Bess*. Translated into Russian. Of course, they didn't pay royalties.

"One day, Dmitri Tiomkin, the composer, came here to visit. He brought along Georges Auric, the French composer—he was one of The Six. They were back from Japan, where they'd been doing something about international copyrights. I said, 'Dimmie, some time ago I received this Russian thing, and I'd like to know what the Russian lyrics are like. So he read them for me. They were more or less faithful to my lyrics, except when it came to 'I Got Plenty of Nothing'— *there* they sneaked in a little propaganda! I asked Dimmie about 'It Ain't Necessarily So,' and he started to read it, and he said '*Little David was* . . . let me see . . . ' He said '*Little David was impotent, but oh my!*' I must say, I found that very curious," grins Mr. Gershwin.

"You know, the Russians never say 'sweetheart' or 'girl friend.' It's always my '*wife.*' Very puritanic. Of course, I knew all about that from the opening night of *Porgy and Bess* in Moscow. In the scene where Bess lifts up her skirt to get some money to give Sporting Life for the bottle of whiskey, there was a gasp all through the opera house. A woman lifting her skirt up like that—unheard of!"

Since its première in 1935 *Porgy and Bess* has achieved a steady international success; somewhat ironically, its acceptance in other countries is far greater than here in America.

"Lehman Engel, the conductor, sent me a ninety-page manuscript of his experiences with *Porgy and Bess* in Turkey. They did it in Ankara. He wrote all about the trouble he had having the thing translated into Turkish. For instance, in 'The Buzzard Song'—they'd never even heard of a buzzard there. So many things were different—idiomatic things like the crap game. They had to hunt for its equivalent in Turkish. Very, very difficult.

"But that goes on all the time. We just signed contracts to have *Porgy and Bess* translated into Dutch for the Amsterdam Opera House. Poland. Czechoslovakia. In France they play it in English. The first translation was in Denmark. Bertolt Brecht had translated it. The Nazis allowed the Danes to have it played, as long as they didn't advertise! Years later I read a book about the German occupation of Denmark. The author told all about how the Nazis would do their regular propaganda broadcasts on the radio, with the fanfares and the music . . . and whenever they'd finished delivering their daily stuff, the underground radio would come on immediately afterward and play 'It Ain't Necessarily So!'

"Even up in Finland—they just wrote me from Helsinki the other day and asked if they might do it there, with a small orchestra. More of a concert version."

What about future productions of *Porgy and Bess* here in its home territory?

"Well," says Gershwin, with a touch of wry, "not too many at this particular moment. It may be that the social climate isn't exactly right. Interestingly enough, there was a very successful performance done last year in Charleston, South Carolina. One hundred and twenty people, all local talent outside of three principals. Sensational, they wrote me; they're going to do it again next year. Afterwards they had a big party." He smiles. "It was the first time the bluebloods mixed with the blackbloods. I remember, that happened when we played Dallas with the touring company a few years back. So perhaps, the show does do some good after all."

A few months after that sunny California afternoon when Gershwin sat in his living room schmoozing about such a variety of subjects, the President of the Nice Guys Association celebrated his seventy-fifth birthday. This happy event elicited greetings and joyful sounds from a vast throng of friends and admirers, all of whom struck up the band in his honor.

ASCAP'S own magazine, *ASCAP Today*, published a special issue of tributes to Mr. G from his friends, replete with fond reminiscences from Harold Arlen, Howard Dietz, Harry Warren, Arthur Schwartz, and other cronies. Ever modest, Gershwin wrote to this author and mentioned the birthday issue of the magazine, adding, "But I had nothing to do with its contents."

An arguable statement, Mr. Gershwin. It could be said that you had everything to do with it.

'My Ideal'

(Richard Whiting)

SONGWRITERS and singers are always supposed to be full of rivalry and jealousy. Not my father," says Margaret Whiting. He loved people, he loved working with other writers, having them come over to the house, he loved it when Kern or Harold Arlen or Harry Warren would come over with something new they'd written and he could be the first to appreciate it."

By the time she was in her late teens, Dick Whiting's daughter Margaret had begun her own musical career; now, twenty-five years after breaking into the business as a band singer with Freddy Slack, she's still singing—not only the songs she grew up hearing in her living room, but the best of what's going today. That ability to roll with the times is one of the lessons she learned from the late Dick Whiting. "He'd say, 'Margaret, there's all kinds of music in the world. I was raised to like popular music, but I love the classical too. And if you're going to be a musician or a singer, you may not be able to create it all, but at least you've got to *understand* it all. There's a whole spectrum of music, just as there are people, and you mustn't shut any of it off. Be exposed to everything.' That was the first thing he taught me," she admits today, "and I'm sure that if he were still alive, he'd be listening to all the new people—the

Beatles, Simon and Garfunkel, Randy Newman, James Taylor, Jim Webb, Carole King, any of them—trying to find out what each of them is doing, and being very excited by the good things he'd uncovered in each one."

Today Margaret, an attractive brunette, sits in her Manhattan apartment, in a study whose shelves are stacked with bound copies of Dick Whiting's ever-green song hits (most of which she has performed and recorded with affection), and talks about her father, the young man from the Midwest who achieved so much success at the complex art of pop songwriting for two decades, from 1918 on.

"My father was born in Peoria, Illinois, but he grew up in Detroit. His family sent him out to school in California— the Harvard Military Academy— but he was always interested in music. He came back to Detroit and got himself a job working at the Jerome H. Remick Music Company. Remick was the only major music publisher to have his offices in Detroit. My father started in as a copy boy—this was about 1916. His job was to hand out sheet music to the various performers who'd come into Remick's looking for new material for their acts.

"Eventually Mr. Remick elevated my father to the job of song-plugger. My father could play marvelous piano, and he was a great demonstrator; he'd go to meet all the stars as they came into Detroit. The big vaudeville theatre was the Temple. They all played it—Nora Bayes, Sophie Tucker, Eddie Cantor, Jolson. That's where he met my mother, Eleanor. She was touring with Maggie, her sister. Maggie would go out and sing the songs—she was what they called a 'coon-shouter.' She'd come back into the wings, and my mother would be standing there, waiting for her with a glass of water. Out would go Maggie, do another encore, then come back for another drink.

"My mother knew everybody. I remember her telling me about the early days with the Marx Brothers. They'd be in some town on the same vaudeville bill, they'd all be living in the same boardinghouse, and my mother always did the cooking for everybody. Groucho would figure out a way to sneak the key to her rooms, and when she'd come back home to start the cooking, he and his brothers would all be there waiting for her in her bathtub, stark naked, just to drive her crazy!"

Young Dick Whiting wrote his first song hit in 1917. Called "When It's Tulip Time in Holland," it sold over a million copies of sheet music. "By that time people in the business had heard of this kid in Detroit, and when they came to town they'd look him up."

A war-song contest was held at the Michigan Theatre. "Anybody, amateur or professional, could enter. My father had written a waltz. Raymond Egan, who lived in Detroit, had written a simple little lyric to fit the tune. My father, who was always a shy, gentle man, obviously thought this wasn't the sort of song that was going to win, with all that competition. So without even pressing Egan to change the lyric, or playing the song for anybody's opinion, he threw the thing into his wastebasket.

"This is really like a Doris Day picture," Margaret comments wryly. "His secretary was dumping out the basket, saw the manuscript, read it through, and then she took it up to Mr. Remick himself. He played it over, and he said, 'Let's not tell Richard. Obviously he threw it away for some reason. If I know Richard, he didn't believe in it.' Remick entered the tune in the war-song contest. Well, it won, three nights in a row. Remick came in to see my father, and he said,

'Richard, you have yourself a nice new hit song,' and my father said, 'But I haven't written anything for quite a while.' 'Yes, you have,' said Remick. He told him that the song had won the contest, that every day they were getting requests for five or six thousand copies. To date, that song has sold nearly seventeen million copies, and I can't imagine how many recordings have been made of it. I suppose you could call it *the* World War I song. It was 'Till We Meet Again.'

"After my mother and father got married, they went to Chicago on their honeymoon. It's always been a family joke with us—my father was so busy writing songs with Gus Kahn in those days that Kahn took a room at the same hotel, the Edgewater Beach. All through the honeymoon they kept on writing!

"He had tremendous hits all through the '20s—'Sleepy Time Gal,' 'Japanese Sandman,' 'Ain't We Got Fun?,' 'Horses, Horses, Horses.' It was my mother who finally got him to leave Detroit. By that time she was handling all his business affairs; she's always been very bright about show business. Eleanor is very much like that woman in *Gypsy*—you remember when the guy tells Rose, 'You're a pioneer woman without a frontier.' She knew what was happening with talking pictures, and she could see what was happening in New York, on Broadway, and she knew my father would have to go one way or the other. She said to him, 'East or West, but you can't stay here in Detroit, because it's a rut.' He got angry, but he finally agreed to go. Went to New York—that's 1928—and he and Neil Moret wrote a song together; a strange thing, because it was my father who did the lyric. It was a love song to Eleanor, back in Detroit, and he called it 'She's Funny That Way.' If you read that lyric, you'll see there's a line at the end: *'I'm only human, coward at best / I'm pretty certain she'd follow me west'* . . . You can see that he didn't think she was going to leave him, but he loved her so much and he was using that as a reason for writing the song."

Whiting was not to concentrate on writing for the Broadway musical theatre; he and Leo Robin were teamed by Max Dreyfus, the publisher, and sent to Hollywood to write songs for the early Chevalier musicals at Paramount. Later he worked with Buddy De Sylva, and tried his hand at one Broadway musical. "It was originally called *Humpty Dumpty*," said Miss Whiting. "Ethel Merman, Jack Whiting, and Sid Silvers were in the cast. When it opened out of town, it was a tremendous bomb, but Buddy De Sylva swore he knew how to make it into a hit, so they closed the show, redid the whole thing, and reopened it with a new title, *Take a Chance*. But by that time my father was so nervous from all the rewrites and changes that he went back to Hollywood. They called him up from New York after opening night and said, 'Congratulations, Dick—you have a smash!'*

"It's ironic how many of my father's songs became theme songs. For years Eddie Cantor used 'One Hour with You.' Fred Waring used 'Breezing Along with the Breeze.' How about 'Hooray for Hollywood,' Jack Benny's theme for twenty years—can you ever see anything about the movies where they don't strike up that song? For years Shirley Temple was associated with 'On the Good Ship Lollipop,' but he wrote that one for me; I always sat next to him at the

---

* Miss Merman brought down the house with the rouser "Eadie Was a Lady" by Whiting, De Sylva, and Nacio Herb Brown. Additional songs by Vincent Youmans, including "Rise and Shine," had been added, but the most lasting song hit from the show was also by Whiting, De Sylva, and Brown, the lilting "You're an Old Smoothie."

piano, sucking a lollipop. And as for 'Louise' and 'My Ideal,' Chevalier loved those songs so much he used them every time he sang."

Whiting's last collaborator was to be the youthful Johnny Mercer, lately arrived in Hollywood from New York in the mid-'30s. They did several films at Warner Bros., and then Whiting died, only forty-six years old, in 1938. Shy, reticent, a very modest man, the fact of his considerable success as a composer never really changed him from the unassuming young song-plugger at Remick's in Detroit. "His greatest pleasure was in finding out what other composers were doing," says his daughter. "He was a very good musician, and he loved to take their new songs and play them. Always accepted the new, adored what was going on with his friends. Jerome Kern always insisted that my father listen to whatever new songs he'd written; he wanted his opinion. My father loved Cole Porter, considered him a real innovator. But his real joy was with Gershwin, whom he'd known in New York as a young man and whom he'd helped out in the early days. When *Porgy and Bess* opened in New York in 1935, he took the train from Los Angeles just to be at the opening. Sat through the whole thing side by side with Gershwin. And he almost died, as did Gershwin, because the reception to that first production was so half-hearted. He resented it so—Gershwin, his friend, his buddy, in whose work he took such pride!

"I was just a kid then," she says. "I hardly knew what he was talking about when he'd say to me, 'Don't they understand what's happened? Don't they realize this is one of the greatest American composers? Don't they see that he's written a classic? What is wrong with these people?' I always sat at the piano next to him. He worked every day, writing something. That was very important; he rarely let a day pass without trying to write something. I'd come home from school and ask to hear what he'd done that day. But after he came back from New York, all he wanted to play were the Gershwin songs—'Summertime' and all the rest.

"If I'm any good at all as a singer," she says today, "a lot of it is due to something my father taught me. He once said, 'Margaret, you have a good voice, you certainly know how to sing. Now, we spend years in perfecting our craft. I hate to think of it as a craft, it's something I love to do, but it is a job, it is work, and we work very hard to write a song and make it work. You must sing this song with great affection and feeling. It takes the men who write the lyrics a long time. Just believe in their words, do them simply and honestly. That's how a singer should interpret a song.' "

'Thanks for the Memory'

(Leo Robin)

As I RECALL the story," said Edward Eliscu, a fellow lyricist and a contemporary of Robin's, "Leo came to New York intending to become a
playwright. It was in the late 1920s, and he had some kind of an intro to George
S. Kaufman, who came from Leo's hometown, Pittsburgh. Kaufman looked at
Leo's plays and he wasn't too impressed, but he was gentle about it, and he
asked, 'What else have you written?' Leo said, 'Well, I've written some songs,'
but he was rather shame-faced about it. 'Let's see'em,' insisted Kaufman, and
Leo showed him one, a lyric he'd written called 'My Cutie's Due at Two to Two
Today!' and Kaufman immediately said, 'That's it—*that's* what you should be
doing!' "

Kaufman displayed acute prescience about young Leo's talent, and his
judgment has been amply justified by the fellow Pittsburghian's extraordinary
lyrical gift. Promptly after the publication of that first paean to his mythical cutie,
Robin went to work with Vincent Youmans and produced, with Clifford Grey,
a song called "Hallelujah!" for the show *Hit the Deck*. And since then he has
never given playwriting another thought.

His collaborators over the years include Youmans, Jerome Kern, Harold

Arlen, Jule Styne, Arthur Schwartz, Johnny Green, and Sigmund Romberg, who, along with the late Richard Whiting and Ralph Rainger, truly comprise a Blue Book of American composers. But Robin is the first to decry his own contributions and talent. In popular music, a fiercely competitive business famous for its back-biting, jealousy, and ego trips, *he* is famous for his modesty. According to Leo, whenever one of his works has been successful, it's usually because of the genius of his collaborator, or because the song was performed by a brilliant talent, or mostly because he "got lucky."

These days Leo Robin lives in a high-rise apartment on Wilshire Boulevard in Beverly Hills. He's a diminutive, alert man whose thick shock of hair is only slightly touched with gray. His rooms are crammed with books and records and pipes. When he talks, he puffs constantly on one of his huge Charatans, and he is a pacer. Since he talks, puffs, and paces in a sort of instinctive contrapuntal rhythm, his pipe is constantly going out.

"How did I start with Dick Whiting? This was way back in 1928, and sound pictures were just getting popular. It was the era of the title song, the theme song, and so forth, and then the studios got an idea that they could branch into larger musicals. There was this big demand for songwriters, for lyric-writers, fellows from New York—what they called the gold rush.

"Well, what happened was that I walked into Max Dreyfus' office one day. Max was the king of the music business, and his publishing firm had the most prestigious, the biggest names under contract. I was a kind of cub lyric-writer around there, just starting in. I was getting an advance of $25 a week or so. I was dabbling in shows, and I'd been lucky enough to be associated with one big hit, 'Hallelujah!,' already. But that was all.

"So I walked into Max's office that day, and he said, 'How would you like to go to Hollywood?' Well, I was footloose and free, unmarried as yet, and I said, 'Sure.' He said, 'You're going to write with a guy named Dick Whiting.' Well, I nearly fell over, because to me, practically a beginner in the business, the name of Dick Whiting had a prestige and a glamour and an aura that floored me. Dreyfus said, 'You'll get such-and-such advance every month, and you'll live in Hollywood for three months—it's a three-month contract.' That three-month contract spread out until I stayed here in Hollywood for over forty years.

"Well, I didn't know Dick Whiting, and he didn't know me. So I called him and I asked, 'When are you leaving, and how do we meet?' He said, 'I'll meet you in the lobby of the Sherman Hotel in Chicago'—he was coming from Detroit—'and we'll take the train from there.' So I get to the Sherman, and I don't even know what Dick looks like! There I am in the lobby, and it suddenly dawned on me to have him paged. Pretty soon a bellboy brings Dick over and says, 'Mr. Robin, meet Mr. Whiting.' Here we are, two strangers, introduced by a bellboy! From that came a very successful and pleasant working experience.

"We get to Hollywood, and, naturally, we register at the Roosevelt— everybody stayed there. We go to the studio the next day, and they say, 'You're going to write a picture for a fellow named Chevalier whom we just signed in Europe.' We'd never heard of him. The name of the picture was . . . oh, hell, my mind doesn't really function until midnight," he complained. Then he contradicted his own statement. "It was *Innocents of Paris*.

"So, we're sitting around in the hotel, and Dick is in another room noodling away at the piano, digging for a tune. Finally he hits something, and from the next room I yell, 'Dick, that's it!' And in his usual modest way he says, 'You really *like* it?' That was Whiting. I said, 'I don't think you have to look any further.'

"Now, the point is this: in those days, if the girl in the picture was named Susie, you wrote a song called 'Susie.' Well, the girl in this picture happened to be Louise. So we called the song 'Louise.' Incidentally, when 'Louise' became a hit, one of the trade papers ran a list of the hit songs of the week, and they topped it with 'Louise.' But through a typo they left the 'i' out, so it was billed as 'Louse.'

"Anyway, it wasn't lousy," said Robin, with characteristic understatement. "It turned out to be, as you know, a standard, and Chevalier, God bless him, even sang it on his last television appearance, very recently. He was an amazing guy. Do you know he'd been in correspondence with Eleanor [Richard Whiting's widow] ever since those days? He loved Dick.

"Chevalier was a very great man, personally," he said. "I've never told this story about 'Louise.' You see, Paramount was not prepared to make sound pictures, especially musical pictures. They didn't even have a sound stage yet. It was a pioneer period, so they took a silent stage, and from the ceiling they hung huge rugs and carpets to deaden the sound outside, because anything rumbling in the street would ruin the take. They didn't use playbacks in those days; everything was recorded right on the set. Back of those carpets, or behind the scenery somewhere, there was a little orchestra, and the musicians would play, and the guy in front of the camera would sing the song. Well, the time came to record 'Louise.' They had to do it in the middle of the night because it was the quietest time. It was probably around two in the morning, when there wasn't any traffic outside the studio, or inside.* It was such an important thing for Paramount—their first musical—that on the set there was every important executive of the company, from Adolph Zukor, the president, on down.

"So they start to play the tune, the intro. The director says, 'Shoot,' the cameras start, and Chevalier starts singing. He sings to a girl sitting on a garden wall, around them trees and flowers. In his kind of demonstrative style, he sings, '*Every little breeze seems to whisper Louise,*' and his fingers imitate a breeze. '*Birds in the trees,*' and he points to the trees, '*seem to twitter Louise.*' And he goes through the song with these gestures of his that are part of his personality and style. Comes the second chorus, and he sings, '*Every little breeze seems to whisper Louise,*' and he does the *same* gestures.

"Now, I was just a novice in the business. I turn to Dick. I say, 'Dick, that's wrong, doing the same gestures in both choruses. The second chorus is an anticlimax. It should be the climax.' Dick says, 'What do you want *me* to do about it?' I say, 'Why don't you go up to Chevalier and tell him?' He says, 'Oh, my God, not me, little me, Dick Whiting. I'd never dare do that. *You* go up and talk to him.' I say, 'Oh, no, not me.' He suggests I tell Dick Wallace, the director. So I go up to Dick Wallace and I tell him I think this is wrong. Dick says, 'My God, Leo, this is an international star. You don't expect *me* to tell him how to sing a song!' I say, 'It's going to ruin the whole thing if somebody doesn't tell him.' He says, 'Okay, if you feel that way, *you* go up and tell him.' The director is giving *me* orders to tell him!

---

* Paramount was in a state of technological crisis. A disastrous fire had burned down several sound stages in construction, and facilities for making sound pictures to compete with Warners' Vitaphone were needed. The rugs and carpets and night shooting were a desperate improvisation, the idea of Sam Jaffe, the studio manager.

"Now, I am absolutely nothing compared to this great star. Just a kid starting in. The set is full of these bigwigs. How can I go up in their presence and tell this guy what to do? Well, I had to. I said, 'Okay, I get fired, but what can I do?' The song was the sacred thing; it had to be right. It was our first, so much depended on it, and it was being done wrong. So I go up to Chevalier, and I say, 'Mr. Chevalier, you are a great international artist, and I don't know very much about the stage or the vaudeville theatre, but here in America we do the songs a little differently than you are doing this, and I think the American public would expect it done our way. In your first chorus you do those wonderful gestures of yours. But in the second chorus you do the same thing. Here in America we first sing the chorus clearly and simply to the girl, then, in the *second* chorus, if you add those marvelous gestures of yours, it becomes great.'

"He looked at me. 'Mr. Ro*ban*, you are wrong.' He called me 'Ro*ban*'— French inflection.

"You can imagine how I felt. I nearly went through the floor. I shrunk away, about three hundred feet down the stage, and hid behind a piece of scenery. Now again the orchestra strikes up, and again Chevalier starts to sing, and he gets to the middle of the chorus, and then I hear the director call, '*Cut,*' and I hear Chevalier say, 'Ro*ban?*' I don't answer. Again he says 'ROBIN!' Then everybody on the set starts to holler, 'Leo, Leo, Leo!' Well, finally I came forward. And here, in front of all these important people, Chevalier says, 'Ro*ban*, you are *right!*'

"Well, I knew then that he was a great man, because this was his first American picture and he didn't have to humiliate himself that way in front of all these people. From then on I adored the guy. Because I was a little nothing, and yet, in front of all these people, he gave me that moment of satisfaction.

"About Zukor. We had a little office upstairs somewhere, one of the side streets off the lot. You had to walk up a long flight of stairs to get there. One day, while we were sitting there, up the stairs and into our office comes little Adolph Zukor himself. One of the gods, a wonderful man, brilliant. Head of the whole company. Asked if he could please hear the songs that we'd written for Chevalier. So we played them, and he said, 'These are very good,' and turning to me, he said, 'I like your lyrics very much.' And that's the first time I heard the word 'lyrics' in Hollywood, because nobody there knew what the hell a lyric meant. They'd refer to *the words*. And I was very pleased to know that Zukor was knowledgeable enough about show business to use a word like that. Amazing human being.*

"Then, Lubitsch was making a picture called *Monte Carlo*. He told us what he wanted. He was the first director that ever wanted the songs integrated into the picture, rather than having them just 'spotted' here and there without any real connection with the story. In those days all the producers wanted were hit songs. They realized a hit was great for exploiting a picture and contributed to its success. But Lubitsch wanted his songs to *come out* of the action of the plot or the situation. In fact, he once used a phrase to me that I've never forgotten. I was back in New York, and he sent for me to come out and fix up some lyrics that some other fellows had written. I'm not going to mention their names, but

---

* In January 1972, when a friend suggested to Mr. Zukor that, come 1973, he planned to take a stage at the Paramount studio and throw a huge party to celebrate Mr. Zukor's hundredth birthday, the old gentleman replied, "Well, *I'll* be around for it . . . but I'm not too sure Paramount will be!

they were very fine songwriters. When I got out here, I said to Lubitsch, 'Why did you have to send to New York for a guy like me when right here on the Paramount lot you have these other great writers?' Lubitsch said, 'I like your style of writing because *you don't turn my characters into performers.*' Isn't that a great line?

"In *Monte Carlo* Lubitsch put on what was probably one of the finest musical scenes, from the visual standpoint, ever done in a picture. It was that scene where Jeanette MacDonald runs away. It had to say what the girl, who was a princess, was thinking while she was on that train. Remember how he shot it—her singing? But then he would shoot away from her onto the fields as she was passing, and he picked up the peasants singing the same song. It was a great *scene.*"

Margaret Whiting adds, "My father had to write train music that would go along with the wheels of the train leaving, and then Jeanette MacDonald started to sing, and she heard the train start to go. My father's music starts to fill in along with the click of the wheels, and she looks out and sees the peasants and she waves to them, and she suddenly realizes that this is a job that she has to do—to be a princess—and she has to go back. But Leo wrote a fantastic lyric to fit what this woman was *thinking*. With the music pounding away, Leo has her say, '*Blow whistle, blow blow blow away, blow away the past. Go engine, anywhere, I don't care how fast. On and on from darkness until dawn, from rain into the rainbow, fly with me.*' As the momentum went along, my father kept up this whole train of excitement going underneath the words. They worked so brilliantly together: '*Beyond the blue horizon waits a beautiful day. Goodbye to things that bore me, joy is waiting for me. I see a blue horizon, my life is only begun. Beyond the blue horizon lies a rising sun.*' Exactly what they wanted this woman to think and to say. So simple, so perfect."

"It *had* to be simple," says Robin. "Remember, the audience in those days was not too sophisticated. In those days it was just a habit to go to the movies. People didn't select, the way they do today. They weren't so educated. So I had to make the lyric—just as any good lyric should be—understandable at first hearing. You couldn't go back and say, 'What did she say?' They had to get it right away.

"Funny, I remember one day Lubitsch came to me, worried about a scene in the picture. Chevalier is knocking at the door, trying to get into Jeanette MacDonald's boudoir, and she says, 'Who is it?' And Lubitsch asks, 'Should he say, "It's *I*"? or "It's *me*"?' I said, 'Have him say 'It's me,' because if he says "It's I" it's too goddam grammatical, and people will stop, and you'll lose them there for a second.' Lubitsch said, 'You're right. We'll say, "It's me." '

"Whiting and I eventually broke up. I had to go back to New York because my mother was very sick, and he went to Fox while I was East. We didn't want to break up that winning combination; it was just circumstances. Then, when I came back—it was when Lubitsch called me to do this little repair job—there was a guy named Ralph Rainger. He was a piano player on the lot, and he came to me and he said, 'Look, they're doing a picture here and there's a chance to write a couple of songs for Bing Crosby.' It was one of those pictures Paramount did every year with various radio stars—*The Big Broadcast of 1935*, I think. 'Why don't you stay on and write them with me?' he asked.

"He wasn't yet established as a songwriter; he'd collaborated on 'Moanin' Low' and some other songs in New York, but he hadn't made it out here. You know, a lot of piano players sometimes write an occasional song that somebody puts words to. I liked the idea of staying in Hollywood at the time; it was an exciting place. So we write these two songs. One of them was 'Please,' which, thanks to Crosby and his power of making songs into hits, became one.

"So Paramount said, 'Well, you two guys look like you can work pretty well together,' and they gave me a contract to stay longer. And with Rainger, as you know, I had a lot of luck.* Thanks mostly to Rainger, and also to my poetic style of writing, we were considered 'classy' writers. I can't think of another word.

"Ralph had very good taste. He had a very good sense of lyric, and he liked the idea of a lyric that wasn't too conventional in style. He encouraged me to dig for distinctive titles. For example, one day he came in and said, 'I hit on a little jingle tune, maybe you'll like it.' He started to play this thing, one of those kind of bouncy schottisches, and I said, 'Let me think about it.' And, as usual, I went out and started to walk around the Paramount lot. That was the way I used to concentrate during the day. When I came back, I said, 'Gee, I've got a great title'—no, not a great one, I *never* said that. I said, 'I've got a title for that.' Because I never thought any of those things were great. In fact, my dear wife used to say, if I had the Number One song on the Hit Parade, I would still say, 'Well, if they'd given me more time, I could have done it better.'

"So I said, 'I got this title. It's "June in January." ' He said, 'You're crazy—June in January?' Sat for a minute, and then he said it again. "What a title!' So he sits down to the piano, and he came up with that great melody for the song. Well, 'June in January,' as you know, is still used in headlines, all kinds of places. Whenever the weather out here gets unusually hot in January, all the headlines use the phrase 'June–in-January weather.' I get a kick out of that more than I do out of anything else, the fact that a song phrase can become part of a language."

Can Robin articulate the creative process which results in such fine lyrics?

"No," he said. "I don't know how you come by them. A phrase just comes out of the air. In this case, the rhythm of Ralph's original tune suggested it. I can't claim any originality. I used to say, someday I'm going to be looking through some old poetry written by some Chinese or Greek three thousand years ago, and I'll see the phrase 'June in January.'

"I don't know where you get ideas for songs. I always did try to reach for a distinctive title. Wasn't always lucky, but I tried it. Ralph was a very good judge of lyrics. We did a song for another picture; I said, 'It'll never be a hit. It's not a song, it's a piece of material.' Ralph said, 'You're crazy.' We bet ten dollars, and I was very glad to pay off. You want to know what it was? Here's what happened.

"They were doing another one of those *Big Broadcast* things, and Mitchell Leisen, the director, comes to us and says he's got a problem. He says, 'I got a scene in this picture and I've had six different writers try to write it, and they can't. It doesn't work. It's dull. And last night,' he says, 'I got a brainstorm. I thought, why don't we put that scene into words and music? Maybe the music will keep it interesting; maybe the rhyme will keep it going. These other guys tried it in dialogue, and it flopped.'

"Leisen says, 'This is a young, sophisticated couple who had been married.

---

* "Luck," in Mr. Robin's ever modest definition stands for six years' worth of such song hits as "June in January," "Love in Bloom," "Love Is Just Around the Corner," and "Thanks for the Memory," which won the Academy Award in 1938.

And they meet by chance on an ocean liner. I want them to show they are still in love, but they dare not say it. It's got to be implied. Now, if you guys can write a song like that, fine.' And I told him, 'Well, it's not easy to say "I love you" without saying it. Most songs come right out and hit it on the nose. But we'll see what we can do.'

"So Ralph and I mulled this thing over for several days. Ralph said, 'Now, this is a piece of special material. Why don't you write the lyrics first?' Ordinarily, he'd do music first. So I wrote some lyrics, brought them to him, he used them as a basis for his melody. We made a few changes, but most of it set the lyric as I had written it. Now, Leisen had said to us, 'This song is going to be sung by Bob Hope. And while it's a serious song, a guy like that has to get laughs.' I thought, 'Oh, my God, now what are we going to do? That really complicates it.' Well, anyway, I finally came up with that completed lyric, and one day about three weeks later we ran into Mitch Leisen in the commissary, and he asks, 'Where the hell is that song I asked you guys to write? I'm ready to go into production and I need that scene.' So we said we had something. I said, 'I haven't wanted to show it to you yet, because I don't think there are any laughs in it.' He said, 'Let *me* hear it.'

"We went over to the office. Ralph gets to the piano, and I, in my usual wavering voice, sing Mitch this song. We get about halfway into the second chorus, and I see that Mitch has pulled out his handkerchief and starts to wipe his eye. And I thought, 'Oh, Christ! What's this! It's supposed to be funny, and here the guy's going to weep!' Well, we finished the song, and Mitch said, sniffing, 'No, it's not funny, but I'll take it.' "

Leo broke into a reminiscent laugh. "Now the song is going to be in the picture and everybody we played it for—we called in guys from the Paramount music department—every guy *cries!* One German composer says, 'Ach, my vife should hear dis song!' Another guy, little Freddy Hollander,* he's wiping the tears out of his eyes like it's Niagara, he was crying so hard. So we never knew what the hell was going to happen to the song. That's when I bet Ralph the ten dollars, and I lost, because it became a big hit, and that's the story of 'Thanks for the Memory.' "

Not quite. Robin had left out the Academy Award he and Rainger won, and the fact that since 1938 the song has never stopped, and that Hope has always used it as his theme song.

"Well, he started using it on the radio, so I guess he's stuck with it," said Leo. "Hope is such a wonderful guy. When Ralph died, in 1942, he spoke about it on his show. He said then, 'As long as I am on the air, I will always use this song.' That was his tribute to Ralph Rainger. So, you see, there are some pretty wonderful people in show business.

"Take 'Love in Bloom.' Jack Benny was being interviewed lately, and they asked him how come he had to pick that one as his theme song. It's a serious ballad and, after all, he's a comedian. He said, 'I don't know, it does seem to be all wrong. But when the song was a big hit, I was doing gags with my fiddle on one of my shows, and I played 'Love in Bloom' because it was the most familiar song at the time, and it went over very big. So I did it several times again. And each time it went over so well that I finally decided to use it as my theme song. Because it had become associated with me through all those gags.'

---

* Frederick Hollander wrote many songs for Marlene Dietrich, including "Falling in Love Again" and "Hands Across the Table."

"We kept doing things that the publishers used to tear their hair about. You know, the publishers had no faith in 'Love in Bloom' at all. They called up and said, 'Who the hell can sing this? Too rangy musically, and the lyrics are too fancy.' But, thanks to Jack Benny and a few other guys, and Bing Crosby's record . . . People don't remember it was written for Bing.

"We used to write all sorts of different songs for Bing, because you could take a chance with him, he could put over anything, no matter whether it was low-down or fancy. We did a picture called *Waikiki Wedding* that had a song in it called 'Sweet Leilani.' We didn't write that one. The producer asked us if we'd mind; Bing had a friend named Harry Owens who'd written it, and he wanted to interpolate it in the picture. We said, 'Sure.' For Bing, we'd have done anything. Anyway, the picture's just about to start, and Ralph and I are sitting around the office, and I tell him I have a funny hunch about the score— we need a hit song, a simple hit. He says, 'You're crazy, we've *got* one in there. The melody is being raved about all through the music department. It can't miss. 'Sweet Is the Word for You'—that will be our smash, don't worry.'

"I said, 'Ralph, do me a favor. When you get up tomorrow morning'—he usually worked in the morning while I was home sleeping—'you sit down at the piano, and the first thing that pops into your head, you just write it down and bring it to me, and I'll write it up.' That afternoon when I came into the studio, Ralph said, 'You want to hear the tune that popped into my head this morning?' I said, 'Fine,' and he played it for me. So I took about half an hour, jotted some words down to it.

"A couple of months later the music proofs come from the publishers in New York. They always sent us the sheet-music proofs for corrections and approval. And Ralph is thumbing through them and he okays one after the other, and suddenly he hits this one proof, and he yells, 'Oh, *no!*' I ask him what's the matter, and he says, 'I'm not going to publish *this* song. This will be a disgrace to us. It's a cheap melody. It's a piece of crap! It'll destroy us. We have a good reputation for writing fine things.'

"I said, 'Wait a minute, the picture's coming out, you can't stop it. I'm willing to take a chance with my reputation.' So finally Ralph gave in and allowed them to publish the song.

"All right, 'Sweet Is the Word for You,' which he and the music department thought was so great, sold about forty thousand copies of sheet music, which is a terrible flop. And this other song that he thought was a cheap piece of trash sold probably ten times as much as the other and turned out to be our most performed song, and *it still is* our most performed song, and the name of that 'dog' is 'Blue Hawaii.' The public loves it. It's played again and again, day after day, all these years. It has something that strikes a responsive chord in the people. So sometimes a creator does not recognize the value of his own thing. Just as I didn't think much of 'Thanks for the Memory,' Ralph hated the melody of 'Blue Hawaii.' "

Would he care to discuss the top-echelon composers he worked with after Ralph Rainger's tragic death in a plane crash? How about Messrs. Arlen, Kern, Jule Styne, Arthur Schwartz, Johnny Green, Vincent Youmans, all of whom have since supplied him with melody?

"Oh, I've been very lucky," he admitted. "Always had great composers to write to. But you know how it is. Sometimes you can't get another guy, so you settle for a Leo Robin."

Settle? Hardly, when one thinks of Robin's score, written with Kern in

1945, for the film *Centennial Summer*, which contained "In Love in Vain." And another set of fine songs he wrote with Harold Arlen for a film called *Casbah*, which includes the haunting 'For Every Man There's a Woman" and the rollicking "Hooray for Love."

"Nothing very big," he insisted. "I would say that the luckiest thing that happened to me after Rainger passed away was a Broadway show called *Gentlemen Prefer Blondes*."

Lucky?

"Oh, *yes*," said Leo. "You know, for years there was always a mystique around Broadway that Hollywood songwriters couldn't ever come back to New York and cut the mustard. Max Dreyfus used to say, 'How come you Hollywood fellows, when you're out *there*, write hit after hit, but when you get back and you write a musical show for the theatre, you come up empty? What is it, Leo?'

"Most of the time Dreyfus was right, you know. Take Ralph and me. We went back once in the '30s to do a show called *Nice Goin'*. Didn't go so nice. We had a young girl playing the lead, she'd just been a sensation the year before in *Leave It to Me*, singing Cole Porter's 'My Heart Belongs to Daddy.' Mary Martin! Now, you'd think that would ensure success, wouldn't you?" He shook his head. 'Flop.'

"I think I know why, though. When Ralph was working on that show, he was terribly self-conscious. He'd come from Broadway, but he had started as a piano player, playing duos in the orchestra pit. In the '20s that was a very popular thing—duets during the entr'acte. Remember how Ohman and Arden played Gershwin? Lovely.

"So I'm sure Ralph had this awe of show business, New York show business, and it was a handicap. He couldn't write as freely as he would have out on the Coast; he was nervous. Out on the Coast he probably felt he wasn't subject to the kind of critics there are in New York. So he strained, and as a result he did not do his best. And that may be the answer to Max Dreyfus' question."

But two Hollywood expatriates, Robin and Jule Styne, certainly confounded the Dreyfusian rule. Their *Gentlemen Prefer Blondes* was a smash-hit score. Not until Carol Channing did *Hello, Dolly!* would she have a more successful number than "Diamonds Are a Girl's Best Friend." The aficionados of first-rate comic lyrics may disagree on the merits of this couplet over that one, and which song will last over another, but it's generally conceeded that Robin's lyrics for that melody of Styne's are as bright and sharp and lasting as any of the best of Larry Hart, or of Porter, or, for that matter, of any of the so-called "Broadway guys."

Leo paced a bit more, puffing on another pipe, and finally shrugged. "Lucky," he finally remarked. "*Blondes* got by because it was a great show, an entertaining show, with a great new star. And, remember, it had all the nostalgia of the '20s that they say today is bringing back the old-style musical. Well, I'll admit that it may not be simply the nostalgia. I read where Walter Kerr wrote recently about *Nanette*, 'It's not nostalgia alone. It's because it's a good show.' "

When Marilyn Monroe did "Diamonds" in the film version of *Gentlemen Prefer Blondes*, it was one of the rare moments in her career that the lady was given a strong piece of comedy material to do, and she did very well with it.

'Funny about that," said Leo. "I had to change some of her lines because they were censorable. I never thought they were so blue, but when Fox did the picture, we were all still stuck with that fear of censorship out here. I guess today it would be quite tame, compared with some of the things I hear. You know how it used to be? I had a censorship problem once on the lyrics to 'Thanks for the Memory.' Can you believe it? Remember the part of the song that went: *Thanks for the memory of transatlantic calls, / China's crumbling walls, / That weekend at Niagara when we never saw the falls, / How lovely it was . . .* ' Well, the censor at Paramount came to me and said, 'Leo, you *can't* say that.' I asked, 'What's dirty about it?' He said, ' "That weekend at Niagara when we never saw the falls." Uh-uh.' So I said, 'Okay, what *can* I say?' He comes back after a while and says, 'Say, "That weekend at Niagara when we *hardly* saw the falls." ' Which *I* think is dirtier!"

After *Blondes* Robin wrote another score, this time for the Broadway production *The Girl in Pink Tights*, which starred Zizi Jeanmaire. His lyrics were fashioned to tunes by the late Sigmund Romberg, and while the score contains such beautiful songs as "My Heart Won't Say Goodbye" and "Lost in Loveliness" (which title seems, alas, prophetic), the show was far from a success.

"Dreyfus pleaded with me not to do that show," said Leo. "He insisted that you cannot do a show after a man has died. But I'd promised Rommy that I'd do the show, and after he died I went on with it for sentimental reasons. Max was right, though. It doesn't work. You simply have to have the composer there *with* you, working throughout. But I'm not sorry I did the show, because one of the greatest people I've ever met in my life was Jeanmaire. Wonderful. Knocked herself out rehearsing and perfecting everything, and completely surprised everybody by the way she could put over a song."

While he lit still another pipe, it seemed an apt time to ask a leading question of a lyricist whose work is so well used by composers and by a vast public which barely, if at all, recognizes his existence. "If somebody brought you a good musical-comedy book today, would you do it?"

He burst into laughter. "You ask *me* that? Me, the guy who turned down *Funny Girl?* See, I thought that book was the same general idea that we'd done in pictures over and over again—the little girl who starts in the ghetto and winds up a star. So I said, 'What's new about this? The critics will never buy it.' And I was wrong. So if somebody brings me a book today—and they have, and I've turned down others, believe me—I think I'd hesitate, because I don't know what will go in the theatre. As a matter of fact, if somebody had told me last year that they were going to do *No, No, Nanette,* I'd have said they were crazy. Because, remember, I was there when that show was produced originally. I only got to work with Youmans on *Hit the Deck* because after *Nanette* he and Caesar had some sort of an argument and Youmans needed a new lyricist, so he settled for me."

He walked over to the window and stared at the helter-skelter sprawl of Beverly Hills below. "But to answer your question," he said, "if somebody came to me with a book—yes, if I could get very excited about it and really had faith in it, I'd probably do it. But I'm not sure. I'm not sure for other reasons. I'm not sure I could take living in New York now."

Is he depressed about the state of music today?

"No, not depressed. Doubtful, maybe, that my style of writing would get very far in this kind of music market. Now, I'm not disparaging the things that the new kids are writing. Some of them are very talented. But they write about the world today, and that world isn't a very pleasant place. So there aren't many pleasant songs. There were always songs of what you could call current interest, and there were also songs that were a little bit disagreeable, but they were usually written within the pattern of other songs of the day—you know, the good old thirty-two-bar song. Remember 'Brother, Can You Spare a Dime?' I doubt whether some of the things written today have the quality that song had, or its *thrust*.

"We've *had* songs about marijuana and dope, remember? They were Harlem songs—'The Reefer Man,' 'Kicking the Gong Around.' These subjects aren't new. Maybe it's just that the conditions are more prevalent today. And the big difference in the songs, as I see it—and I can be wrong—is that the song of yesterday appealed to the general public. Almost everybody could identify with it. The song of today appeals mostly to just one section of the public. It's aimed at the young, it expresses feelings of the young, and the young can identify. But the over-thirty people *can't*. There's the big difference.

"Today, even the construction of the songs is unconventional, and the language is the sort of language that only the young can understand. I don't think the kids are writing for anyone except themselves. They don't really want to reach anyone else. It's as if they're saying, "This is a music *for us*. This is our music.' I don't know whether they even reason it out that way. They just—well, these young writers express themselves and react only to what's going on. And they just write.

"But listen, that is not a criticism of rock-and-roll songs. I don't want to pan these kids who are writing today. The things they're writing are at least honest expressions of how they feel, in relation to the conditions of their world, and how they react to their own lives and futures. I'm sure you cannot fault these kids for their attitudes. Not the way you could fault some hack Tin Pan Alley songwriter back in 1925 who was writing second-rate mechanical songs about how sweet it would be to be back in dear old Dixie with his dear old mammy or his lovely little tootsie-wootsie baby. Maybe he was doing a professional job, but he was peddling a totally false picture. Today these kids are, at the very least, *honest*."

There were half a dozen or so discarded pipes stacked in the ashtray between us, and Leo abruptly ceased his pacing. "I've really talked enough," he said. "I warned you before—I don't make much sense until after midnight."

So when he wrote "Up with the Lark" with Jerome Kern for *Centennial Summer* all those years back, the lyric wasn't autobiographical?

He grinned. "No, not me. Funny about that song. Every now and then I go over the lyric. I like it, but there are one or two spots I'd like to improve. Listen, why don't we meet again sometime at night when I can really make some sense?"

Morning, noon, or midnight . . . any time, Mr. Robin.

'Make Someone Happy'

(Betty Comden)

MRS. STEVEN KYLE, who is known to film and theatrical producers and music publishers as Betty Comden, sits in her tasteful East Side townhouse living room *toute seule*. Her professional partner, Adolph Green, is off for an extended session at his dentist's. "You may have wanted the team," she says, dead-panning a paraphrase of the old film-musical cliché, 'but you'll simply have to settle for me."

It comes as something of a shock to anyone who is a contemporary of Comden and Green to realize that this graceful, attractive mother of two grown children has been writing with Mr. Green for a quarter of a century. *Applause*, for which they did the book, is enjoying a long Broadway run; their first Broadway musical, *On the Town*, which they wrote with Leonard Bernstein in 1944, was revived last winter. In between they wrote music and lyrics for *Wonderful Town*, Mary Martin's *Peter Pan, Billion Dollar Baby*, the revue *Two on the Aisle, Bells Are Ringing, Subways Are for Sleeping*, and *Fade Out—Fade In*. They have also had extensive experience in the postwar Hollywood scene; among their most successful musical films were *The Band Wagon* and *Singin' in the Rain*. ("Can you believe it? It's one of those movies that gets 'studied' in college cinema courses," she says incredulously.)

The Comden-Green career began when the two were part of a talented group, The Revuers, whose second female member was the late, great Judy Holliday. In the early 1940s the Revuers specialized in writing and performing their own satiric musical-comedy material in Greenwich Village night clubs. "We couldn't afford to pay for material, so we just said, 'Gee, maybe we can write some and get by.' We started writing out of necessity. No particular preparation or training. We sort of sat around and wrote. We wrote music then, too. I had a friend who taught me four, five chords on the piano, and I wrote all kinds of things on the basis of those few chords, judiciously arranged. One of the others in our group really could play the piano, and we used to sing melodies at him and he'd play them. Of course, as you get to know more, you lose that sort of tremendous nerve and courage of youth. When we came to do our first show, from that time on, we wouldn't dream of writing music!"

That first show was *On the Town*, and its score was a collaboration with young Leonard Bernstein. He had written the music for a ballet, *Fancy Free*, that was choreographed by Jerome Robbins; the ballet, which dealt with three young sailors on leave in Manhattan, was such a success that it was decided to enlarge it into a Broadway show. With the veteran George Abbott, the only over-forty talent around the production, as director, *On the Town* exploded a burst of Roman-candle talents on Broadway in December 1944; Comden and Green not only provided Bernstein with lyrics but performed in the show as well. The score of *On the Town* was replete with Comden-Green-Bernstein pleasures. The rollicking "New York, New York," the lovely ballad "Lonely Town," and the satiric comedy of the duet which the two lyricists had written for themselves, "I Get Carried Away"—all of them were to captivate delighted audiences, not only on Broadway but when the show was made into a film at Metro-Goldwyn-Mayer, with Gene Kelly as its star.

"We were very close friends with Leonard," says Miss Comden. "We'd known him forever. When he works on something, he works very much from a base of trying to get an entire concept, or one clue that's going to make the whole score fall into place for him. He thinks in terms of the whole show, and there's a kind of texture to his music that's unmistakably his. Nobody writes for the theatre the way Leonard does. And he never feels that because he's doing something for the commercial theatre he's in any sense writing *down*."

On the Town was revived in the fall of 1971. "It was fun to see audiences responding to it in the same way they did in 1944," remarks Miss Comden. "What's most interesting to me is the song 'Some Other Time,' which is much less known than the others but which seemed to overwhelm 1971 audiences. It had been a very moving moment in the show back then, but in the revival, perhaps because there was that sense of time having passed and the world being so different from those World War II days, it seemed to affect people very deeply. Funny, my daughter, who had never seen the show, and who's twenty-two, found it one of the most moving songs she'd ever heard. And I don't understand it, because she was certainly not being nostalgic about it."

After *On the Town* the young team collaborated with composer Morton Gould on the score for *Billion Dollar Baby*. They also began to work in Hollywood, where they were signed to write scripts at Metro for producer Arthur Freed. But, unlike other Broadway talents who were lured to Culver City by fat salaries and the affluent ambience of the movies (never to return to Broadway), Comden and Green were only annual N.Y.-to-L.A. commuters; they never settled permanently in Beverly Hills. Nor were they "corrupted."

"Oh *no!*" sighs Miss Comden today. "We worked our heads off. It wasn't any swimming pools and mad nights; it was going to the office every day and *working*. Alan Jay Lerner found that out too. We worked like brutes. Salt mines! All that stuff about 'Oh yes, you'll get to Hollywood and you'll lead the lush life, and they'll slip those checks under your doors'—forget it! That was a different era from ours, believe me. We were always working for Arthur Freed on a specific project, it wasn't a question of writing and then having fourteen other writers assigned to our scripts. We wrote, and we did some music and lyrics, and then, in almost every case, we saw it go right into production. We worked night and day with Roger Edens, who was Arthur Freed's associate producer—an invaluable man, quite remarkable."

It was indeed a different era, and the films on which Comden and Green worked were far removed from the old-style Esther Williams/Eleanor Powell/Tommy Dorsey/Red Skelton/etc. Metro musicals. What they produced were literate, integrated films where story and music and lyrics meshed into brilliant highlights such as *Singin' in the Rain, The Band Wagon*, and *It's Always Fair Weather*.

In 1951 they embarked on their first collaboration with songwriter Jule Styne when they did the score for the revue *Two on the Aisle*. Was it a problem to adopt their style of writing to his music?

"No," she says. "None at all. True, there's a big difference in the sort of music Jule writes, as compared to the way Leonard writes, but they're both creative men of the theatre—they *think* theatrically, they think dramatically, they're not just composers or songwriters. And they're both extremely easy to work with. Jule is less apt to think in terms of the entire concept the way Leonard does, but he's tremendously involved in characters, story, book, everything that's happening. Very much a dramatist—as composers have to be in the theatre."

Since 1953, when Comden and Green were reunited with Bernstein to write the score for *Wonderful Town*, which starred Rosalind Russell, the two have worked mostly with Jule Styne. But Miss Comden feels that the score for *Wonderful Town* represented a definite change in the team's style of writing. "For a long time we were known as 'those kids without any heart, who write all this brittle stuff.' When we did that show, which was based on *My Sister Eileen*, we didn't drop the satiric approach, but we had songs like 'A Quiet Girl' and 'It's Love' and 'Why Oh Why Did I Leave Ohio' that were *pretty* songs.

"Adolph and I have never written popular songs, you know. We have only written in connection with shows. We've never sat down and said, 'Hey, let's write a song called . . . ' and then do it to a title. So it's very hard for us to come up with the kind of song that's possibly going to be a hit. Sometimes, when everything is just working right, you may come up with the right situation, and the right thing for a character, and also come up with a hit. But why that happens, or what those elements are, I don't know exactly. In all these years we've had only three big standards."

Two of those standards were part of the Comden-Green-Styne score for *Bells Are Ringing*, which starred their old friend and partner from the Revuers days, Judy Holliday. "At one point we were talking to Jule, and said, 'Wouldn't it be nice to have something in the show like an old Youmans tune, where there's two notes, but the bass keeps changing and moving under the notes, making different harmonies and moving a melody.' Very simple. Jule went to the piano and started playing a simple thing—*da*, dee *dah*. He asked if that was what we meant, and we said absolutely! And he started finishing the melody, sort of laughing about it because there were just the two notes, and a moving succession of chords under it . . . and then he developed it, and it was a tune! Well, we all fell in love with it. But we had no idea where it would go. No name, no words. A big hit at parties with Jule singing *'Da* dee *dah,* da *dee* da *dah* dee *dah!'* and killing the people. It was a very big hit as *'Da* dee *dah!'*

"And it might never have been in the show except that as the book we were writing developed, we came to a place where the leading male character feels that his life has been saved by the arrival of this curious girl Judy Holliday, who played the telephone operator at his answering service. So there was a place for him to express that to her. Suddenly it came to one of us—don't ask me which one—the right words for that situation and that character. And they fitted the melody Jule had been playing at parties—*Da*-dee-*da*—'*Just in time, I found you just in time!'*"

There was a second big hit from *Bells Are Ringing,* a Comden-Green-Styne standard that has become a traditional closing number for every night-club chanteuse who needs to tickle her audience's tear ducts—"The Party's Over."

"Well" says Miss Comden, "that just evolved. We had a scene in the show where Judy had gone to a big fancy party, and after all the guests left, she stood there and sang. When we got the idea for the title, we told Jule about it, and he sat right down at the piano and set it. Sometimes you give a composer a lyric and he goes away with it and you hear from him much later. But with Jule we very often work on a spontaneous-combustion principle. We stand around him singing it while he's writing.

"I remember something curious about 'The Party's Over.' About Judy.* She'd been in the Revuers with us, and she trusted herself as a comedienne and an actress, but she hadn't been in a musical before. So she said, 'Look, I'll do anything in the show but *don't* ask me to sing any straight ballads, because I can't do that.' Well, we knew she could—we'd worked with her long enough. We also knew that Judy liked to sing harmony parts. She used to love to embellish on a melody and sing around it, or sing a third above, or a third below, and have fun at the piano. So when Jule finished this song, he took Judy aside and he said, 'Look, Judy, we have an idea for a musical spot, and this is your part.' He taught her the song as if it were a harmony part—a melodic line that went against something else. She learned it—and of course she could sing it, it presented no problems at all. Then we all said, 'All right, Judy, that's your song. So now you can't say you can't sing it . . . you just have!' But then, Judy could do practically anything. Adolph and I miss her so damned much . . . "

The third big Comden-Green-Styne standard is another universal favorite with singers, a song that is as well suited to Tony Bennett's rhythmic drive as it is adaptable to the softer vocal touch of an Eydie Gorme—"Make Someone Happy."

"That came from a show Garson Kanin wrote called *Do Re Mi,* and again Jule wrote us a beautiful melody. It was a duet that took place in the middle of the second act, and it stopped the show and, believe me, very seldom do you have a ballad that does *that* in that spot. Jule wrote a very big climax to the song. It actually has two of them. The end starts coming, and then you think it's almost over"—she hums the melody in a high, pleasant voice—"and then

* Miss Holliday, who had captivated theatre and film audiences since her enormous success in *Born Yesterday,* died a few years after the long run of *Bells Are Ringing.*

he goes on to a slightly bigger ending. It's a song you *enjoy* singing. I only thought of that this second, but it's true! There are songs that people like to sing, or bellow, or croon for their own pleasure . . . the singable song. 'Make Someone Happy' is a simple idea, and I guess it affects people. That's the only way I can explain it. I've been thinking about that, too. We've written dozens of songs, but had only three big hits. And lately it seems as if there are fewer and fewer chances in Broadway shows to score with songs the way there used to be.

"I'm very uneasy about things, you know. Everything *costs* so much. The revival of *On the Town* cost five times as much in 1971 as it did back in 1944.* When it's that much of a gamble, it really gets too scary. All the fun has gone out of it. That sense we used to have, when we were just starting in, of 'Let's do it. Let's get an idea and let's do the show!' No more . . . And I'm afraid lately we don't have too many moments on Broadway where one producer comes up to his partner during intermission and says, 'Well, J.R., it looks as if we have a hit on our hands!'

"I haven't got any anecdotes about how songs were written, or what happened when we were trying out in Detroit. I think there's something about the creative process—whether it's painting or writing or songwriting, anything— which is that you can't *talk* about it. You try to think of anecdotes about it, and you try to explain, 'Yes, I was sitting in this room and this happened, and then that happened.' But you're never really saying what happened, because in the middle and surrounding all of it is a very mysterious thing. I mean, it's a kind of instinctual something that just *happens* when talented people are creating something. And it can't be described, it's a combination of that sort of happy accident that the best creative thing always is."

She thinks for a moment. "When I say accident, I mean you bring everything in your life that's been in it up to that moment to it—but there's still a tremendously accidental, unanalytical thing that happens at the actual moment of . . . of making something. And when people sit down and are interviewed and say solemnly, 'Well, you see, what I tried to do *here* is . . . ' that usually turns out to be a lot of baloney. You cannot describe this process in so many words. It's not like making a product—a box, a car, or a bowl of chowder. It's unique . . . and I can't describe it."

Later, standing in the front doorway of her house on East 95th Street, Betty Comden says, "If you ever come across the secret of what makes one song a hit, and not another—call me. Immediately!"

---

* Not only was the revival costly to mount, but it proved to be a box-office failure.

'Lullaby of Broadway'

(Harry Warren)

AS HE HIMSELF is usually the first to point out, genial Harry Warren is probably the most successful composer of popular music who has ever remained completely unknown to his vast American public. For nearly half a century, generations have hummed to, sung to, danced to, wooed and won wives to, bellowed in the shower and even marched to such Warren melodies as "Nagasaki," "I Found a Million Dollar Baby in a Five and Ten Cent Store," "That's Amore," "Jeepers, Creepers," "The Atchison, Topeka and the Santa Fe." And for all those same years the spotlight has stubbornly avoided round, five-foot-tall Mr. Warren.

Philosophic in his anonymity, pushing eighty, Warren is not completely reconciled to it. He has developed a certain snappish defense mechanism. "I never had publicity," he says. "And now I'm at the stage where I don't give a damn."

As remarkable as the lack of Warren's personal fame is the extent to which his songs remain firmly imbedded in the mass consciousness. Even today, among the latest generation of the early '70s, those bushy-haired, granny-glassesed, passionately intense film devotees, there is keen awareness of Warren's songs.

The Elgin Cinema buffs and the Cahiers du Cinéma crowd may not recall his name, but they can all discuss his catchy ditties for such landmark early musicals as *42nd Street*, *Gold Diggers of 1933* (as well as *1935*, *1937*, and *in Paris*), *Footlight Parade*, *Dames*, and a dozen-odd other vintage Warner, Fox, and Goldwyn oeuvres. Camp he may be to the children; to their grandparents he has been a Pied Piper ever since that long-ago year of 1922, when his first hit song, "Rose of the Rio Grande," was knocking 'em dead in vaudeville.

Bing Crosby, Al Jolson, Fred Astaire, Judy Garland, Alice Faye—name a star performer, pick your favorite, and there'll be Warren standards galore in his or her repertoire. So how is it that such deafening silence surrounds the composer?

Harry, who shows no sign of age beyond his snowy white hair, ventures an explanation. "I'm a Capricorn," he says. "They call the Capricorn the hard-way guy, you know, you always have to go the hard way. If there's a hot-dog stand and there's a lot of people standing around and I keep saying, 'Give me a hot dog,' he probably waits on everybody but me, and finally when it gets to me, he says, 'Wait your turn.' Even when they had the ASCAP show in New York at Lincoln Center, I arrived in a tuxedo at the door, and the fellow stopped me. He didn't stop the other people. He stopped *me*. He said to me, 'Where are you going?' I said, 'Where the hell do you think I'm going?' That's the story of my life."

But he's not gone completely without recognition. What about his three Oscars for best film songs?

"Ah, I use 'em for doorstops!" Warren grins, lighting up a thick black Italian stogie.

It is a damp California morning with fog still shrouding the foothills above, and that same air that Harry Warren has been breathing since those days back in 1932 when he and Al Dubin were pounding out hit songs for Busby Berkeley to stage is now slightly acrid with smog. Warren still maintains a large home, early '30s style, off Sunset Boulevard, in Beverly Hills. Some yards away is his work studio, and here is his piano. He snaps on a small gas heater to warm up the room. "So, you really want to talk about *me?*" he says, with amiable sarcasm. "Isn't it a little late for that?"

Can he perhaps explain how so little personal recognition has accrued over the years to his massive output of melody?

"Well, I never was a publicity seeker," he admits. "They always wrote about the guys who were publicized. Like, the other day this guy comes to me and interviews me about Burt Bacharach. Like he's the second coming of Jesus. He's telling me this guy has just upset the whole music world. I said, 'No! He's just getting a lot of publicity.' Another thing, he's an *entertaining* songwriter. He's an *actor* songwriter. He goes out and plays his songs with a big orchestra. Have you seen any songwriter doing that, except maybe Mancini? He and Mancini, they're the only two. It's like the old days, when Johnny Mercer used to go on a lot of radio shows. So did Hoagy Carmichael. They got publicized. Years ago, when Berlin had his own publicity department, with his own company, he did the same thing."

The walls of the small studio are covered with framed photos: a much younger, black-haired Warren pounding the piano, Dick Powell leaning on his shoulder, reading the music. Affectionately inscribed photos of Al Jolson, Alice Faye, and Warren's later collaborators, Ira Gershwin, Johnny Mercer, Dorothy

Fields. "So many people out here did so much," he murmurs. "Look at little Leo Robin there. You ever hear anybody mention *him?*"

It is a pleasure to inform him that Mr. Robin has supplied fascinating material for a section of this book dealing exclusively with his accomplishments. "And of course he won't take bows for anything he did," says Warren. "You know, I nicknamed Leo the Mary Pickford of the songwriters."

Against another wall is an elaborate tape system on which Warren plays his favorite music, notably the works of Puccini. "My favorite composer," he says. "Not just because I'm of Italian extraction but because he was such an innovator. I just love his music." There hangs a framed sheet of one of Puccini's original manuscripts. "They presented me that when I was on *This Is Your Life*," he says, caressing it with affection. "Sometimes I go off on a Puccini kick for days. I'm also hooked on *Der Rosenkavalier*. You know that was Jerry Kern's favorite opera? He got me started on it. I used to say you'd have to have buttons in the belly to sing Richard Strauss' music. I don't know how the singers did it, because sometimes there isn't even a cue note for them. They have to hit it like that. You know who's great at that? Bing Crosby. He knows just where to come in. You never have to give him a 'da' to tell him where he has to start singing, he just *knows*."

How did he get started writing songs? What was the impulse?

"Oh, I always had it. It's a craving, says Warren. "My family was the same; my sister was in show business, my brother was a singer, and I always wanted to learn to play an instrument. But we didn't have the money for me to learn to play one, so little by little I started saving money. My father was a bootmaker, he felt you should have a trade. But by the time I was fourteen I was a drummer in a band. Snare drum and bass drum. I got a job in Canarsie: you know where that is? That's the roughest end of Brooklyn. Played in a dance hall. Oh boy, that one-o'clock train leaving Canarsie, it was a corker. One long blast of the whistle, and at the next station the whole platform would be lined up with cops with their clubs out.

"You know, sometimes I can't realize how old I am. Look at all the things I've done. I worked at the Liberty Theatre in Brownsville when Jacob P. Adler ran the Yiddish stock company there. I used to sell fruit, you know, walking down the aisles and everybody clamoring to buy an orange or a lemon, and everybody with tears flowing from the melodrama up on stage. I remember a guy there who was the cop, Hymie—he became the Democratic leader of Brownsville, this guy. Couldn't read or write. When the lights went down before the curtain, he had a cane, and he'd go around the theatre and hit people in the back and yell. 'Hats *off!*'

"Then I got a job at the Loew Theatre on Liberty Avenue as a stagehand. Twelve dollars a week. Saw all the vaudeville acts. They used to have little signals, you know, for actors that didn't tip us stagehands. Guys lifting their trunks to take them out at the end of a date, they'd tie a shoelace to the trunk. When the act got to the next theatre and the next stagehands saw the shoelaces, they'd know this bum didn't tip. So anything that vaudevillian would ask for, he couldn't get!"

That was before World War I. When the unions came in to organize the stagehands, Warren went on to other pursuits. By now he had picked up a little piano playing. He found a job at the Vitagraph movie studio in Brooklyn and graduated to the rough-and-ready job of assistant director. He also became unofficial pianist for Corinne Griffith, a reigning star of the silents. While Miss Griffith emoted for the camera, Warren would improvise background music to create the proper "mood" for her dramatic scenes.

"From that, I got a job playing in silent movie houses. Out in East New York there was a movie house where I got $12 a week. They used to pay me off in nickels and dimes. Weighed a ton. I used to get on a trolley car with one half of me lopsided."

Came World War I, and Warren joined the Navy. He was stationed at Montauk Point Naval Air Station, where he was assigned to play piano and to lead a small band. "A flying piano player," he remarks. After the war ended, he returned to the local cafés. "I didn't play so good," he admits. "I still don't play *well*. I play better than Berlin, though. And Jerry Kern, too—I play better than he did. Cole Porter was a lousy pianist. Anyhow, one night two guys came into this place, they were a little *farshnashkied* [Brownsville Yiddish for drunk], and we got talking. I found out they worked for a music publisher and I said, 'Gee, I got a song,' like that. I had written one called 'I Learned to Love You When I Learned My ABC's,' which is my pet song even now. So they heard it and asked me to come play it for their boss on Monday. That's how I got my first job, with Stark and Cowan Music Company. Twenty a week. I was in the music business! But my song didn't get published because just that week Woolworth's, a big outlet, decided to go out of the sheet-music business, and that sort of put an end to things for a while. They'd give me a paycheck and say, 'Don't cash it till next Tuesday.' My next tune did get published—'Rose of the Rio Grande.' Became very big. But I never collected a nickel royalty. They gave me a promissory note on it, and by the time the note came due, the bank had folded!"

Warren went on to learn the niceties of composition very quickly. "I learned the mathematics," he says. "That's all music is—mathematics. I asked questions along the way. You had to learn. You had to transpose. How else could you play songs for big acts like Sophie Tucker and Belle Baker and all those people you needed to plug your songs?"

During the mid-'20s Warren's melodies began to achieve a certain steady acceptance. He wrote "I Love My Baby, My Baby Loves Me" with Bud Greene, as well as "In My Gondola" and "Nagasaki," and soon began to find a niche on Broadway, writing for sophisticated revues. By 1930 he was writing with Ira Gershwin and others, and composing the melodies for "Cheerful Little Earful" and "Would You Like to Take a Walk?" with Billy Rose and Mort Dixon for a show called *Sweet and Low*. The following year, for Rose's show *Crazy Quilt*, there emerged "I Found a Million Dollar Baby in a Five and Ten Cent Store."

Warren had ventured westward in 1929 to work on a film called *Spring Is Here*, notable only for the song "Crying for the Carolines," but he quickly returned to New York. "I couldn't stand it here then," he admits. "I missed Lindy's. This place was nothing. Then I came out in 1932, to do another picture. Al Dubin was already here; they'd assigned me to work with him.* Summertime. The studio was closed. Probably only two or three writers on the Warner lot, nobody else, and Zanuck was running the production department; he had an idea about making a picture, but he didn't know what. A something. He was

---

* Dubin, a prolific lyricist, had already written "My Dream of the Big Parade," "Dancing with Tears in My Eyes," "Tiptoe Through the Tulips," and "Painting the Clouds with Sunshine," among other hits.

going to make something with music. Of course, musicals were dead at the time. And Warners was in a lot of financial trouble. So was everybody else. Zanuck got a set of galley proofs of this book called *42nd Street* from the New York story department, and he read it and said, 'I think this would make a good musical. Why don't you stay on?' "

Warren shakes his head. "Burbank in the summertime. No buildings anywhere, just fields. It was like being at an Indian outpost. Hotter than hell. No air-conditioning.

"Dubin and I sat down and we wrote this score practically from the galleys. They had Dick Powell, and Zanuck told us he was putting Jolson's wife, Ruby Keeler, in it, and they had Buzz Berkeley sitting around, so we sat down and began to write songs. 'You're Getting to Be a Habit With Me,' 'Young and Healthy,' 'Shuffle Off to Buffalo.' *Afterwards* they wrote the screenplay. Of course today Berkeley tells everybody he told the writers what to write . . . but you know"— Warren winks broadly—"you never heard of a dancer or a choreographer telling anybody what to write, did you? He used to sit down on the stage for days with about a hundred girls, waiting for us to write him something."

Did Warren and his partner Dubin have any idea that this modest film was going to become a landmark? That it would go on to be a huge financial success, to revive the public's craze for film musicals, to earn so much profit that the film's returns would rescue Warner Brothers from near bankruptcy?

Warren shrugs philosophically. "Not at the time. Who knew? We just worked hard. I remember Al Dubin—he was a terrific eater, weighed about three hundred pounds—he'd disappear on me. Carried a little stub of a pencil, wrote lyrics on scrap paper. I'd write a tune and hand him a lead sheet and then I'd never hear a word. All of a sudden, he'd come back and he'd have the lyric. Once he brought in 'Shuffle Off to Buffalo' on the back of a menu from a San Francisco restaurant! There weren't too many good restaurants here in those days. I always say that with all the wonderful ones we have now, if Al were only alive he could be doing some great lyrics!"

The Warner lot was smaller then, more compact, everyone more cooperative, especially in the face of the dire economic adversity that loomed everywhere outside those Burbank sound stages. "It was something like a stock company," remarks Warren. "Even though the Warners could be cruel in some ways. I remember later, when we were doing *Gold Diggers of 1933*, we're sitting in the projection room and they ran our number 'Remember My Forgotten Man.' Now, we'd thought that number up out of the blue, which we had to do all the time. It's like writing for a revue, you know—you had to get ideas. Berkeley had done a great job on this. And they're all sitting in the projection room, Mervyn LeRoy and Mike Curtiz and all of Zanuck's cohorts and Jack Warner, and then the lights came up. Everybody is raving about this number, and Jack turns around to me and Dubin and he says, 'What're *you* guys doing here? You were laid off last week!'*

"We thought he was kidding. But we *were* laid off, and we didn't know it yet! Another time Bill Koenig, who was studio manager, called us in and asked us to take a cut. I was getting $1,500 a week—darn good dough in those days. The money was the only real reason I could stand staying out here in California.

---

* Studio contracts contained clauses which guaranteed only so many weeks of paid employment per term; the weeks of "layoff" could be exercised at the producer's option.

I said, 'Why should we take a cut?' and he says, 'We're losing money.' I said, 'Not on *musicals!*' He says, 'Forget it.' "

The roster of Harry Warren–Al Dubin scores bears ample witness to the composer's angry retort. *42nd Street* was followed by *Gold Diggers of 1933*, then an Eddie Cantor film for Sam Goldwyn, *Roman Scandals*, and *Footlight Parade*. In the same year, when Zanuck departed Burbank to form Twentieth Century, the team wrote the score for his first independent musical, *Moulin Rouge*.

In the following year, 1934, the team churned out scores for *Twenty Million Sweethearts*, Al Jolson's *Wonder Bar*, *Dames*, and *Sweet Music*, which starred Rudy Vallee. And in 1935 their output was truly prodigious. No less than eight Warner musicals featured huge phalanxes of beautiful girls dancing and singing Warren-Dubin tunes. Rarely did they turn up with fewer than two hits in any of their films. In *Gold Diggers of 1935* they won the Academy Award for "Lullaby of Broadway."

"I guess we made an impact all right," Warren admits. "It was thirty, forty years ago; you don't remember those plots, but the songs still hold up, don't they? They still play 'About a Quarter to Nine,' from Jolson's *Go into Your Dance*, and 'I Only Have Eyes for You,' and a lot of the others, all alive, still alive. Funny, though, we did all the pictures, made them all that money, but in most of them they never even mentioned *us*. Publicity? Nothing. But, as I told you, I never looked for it . . ." He lights up another stogie.

"But then we went to Europe with Buddy Morris, who was the head of the Warner music publishers—he and his wife, my wife and I, and Benny Goodman—and we were at the George V Hotel in Paris. They sent a sound truck over to the hotel and did a big interview on the radio. *They* knew all about our musicals over there, they were big fans of the composers already. Not only the French, the Germans too. After Hitler came in, every refugee who came here from Germany who was a music-writer knew me. They'd call me up and want to meet me—because they had seen those musicals!

"Maybe I should have gone and played piano at producers' parties. That's how you got attention out here. But the hell with that. I'm a family man. Always was. Most guys who got ahead in the picture business lived like single men, even if they were married. Played cards with the boss, went to the tracks, partied. But not me. I always came home. I didn't go out nights. You know, I've been living here since '32, forty years, and I never went to a Hollywood party?

"And sometimes somebody would say, 'Did you write "Lullaby of Broadway," really *you?*' I got that with all my songs. 'Now, don't tell me you wrote *that* one too?' But that was all part of the game. Out here in Hollywood a songwriter was always the lowest form of animal life. Unless, of course, you were a Broadway show-writer. Then they paid you respect. I remember once in the café at the Warner lot Eddie Chodorov was there. He was a Broadway playwright, and he was explaining something to Jack Warner with a few of those college expressions he had. And Jack Warner, after he left, said, 'Smart guy, great guy!' See, the guy had gone to college. Jack never went. He was impressed by Eddie's education. And that's a throwback from the old days. My father always said, 'You tip your hat for the doctor.' I'm of Italian descent; with us it was a tradition. My father had great respect for anybody who was a professional man, a lawyer, a doctor. You tipped your hat—that came from the old country. The judge, the doctor. You kissed your midwife's hand too, you know. That's a mark of respect for the woman who delivered you. So I guess the respect these guys here had for the Broadway show-writers was probably part of the same tradition."

Warren stares out the window for a long moment. The morning sun is about to break through the dense gray landscape; bright light is beginning to spread outside, revealing broad lawns and colorful flowers. "Most of those guys were illiterate, anyway," he murmurs, calling back his memories. "I could tell you such stories. I remember when Hal Wallis was producing *Hollywood Hotel* and I prevailed on him to hire Johnny Mercer and Dick Whiting to do their first picture for him. Very talented men. So Wallis calls me after. 'Come on down, I want you to hear their songs.' I said, 'Hal, don't ask me to go down and pass on their songs, that wouldn't be right. I'm not the producer; *you're* the one to decide.' He said, 'But *you* told me to hire them!' He didn't know. That's what you were up against.

"We had a waltz in a picture, *Broadway Gondolier*. It was called 'A Rose in Her Hair.' We played it for Wallis and he said, 'I'll bet it only took you five minutes to write that one, didn't it?' I said, 'Why?' He said, 'It's very short.' I said to him, 'What do you mean? It might take five days to write a short song! That's got nothing to do with it!' But, you see, they didn't know. . . .

"We had another song, called 'With Plenty of Money and You.' Wallis came to our bungalow, walked in. He picked up a newspaper that was lying there and he says, 'Okay, play me the song.' So I said to him, 'Are you going to read or are you going to listen to the song?' He said, 'Come on, play me the song.' So we played it for him, and he got up and threw the paper down. He says, 'It stinks. Write a new song.' And he walked out. So I opened the door and I said, '*You* stink! Get a new boy!' He turned around and laughed, but he kept on walking. So now we had to figure, how're we going to get the song in the picture? Well, we knew there was another way we could do it. We knew Jack Warner and Hal Wallis were feuding. So we called Scotty, who was Warner's secretary, and we told him we had a song we wanted J.W. to hear. He calls back and says Warner wants us to come right up. So we went up and said to Warner we wanted him to hear a song that Wallis didn't like. We played it. He said, 'That's swell! What the hell does *he* know about songs? Great, it goes in the picture!' That's how the song got into *Gold Diggers of 1937*."

He chuckles at the recollection. "Big hit. Opened the picture. Depths of the Depression. Marvelous idea in the title—'*Oh, Baby, what I couldn't do, with plenty of money and you* . . . ' But those were the little devices. We had to do that in reverse, too. With Wallis. We'd go to Warner and play him one, and if he didn't like it, we'd play it for Wallis and tell him *Jack* didn't like it. Again, in it went!

"Illiterates, you know? Illiterates in that they didn't know whom to respect. I grew up knowing that you respected talent, no matter who had it—it could even be the stagehand or the electricians. You know, I was very close friends with Jerry Kern, who was working on the Metro lot before I went there, years later. And he was getting something like $3,000–$4,000 a week. And David Selznick, who was then head of his own unit there, was going to do a picture called *Ebbtide*. He sent for Jerry; Jerry had a bungalow at Metro. He came in. Jerry was a little martinet, you know. He always had his coat buttoned in the wrong place, and he always had his sleeves rolled up, and he always cocked his head this way, on a slant. And Selznick said, 'Mr. Kern, I'm doing a picture called *Ebbtide*. Play me some melodies.' And Jerry looked at him and he said, 'I'm sorry, I don't play samples.' Walked out.

"There was another guy, I think it was Pandro Berman, who was producing *Roberta* at RKO, before this, and Jerry had a song—it was called 'Lovely to Look At' after Dorothy Fields set the lyrics to it. He came in and played the melody for Berman, and Berman heard it and said, 'Isn't that kind of short?' Jerry looked at him and he said, 'That's all I had to say.' Ah, Jerry, he was fantastic . . . 'That's all I had to say.'"

Al Dubin died tragically young, in 1945. By that time Warren had left Warners and moved his piano over to 20th Century-Fox. But before he departed Burbank for West Pico Boulevard, he did a set of songs with young Johnny Mercer, the talented lyricist he had recommended to Hal Wallis. One of their creations, introduced by Louis Armstrong in a Warner remake of a play called *The Hottentot* and renamed *Going Places*, was the joyful "Jeepers, Creepers." And for an equally forgettable film called *Hard to Get* they produced "You Must Have Been a Beautiful Baby." Later he and Mercer were to team up again with equal success. But when Warren moved to Fox, it was to work with another king-sized gourmand, the legendary Mack Gordon. From 1938 up to and throughout the war years came a seemingly endless string of Darryl Zanuck's musicals, equipped with Alice Faye, Carmen Miranda, Sonja Henie, Betty Grable, Tony Martin, Don Ameche—and Gordon-Warren tunes.

"Funny, all those years I never felt like a native Californian. Lots of times I'd think about throwing it all up and going back to New York. You know, in the old days here we would say, 'Don't buy anything here you can't take with you on the Chief'—that was the train that took you back East. So we never bought anything. We could have been millionaires with real estate; we never gave it a thought. Property on Rodeo Drive that was $10,000–$15,000 a lot— today it's worth millions. But it always was that kind of a business to me—it never felt permanent."

Whether or not Warren personally felt stable becomes irrelevant when one runs through even a partial listing of what he and Mack Gordon produced in their studio years at Fox. There were massive successes, such as "I've Got a Gal in Kalamazoo," which Glenn Miller's orchestra made permanent in *Orchestra Wives*, "Chattanooga Choo Choo," lovely ballads of the quality of "You'll Never Know," "At Last," "Serenade in Blue," and "There Will Never Be Another You."

The inevitable question becomes, did Zanuck know anything about musicals?

Warren's answer is short and to the point. "Nope. Although he was great with songwriters. I've never heard him say—and I did a lot of work with him —'That's a lousy song, we can't use it.' Never. Though for some reason he was tough as hell with scriptwriters. But don't forget one thing: we *delivered*. Hell, sometimes we were working on two pictures at a time. They used you. It was always, 'C'mon, fellas, help us out, we're in a spot here with the picture, put in a little extra time for us, you're part of the family.'"

Such intense pressure-cooker-type atmosphere can often induce bursts of creativity . . . or force the complete collapse of the muse.

"Well," says Warren, with the magnificent candor of one who has made many trips to the well and rarely come up dry, "you either have it or you don't. You can't be trained, you can't go to school and learn it. You get a script and you read it, and then your subconscious mind goes to work. When I do a picture, I must write reams of melodies. I might write maybe fifteen, twenty tunes before I get the right one, the one that *I* like. I write 'em and I think about one—I always try to get the tune first, because the lyric-writer can always fit the tune.

If I don't get anything, I go away. Sometimes I get them *away* from the piano. Then, when I get the one I like, I say, 'I think we'll use this!' But I always know going in what I'm looking for. When I did *An Affair to Remember* for Leo McCarey in 1957—Cary Grant and Deborah Kerr—I knew I had to get some sort of a melody that would sound good with the old lady playing it on the piano, one that would sound almost classical. Well, I must've written about twenty-five tunes before I finally hit that one."

In 1945 Warren once again moved his piano—this time over to Culver City, where he became enfiefed to MGM and its feudal lord, Louis B. Mayer. One of his first assignments was to do the music for a film called *Yolanda and the Thief*, notable now as then for the fact that Mayer had cast Fred Astaire opposite a complete unknown, Lucille Bremer, a lovely dancer whom the great L.B. had spotted in the chorus line of New York's Copacabana. The results were disastrous. Yolanda and Miss Bremer faded into the sunset. Astaire and Warren survived Mr. Mayer's momentary whim.

"Oh, sure, it's fashionable to knock Mayer now," says Warren with a flash of truculence. "But it's easy to forget what a really good producer he could be. I thought he was great. He did more for musical pictures than anybody. He really liked music, and he liked to make musicals, and that to me was more important than these dramatic producers or another guy who wanted to make gangster pictures. He had a whole school of sopranos over there, all kinds of singers, vocal teachers, a stock company of singers and dancers. That lot was really jumping. I got the biggest salary of my life at Metro. Funny thing, though, the only song I ever scored with over there was in my next picture, *The Harvey Girls*, which I wrote with Johnny Mercer. Judy Garland sang it—'On the Atchison, Topeka and the Sante Fe.' Look over here . . ."

He jumps up, goes to the wall, removes an elaborate gold-encrusted plaque, and proffers it for display. "Out of a clear blue sky, this came last year. The president of the Santa Fe Railroad himself sends it with a letter. He says this is to celebrate the twenty-fifth anniversary of the song Mercer and I wrote. Sends a guy up here personally to deliver it. They took pictures. My God, it's been twenty-five years!"

He replaces the plaque with care, next to the assorted photos of Bing Crosby, Dean Martin, Jolson, and framed copies of his own sheet music four and five decades old, all "standards" now.

"Maybe people didn't like Mayer's politics, or maybe that was just an excuse for not liking him, I don't know which. I know one thing. If Judy Garland had been working at Warner's you never would have heard of her again. First time she didn't show up at a rehearsal or a date for something, Jack Warner would have taken her right off salary! He did it with Bette Davis, anybody. Anybody who argued with him—out! But Mayer was never like that. He used to send Judy *flowers*. And she cost them a fortune over there; a lot of people don't realize that. We did a couple of pictures with her. She started on one called *Summer Stock*. Nobody knew where she was. She never showed up. And, you know, the day of shooting there could be a thousand extras there? They had to send everybody home and pay them. No explanation. You think she could have done that at Warner's? Only with Louis Mayer . . ."

The opulent majesty that was L.B.'s domain, his glorious monolithic Metro, has long since crumbled. All that remains are the cans of film, and a few vivid memories of Mayer, the private property of veterans like Warren. "You know what he did to Robert Walker, who was quite a tippler in those days? He got him in there one day, and said, 'How would you like to be an extra who lives way down in Hollywood and you have to get up at five in the morning and take three or four buses to get to Culver City and get out here to find out they're not shooting because the star, somebody like *you*, didn't show up?' He said to Walker, 'You're depriving these people of their livelihood, their means of getting some food.' Walker really cracked up at that. 'Mr. Mayer, I never thought of that,' he apologized. 'Well, you should!' said Mayer.

"Because back in those days, you know, if you lived out here, it was complicated to get from Hollywood out to Culver City. Or going out to work in the Valley. They used to ask me, 'Harry, how come you never worked for Universal?' I said, 'I never did get a passport to get over there.'

"Oh, Mayer was a tough man, sure. After some years I figured I'd had it there and it was time to quit." Warren had by that time crafted an excellent score with lyricist Ira Gershwin for *The Barkleys of Broadway*, which had re-united Fred Astaire and Ginger Rogers in 1949. "Fred, that's another guy with great magnetism," he comments, with obvious affection. "He isn't vocally good, he hasn't got a great voice, but there's something about Fred—when he sings a lyric, it really comes out.

"To get back to Mayer. We were out on the stage, I think it was *Summer Stock*, and somebody called me and said, 'Mr. Mayer wants to see you.' I don't know, I guess I kind of forgot about it. They were shooting a number, Gene Kelly was in it—I think it was 'Dig for Your Dinner.' All of a sudden, two cops come in and say, 'Come here, Mr. Mayer wants to see you.' And they grab me by the arm and take me up to his office. I didn't know what the hell was up. So he said to me, 'What is this I hear about you quitting?' I said, 'Well, I am, because it's not a good lot for me. This is a songwriter's graveyard here. You don't get the plugs, your publishing companies are not good. We don't get enough records on our songs, not enough noise is being made.' It was the truth; I'd had much more success at Warners and Fox. So Mayer said, 'I'm not going to let you quit. I'll give you your own publishing company. How would you like that?' I said that would be fine. But I didn't realize that even when I had forty percent of it—and they had sixty—the same inefficient people who were handling the Metro music publishers would be promoting *mine!* It was just one of Mayer's cute gimmicks!

"Later on, when it turned out that the firm I owned was losing money, we had a big meeting in New York. There were all the Metro lawyers and hatchet men sitting around, big cigars in their kissers, and one of them, the head killer, he's reading the company report, like he's a Supreme Court judge or something. He looks at me like I'm some criminal, and he says, 'What are we going to tell our Metro stockholders? You know your firm has lost $150,000? What are we going to say to *them?*'

"He wasn't kidding *me*," says Warren truculently. "They could write that off. It was pennies. Lots of times people don't think you know anything—you're a songwriter, that means you're a dope. But I said to this guy, 'Tell them what you tell them when *you* lose a couple of million on one bad picture.' He almost fell off his company chair.

"I don't know exactly what it was, all that hostility toward us songwriters," Warren continues, lighting another stogie. "Maybe it was because most of the time you were making more dough than the producer and he sort of resented that. He knew he needed you—that probably made him hate your guts all the more. The only guy that ever really gave us respect was Arthur Freed. He'd been a songwriter himself, and he *knew*. Hired the best people he could get, took big chances on young talent. I remember years ago he called me up, I was still at Metro, and he asked me to come over. 'I got a couple of young kids coming in from New York. They've done some shows and they're going to play me some stuff.' I went over there and Vincente Minnelli was there, and a couple of studio people, and in walk these two guys from New York, with their little raincoats on, with horn-rimmed glasses; they looked like two little comics. They played a lot of tunes, and when they left, somebody asked Freed what he thought of them, and he said, 'I think they stink.' Alan Lerner and Fred Loewe! But here's the point—right after that he was bright enough to see that he'd made a big mistake, and he reversed himself and hired Alan Lerner, who's a great big talent. Matter of fact, I was supposed to work with Alan on *Royal Wedding*, but I was so busy on something else that they got him Burton Lane instead.

"Later on, a funny thing happened with me and Alan. I'm now out of Metro, and I'm sitting home, and the phone rings, it's New York and Alan calling. He says, 'How would you like to do a New York show with me?' I said, 'I'd love to.' He says, 'Don't tell anybody—I'm splitting with Freddy Loewe—it's a secret—and I want you to do the show. I'll get back to you.'

"After that, nothing. Silence. Ten years go by. One day I'm over at Warners, looking for some sheet music I'd done there, and they tell me Alan Lerner's there, recording the score for *My Fair Lady*—that's the show he called me to do! So I walk down to the recording stage, and there he was. Alan's a very European sort of guy. When he meets you, he kisses you. So he gives me a big hello, and I say, 'Alan, you never called me back.' He goes blank and says, 'Gee, I don't know what you mean.' I say, 'Don't you remember when you called me up ten years back and said you and Freddy were breaking up and you wanted me to write this thing from *Pygmalion* into a show?' He says, 'Oh, my God—Harry, you're right!' And I said to him, 'Now, aren't you glad you *didn't* get me?'"

From Metro, Warren made still another move, this time to Paramount, where throughout the 1950s he continued to turn out successful film scores. For Bing Crosby's film *Just for You*, he wrote "Zing a Little Zong." And in the Martin-and-Lewis comedy *The Caddy*, he provided Dean Martin with "That's Amore," a hit song with firm Italian ethnic roots.

In 1956 he ventured back to his old stamping ground, Broadway, to write the score for a musical version of James Hilton's *Lost Horizon. Shangri-La*, as it was retitled, proved to be a mammoth mistake when it opened in New Haven for its tryout. It was not Warren's score, written with Jerome Lawrence and Robert E. Lee, which was at fault; the physical production of the musical proved too massive and cumbersome for the stage. *Shangri-La* died a-borning, after twenty-one performances in New York. "Too bad, too," says Warren ruefully. "I thought some of the stuff I had in there was as good as anything I'd ever written."

Then came McCarey's *An Affair to Remember* and a batch of scores for Jerry Lewis, in the days when that gentleman was still providing Paramount with a steady flow of black ink for its corporate books. By the early 1960s Hollywood's musical-comedy era was winding down after nearly three decades of all-singing, all-dancing profitability. Nowadays the original musical comedy, written directly for the screen, is a museum exhibit. Aficionados of the early Alice Faye/Don Ameche/Cesar Romero/Betty Grable/Dick Powell/Ruby Keeler era must sit up until 2 A.M. to hum along with their favorites on the Late Late Show, or seek out their favorite long-lost Carmen Miranda/Ritz Brothers/John Payne gaiety in some out-of-the-way theatre dedicated to the renaissance of Zanuckian musicomedy.

"Oh sure, the pictures may be old pieces of junk," admits Warren, 'but, damn it, the songs still go on. They have a sort of life of their own. Sometimes I hear them, and it brings back all kinds of crazy memories. Like when we were doing a picture at Warners for Clark Gable and Marion Davies. It was called *Cain and Mabel*. What a title! You know, Marion was a great girl. She always had music on the set. She had a piano, an organ, or something going all afternoon. When she walked on the stage in the morning with her little retinue of people, the orchestra would play something like 'Pomp and Circumstance' for her entrance!

"Anyway, we had to go over there to the stage to play some songs. One of them was 'I'll Sing You a Thousand Love Songs.' Mr. Hearst himself was over there, and when we got to the stage, there were these two cops guarding the door. They wouldn't let us go on the stage. So we went back to our bungalow. And we get a phone call. 'Where are you guys? Come on over!' I said, 'They won't let us in!' 'Come on over!' We went over, the cops stopped us again! So we went back, and again they called us, and I said, 'You go screw yourself! If you want us, you better tell those two cops to leave, or we're not coming any more!' We did another one for Marion called *Hearts Divided*. Dick Powell was her leading man in that one. He was scared stiff of doing love scenes with her; whenever they shot one, Hearst would be sitting right there on the sound stage watching, and Dick never knew whether or not the old man would get sore if he started getting ardent with Marion. A hell of a way to have to act, believe me! Anyway, when we wrote the songs for *Hearts Divided*, we had to play them for Hearst. He was in New York, and we had to do them for him over the telephone! I mean, what the hell can you hear over a telephone? He didn't know what he was listening to, anyway. But he never turned anything down. Neither did the other producers. They took what we wrote, and onto the screen it would go. What the hell did they know? *We* were the ones who were coming up with the hits!"

The midday sun shines down on Beverly Hills. The canyons above, which were once covered with wild brush and populated mainly by animals running free in those earlier, less complicated days, are now studded with rows of expensive houses that march upward toward the flattened summits of the Santa Monica Mountains. Few of the inhabitants have anything to do with the business of film-making; those who do are involved with the sausage-style packaging of television half-hours, or with cable TV, video cassettes, and other visionary methods of making less taxable capital gains. Popular music has long since drifted away from the personality-cult era of Crosby, Astaire, and Alice Faye. We've come into a new world of LPs and college one-night concerts, performed by bearded bards with eight-stringed amplified guitars and folk-singing ladies with long golden hair who croon endless choruses of atonal anguish. And what does Harry Warren think of the musical scene, circa 1972?

"I think it's awful," he complains. "Mancini's good, Elmer Bernstein writes good picture music, and Johnny Mandel, he's great. But most of the rest of them . . ." He shakes his head. "They don't do anything for me. I'd rather sit here and play my tapes. I can run the gamut of all music because I love music so much. I used to know all the overtures by heart. 'Light Cavalry,' 'Poet and Peasant,' 'Morning, Noon, and Night,' any one you could think of, I knew them all. I knew all the church music, all the Catholic mass music. I knew all the Debussy, I knew all the Ravel. I love them . . . and, of course, Puccini. I'm his slave. *That's* music."

We walk outside into the clear sunlight. Below us, behind a thick hedge, we can hear the steady rumble of that incessant California traffic. "Say, was I any help to you?" he inquires.

In these past two hours he has footnoted forty years of Hollywood's history. He is, in fact, a walking compendium of film history, this short, voluble gentleman who once played drums in Canarsie, who wasn't completely sure that anything in Southern California was going to be permanent when he reluctantly stepped off the Chief back in 1932.

"History?" he says, beaming. "Say—I like that. I like being part of history. Think how many people live out all their lives and they're *never* part of it. Just look at all the things I've done that have been a pleasure. Started as a drummer, then a piano player, then in the studios as an assistant director. I get to Broadway, I'm a song-plugger, then a composer. And then I come out here and I get to write a lot of hits with a marvelous bunch of guys I always enjoyed being around—Jerry Kern, Ira Gershwin, Johnny Mercer, Dorothy Fields, all of them. It's been a hell of a good life, and I'm grateful for it."

He tramps away toward a parked sedan, humming softly . . . Obviously something from Puccini.

'Moon River'

(Johnny Mercer)

IT'S NOT a quarter to three, it's a good deal earlier—ten A.M. And there's no one in the place except Mercer and me. The place is a tiny, snug New York hideaway in the East Sixties that Mr. M and his wife retain as *pied-à-terre* for their frequent visits to town. In the mini-living room there's hardly enough space for both a sofa and Mr. Mercer's working equipment, an upright piano covered with sheet music. Hidden off a hallway are two Pullman-size bedrooms. In his pajamas, Mercer is prowling about, brewing instant coffee in a cubbyhole that would make the galley of a large cabin cruiser seem like the kitchen at the Waldorf. "We don't pay the size of this place much mind," he remarks. "Matter of fact, my wife Ginger once said the motto of this apartment has to be 'I'll be loving you sideways.'"

Very early in the morning to be making jokes, but somehow wit has always come naturally to Johnny Mercer, even after last night, which seems to have been strenuous. "I come to New York every so often on business, and it never fails to charge my batteries," he admits. "New York was always The Place in my world. First came up here when I was nineteen. Been coming back ever since. Maybe it's not as relaxed as it used to be, but I'm still hooked on the place."

That first arrival would be in 1928, when young John Mercer migrated from Savannah, Georgia (birthplace also of the fabled "Hard-Hearted Hannah"), and since then he has indeed traveled more than a country mile, with most of his progress steadily forward. He's made it big in New York and Hollywood, and yet the home ties are still strong; he has just returned from a municipal celebration down in Savannah, where he and another hometown boy who made good, Hal Kanter, the producer-writer, staged a show for the people. "Big doin's," he says. That familiar Georgia twang is still very much in evidence, even after all his years up North and out in those Beverly Hills. "Savannah's still like it used to be, you know—hospitable, warm, friendly. Everybody goes around and sings songs, drinks, and loves one another."

Mercer's first few jobs in New York were as a tyro actor. But then he turned to singing and the writing of lyrics. "I guess I gradually just gravitated to songwriting," he remembers. "I think I absorbed it. I don't think I actually studied it consciously. But my aunt once said that when I was six months old she hummed to me and I hummed right back. Now, *that's* pretty early. Three or four years old, I began to like songs and listen to'em. Always listened to records—the old cylindrical ones, then the big thick Edison ones, and then when they got to the regular 78s, we had all those. By the time I was eleven or twelve I really knew most of the songs that came out, by heart. Knew the verses. We'd get around the piano and play hundreds of songs, the way folks did in those days. I'd always look at the writers, see who they were. Victor Herbert was one of my very favorites, and I can remember liking Kern's 'They Didn't Believe Me' when it came out. Couldn't have been more than four or five then.

"When I got a little older, I remember asking my brother who was the greatest songwriter in America. He said Irving Berlin. I suppose Irving was getting a lot of publicity even at that time. That would be around the war, maybe right after it, 1919. Later on, when I worked for Paul Whiteman and began to meet all those guys, it was a big thrill. They liked me, and they were particularly surprised because I knew all their songs. And I didn't do it to flatter them. I really *knew* them."

The very first Mercer lyric appeared in a rather auspicious showcase, the third edition of *The Garrick Gaieties*, in 1930. In a collected revue, which also featured the burgeoning talents of E. Y. Harburg and the late Vernon Duke, Mercer contributed a song called "Out of Breath (and Scared to Death of You)." It was in that same production that he met and married Ginger, who is at this moment minding their California house. Which is fortunate, because in this small apartment three would definitely be a crowd.

"Met lots of different writers after I had that song," Mercer says. "Hoagy Carmichael, for one. Marvelous writer. The two of us had a great big hit called 'Lazy Bones.' After that, he quit what he was doing to earn a living and started writing songs exclusively, and I got the job working for Paul Whiteman. Wrote a song every week. Paul had the Kraft radio show then, with Al Jolson, and I wrote for his singers. One of them was Jack Teagarden, the trombonist. Brilliant horn player . . . a genius."

After those intensive days Mercer was hired to go to Hollywood to write songs and act in low-budget musicals at RKO. "Did two there," he recalls. "Right after that they sent me back to the typewriter, and I've been there ever since. My first big song was 'I'm an Old Cowhand from the Rio Grande,' which Bing Crosby put into a picture called *Rhythm on the Range*, and then I did rhythm songs like 'Bob White,' made records like 'Last Night on the Back Porch,' with

Jerry Colonna, 'Jamboree Jones,' and it just kept on going like that from there. Got to performing less and less and writing more and more."

Mercer's list of subsequent collaborators is formidable. It ranges from the late Richard Whiting through Harry Warren, the late Jerome Kern, Harold Arlen, Jimmy Van Heusen, Henry Mancini, Gene DePaul, Arthur Schwartz, the late Bobby Dolan, Michel LeGrand. And the resultant roster of hit songs is a remarkable thing to contemplate, one which extends from "Jeepers, Creepers" (Warren), "That Old Black Magic" (Arlen), "You Were Never Lovelier" (Kern), "Satin Doll" (Ellington), "Hooray for Hollywood" (Whiting), "The Atchison, Topeka and the Santa Fe" (again Warren), "In the Cool, Cool, Cool of the Evening" (Van Heusen), all the way up to "Moon River" and "Days of Wine and Roses" (Mancini), and even to "I Want to Be Around (to Pick Up the Pieces When You Break Your Heart)," which title was mailed in by a lady from Youngstown, Ohio. "That one was a natural," he once said, with his customary modesty. "She did the title and I did everything else, but I figure that's fifty-fifty. Because, as far as I'm concerned, that's a hit *title*. The guy who has it is a lucky guy, because he's got half the battle won if the general public already likes the title . . . which they did."

Mercer always makes it sound easy. But anyone who's ever sharpened a pencil and tried to write a lyric to a tune knows better. "Johnny *studied*," said his good friend Bobby Dolan, with whom Mercer wrote two Broadway scores —*Texas, Li'l Darlin'* and *Foxy.* "He listened, and he learned the basics. He absorbed everything, and then transformed it with his own style. Believe me, it's no accident that he's been able to work with so many great composers."

What about this remarkable adaptability?

"It's the secret of any success I've had," admits Mercer. "There are certain writers who have a great feeling for *tunes*, no matter where they come from. I think I'm one of them. I don't mean that in any egotistical way. I think Dorothy Fields is one, too. She's written with a lot of guys and she's always written well. She has a *feel* for the tune. I think Gus Kahn was a terrific tune-picker, had magnificent hit songs, probably because he recognized a great tune when he heard one. Today I think Paul Simon is probably going to be one of those. I think Jimmy Webb is one of them; of course, he writes his own tunes. Most of the young people of today do.

"But to get back to Dorothy—to me she's like John O'Hara. He had such a terrific *ear* for dialogue; she's got it for lyrics. For the way a thing should be said. You find it time after time in her lyrics." Mercer begins to sing: " *'I know why I've waited, know why I've been blue . . . I know why my mother taught me to be true, she meant me for someone exactly like you.'* Now, that doesn't rhyme or anything, it's not difficult, but it just says what the melody says, and it's wonderful. Listen to this one—it's the start of a verse, and she writes, *'Gee, but it's tough to be broke, kid, but that's oke, kid . . . ,'* and then she goes, *'I can't give you anything but love, baby,'* Wow! What an idea for a poor boy and girl—*every* boy and girl, you know. Rich or poor, but especially if they're poor. And later on, when she wrote with Kern, Dorothy did that beautifully, too. She rose right up to his melodies. Her lyrics *enhanced* his tunes—'Lovely to Look At,' 'Remind Me.' My God, what a good lyric *that* is!" Again Mercer sings, in that high, distinctive voice that was heard so many nights on the old Bing Crosby Kraft Music Hall shows in pre-World War II days. *"Remind me not to find you so attractive.'* Marvelous! It just *makes* that tune!

"Oh, Bobby Dolan was right," he concedes. "I did study them all, from the very beginning, to learn what made a good song. I'd always loved Walter Donaldson's* songs, and when I finally got to work with him, it was a big kick for me. He'd had lots of hits, and I knew them all, the lyrics, even the verses. He had the kind of hits that everybody sang on the street. 'My Buddy,' 'Blue Heaven,' 'Little White Lies.' Truck drivers would sing'em. It's a terrific thrill for me to write a song that truck drivers like and laborers like. Say, a 'Strip Polka.' You know, they all sing, *'Take it off, take it off'*—they love that, you know? I had one called 'Goody, Goody,' a big popular song. People love to sing it when it comes to the title. Well, Donaldson was that sort of writer. He impressed the hell out of me. There was a big difference in our ages—I was young and impressionable—but there was a nice twinkle in his eye, and he was kind to young people. He was kind of at the tag end of his career, this great, gifted songwriter. He was improvident, a spendthrift. He'd give away his ideas, just like his money. I'd sing him one of his songs like 'My Best Girl,' even the verse to it, and he would say, 'Where'd you learn that?' Because it hadn't been a hit, but I knew the song.

"Later I found out that one of the vagaries of this business, if you can call it a business, is that you can make a big hit but you can also lose a big hit. Depends on the records you get, and the plugs you get, and everything else. But it's very hard to hide a really great song, 'cause it will eventually surface *somewhere*. Take 'Begin the Beguine.' I knew that was a hit the night I saw Porter's show *Jubilee*. And yet it took two years for it to become a popular hit.

"Anyway, I got to work with Donaldson; we did a few songs that worked. One of them was 'Mr. Meadowlark.' That was sort of cute. Then Buddy Morris at Warners asked me who I'd like to write with, and I said, 'I'd rather work with Dick Whiting than anybody.' Another one of my idols. I had heard all his songs, I loved them. 'Japanese Sandman,' 'Till We Meet Again,' 'My Ideal,' 'Sleepy Time Gal,' and those songs he'd done with Leo Robin for Chevalier—'Louise' and 'One Hour with You.' He had a lot of quality, and he was an original. A dear fellow, too. Modest and sweet, and not at all pushy like a lot of New York writers are. He came from Detroit, and he was kind of a shy man. He wasn't too well by that time, but we were really good friends. We went to work at Warners, did a couple of pictures together. They worked you pretty hard then, you were at it every day. We did *Hollywood Hotel* and *Varsity Show*, and a picture called *Ready, Willing and Able*."

Mercer pauses, stares out the ground-floor window at the tiny garden outside, perhaps thinking back to the sunnier days of the '30s when he and Whiting turned out songs in a Burbank office. 'We did have one big hit together, a song called 'Too Marvelous for Words.' "

Margaret Whiting recalls: "My father always said that the genius of Mercer really comes out in that lyric. They staged that number in a typical Busby Berkeley style—a huge typewriter with all the girls lying on their backs; their legs were the keys, and they tapped out the words on a huge roll of paper, can you believe it? But Mercer had written such an *idea!* The guy is trying to tell his girl how he feels about her, and he says, *'You're just too marvelous, too*

---

* Donaldson, who died in 1947, left behind a catalogue brimming with "standards"—"How Ya Gonna Keep'Em Down on the Farm?," "Love Me or Leave Me," "Making Whoopee," "Carolina in the Morning," "You, You're Driving Me Crazy," and dozens of others.

marvelous for words like glorious, glamorous, and that old stand-by, amorous.' And then he gets to, *'You're just too much, you're just too very, very, to ever be in Webster's dictionary,'* Now, every word is supposed to be in Webster's, and here's Mercer having him say she's so much that he can't find the words. Just think about it in terms of the '30s, as an enormously original approach to saying 'I love you, honey.' It was unique!"

That particular brand of wordsmithing, that special turn of phrase, Mercer has been coming up with all these years. Can he explain where it comes from?

He grins. "No. I get lyric ideas from anywhere. Maybe from a billboard on the street, or something I read. An idea will hit me and I jot it down. I'm an inside-the-matchcover type of writer. They don't always come fast, believe me. I remember once Hoagy Carmichael gave me two tunes to set. Well, I struggled over them for a long time. Must have been a year before I got one; I called it 'Skylark.' I called up Hoagy and I said, 'Hey, I think I got a lyric for your tune.' He said, 'What tune is that?' He'd *forgotten* it!"

After the death of his friend Whiting, Mercer began working with Harry Warren. "Probably one of the two or three best popular songwriters America's ever had. And probably the best movie composer that we had. Don't think there's anybody else who's had the record of writing for movies that Harry's had. You realize that he had not only one but sometimes two, three hits in his pictures?" Quite a few of those Warren hits—"You Must Have Been a Beautiful Baby," "Jeepers, Creepers," and "Atchison, Topeka and the Santa Fe," among others—were with Mercer.

Then came the immensely fruitful collaboration with Harold Arlen, one that was to continue sporadically from the late '30s until now.

"Well, Harold and I have a good feeling about songs," says Mercer. "I don't know why that is, 'cause we don't come from the same neck of the woods or anything, but we really have a thing about jazz and blues, and creativity and originality, and structure. I appreciate *his* work so much that possibly he thinks I get the right words to it."

Among those "right words" that Mercer has fitted to Arlen's melodies would be the lyrics to "That Old Black Magic," a lush ballad which the late Billy Daniels single-handedly made into a rhythm hit. "That one came from one of the early Cole Porter songs I heard when I first came to New York," Mercer says. "It was a song called 'You Do Something to Me,' and it had a phrase in it—'*do* do that *voo*-doo that *you* do so well.' I've always loved Porter—those early songs of his were so clever, and later on his melodies became so rich and full. Anyway, that thing about voodoo must have stuck with me, because I paraphrased it in 'Old Black Magic.' "

The Arlen-Mercer collaboration also produced "My Shining Hour," "Come Rain or Come Shine," "Hit the Road to Dreamland," and a song that is easily the great torch lament of our times, "One for My Baby."

"Well, I have to tell you that those are luck," explains Mercer. "When you get a tune like 'Baby' and you find the right mood for it, that is the luckiest thing that can happen to a lyric-writer. The thing about it is recognizing it when you think of it. You say, 'That's right for this tune. That conversational way to write this is gonna make this tune.' And that's the same thing that happened with 'Come Rain or Come Shine.' A really simple way of saying 'I love you' or 'I'm unhappy' the way a guy in a saloon would feel it. Pure luck. I don't know, maybe it is some sort of gift. Somebody up there is writing it for you."

Pure luck, or the meeting of talent, idea, and timing, all coming together at the same creative moment?

"Well, that's so, too," he admits. "Sort of like a baseball player getting a hit at the right time. He knows how to play ball, he knows how to hit. But he's not always gonna get a hit, especially with two men on base and two guys out. Well, that's the way it is with a song. Sometimes you get a little luckier than others. When I wrote 'Days of Wine and Roses' I could not get the words down fast enough. It was as if I was taking dictation! Not that it's such a great lyric, but it just seemed to write itself. Of course, you know the title wasn't mine, it was Ernest Dowson's."

But the fact remains that those lucky "accidents," those fortuitous matings of music with Mercer's appropriate words, have been happening with regularity for a long, long time. Mercer's batting average is so consistently better than .400 that the word "lucky" has to be discarded.

Margaret Whiting vividly recalls the time she first heard "Blues in the Night." "We always had a Saturday-night get-together at our house in those days. People came and went, songwriters dropped by, we were a show-business family, and everybody sort of hung together. All of us were Hollywood kids then. Mickey Rooney was there, and Judy Garland, Martha Raye, an old friend, and Mel Torme. And around nine thirty or ten Harold and Johnny came by, they'd just finished the song, and they went to our piano and did 'Blues' for the first time. Well, I want to tell you, it was like a Paramount Pictures finish— socko, boffo, *wham!* At one end of the room, Martha Raye almost passed out; for once, she didn't have a funny line. Torme was so knocked out by the musicianship, he just sat there. Mickey Rooney kept saying, 'My God, this is unbelievable!' And Judy and I raced over to the piano to see which of us could learn the song first! You knew right away the song was so *important.* When they put it into the picture, they really murdered it. But the song had its own strength . . . that whole thing about the whistle blowing in the night, the associations that were built into Johnny's lyric. And Harold had written that kind of steady blues refrain that kept on repeating itself. Trains are such a marvelous symbol. Somebody's always coming in, or leaving on one, so it's neither sadness nor happiness, but it's the way *you* react to it, how *you* respond."

"Took us about a week," Mercer comments today. "We wrote a lot of songs pretty fast. I remember we wrote 'Come Rain or Come Shine' in only one evening at Harold's house. Harold's a magnificently original writer, you know, and it's something to write with him."

Mercer joined with the late Jerome Kern to provide a trio of near-perfect ballads for the 1942 Fred Astaire—Rita Hayworth musical *You Were Never Lovelier.* "Oh, I loved working with Kern," he says. "He was everybody's favorite composer. Dick Rodgers once said, 'There's nobody who hasn't learned from Kern.' Little short man, stood up very straight, took everything very seriously. He was interested in everything that had to do with the project—the scenery, the costumes, the props, everything. That was part of his meticulous craftsmanship. He was the best theatrical writer we've ever had. No seconds. Gershwin and Rodgers are great writers, but Kern's my particular favorite."

Besides the lovely title song for *You Were Never Lovelier*, that collaboration produced "I'm Old Fashioned" and "Dearly Beloved." Carmichael, Donaldson, then Whiting, Warren, Arlen, and Kern. Six remarkably different composers; each man very much his own. Yet Mercer functioned supremely well with each of them. How so?

"Well, I never let personality get in the way of the work," he says today. "The song is the main thing. And I find that if it's getting a little, say, rough, personality-wise, I just clam up and sit in a corner, or I say, 'Well, I'm gonna take this home and try to work on it.' I never let anything bother me. It's only when a guy tends to force his work in your department that it gets a little annoying, you know? It's as if I were to tell Kern, 'I don't like that middle, why don't you do it this way?' Now, how the hell are you going to tell Jerome Kern or anybody else that? So I don't do that. I just say, 'Is that the way you like it?' Or I say, 'Maybe that middle sounds a little like something else,' or 'Don't you think it's a little bit long? Or short?' That's as far as my criticism goes.

"Composers don't mind usually when I say I'm going to take something home to work on. As long as you come back with the lyric, it's okay. I prefer having the music first, because I seem to catch the mood of the tune. If I have any gift at all, that's it, being able to write the mood properly."

Work habits? "I'm best when I get up. First hour, I feel good. I work maybe for half a morning or half a day. If I get tired, I quit. Don't come back. Let my subconscious do the work; it's a remarkable instrument. I have a study—always have had a room where people will leave me alone. I lie down, and Ginger will say, 'Daddy's working.' And you can get ideas when you're out drinking, or when you're driving, or playing golf. You can't ever tell when that idea's going to come, but you'd better have a little something to put it down on. It's liable to slip away. When I really start to work at it, I get a lot of paper and I go to the typewriter and I type dozens of alternative lines. Then I look at those lines, and I gradually weed out the poor ones until I think, 'Now I've got the best.' I guess it's taking pains," Mercer remarks. "Yip Harburg taught me about that. He's a terrific writer. God, he'll sit in a room all day and he'll dig and he'll dig and he'll dig. And it shows, I think. He's witty, he has inventive words. When Yip writes a comedy song for the stage, I think he's almost without equal. Yip was a big influence in teaching me how hard to work. Sometimes we'd get a rhyming dictionary and Roget's and we'd *sweat*.

"Oh, sure, I'd studied other people's lyrics. De Sylva, Brown and Henderson*—they had great ideas. Berlin's lyrics—such an economy of words. Cole Porter—such a fund of ideas, such rhyming and style. And Larry Hart was marvelous; he could write beautiful ballads and he'd turn right around and write a funny song, and a wry song, and a sardonic song . . . Well, Yip can do that too. He can do practically everything."

The fact remains that Mercer's assessment of Harburg holds true for his own work. His "ideas" ("Something's Gotta Give," "Ac-Cent-Tchu-Ate the Positive"), his ballads ("Laura," "Autumn Leaves"), his patter lyrics ("Jubilation T. Cornpone," "Legalize My Name") demonstrate an astonishing versatility.

Mercer shrugs. "Well, I like to think I'm a well-rounded writer. They always used to say, 'I'd like to write a college show with you,' or a Southern show, and I thought, Oh, that's a pain in the ass, because I can write those, sure I can, but I want to write something else, you know? I might be able to write Southern things a little better because I *am* a Southerner. But the Southern

---

* Which include "You're the Cream in My Coffee," "Varsity Drag," "The Best Things in Life Are Free," "Button Up Your Overcoat," "Sunny Side Up," and "If I Had a Talking Picture of You." The trio flourished in the late '20s and early '30s. De Sylva later became a hugely successful Broadway and Hollywood producer; at one point he ran the entire Paramount studio.

stuff got the attention first off because it was Southern in a different way. Nobody had brought in a song like 'Pardon My Southern Accent' or 'Lazy Bones' before. Up to then it had all been Tin Pan Alley Southern, you know? Stuff like 'Is It True What They Say About Dixie?' Sure, it was a big hit, even in the South, but it's not Southern like, say, Roark Bradford would have written, or DuBose Heyward. It's not Southern like 'Moon River.' "

"Moon River," which Mercer wrote with Henry Mancini as a song for *Breakfast at Tiffany's,* and which won one of his several Academy Awards (this one in 1961), contains that remarkable lyric phrase "my huckleberry friend."

"I don't know *why* I thought of it," he says. "Probably stems from the days of my childhood, when we'd go out in the fields and pick wild berries; they were everywhere. I was free-associating about the South for that song. The heroine, Holly Golightly, was from down there. For a while I called that song 'Red River,' because all the rivers down there are so muddy. I figured, it's springtime, she's in New York, but she's thinking of her home down there when she was a child. And when I thought 'huckleberry,' I said, 'That's the right word. I know it.' It's an odd word, but that's why it's so attractive."

Mercer chuckles. "We had that song in the picture; Holly sat on the fire escape and sang it, remember? Well, we all went up to the first preview in San Francisco, and afterwards we went back for the usual post-mortem. The verdict was the picture was too long. First thing the producer said was, 'Well, I know *one* thing we can cut—that song 'Moon River.' *It* can go."

Still relishing that irony, he ducks into one of the small bedrooms and returns a few moments later dressed for the day in somewhat sober gray and a Brooks Brothers button-down. It's nearing lunchtime, and he's ready to move in that direction, but with those Ben Franklin spectacles he now wears, plus a short goatee, he might well be Professor J. Mercer on his way to conduct a seminar.

"Let's not kid ourselves," he says, most unacademically. "We can all make those mistakes. Couple of years ago they asked me to do the song for a picture called *The Sandpiper.* I worked up a lyric and brought it in, and the producer turned it down. He went and got another one—'The Shadow of Your Smile.' Huge hit. That can be pretty depressing."

Did Mercer like the replacement song?

He grins. "Well, it sort of sounded to me as if it were about a lady with a slight mustache . . ."

But such unhappy incidents are rare in Mercer's career, are they not?"

"Luckily," he says. "The more you write, the easier it is. It's like developing a muscle. You get to be an amateur golfer, and then when you get down to the seventies, you get better and better. And you don't make that many mistakes. The same thing about writing songs. I know I'm much more skillful than I was when I was twenty. Maybe I don't have as many original ideas as I had then, maybe they're not as far out or as wildly imaginative. But I can write'em. When I get'em, I know what to do with'em. Don't waste any time fooling around, writing four or five versions. It's knowing where to go with the words, to recognize the thought when it comes, to recognize the proper word. But there *is* something else to that," he says most soberly. "If any young writer is going to pay attention to what I'm saying, he might learn a lesson. It's the *extra* hour of work that does it. Kern taught that to Hammerstein—Oscar always admitted it. You go back in the room and say, 'Now, that's the way it is, but is there something

I can improve here? Or something that can be a little more original than it is?' I really think that's the trouble with many kids today. I don't think they *work* on the songs. Well, hell, I don't think they have to. They get such a fast record. I get them coming up to me with things they've written. I had one a few days back. I heard this thing and I said, 'Very nice, but why don't you work on it a little bit longer? Why don't you take out this part, because it sounds too much like some of the rest? Why don't you improve these two lines? They could be so much better.' "

Mercer suddenly grins, and even behind that sober Brooks Brothers façade he's the same impish chap who sang carefree duets with Crosby and Colonna in the Kraft Music Hall, always having himself a ball and letting everyone know it. "The kid looked at me kind of blankly, but I think *maybe* I got through to him. I sure hope so."

As for the Mercer-Arlen collaboration, the two have remained extremely close over the years. It's unique in that both men are first-rate performers of their own work. Both sang professionally and are more than capable of performing, in many cases superior to the phalanx of weepy torch singers who use "One for My Baby" as a sure tear-getter, or who wail "That Old Black Magic" for effect rather than for honesty. Arlen and Mercer are both vocal masters of their own work. "Oh well, anybody can do *that* these days," he says, passing it off far too lightly. "All the kids who're around, they're just hollerin' and screamin' and they're just great, you know? Those groups like Blood, Sweat and Tears, and The Cream, and Credence Clearwater—they all write, and they're damned good at performing what they write, too!"

And what about Mercer's own tunes?

"Oh, I don't think my stuff compares with Kern's tunes, or Warren's, or Harold's. I think they write music a lot better than I can. I can do a song like 'Dream' or 'Old Cowhand' or 'Something's Gotta Give,' but I'm not kidding myself. I've got a son-in-law who's a pianist and he works with me. Before that, I'd get in an arranger and we'd work together. I'd sing it to him, or I'd try to play it with one finger. He'd play the chords and ask, 'Do you mean *that* chord?' and I'd say, 'No, that's not the right chord.' Together, we'd find the chord, and he'd write them down for me."*

It's Park Avenue now, near lunchtime. We're headed downtown. Mercer glances down an East Side block jammed with stalled traffic. "This town is so different from the old days," he says sadly. "I dunno, maybe it's just my imagination, but everything seemed so much more relaxed and pleasant back then. Nobody seems to have any fun here any more. Maybe that's what's wrong with music today, too. The kids don't have any sense of humor. They're worried, and they're scared, and they're competing fiercely with each other to get a foothold in a profession that's overcrowded. Everybody plays the guitar, everybody makes records, everybody has his own group, his own company. And the competition is really fierce. It's like a school of fighting fish."

There is no hostility in his tone. Many of Mercer's contemporaries have "tuned out" on the under-twenty-fives and react with Pavlovian distaste to anything played or sung by the emerging talents. "Johnny is one of the few composers

* Note the parallel to the pattern of some of Irving Berlin's composition, as recounted later by Robert Russell Bennett, who observed, "Irving can't play it, but he can *hear* it."

of his age group who stay close to what's happening today," says Margaret Whiting. "He keeps the lines open. He pays attention, and he really digs what's happening."

"Out of competition come superior writers," muses Mercer. "The more the competition, the better the writers will be. But there's no humor. When things get back, if they ever do, to a more peaceful way . . . You know, I think the scare technique in our society has stultified creativity a lot. The headlines every day, something horrible—war, or a threat of war, or violence, or racial tension, or some goddam thing. Well, we never had that back in the '30s or the '20s. We had a golden age of productivity. People had time to laugh then. You want to laugh now, but what's there to laugh at? You try making a joke about somebody, see what happens. They take it personally, and they say it's racial, or they say it's ethnic, or they say, 'You're laughin' at me because I'm a fag, or because I'm fat, or because I'm a woman.' Hell, you don't dare say anything about *anybody!*"

In the current atmosphere, one might not even dare to write a "Pardon My Southern Accent."

"Nope, they wouldn't like that. They didn't like it *then!* Somebody, a lady from Atlanta, wrote and said, 'Nobody but an ignorant Yankee would write that!' She meant you don't say 'you-all' to one person! Hell," he snorts, "if I didn't say 'you-all,' I wouldn't have had a song! Oh, it's a damn shame about the way things are now, because to make fun of the human weaknesses is what gives us, has given us, most of our laughter for centuries."

Does he believe that the younger crop of songwriters, the Jim Webbs, the Harry Nilssons, the Bert Bacharachs, the Randy Newmans, will demonstrate the same span of accomplishment that is his? Are they merely this year's talents, or will they be around for a while?

"Depends on the opportunities they get to write, more than on what they're writing now," he comments. "See, what they're doing today is making up complete albums; it's sort of like writing little short stories, all strung together and set to music. I think they'll get fed up with this hard-rock stuff soon. I know *I'm* bored to death with it. They found all the old Elizabethan songs, and they've had a run at that. Now they've dug up the folk songs, the Tennessee mountain songs, and they've been doing that. Do you think maybe," he asks somewhat wistfully, "they might come back and like some Jerome Kern and Victor Herbert?"

In the world of musical tastes, all things are possible, aren't they?

"I sure hope so," he says. "I miss them the most. And Gershwin. *Melodic* Gershwin, you know? And Youmans. That's why I think *No, No, Nanette* has been such a smash. Lots of other people must miss that melody era too."

A current manifestation of that desire for things past must be the publication of a $25 documentation of Cole Porter's life and works—the book *Cole.*

"Smash!" says Mercer happily. "And rightfully so. But I think there's another reason for the Porter book being such a runaway. Cole Porter is definitive of an era. He *is* those years, you know? He is the style of all those shows, all that period. He represents it better than anybody else, better than even Kern or Berlin. Porter's so . . . thirties! Jerry and Irving have had an enormous, probably a bigger, influence than Cole, but they didn't have that particular sophistication or . . ." He pauses, again hunting in his mental Roget for the exact word. "*Flair,* I guess."

Lower Fifties now, on Park, headed in the direction of what's left of the once flourishing theatrical district. Where dozens of Broadway musicals once played to cheerfully packed houses, there are now only a handful of super-smashes, with $15-top seats separating the big spenders from the true appreciators. Over there, in the past three decades, Mercer has only sporadically tried his luck. He and Arlen did *St. Louis Woman*. The show failed, but the songs like "Come Rain or Come Shine" will survive. He and Bobby Dolan collaborated on *Texas, Li'l Darlin'*, which was a moderate success, and in the early '50s Mercer and Gene DePaul provided *Li'l Abner* with a fine score. There was also the Phil Silvers starring vehicle *Top Banana*; a show called *Foxy*, which he and Dolan wrote for the late Bert Lahr and which contains some as-yet-undiscovered musical-comedy treasures, due someday for revival; and a show with Arlen called *Saratoga*, which collapsed beneath the weight of a soggy adaptation of the Edna Ferber novel.

Is Mercer masochistic enough to tackle that scene again?

"Yes, but I don't want to do the wrong one. I want to do a show that's really good, a show that's a credit to myself and the composer. And you don't know where those books are going to come from any more.

"What you *do* know, though, is, it's got to be different. It can't be just another damn show. There are so many of those. Almost all the shows that come into town are not original, they're all like something else. And I—well, this will sound conceited to you, but I just don't want to write *Hello, Dolly!* I think it's a dreary show. *West Side Story* was a strong show, or *King and I*. That'd be the kind of show I'd like to write, one that has some substance, with a lot of original ideas and a lot of great songs." He trudges on. "Wouldn't that be wonderful to come in with—a show like that? But it's tough as hell to come by one, I can tell you," he says fervently.

Now it's crosstown. He makes for a seafood restaurant in the Fifties, one which features delicacies notoriously absent from Southern California menus.

"So I'll just keep on looking," he says, "It's the humor thing that's so tough to get past. So damn little of it around these days. Or maybe we all get to a certain age and we're past our time, you know? We can't laugh at the things that tickled us so when we were young . . ."

It comes as something of a shock to consider that Mercer has reached the age where down in Savannah he'd probably be referred to as "spry." Somehow, one refuses to accept middle age in this cheerful gentleman whose impish wit has brightened so many corners; maturity, perhaps, but Golden Age retirement, never.

Nor does he, happily. "You've got to be involved in *something*," he insists as we approach the restaurant. "Damn it, you can't just sit in a room and stare out the window in a catatonic state. You've got to *do* something. But you know, I'd rather keep busy traveling, or going to the supermarket, or driving in my car, than just sitting there. I certainly don't get any kick out of writing things and putting them in a drawer. If I write a song today and I can't get it recorded, it's embarrassing. It really is. So if somebody calls me up and asks me will I write even a title song for a picture, I don't care, I jump at the chance, as long as they pay money.

"But to write 'em, and take 'em around and have people say *no*, turn my stuff down—man, that's *demeaning*. It would be as if Dick Rodgers were to go to Motown Records* with some melodies and they said to him, 'Oh, we don't like those tunes, buddy.' "

As we enter the restaurant, the owner recognizes Mercer and has news for him. One of his old friends was in two nights before, enjoying seafood with the dean himself, Irving Berlin, who rarely goes out these days. "A big week for songwriters hereabouts," says Mercer. "Maybe we *are* making a comeback, eh?"

He orders an immediate Dewar's. "Strictly medicinal," he explains. "Last night was a little . . . debilitating, and I'm still recovering from the effects."

The true mark of a Georgia gentleman. Not once this morning has he betrayed any sign of morning *mal de tête*.

"No problem," says Mercer, imbibing his therapeutic potation. "You had me talking about songwriters, which is always a pleasure. Did Bobby Dolan ever tell you the story about Irving Berlin when they were making *White Christmas* at Paramount? They were discussing a sequence in the picture, one that didn't have an actual musical number in it but would be underscored with music. Bobby was the producer, and in the conference he said, 'Now, at this point I'd like the background music to be one single note.' And Berlin waved his finger and said, '*My* note!'

"I've always written what I think I want to do, and the way I want it to be," says Mercer thoughtfully. "Berlin once said about me, 'Mercer will always write what he wants to write, and then let the public find out about it.' And that's absolutely right."

Absolutely, Mr. Mercer. Positively, Mr. Berlin.

---

* A vastly successful Detroit-based recording company specializing in hard-rock and rhythm-and-blues. Its product is aimed specifically at the under-twenty-fives, those record buyers who allegedly make up the majority of today's market.

'Over the Rainbow'

(Harold Arlen)

WHEN I CALLED Harold Arlen to ask him if he'd care to talk to me about songwriting, his response was a trifle sardonic. Why was a grown man wasting his time on such pursuits? "You're kidding yourself that anybody *really* wants to hear what *I* have to say," he chided me. But we arranged a date for the following week.

By some absolute fluke of coincidence, the morning of the day of our appointment I came into New York from Connecticut, started walking through the bright midsummer heat up Park Avenue, and coming toward me on the sidewalk I saw a lean, dapper man, immaculately tailored, sporting the familiar mustache and horn-rims, the same face that graces the cover of his latest LP (made with Barbra Streisand)—Mr. Arlen himself.

I stopped him and introduced myself. We had a date for three P.M., but perhaps he might enjoy beginning sooner, perhaps we might have lunch?

Arlen shook his head. "Thanks, no," he said. "That's socializing. We made a date for an interview—that's *commerce*. Don't believe in mixing the two. First we attend to commerce, *then* we can socialize."

At the agreed time I arrived at his apartment, which is in one of those spacious old Central Park West buildings with vestigial parquet floors, large pleasant rooms, and high ceilings. Arlen's walls are hung with a stunning collection of paintings, drawings, and prints, not chosen by a decorator but selected by their owner with taste and love. (A number of his oils are the work of his great friend Irving Berlin, with whom he chats on the telephone every day.) We went into his study-workroom, and sat down to talk.

To begin, the biographical facts. Harold Arlen was born in Buffalo, New York, in 1905. His father was the cantor in the local synagogue; he and Irving Berlin are as one in their musical heritage. At the age of seven Harold was singing in the synagogue choir.

"My father gave me piano lessons so I would be a teacher and not have to work on *shabbas*," said Arlen, who chuckled at the irony of his late father's intention. "Mine was a marvelous family—all kinds of love. But that was the first reason I went to the piano. I found other reasons soon enough, needless to say!" He laughed.

His musical career developed with all possible speed. By the time Harold was fifteen he had his own instrumental group, The Snappy Trio. Soon after, he joined another jazz-oriented outfit called first The Southbound Shufflers, then The Yankee Six. They expanded into a dance orchestra known as The Buffalodians. When that group became successful enough to go on tour, they headed for New York, with the very young Arlen playing piano, arranging popular tunes, and singing vocals. He was heard by a bandleader named Arnold Johnson, who hired him to be part of his own orchestra.

"It was a very strange pattern, when I look back," Arlen said. "You have to believe me, I never had *any* notion of being a composer. As a kid, I loved to sing. I wanted to be a singer. Never dreamed of songwriting. I have to be a fatalist and say somebody, something, moved me on the chessboard. I was taken by the neck and put here, and put there, and put there—and then things happened to me. Because listen to how it all worked out for me."

Johnson's orchestra appeared on Broadway in *George White's Scandals of 1928* for a six-month run. To satisfy his young vocalist's basic urge to sing, Johnson allowed the Buffalo fugitive to reprise, during the show's intermission, a DeSylva-Brown-Henderson hit song from the show, "I'm on the Crest of a Wave" (performed in the same show by Harry Richman).

"Vincent Youmans, the composer, heard me and liked my singing. He hired me to sing in a show he was preparing called *Great Day*—the first version, in 1929. I had a song to do called 'Doo-Dah-Dey,' as a character called Cokey Joe. It didn't work. After our first tryout performance it was cut.

"Now, you'd ordinarily figure that was the end. I could go back to singing—I'd also been in a vaudeville act for Arthur and Sam Lyons called *Maytime Melodies* and sung on the radio with Johnson's band, a show called *The Majestic Hour*. But just listen to how things happened. Fletcher Henderson was doing arrangements for Youmans' show. Henderson was one hell of a great musician; later he was to do all of Benny Goodman's best arrangements. He asked me if I'd like to help him arrange music for his pit orchestra. I jumped at the chance. I was jazz crazy, and I loved his music and style.

"Now, Fletcher is working and he takes sick. He asks me if I'll take over for him at rehearsals. And I'm leading the singers at rehearsals, playing piano for them, and I sit at the piano and give them the regular opening vamp. You know how it goes: *Da-dum, da-dum* DUM DUM! That's how you always did it for an opening.

"But after a couple of times I get bored with that vamp, and I start fooling around with it, and I give the chorus singers *dadada dadadada* DUM-DUM! And another time I go *Da dee da deeda da da da dum dum!* And I keep working away, fiddling with the chords, and one day one of the people there says to me, 'What *is* that you're playing?'

"I didn't know I was composing anything. I was just improvising, naturally! And one day along comes a guy I've met named Harry Warren, and he introduces me to a guy named Ted Koehler, who writes lyrics. Koehler sits down and writes a set of words to my little vamp, and he calls it 'Get Happy.' I didn't seek it out, or ask for it—it just *happened.*"

The song so inadvertently written was auditioned for a lady named Ruth Selwyn, who was preparing to produce The *9:15 Revue.* She promptly took it for her first-act finale, where it would be sung by that popular vocalist of the day, Ruth Etting (whose somewhat lurid life story was later made into the film *Love Me or Leave Me,* starring Doris Day).

The Selwyn show was somewhat less than a success, but Arlen was already launched on a songwriting career. "I started getting $50 a week from Al Piantadosi, who was running a subsidiary of Remick's Music Company, as a regular advance against royalties. I didn't even have to come in. Every week they sent me $50 a week for whatever I felt like writing. Marvelous!

"After that, I did another show, *Earl Carroll's Vanities,* with Koehler, but that didn't give us anything much in the way of hit songs. What it did do was to get us a job writing the score for a night-club show in the famous Cotton Club. We do that. They up my weekly advance to $100 a week. Here I am, still a kid, getting $100 a week. I made enough to have myself a *penthouse.* Because I'm still playing piano for Ethel Merman and Lyda Roberti and Frances Williams, singers who do night clubs and play the Palace in vaudeville.

"But do you see what I mean by other forces? Somebody, or some mysterious thing, always in motion. Each step that happened was part of a chain."

Arlen shook his head, as if still amazed by the peculiar nature of his success story. "Now, I don't know how many men in the creative arts start that way," he said. "It seems to me that the 'bug' is there early in most authors, or composers, or lyricists. But I didn't have that bug at all. And I didn't study other composers, I didn't worry about lyrics, not me. I was only interested in the Memphis Five, a jazz band, or Benny Goodman. Because I had always been a jazz buff.

"I started pretty late in life developing tastes, for paintings, whether they're good or bad, or a taste for Kern and Gershwin. I didn't really study other composers and their work until I got to the point where I had to write eight or ten or fifteen songs for a show. Then I asked myself, 'What do they do?' *Then* I began to study them, to realize their ideas and their styles, to appreciate what they were doing . . . mostly after I'd gotten to know them personally. But my beginnings were never centered on those guys, only jazz.

"I'll give you an example. I sang in a night club one night. Just got up and sang. And Bix Beiderbecke [the legendary jazz cornetist of the '20s and the early '30s] was there, and when I finished, he said, 'Great, kid.' Holy Jesus, that meant so much to me!"

Could he remember his first experience with the blues, the echoing strain of which permeates so many of his greatest songs?

"When I left home and came to New York, I went to Roseland in Brooklyn and I heard the original Memphis Five, a really great group. When they came off the stand, I stood there with as much awe as if the President of the United States had just finished speaking."

What about the end result of his father being a cantor in a Jewish *shul* in Buffalo, and his deep affinity for black-oriented jazz and blues? That unique meld of the two cultures, that strain, seems to be the strength of his highly original melodic gifts, both in writing and in singing.

Arlen shook his head. "Oh *boy*, I don't know how the hell to explain it— except I hear in jazz and in gospel my father singing. He was one of the greatest *improvisers* I've ever heard. Let me tell you a story about him. I brought home a record of Louis Armstrong, I don't remember now which it was. My father spoke in Yiddish. And you have to remember, he was brought into this country originally to Louisville, Kentucky, so he must have picked up some of the blacks' inflections down there.

"Anyway, I played him this record, and there was a musical riff in there —we used to call it a 'hot lick'—that Louis did. And my father looked at me, and he was stunned. And he asked in Yiddish, 'Where did *he* get it?' Because he thought it was something that *he* knew, you see.

"I can remember improvisations of my father's that are just like Louis Armstrong's—and, remember, my father came from Eastern Europe when he was eleven years old. He knew nothing about jazz, but there was something in his style that's in the style of jazz musicians . . . Louis' riffs.

"You know, later on, when I started writing hit songs, he would always sing my songs in the *shul!* It got so that his congregation would expect to hear him sing one of my so-called 'hits' . . . of which I began to have a fair amount. Whatever of mine was going at the time, he'd use it in the musical text of the service. He'd sing 'Stormy Weather' or 'My Shining Hour' as one of his solo passages!

"No, I never dreamed of aping my father, but I know damned well now that his glorious improvisations must have had some effect on me and my own style."

When lyricist E. Y. Harburg fell to analyzing Harold Arlen's music, he said, "You know, a lot of George Gershwin rubbed off on Harold. George was Harold's deity, he really was. George, you must see, changed the whole face of chords and music and development. He brought to American music a combination of his own Semitic background and melded it to the Negro jazz. Put them together, made new rhythms. It was really a melting pot of America, a great contribution to music.

"But later Harold went off in a different direction. True, his background was much more of the cantor, and also, Harold had a completely different psyche from George's. That's another thing that matters deeply, a fellow's psychological equipment. Harold is a very, very melancholy person. Inside, deeply religious. But he's very superstitious. When he gets to the piano, it's a feeling of witchcraft. He'll spit three times and almost talk to the chords, talk to God. He does it humorously, but behind the humor are all sorts of superstitions and beliefs.

"Behind every song that Harold writes is great sadness and melancholy.

Even his happy songs. You take a song like his rousing hit 'Get Happy.' Sing it slowly. Examine it. It's painful! Everything he does, he's never liberated from that . . . *thing* hanging over him."

Was it difficult, then, to write light lyrics to Arlen's music?

"Not for me," said Harburg. "Because I realize that the best of humor has pathos in it."

Arlen and Koehler wrote several *Cotton Club Revue* scores in the early 1930s, and they came up with an extraordinary string of song hits that have remained popular standards. "Ah, but it was a different time," Arlen said modestly. "Look how difficult it is today. You do a Broadway show and the songs better be damned good, or you get absolutely nothing out of it. But in those days, can you imagine writing for a nightclub show and getting 'Stormy Weather,' 'Between the Devil and the Deep Blue Sea,' 'I've Got the World on a String,' 'As Long as I Live'—even 'I Love a Parade'? And I might even be missing some of them we did then."

As in fact he was. He'd omitted the haunting ballad "Ill Wind" and "Kicking the Gong Around," as well as a song that Louis Armstrong was to make famous, "I've Got a Right to Sing the Blues."

He moved rapidly into the most difficult kind of Broadway show-writing, the satiric revue, in company with Ira Gershwin and E. Y. Harburg—*Life Begins at 8:40.*

"Well, that's another link in that chain I mentioned," said Arlen. "I'd already had my turn at the luck wheel, in the Cotton Club. I wanted to break out of that and try my luck on Broadway. And it was tough for me, because to this day I'm essentially not a smart writer, I'm a blues writer. I talked to somebody just yesterday, and when he asked me how I felt, I said, 'The blues is hanging over my head.'

"But I did the Broadway show, the revue. Tough as hell. The amount of material you need in a revue, as opposed to a show with a libretto, is enormous. It was a pretty hard job, that show. One composer, two lyricists. They collaborated on the lyrics. I did the music alone."

"It was a joyous experience," said Harburg about *Life Begins at 8:40.* "John Murray Anderson was producing the show for the Shuberts, and I loved Murray. He was a very smart man. Had such class, style, taste, sophistication—everything. Always put on such beautiful sets and décor. It was my big chance too. And I went to Ira Gershwin, whom I'd known since my early college days, and said, 'All right, your brother George is working on *Porgy and Bess* and you're not doing anything, whatta you say we write a revue? I've got a lot of ideas for it.' And Ira said, 'All right, who'll we use for music?' I said, 'How about Harold Arlen?' He said, 'Yes, I think a lot of him.' So the three of us got together with Murray Anderson and said we'd do the show for him.

"We had this darling notion for the opening—that life begins at 8:40 P.M. A parody on a current best-seller by a man named Walter Pitkin; it was called *Life Begins at Forty.* Our idea was that life begins when the curtain of the show goes up. We had this big Munich clock onstage, and out of the clock came all the characters that would appear in the revue. The husband, the lover, the wife, the blues singer, the comedian, the dancers, and so on. And in the words for the opening we said, '*At exactly eight forty or thereabouts, this little playworld, not of the dayworld, comes to life.'* And then out came all the people who were working in the theatre itself, show-business types, who said we're *not* the average run of people who sleep all night and work all day. We reverse the process.

"Ira would come in with one idea, I'd come in with something, then Harold would come up with a tune. It was a very happy few months there, and we got a great score out of it."

"Yes," Arlen agreed, "out of that show came 'Fun to Be Fooled,' 'You're a Builder Upper,' 'Let's Take a Walk Around the Block,' and 'What Can You Say in a Love Song?' Pretty smart stuff. And to be asked to do it, and to take it on, took *guts*. So I proved that I could come out of the Cotton Club. That's not a big deal, it's not as hard, say, as getting out of Vietnam," Arlen said, chuckling, "but it was an interesting road to travel."

That was the summer of 1934, and the Broadway theatrical scene was far from the most solvent area of show business. Out in Hollywood, the studios had rediscovered an audience for musical films. For the price of a movie ticket the public could sit in the neighborhood movie house and forget how tough things were outside its walls. Ballads and Busby Berkeley, tap dancers and tenors provided twenty-five cents' worth of Nepenthe. Good songwriters were in demand, and the studios offered long-term security. Arlen and Ted Koehler went to Hollywood on one writing contract; Harburg went on another.

Eventually, after a couple of films with Koehler, Arlen rejoined Harburg, and the two men went to work at Warner Brothers in Burbank, writing, among other films, *The Singing Kid* for Al Jolson, and *Gold Diggers of 1937*.

"Then Yipper got an idea for a Broadway musical show—a satiric story about war, and how stupid it was. He called it *Hooray for What?* and we wrote the score.* Came back to Broadway.

"Now just see how strange things are in this business. We had some good songs in that show—'Down with Love' and 'God's Country.' That's where Yip wrote that instead of Hitler and Sir Oswald Mosley, we had Popeye and Gypsy Rose Lee. But there was one sweet little ballad that was called 'In the Shade of the New Apple Tree,' and *that* song got us *Wizard of Oz*. Because, as we found out later, Arthur Freed, the producer at Metro, based his choice of Yip and me to do *Oz* on that one song. He felt it had the quality of naïveté and sincerity that Dorothy in Oz should have. And I can tell you, there were plenty of other major songwriters who were damned unhappy and shocked when they heard that we'd gotten it, because they'd all been sitting around, *waiting* for that job."

What about the score for *The Wizard of Oz*, which has long since become classic, and includes the touching "Over the Rainbow"? Had its composer and lyricist any inkling of how great a success that would eventually be?

Arlen shook his head and shrugged. "Sometimes in this business you get fortunate."

It was a warm afternoon, and we were both in shirt sleeves, sipping iced tea. Arlen sat silently, perhaps remembering the days in 1938 when he and Harburg worked in a California office, preparing "Ding Dong, the Witch Is Dead," "If I Only Had a Brain," and all the rest of those joyous songs which echo from millions of television sets like some happy ritual every year.

---

* Howard Lindsay and Russel Crouse did the book. The leading role went to Ed Wynn, whose performance as a naïve inventor who develops a gas that will eliminate war was a delight.

"I guess the story's been around a long time," he said finally, smiling, "about how Yip didn't like my original melody for 'Over the Rainbow.' He thought it was something for Nelson Eddy to sing . . . ."

"As far as that music is concerned," said Harburg later, "Harold struck a brave and inspired symphonic theme. It is not a little child's nursery song. It's a great big theme that you could easily build a symphony around. Hum those first bars of 'Over the Rainbow'—da *dum*, da da da da *dum*. It's strong. And the fact that we covered it up in a nursery story—behind it is this big, sad statement.

"I'll admit that at first the song bothered me because it was so powerful. But then we brought it down with those colorful and childlike words. I don't think there's more poignancy to anything that is adult than there is in a child's idea. Children are so clear about life . . . and they never cover up."

"You wonder later," mused Arlen, "in mystery, how it all happens. It seems so natural. It seems like they were all born together, the music and the lyrics. They're not apart, you can't separate them."

"Rainbow" is also unique because it's basically identified with *Wizard of Oz*. That period of Hollywood in the '30s was a fruitful one, and yet, thirty years later, it's the *songs* that survive. Outside of *Oz* it's sometimes impossible to remember what the pictures actually were, but the scores remain rich.

"It was a great period!" continues Arlen. "Maybe it was the accident of all of us working there because of the Depression. Practically every talent you can name. So many. Jerry Kern, Harry Warren, the Gershwins, Dorothy Fields and Jimmy McHugh, Oscar Hammerstein—even Berlin, although he didn't stick around. All of us, writing pictures so well. We were all on the weekly radio Hit Parade. If we weren't first, we were second; if we weren't second, we were fourth. A sensational period. Lovely for me. I went to the studio when I damned well pleased, or when they called me. Got my check every week. And we were pouring it out!

"Oh sure, we all wrote picture scores that were bad. But people were having flops on Broadway, too, weren't they? It was a great life. Most of us played golf or tennis, or swam, and did our writing at the same time. I wrote at home. I could write at midnight, or at five in the afternoon, at nine—it made no difference. As long as I came in with something that the so-called producers liked." Again Arlen grinned. "And, believe me, when it came to matters of quality, their guess was as good as mine."

It was during the late '30s that Arlen began working with a young Southerner named Johnny Mercer, and for a relatively minor Warner film about jazz musicians on tour the two men crafted what has become still another American popular classic, "Blues in the Night."

"It wasn't even a musical. The song was incidental," said Arlen. "The script—it was called *Hot Nocturne*, or something else—called for the jazz band to be in jail, and for a black man in the cell next to them to sing the blues. So I said to myself, any jazz musician can put his *foot* on a piano and write a blues song! I've got to write one that sounds authentic, that sounds as if it were born in New Orleans or St. Louis. So I did a little very minor research. I found out that the blues was always written in three stanzas, with twelve bars each. That was the first thing.

"Then I told my late wife—it was the only time I ever said such a thing to her, bless her—'Don't trouble me, don't bother me, until I knock or come into the house.' I had a little studio off behind the place. It took me a day and a half. That's long for me, because when you haven't got an idea—well, most times you have what I call 'jots' stored away. They're not indexed, they're not written out yet, but they're around somewhere for when you need them. Possibilities, for shows, or for other lyric-writers, or for other situations where I'll be needing a number. That way, at least, you've got some notion. It's kind of a *handle*.

"I didn't have a handle for this blues thing, but I knew I could write a blues. Along the way, I got this little notion. You know how it is sometimes when you're writing—you get an idea and it works itself out. Sometimes it stumbles. Not this one. You see, the thirty-two bars that you usually write a popular song in is a cameo form, but it is an art form. You have to get something that's melodically arresting. Something that's immediate. There are some songs, for example, like the things that Dick Rodgers wrote when he began to work with Oscar Hammerstein, that you had to play two or three times, over four or five days, to get yourself familiarized with. They weren't on the beam, so to speak, but they were glorious. You knew what Dick was trying to say, but it took some learning.

"But here I am with this notion, a musical idea, and, brother, the fires went up and the whole thing *poured* out! The first stanza, second stanza, the third, the repeat of the first, and the coda—just as my research had told me it had to.

"And I hollered, 'Annie!' She came down and listened. She always listened . . . she was always there. And I played it and I knew in my guts, without even thinking of what John could write for a lyric, that this was strong, strong, *strong!* You can't say that about all melodies. I can't tell about melodies until I get a lyric. And if it's happily wedded, fine. If not, I'm in trouble. But this I knew was strong. As a matter of fact, it was one of the high points of *knowing* in my whole life. . . .

"So, casually, not with work in mind, I went over to John's house and I caught him at his desk. He used to come and visit me, and he'd wink at me, and that was supposed to mean that he'd had a big night, no work today. But this day I didn't stay around long. I played him the melody. No questions asked, no experiments, no saying, 'This needs another two bars' or 'I don't like the third stanza'—nothing. He just listened. I played it a couple of times, and then I went away.

"I came back later and he had written it down. He had everything as you know it today, except the first twelve bars! I can't remember what he had for the first twelve, but they didn't hang together.

"He had a piece of lyric lying around on his desk that he'd probably forgotten. I'd never done this before with John, but I picked up this piece of paper, and on it was written out, '*My momma done tole me, when I was in knee-pants, my momma done tole me, "Son, a woman's a sweet-talk, who'll give you the big-eye,"* ' and so on. All the rest of it! The words were just hanging there, nowhere. And we put them into the first twelve bars. That's how *that* happened.

"After we finished the song, we took it to Jimmy Lunceford [a popular jazz band leader of the late '30s]. He refused to record it. Hated it! He was forced to do it by the Decca company—Jack Kapp insisted. Not only one side, but *both* sides of a seventy-eight record. In those days, remarkable. You just didn't do a song on both sides of a record, *ever*. Got Lunceford a big hit.

"We were hoping to get Ethel Waters out of retirement to record it, hoping she'd make it into a hit, but before Ethel could do it, the song had become a smash. Overnight.

"Funny, if we hadn't had that phrase '*My momma done tole me*' as the statement . . . But then, everything in 'Blues in the Night' was wedded well. There is no such thing as a melody doing it, or the lyric doing it alone. It's got to be a combination. There's just no other way. And I can shoot holes into any and all arguments to the contrary. Mention any song you want to, and I can show you the title you remember, or a phrase you remember, and if it weren't for that phrase *with* the melody, it wouldn't have happened.

"I can tell you how this fact was illustrated to me some time back. I wrote a song with a pretty goddam wonderful lyric-writer. He brought in a lyric that didn't have any strength. Sometimes a lyric depletes a melody, just as a poor melody can deplete a good lyric. The lyric he brought in didn't really weaken it, it just made nothing out of the song.

"Fortunately, it came out of the show I was doing, and then later I got another assignment and I knew that this other lyricist might like it." Arlen waved a defensive hand. "No, I'm not going to tell you their names. They're both good friends of mine. Anyway, the other writer agreed to try to use that original melody. And I want to tell you, if there was ever an example of how that 'wedding' works . . . The new lyric was glorious. It isn't that the other fellow wasn't capable; he just wasn't in tune that day, or something. But the second lyric made that melody sound like the Rock of Gibraltar! The first lyric had made my melody sound so puny, it was unbelievable. It has nothing to do with their two talents. One is different from the other, but they're both excellent lyric-writers. I wrote well with both of them. But, believe me, with one man's words the song was enormous in its strength, and with the other's it was puny. One lyric made life glorious, the other deadened it.

"That's what a wedding means. I don't know whether other songwriters have the same feeling, but I always have. Happy collaboration is a good wedding."

Arlen has been remarkably successful in finding that "happy wedding" with his various lyricists. Most of them—Harburg, Mercer, Ira Gershwin, Koehler, Leo Robin—have seemed to "meld" with his music to a high degree of perfection.

"Mostly a question of styles and assignments, I think," said Arlen. "My first four years were with Ted Koehler. I didn't know then how important and big they were. Others told me how good they were, but I just looked and stared at them, because I was a freshman at this. Later, with John, fine. Yipper, another good one. Look how he writes! Talk about the protest songs today . . . You know, this generation didn't originate message songs. Bob Dylan may say it in four or five choruses, takes fifteen minutes. But Yip, he wrapped it up in thirty-two bars, thirty-five years ago, with 'Brother, Can You Spare a Dime?' He told it all. Exactly what they're trying to say now. Everything today is a message, but they're not saying it as well as Yipper already has."

In 1944 Harburg collaborated with Arlen on the score for another Broadway musical, *Bloomer Girl.* Laid in a small American town in the Civil War period, the story of Amelia Bloomer, one of the first suffragettes, made a strong book, and the two men enhanced it with a score of great charm, haunting melody, and strength. In it were "Evalina," "Right as the Rain," and "It Was Good Enough for Grandma." The subject of slavery coupled with Arlen's affinity for black music made for such hits as "I Got a Song" and the unforgettable "The Eagle and Me."

Fellow songwriter Stephen Sondheim has remarked that his favorite single line among all the lyrics he has heard was written by Harburg, to Arlen's music in "The Eagle and Me": "*Ever since the day when the world was an onion*" . . . "I don't know how an idea like that ever occurs to somebody," marveled Sondheim. "It's too good!"

In 1946 Arlen and Mercer collaborated on the score for the all-black musical *St. Louis Woman,* out of which came "Come Rain or Come Shine." Pearl Bailey was a huge personal success singing the two comedy songs they crafted for her, "Legalize My Name" and "A Woman's Prerogative," but the show was only a modest success.

"I always went back to Hollywood," mused Arlen. "To the comforts of a home in Beverly Hills. Kept on writing pictures. Some good, some bad. Kept on wandering from one lyricist to the other. I don't know what the reason for that was. I suppose I didn't want to be pinned down.

"Mercer and I did very well. I remember doing 'One for My Baby.' I wrote it as if it were natural to me to write that kind of song, but then I started thinking, 'Jesus, how could a lyric-writer dig *this,* or even understand it?' Because I'd started in one key—I didn't even realize it at the time—and I wound up in another key. Unlike anything I'd ever done, or heard. And yet John put on that line the best torch-song lyric of our time. The *right* lyric. That was a song that didn't 'happen' for a couple of years. A delayed reaction.

"I knew 'Over the Rainbow' was a strong song, but I never knew its true strength until afterwards. 'Blues in the Night'—that was the high point of immediacy. It was wham, *that's it!* But 'Old Black Magic' was another song that took a couple of years. I knew that one was different. It wasn't complicated as far as *I* was concerned, but I thought it would be complicated for an *audience.*"

Also written with Mercer, "That Old Black Magic" is a crowning example of a song which breaks with the accepted thirty-two-bar pattern, being more than twice as long in musical form, attenuated far past most popular-music statements. "The singer Billy Daniels got hold of it, and he did it, not the way I wrote it, but in an up tempo. Mine was a sultry, lush song; Billy's version was rhythmic and terribly original. Still is. It could still go. Even today, I hope."

The long list of songs which Arlen collaborated on for various films also includes "Hit the Road to Dreamland," "Ac-Cen-Tchu-Ate the Positive," "For Every Man There's a Woman," "My Shining Hour," "Hooray for Love." Only dedicated film buffs will be able to name the pictures from which they come.

When Harburg went to work at Metro as the producer of the film version of *Cabin in the Sky,* the Broadway hit musical, he and Arlen collaborated on two additional songs for the picture—a rollicking number for Dooley Wilson called "Consequences," and a song which many of Arlen's fans consider as good as anything he's ever done, "Happiness Is Just a Thing Called Joe."

In 1954 Arlen returned to Broadway, once again drawn by his affinity for black music, to write the score for Truman Capote's book and lyrics about the Caribbean, *House of Flowers.*

"Maybe I should have written more for the theatre, but it isn't so easy to write for the theatre any more," sighed Arlen. "You have to be so goddam lucky. And you talk about weddings—it makes no difference how lovely your score is, if something doesn't happen up there on the stage, the stardust doesn't fall. The book for the show—without that for a spine, you're nothing. *St. Louis Woman,* beautiful score, most people agree on that. But no book, the book fell out on us. Lovers of songs remember it, that's all.

"And the same thing is true of *House of Flowers*. They keep saying how they love our score—they forget about the fact that we never had a second act. But there is something about that show that keeps it alive in the minds of people. Whether it is the charm of the music and lyrics or what, I don't know.

"On the first night of that show, at the end of the first act, Walter Winchell, who was sitting in front of me, turned around and winked, as if to say, 'You're in.' But after the second act he had a whole different attitude. Well, we never had a second act, and we deserved what we got."

Is there a way to define what made those weddings with the many talents he'd written with so happy? What were they all like?

"Well, with Ted Koehler," said Arlen, "you had to sit at the piano and play for days and days. Sometimes all night. I don't know why, I had the feeling sometimes that he just couldn't stand being alone, and desperately wanted company.

"With Johnny Mercer . . ." Arlen threw up his hands. "You trust him. That's all. You have faith. He takes your melody away and comes back with the words.

"Worked only once with my good friend Dorothy Fields, we'd known each other for years. I'd played tennis with her, but I'd never written with her. She's a hell of a lyric-writer. We did a picture at Metro called *Mr. Imperium*—wrote three other good songs that didn't get into the picture, but we did come up with 'Today, I Love Everybody.'

"Now, about Leo Robin. The two of us wrote 'Hooray for Love' and 'For Every Man There's a Woman' and a few others. Very talented man, Leo, but he's never sure. He tightens up. Comes back and hands you a lyric and then he says, almost as if he's apologizing, 'This is just a dummy lyric.' Of course, that dummy *stays!*

"But Leo isn't the only guy who tightens up. Ira Gershwin is the same way. He seems to hate writing ballads. Absolutely loathes doing them. And *he's* the guy who wrote 'Love Walked In' *and* 'They Can't Take That Away from Me' *and* 'Embraceable You,' among others.

"Ira tightens up so before he starts an assignment, I always had the feeling that when there was a ballad coming on, he immediately took to his bed! When we started working on *A Star Is Born* for Judy Garland, the big musical version in 1954, I went over to see him, and we were talking, and I casually said, 'Well, Ira, it looks to me as if we'll need about five ballads here.' I was just kidding him, but, so help me, he had to get in a nurse!

"Ira is very much like Yip Harburg. Two very interesting guys, always experimenting with words. Using the language, twisting it, bending it. I remember back when both of them were working with me on *Life Begins at 8:40*—man, they sure gave me an interesting time!"

Harburg has said, in turn, "The communication problem is a very important one, a very special one, and a very tough one between collaborators. Sometimes it doesn't work out because either the people are impatient with each other or don't understand each other's psyches. Or one happens to be not on the same creative level as the other. But not with Harold. He is always aiming for something. Bending over backwards to get the best."

Arlen continued. "I guess I've always been very lucky in my collaborators. And lucky because I've always had something in my music that 'lights them up,' gets them enthusiastic. I don't know where it comes from. Every time I face a job, part of myself says, 'Jesus, how will I do it?' And then some other part of myself says, 'Go ahead—you have to.' Brother, you have to keep reminding yourself that you're a writer, to stand off and tell yourself, '*Go. Do it.*'

"Memorable songs?" Arlen asked, half to himself. "How do you know? A song becomes memorable *despite* its author. Oh sure, you know if what you've written is good, or melodic, or well made, or all three. But nobody can sit down to write a hit. Think about how accidental it all was! I became a songwriter by accident!

"Why, I was *so* naïve, I didn't even realize how demeaning it was to audition as a singer, to sing in front of all those potential hirers, with all those glaring, staring faces. I remember singing for Jake Shubert, back in the early days, ten songs at the piano. I stopped singing. He yelled, 'What happened?' I said, 'I ran out of throat!' He was so callous. He didn't even stop to think about that. . . . But after I started getting that $50 a week for 'Get Happy' and I was able to buy my privacy, that was it. It wasn't really so much the songwriting, because, as I told you before, I did not *know*. I took on the job of writing songs without even being conscious of all the problems that would make. As if I'd done it all my life! But that privacy . . . that was what rang the bell for me and made me stick to songwriting. That's what hit me then, and to this very day. I love my privacy."

He waved a hand at the walls, covered with fine pictures; at the bookshelves filled with volumes, with awards for songwriting, with autographed pictures of his many friends; at the stacks of records and the hi-fi . . . and then at his grand piano. "I can sit in here at my piano and be as goddam nutty melodically as I want to. And when I catch something, down it goes. Another 'jot.' And when I like it, I pray that the lyric-writer will like it, and it'll raise a storm sometimes. Most times not, but my batting average has been pretty good."

We had been in his study for almost two hours. "Are you running out of throat now?" I asked.

He nodded. "Don't usually talk so much."

"Just a couple of things more," I said. "What about the music today?"

He groaned. "I don't know. You can't tell any more. Nobody wants melody. The kids are ignoring it so completely. This is such a percussive era, you know? Could be a fellow like me is out of date. But there are some signs of hope. *No, No, Nanette* is one of them. Singers like Sonny and Cher are moving away from singing that *farkakteh** stuff, to singing old standards. There are signs of change, of getting back to what I could call the art of pop, the well-knit, the well-written song—away from those percussive things that say nothing."

I gathered up my notes and put them away—and offered one final query. "I know a lot of your fellow composers are ducking the theatre, staying far away from it. But supposing somebody brought you a book you liked—would you do a show on Broadway *now*?"

And as quickly as the question was out, there came Arlen's answer: "Try me."

---

* A Yiddish word, which translates (politely) into "junk."

'People Who Need People'

(Jule Styne)

IT IS a sultry mid-August afternoon in 1971. Anyone in Manhattan who can get up the price of a ticket or a Kinney car rental has fled the borough for Fire Island, or the Hamptons, Fairfield County, Bucks, or the Jersey shore.

Not Jule Styne. He is in his office. To reach him, take a walk down 51st Street, cross Broadway, and go to the stage door of the Mark Hellinger Theatre. No, there's nothing playing there; it's been dark since *Coco* left months ago. There isn't even a stage doorman on duty to bar the way. Inside the backstage, dim light, the lingering odor of old canvas scenery and dancers' rehearsal shoes. The vast stage is bare. This fall it will be filled with the trappings of *Jesus Christ Superstar*, but today the place is as silent as the waiting room of Frank E. Campbell's funeral home.

Where's Jule? Up two flights of the dingy stairs, in a small converted dressing-room suite. There's a small piano in the corner. The desk is littered with books and manuscripts. And the walls are hung with window cards advertising all his past shows, the hits along with the flops. *Gypsy* cheek by jowl with *Say, Darling, Gentlemen Prefer Blondes* and *High Button Shoes*, side by side with *Something More, Peter Pan* next to *Subways Are for Sleeping*. It's a brave display; most show-business people are reluctant to be reminded of their failures. Not Jule Styne.

He's a short man in his mid-sixties, wearing a pair of slacks and a sport shirt, his sparse hair is grown long in today's style, and he exudes energy, both physical and verbal. Jule never sits down. The thoughts keep tumbling out of his head in rapid-fire clusters. Sometimes he speaks so rapidly that he changes subject in mid-sentence. "Jule," remarked one of his friends, "speaks pure Martian."

Manhattan has been temporarily evacuated, but on this muggy afternoon Jule is working. He and Bob Merrill, lyricist of *Funny Girl*, are doing the score for *Sugar*, the musical-comedy version of the film *Some Like It Hot*. By putting it into rehearsal, David Merrick rolled the dice (and $700,000 to $800,000 cash) in what gamblers refer to as a very long shot. These days there are few producers who have the guts and the bankroll to try their luck with a musical comedy. You can count on the fingers of one hand the composers who are still gainfully employed writing original music for potential Broadway shows. Jule Styne is one of them.

When this fact is mentioned, Jule shrugs it off as if it were of no importance. "It's always a gamble," he says. "If it weren't, everybody would be doing it. The bigger the odds, the bigger the payoff. So what do you want to know about me?"

Before one can even pose a question, he has begun to talk. Which is par for the course with Jule. ("I'll tell you what it's like, working with Jule," said one of his collaborators. "You're driving in a small sports car, with the windows closed and the top up, and you're in the mountains, and you go down a pass at seventy miles an hour, your brakes are locked, you're skidding—and all the time there's this hornet inside the car with you, buzzing around your head. That buzzing is Jule!")

The basic vital statistics are already known. Born in London in 1905. Eight years later his parents moved to Chicago. Of such musical talent was young Jule that at the age of nine he was a piano soloist with the Chicago and Detroit symphony orchestras. By the age of thirteen he'd won a scholarship to the Chicago School of Music. There he amassed a thorough education in harmony, theory, and composition. But instead of following a classical-music career, Jule was seduced by the new rhythms of jazz and pop. He took a job as pianist with various Chicago bands, and played with Phil Spitalny, who had one of the leading dance orchestras of the day. In 1931 he organized his own musical group and began writing songs. One of them was a hit; it was called "Sunday." Then he came to New York, which, as today, was Mecca.

"I used to be the top vocal coach out of New York—teaching people how to sing the songs, how to use their hands, how to get a charisma, have some relationship with the audience. I did a good job with Harry Richman [a singing star of the early '30s], and Joe Schenck got to know me and my work. He was a very big man in the movie business; sent me out to California to work at Fox, for Zanuck, as a vocal coach for all the people who were in Fox musicals. That was in the mid-'30s when Zanuck had all those people—Alice Faye, Tony Martin, the Ritz Brothers.

"After I'd worked for Zanuck for about a year, he said to me, 'Jule, you're in a luxury business. You ought to write songs. Have you written a song?' 'Yes,' I told him, 'I wrote two songs back there, but I thought it was square to write songs. I thought old people write songs.' Zanuck said, 'No, that is a commodity

out here. Coaching people they will eventually do away with, but songs they
have to have out here—it's your secondary asset.' So I said, 'Why don't you give
me a job here at Fox writing songs?' He said, 'Here we only hire $2,500-a-week
songwriters. You have to go somewhere else and then I'll bring you back here.'
So I said, 'Then get me a job.' He said, 'I'll tell you what. I have a good friend
at Republic Studios, Moe Siegel, and he's talked to me. He wants to know how
to make musicals, a cheap musical. I told him there is a market for it. So let me
call him.' And Zanuck called him up right in front of me. And he hung up and
said, 'I'll tell you what. You've got to gamble. I gamble. Everybody who wants
to do something else has got to gamble. You get $900 a week coaching people,
you're going to get $165 a week over there at Republic, but you're going to write
songs. You'll be the only one there to write. So just pretend that you're investing,
betting on yourself. You're a gambling guy, *bet.*'

"So I went to Republic to write songs, but I found out that plus writing
the songs, I had to wash the sink, wash Roy Rogers and his horse, Gene Autry
and *his* horse—everything. I found out I was walking in the slush with the
wagons in their Westerns, I was conducting the orchestra and arranging
the music, everything—but songs I'd get to write. I started writing songs, and the
first script I had to work on was a movie called *Sis Hopkins.* They had Judy
Canova there.* They also had John Wayne at Republic. So they said, 'Who do
you want to write the words?' I said, 'Frank Loesser.' 'Where's he?' 'Paramount.'
So they made a trade. They swapped John Wayne for a picture to get Frank
Loesser; that was the deal. Well, Frank Loesser came over to Republic and I
played him some tunes—he hated me because I'd degraded him. He was on
his way up at Paramount, and here he drops down to nothing—not to Metro
was he loaned out, but *Republic!* I knew him because I had been loaned out
from 20th Century-Fox to Paramount on one of his pictures. But now he said
he hated me. He said, 'Look, I'm here for three weeks. I want to finish everything
we have to do in a week—not turn it in until three weeks, but I won't be here
the last two weeks.' He gave me that kind of big-time stuff. I said all right. He
said, 'Well, play me some tunes.' So the first song I played him was a tune that
went *da-da da da da da.*" And Styne sings a very familiar melodic refrain in a
true, high voice.

"Loesser said, 'What's that tune? It has something! Gee, that's a great song.
Shhh! We won't write that *here.* I'll borrow you from here to Paramount. *Don't
write that here.*' He was that kind of a schemer. So, later he called that 'I Don't
Want to Walk Without You, Baby.' But we weren't going to write that at Republic. 'Quiet. Don't play. Lock that up. I've got a picture coming up there in
three months. Because of this tune, I borrow you *now.* Right?' I said, 'Gee,
that's great.' So we wrote the picture *Sis Hopkins* for Judy Canova. It was much
too good a score, a marvelous score, some marvelous songs, but much too good,

* Republic, a San Fernando Valley studio, specialized in low-budget "quickies."
Miss Canova's appeal was rural-based. A Republic executive once said, "City people we
don't need. We make these pictures to play in theatres you never heard of, to people
you never met—and the profit is guaranteed." Republic musicals, usually barnyard-
oriented, starred Miss Canova, the Weaver Brothers and Elviry, and Shug Fisher, and
in the trade were fondly referred to as "shit-kickers." Their plots were simplistic to a
point where the story often became invisible. But the resultant black ink on the Republic
books was not.

they didn't even understand it. We had Gabby Hayes there. If Gabby was eating a piece of watermelon, the song would be called 'I Like Watermelon.' Right on the head. Not 'The Sun is Shining Today and You're Happy,' just 'I Like Watermelon!' I wrote about 150 songs there. And I learned a lot. Listen, you know who the writers were on the lot then? Isobel Lennart, Mike Frankovich, Jerry Chodorov, Joe Fields*—everybody was learning. You know, we were having a lot of fun!

"But Loesser was responsible for me, because the first song I wrote in the big time was 'I Don't Want to Walk Without You, Baby' and then 'I Said Yes, She Said No'—in the same Paramount movie! So then I got two more pictures with Frank at Paramount based on those two hits, and we were really going together. I mean, Christ, we just had a great time. And then he went into the Army. When he went into the Army, I asked him who should I write with now. Unashamed, he said, 'You've been spoiled, there's no one like me.' He said, 'I'll tell you what. If you want someone like me, don't get a clever rhymer, because there is a thing called a rhyming dictionary. Anybody can rhyme, you can find a rhyme for anything. But get a guy who can say something clever and warm, because you need warm lyrics for your music.'

"So there was a picture called *Youth on Parade* that a fellow named Cohen, Al Cohen, was producing. He's no longer alive. Very nice fellow. And now, when I come back to Republic with two hit songs at Paramount, you know, it's a whole different ballgame. They now *ask* me, and now they're recording there with forty-six men! They never paid a flute $135 for a date before. The music contractor says, 'Why do we need a flute? We never used a flute here.' I said, 'It's a very important instrument.' 'Harps? We're walking in the mud and you want *harps?*' They're paying $10 a page for orchestration—always paid $3. They were kind of shaken, but they went with me because it must be right. I must be right if I've written hit songs with Frank Loesser. Then they said, 'Why didn't you write the song hits *here?* We had Frank Loesser here.' I said, 'Because it's the quality. You didn't record well enough, you didn't give it class—but from now on it will be fine.'

"So this producer, Al Cohen, tells me about Sammy Cahn. He had just broken with Saul Chaplin. I'll be frank, I didn't want to write with Sammy Cahn because Sammy then was a rhymer. Rather than going back to his plain Jewish ethnic simplicity, he was now going to become Johnny Mercer. And Johnny Mercer then wasn't fancy, he wrote what he knew. Everybody writes best what they know. Like Al Dubin† around that time. They all wrote simple. Cohen told me, 'You know, Cahn is a talented guy.' I said, 'Sure, he's talented, but I just came off Frank Loesser and I want to go further.' He said, 'You'll go further, but I tell you, Jule, he's good enough for this job, and he needs a job. He's had a lot of experience—in fact, more than you.'

"I said, 'You want him, Al? Okay. I'm under contract here by the week, so what I write I don't get any extra money for. Will Sammy, who's not under

---

* Isobel Lennart became an enormously successful screenwriter, and wrote the book for *Funny Girl* on Broadway. Mike Frankovich became the head of production at Columbia Pictures. Jerome Chodorov and Joseph Fields went on to write such Broadway hits as *My Sister Eileen, Junior Miss,* and *Wonderful Town.*

† Lyricist for a long string of successes, especially with Harry Warren, at Warner Brothers including *42nd Street* and the *Gold Diggers* films.

contract, write twelve songs for $1,100? It's unbelievable.' He said, 'Believe me, he'll write for $400, he wants to work with you.'

"So we sat down and I played Sammy a song; actually, I played him some of the tunes that I started with Loesser for a movie that never materialized at Paramount. And Sammy hears the song and the first thing he says is 'I heard that song.' I said, 'You never heard this song! Only one guy has heard this song, Frank Loesser.' 'No,' he said, 'the *name* of the song is going to be "I've Heard That Song Before"!' That was the first song I wrote with Sammy—this is about 1942. A tremendous hit. And we had unbelievable success. We went, according to ASCAP [you were elevated from one class to another by performance], from $400 a quarter, $1,600 a year, to Double A—the top rating—in seven and a half years! That's the amount of hits we had. What it takes some fellows twenty-five years to get, we did in seven and a half—and we never asked for the raises. It was phenomenal. We had as many as three and four songs on the Hit Parade at one time. One time we had the number-*one*, number-*two*, number-*three* songs! It was just hit after hit. Rather embarrassing. I melodically wrote for singers, because I was coaching singers, and I knew, every song I was writing, where the singers would fall apart. Sammy was coming in there with fresh ideas and we just caught on. We started out with 'I Heard That Song Before,' tremendous hit. Then we wrote 'It's Been a Long, Long Time,' 'I'll Walk Alone,' 'Victory Polka,' 'It's Magic,' 'Five Minutes More,' 'Time After Time.' Oh God, I can't tell you, but every year we had three or four big songs going all the time. Big ones. Million-copy song hits, and two, three-million record singles."

Jule pauses to catch his breath.

"We got many pictures, clippings of guys overseas, our soldiers when they were taking over. 'I'll Walk Alone' spelled out on a German fence: 'I'll Walk *Cologne.*' When we landed on the Anzio beachhead, 'Victory Polka.' When they came back, 'It's Been a Long, Long Time.' While they were away, 'Saturday Night Is the Loneliest Night of the Week.' 'Let It Snow, Let It Snow.' 'Time After Time' was a Sinatra. We wrote a lot of songs for Sinatra, tremendous amount. For *Anchors Aweigh* we did the whole score . . . we couldn't get out of our own way! But writing songs was kind of a professional thing for me. I didn't have to be inspired because I knew where I was going all the time.

"I began to hate California, because I saw things happening. It was no place where I could rise higher and stay there and move ahead on my own, because it was a belt, it was a factory. Too many people participated. They were scavenging on what I created. By the time it got through, it didn't make any sense. I saw fellows around me who were big when I came to California and in just a short span of three or four years they were getting less and less. Fellas like Harry Warren. I saw them dismissing him. I saw that. And I didn't want to be one of those dismissed people, because I didn't start to write songs until late in my life, until I was thirty-five. You know, it wasn't as if I started like those other guys when they were twenty years old, back in New York. So I wanted some place to show my talents. Something that would draw on my talents. I knew California didn't draw on your talents, because you were *told* what to do. And I decided that the best way was to go to some medium where you either fail or achieve success, but you are betting on yourself.

"I was very enamored of the Dramatists Guild contract here in New York—to think that what I write *has* to be played unless *I* decide to rewrite it. I'd met some fellas here, playwrights, and I was enamored of it all. So in California

I decided that I must do a show, and we found this thing in the paper, in the Sunday magazine section of the *New York Times*. It showed a Model-T Ford and the whole family. I said, 'My God, there's a good idea for a musical, go back to the turn of the century.'

"I got Sammy, who was very reluctant to do the show, because he now had the thing he was looking for. He liked the swimming pool, you know. He was big there, he could go from house to house and play his parodies, and he loved that, but I wanted to get another environment. I finally convinced him to do the show anyhow, *High Button Shoes*. We got Jerome Robbins and all the big people, and it was a tremendous success.* A big leap for me. But I knew that I hadn't succeeded yet, even though there were the two big songs in it.

"And also, in that first show, I worked with George Abbott and Robbins and Oliver Smith and Miles White—it was kind of a class thing. And I *learned*—oh, did I learn what I didn't know! In California they would have you believe that you know it all. 'He's the best.' *Why?* Because I wrote a song? Because you write a hit song for a movie? My God, you had the publisher hammering away, because the publishing company was owned by the movie company, and they hammer away on it! *No!* There's more to it! I saw there is something very fascinating to this composing thing. What about those other fellows, Rodgers and Cole Porter? How about that avenue for me? I said, 'I'm starting late in life, but I'll give it a try.' The theatre was kind of a closed shop then, you know—Cole Porter was doing a show, or Berlin was doing a show, or Kurt Weill, or it was Kern, but it was a closed shop. And right on top of *High Button Shoes* I decided to stay here. I decided that I wouldn't build my career around Sinatra. Why should I build my career around Sinatra? I'd found myself writing out there with Sinatra in my mind all the time; it's like that, the Hollywood pattern. You get one hit, you write another Dick Powell song, another Alice Faye song. 'Gee, Alice Faye will sing that.' Or, 'I bet Judy Garland will sing that.' It took me a long time to break away, but finally I said, 'When Dick Rodgers writes a song, he doesn't know who's going to sing it yet. Somebody along the way, but it's for *everybody*.'

"I was studying librettos, too, looking at what Gershwin had written, what Kurt Weill had written. I was looking at stuff and examining it. See, the whole thing here in New York—nobody knew what anyone else was doing, they only knew what you were doing when you went to bat. A publisher called me up and said, "Do you want to do a musical for me called *Gentlemen Prefer Blondes?*' This was right after I'd written *Shoes*. They said, 'We know you, you can write the hell out of that period.' Because in that period I'd been playing piano for Harry Richman and for Fannie Brice, and for many, many stars that came to the Chez Paree,† you know, so I knew that period well. I knew where it was. So I did it. We cast around for the lead. I said, 'Listen, I saw a girl in a revue in California that is the greatest Lorelei, and incidentally her revue is coming here next week, *Lend an Ear*.' I brought the girl up to an audition; they thought I was crazy. Anita Loos said, 'It's got to be a *tiny* little gold digger.' 'Look,' I said, 'that's what's going to make it different. You're not going to do it the way you did it ten years ago. This girl will be the caricature of *all* blondes,' and it was Carol Channing. I got three or four hits in that thing.

* In the score were "Papa, Won't You Dance with Me?," "I Still Get Jealous," and a classic Keystone Kops ballet choreographed by Robbins.
† A popular night club of the '20s and '30s in Chicago.

"But then, want to hear something amazing? What *really* made me? See, you have to be kind of a person here on Broadway, you have to be a *mensch** here too, in New York more than California, 'cause here they watch you work. It was back during the McCarthy witch-hunt, when the writers in Hollywood, all those talented guys, were blacklisted, not allowed to work or write, that I did *Pal Joey*. That was the first time I *produced* a show. Won the Drama Critics' Award—first time a revival had won it. And this is what made me, now; on top of two hits, this happened.

"When I'm producing *Pal Joey*, I say to myself, 'Gee, I worked with Sammy long enough, I know how this ballgame goes in producing, there's more to it than getting an actor cheaper or a writer cheaper. You've got to get the *right* people. So I got the author, the late John O'Hara, and Richard Rodgers, the composer of *Joey*, and I find that they don't speak to each other. Which is a terrible thing. I'm doing a revival and they don't speak to each other, and what if I want to make a change, a dramatic change or a musical change? At least if they were in good shape, I'd be able to talk to them together. You know, when the show originally opened, Mr. Atkinson of the *Times* said, 'You can't pour sweet water from a sour well.' He loathed it. Yet *Joey* was the inside thing, the okay thing, the flip thing with all the gay ones and the sad ones, all the lost souls. So we come to casting. I say, 'I don't want the original guy who played the part of the agent, Jack Durant; I want a guy that is really a kind of mod-looking guy.' I wanted Lionel Stander, and you will never believe what the newspapers did to me personally. They accused me of being a Communist because Lionel Stander took the Fifth Amendment. And I started getting stuff from some guy, must have been a Bircher, sent me magazines and testimonies that prove Stander's un-American, and Dick Rodgers was being pressured and John O'Hara was being pressured.

"And John O'Hara and Dick Rodgers walked up to me one day—they had had lunch for the *first* time—and they told me, 'We hope you will not be intimidated by all this adverse propaganda because the only thing that counts is can Lionel Stander play this part.' I said, 'What a thing that is. Thank you, guys, because whether you liked it or not I had no intention of anything else. I'd walk away, give me my money, I don't do the show. *If* Lionel Stander misbehaves in the part, he gets fired because he didn't do his part right, but as far as that other goes, nothing.' I walked down 44th Street, and I had more fellas slap me on the back. It didn't dawn on me that it was because I did that. Lionel Stander was still in the part. . . . Well, I found such enthusiasm, such marvelous things in the theatre, that I couldn't help but say the theatre is the place.†

"I'd like to skip to another show I produced, *Mr. Wonderful*. I saw Sammy Davis at Ciro's when he made his big debut. Twenty-four out of twenty-six performances. I decided to bring this kid to the Street. He wanted to do an evening—first half of the Palace kind of thing. I said, 'No, you're a talented little guy. I'm going to try and find something for you.' Then I go up to the William

---

* Yiddish for "man," but meaning someone who has proved himself.

† Styne is making another very large point. The time he referred to, the '50s, the McCarthy era of blacklisting, was a nightmarish period in the arts. Films, television, radio, all such public media were subject to acute pressures from self-appointed censors. Talented performers were tried and convicted by shadowy behind-the-scenes figures. Many were hounded out of the country. The New York theatre was one of the few bastions—albeit a shaky one—of constitutional freedoms.

Morris agency and get Joe Stein—the very kind of fellow who had a heart full of things he wanted to say, but where he was, in TV, he could never even write that kind of joke. Everything there was 'Be careful or we scratch it out.'

"Anyway, in *Mr. Wonderful* we had a scene which I think was ironic, because I was in Florida playing in a band in 1927–8–9, and I know how the black thing was going down there. Christ's sake, they were lynching them and everything else. Georgia, Florida, it was unbelievable. We had a Jewish banjo player in our band, Leo Kaplan, who was taken off the train by a mob of guys because he had a date with some little girl! They just pulled him off the train. Guys came in, we were afraid, we were in a private car, no policeman. They stopped that train right out of West Palm Beach and took this boy off! Beat the hell out of him and left him in the road, and he was picked up and taken to the hospital and sent back. So I know about that.

"In the scene, in Joe Stein's scene, I said, 'Fellas, look, this is 1956. There are going to be half black actors and half white actors in this scene.' The director said, 'You mean you're going to have black people in Florida, back then, when you're doing a period show?' I said, 'What's the difference? There they are now walking along Miami Beach, blacks and whites.' They weren't black; they were people. They were *tourists*. With big sport shirts. And I want to let you know, the critics hated me for that. They knocked this show out, eight for eight. *Mr. Wonderful*. And because Sammy wore horn-rimmed glasses and spoke in kind of an intellectual manner with Jack Carter, who was his buddy, a white boy who discovered him—that was the story.

"So I got the theatre in my blood, I *felt* it. My God, I belonged to some kind of society. I found here a very enthusiastic society of creative people and they were giving of themselves and there was a great spirit of something. I came from a company town to an open shop, and I said, 'Isn't it marvelous that I can come to a place where I say "I am a *producer*"?' I couldn't say I'm a producer in California. 'What do you mean you're a producer? We won't give you a job as a producer.' So here I'm the producer. I've a hit show, *Pal Joey*. I'm doing what I want, I'm doing the kind of show with Sammy Davis, Jr., nobody else wants to put on. I don't care if it failed, we got all our money, we didn't lose any money. Jesus, what a wonderful thing.

"I wanted once in a while to do a movie, but I found that I was in a way ostracized in California because, well, everybody knew my temperament pretty good, because I told off all those guys, including Harry Cohn, with whom I did six pictures, Zanuck, Sam Goldwyn. Zanuck—I must say that was the biggest day in my life, when he hired me back and gave me $75,000 to write the music for a picture as a composer, when he was the first one who gave me a start. It was a movie for Betty Grable. A very bad one. Something about springtime. Leo Robin did the lyrics. Very bad movie. Gwen Verdon was in it, and Shirley MacLaine—she was a dancer.

"I had some very good friends in California, like Sol Siegel and Buddy Adler, and I came back out to work. It's 1953, and Sinatra is invited to do a movie with Marilyn Monroe, just these two talents, and I'm back working with my old partner Sammy Cahn. I walked in to Sol Siegel. Now, I'm coming off three big hits, *Shoes*, *Blondes*, and I'm the producer of *Pal Joey*. And Sol Siegel doesn't like me around because I won the Drama Critics' Award. I'm a producer and I'm a fink. He's the kind that doesn't want to take a back seat to me. He figures I'll probably save my best songs for my next show. I said, 'Listen, Sol, let me straighten you out. You're the producer and I'm a Hollywood songwriter and I know how it goes, Sol.' Well, we wrote this marvelous score which was never done, and the score is finished, and we're told they are not going to make the film. And Sol calls me in and says, 'I got a picture that is terrible, I made it in Italy, it's awful. We need a title song.' So we write him a song called 'Three Coins in the Fountain.' As you know, without the song the picture would have gotten nothing; *with* the song it got about $8,000,000 or $9,000,000 gross at that time. That was my last collaboration with Sammy and goodbye again.*

"Then I looked over the whole Hollywood thing good again. I had said, 'I am going to go with a different kind of lyric-writer now. I'm going with the so-called "in" group,' and I did a revue with Comden and Green, *Two on the Aisle*. I knew their shortcomings, but I also knew what they gave me. They gave me a lot, too; they added to my cranium, another level. It's a marvelous thing, what it does, your knowing people and understanding comedy and knowing what people can do. You know, you *say*, 'Oh, Bert Lahr is funny.' But you really don't know Bert Lahr until you *work* with him to see how really talented and gifted he is. Tremendous, a classic comedian, not just a fellow who can buy you a cheap laugh with a *Gnong, gnong, gnong!* I found him to be a man with great, great understanding, and he did a thing to me as great as anything Chaplin ever did. It was grandiose. The character Bert was playing was Siegfried, and we mixed up a finale. Brünnhilde was in a fire up there and Bert walked down and looked at her upstage, and she was screaming to him, '*Ho yo to ho, ho yo to ho.*' The fire was burning and whatnot, the Rhinemaidens on the side, it was a combination of all Wagner girls, nude in the forest, nude girls in the trees, and Bert walked down, very noble, almost like Richard II, and he looked at the fire and took out a seltzer bottle and put the whole fire out. But with such great dignity; he wasn't doing just a burlesque act, he played it as if he had a chore, like 'My God, there's a fire, and I'll put it out and save this girl,' and he just squirted the seltzer out, and he came down and said, 'And *that* was that.' Such a scream I never heard from an audience.

"And so you learn. From Comden and Green I then met Leland Hayward and *Peter Pan* with Mary Martin, and then I came back with Comden and Green. One day they walked in to me and they said, 'We gotta see you.' At my apartment they held up the back page of the telephone book and there was a girl with all kinds of wires plugged into her body and she says, 'Answer phones?' They said, 'Is this a musical?' and I said, 'My God, it is sensational,' and they sat down and wrote a story of *Bells Are Ringing*. And then we did a couple of things of lesser importance—but all the time batting.

"I went to bat twice a year. I did two shows every season because I wanted to practice my art. Because I went back to the old days—how did Rodgers and Hart, and how did Gershwin, and how did Kern, how did Cole Porter acquire such a catalogue? Fifteen hundred or two thousand songs, which I hadn't. How? Because then, in those days, a hit show only ran for four, five months. All of those shows—Ethel Merman in her biggest hit, eight months, and then she started a new one. So I wasn't doing it for that; I was practicing, I was acquiring, because out of every show, good or not good, comes a song. Like out of *Do, Re, Mi* came 'Make Someone Happy,' which is a giant; out of *Peter Pan* came 'Never Never Land.' Of course, out of *Bells Are Ringing* came three songs—'The Party's

* See Sammy Cahn's account of their collaboration, in the next chapter.

Over,' 'Just in Time,' and 'Long Before I Knew You.' And from Comden and Green I learned a technique—that in accompanying comedy you had to be a dramatist; the *music* had to be funny, too. All the Hollywood composers—and I have respect for all of them, Mancini or whoever it might be—they are not dramatists, because when they get a picture, the score has *already* been dramatized. The director has directed the picture; they are only *accompanying* the drama.

"In some strange way, all the guys that have made their way in the musical theatre as composers are *dramatists*, because they have given the character. When you can give characterization, you are a dramatist. So I was growing up with this all the time, layer upon layer of know-how, and then came *Gypsy*. Of course, that was the biggest kind of landmark that ever was for me. I became the superb dramatist out of that because, God, I mean, to me that was like *Traviata*—that first act, writing a thing like 'Everything's Coming Up Roses,' which was so macabre, with this child thing, and the woman crying, and all that. It was just unbelievable. It was, of course, one of the greatest shows I have done.

"And then came *Funny Girl*, which brought Barbra Streisand, who scored a tremendous hit. A very big dramatic score, and in it a song called 'People' and 'Don't Rain on My Parade.' In the theatre I never go out of my way to write a hit song. When we wrote 'Just in Time' in *Bells Are Ringing*, we didn't write it for a hit song; we wrote the *character*, a flip kind of character who was taken out of the gutter by a girl who was actually an answering-service girl who couldn't be herself but had to be someone else because of the complex psychological problem. And the song happened to fit the situation—it was a comedy situation, mind you. In the scene people were watching them dancing in the park, and they were doing a comedy routine, but the song *emerged*. And 'The Party's Over' was not written for a hit song, but it happened. In the movies you get assignments *only* if you write hit songs. Since *Funny Girl* in '63, it's been hard to come by a good libretto.

"The thing I have got to go by, I tell you, with all my dramatic know-how and everything, is if they don't *understand* what I am writing about, then it is for naught. I found that *Gypsy* was understood. Well, it had four powerful big songs in it.* And that is what I am supposed to do, not write hit songs but *music* they'll remember from that dramatic entity, as they remember an aria of Verdi's from an opera. You can't just write special material. You remember nothing in *Follies*, nothing in *Company*, nothing in *Applause*. The point is you shouldn't *try* for the popular song, but, indeed, what do you whistle when you walk up an aisle? Out of an opera you remember an aria, whatever it is, you walk up the aisle, the music is playing, yes, it was a beautiful thing, whatever it might be!"

Gypsy was everything Styne says it was, a landmark in American musical comedy, with a near-perfect book by Arthur Laurents, Sondheim's superb lyrics, and the whole staged brilliantly by Jerome Robbins. But talk about it? No way. Jule has caught his breath and is gone, twenty conversational yards ahead.

"I've always done things to prove things to myself. I never wanted to live in a dream and say, 'Boy, if I had a chance, how I would have done it!' I said to myself, 'Jule Styne, take it on.' Tony Richardson called me and asked if I'd

---

* Six, Mr. Styne: "Everything's Coming Up Roses," "Together," "You'll Never Get Away from Me," "Let Me Entertain You," "Some People," "Rose's Turn."

like to score a play, Bertolt Brecht's *Arturo Ui.* I said I'd always wanted to score
a picture and they would never let me. Yeah, *why not?* Two hours of music I
did, pages and pages. What I used was a Dixieland band and an organ. Took
place in Chicago. In Chicago, Dixieland was the thing, and the organ gave it a
dramatic tonality, overtones of tragedy. You don't hold up signs and say 'Listen
to this,' but it spelled it. I was very satirical. I knew that Mr. Brecht had done
it and so I was competing with Mr. Brecht. Some notices said Brecht would
have loved what I had done.

"Then, all of a sudden, a certain respect grows, not because of what you
did but *how* you did it, and your understanding. And, incidentally, they always
expect more from you. The only trouble with the theatre critics is that if you
do something that five years ago they said was sensational, they expect better
this time, you are supposed to do better. That is a very tough thing. Like with
Irving Berlin, they said *Annie Get Your Gun* was not one of his best scores.
Now, for God's sakes! Or Cole Porter, they said *Can-Can* was not one of *his*
best scores. They expected more, my God! But there were five or six hits in
each one of those shows I mentioned, so what did they want?

"But I'll tell you what it does do—it makes you sit up straight all the time
when you are working. You become important to yourself. You really do. Even
though they don't like it or they do like it, it becomes secondary to you yourself.
There you are, you're going to work, you're writing. I write here with a bench
and a piano. I give it my all, which I find I cannot do in California. I find some
of these younger kids getting together with a dollar and a half, like that movie
Joe, where they work and put it together and must work twenty-four hours a
day. And that kind of enthusiasm is hardly inspiration, it's perspiration. I think
only amateurs have to be inspired in some ways. You're a professional, you do
your job. The inspiration comes later on when you have already got something
and are inspired to make it better, better than it is. Write. When I write a score
for a play, just to give you an idea, I write between forty and fifty songs to get
sixteen. Sometimes they accept this, and I come back, but I *change* this, and
they say, 'Gee, this is better,' or 'No, we'll keep the original.' But I test. I *draw*
on myself. I'm that enthusiastic.

"I want to tell you something. I have done six shows with Jerome Robbins,
and if there is such a word as genius, he is the only genius I have met in motion
pictures, theatre, or any medium. Truly an ingenious man. All this work in the
ballet, and the things he has done such as *Fiddler on the Roof* and *West Side
Story* and *Gypsy* and all the things—you just pile one on top of the other. Say
that he is something very, very special. And the theatre allows you to mingle
with these fellows, and discuss with these fellows, and really, whether they use
your ideas or not, you can tell them how you feel, and you become part of it.
Whereas in motion pictures you have no license to discuss. How can you walk
up to any major director and say, 'Listen, I'd like to tell you something—I don't
think you're getting all the comedy out of that'? He'd say, 'Well, do *you* want
to direct the picture?' The guy says, 'Get him off.' I'm talking about the old days
especially. Now *here*, in New York, you say this to a man, and you're in hearing
distance of three or four people. And the lyric-writer comes and says so-and-so,
and a choreographer comes to say such-and-such, and it's a thing called collaboration. There's a collaboration between an actor and a director; if it works, you
get the greatest thing of all time. But if you get that director who says, 'No, do
it *my* way,' you're only getting half of the actor. You know, it's a Garbo directed

by Lubitsch, as against a Garbo directed by someone else like Victor Fleming. It's McCarey at his best getting that performance *going* for you—or Capra. It's nobody at Metro making it with Gable until he came to Columbia, and then there was something going.* It was nobody getting a thing out of Gene Kelly at Metro until he came to Columbia to make *Cover Girl.* You know, sometimes it's the head of the studio that says, 'Gee, you're the greatest.' Like Harry Cohn was mad about Gene Kelly.

"Robbins has always gotten something out of me; he never settled with me, but he's allowed me to *say.* He said, 'Let Jule *talk.* He'll say how many things, but he's intuitively on to something. He may say eighty-one things no good, but *watch out* for the eighty-second thing—it may be the whole play!' He doesn't let everybody talk—he can tell whether you know it or not.

"I had the biggest fight with Jerome Robbins on my first show, *High Button Shoes.* I said, 'You get Lenny Bernstein or Morton Gould. You have to *tell* me what you *want* or I can't give it to you. Goodbye.' He's doing the ballet. He calls me up in about an hour and says, 'Can you come to my house for dinner tonight?' So I go and we sit down—no anger or nothing—and he says, 'I want to play you some records.' Then he played me a Richard Strauss piece and he played a couple of piano etudes, Scarlatti etudes, and I said, 'What has *that* got?' And he said, 'Nothing. I thought I would just cleanse the atmosphere.' Then he said, 'You will write, probably—because I know you have the greatest sense of humor of any composer I ever worked with, and I have worked with a lot of them like Bernstein, Gould, but *you*—you have a sense of humor that is un-believable. Whether you can execute it, I don't know, but you are damn well going to make a try at it. I want you to write me forty-five minutes of music about a day at the beach—any beach. I am going to be a little more specific than that. You see, when I tell a fellow to write me a ballet, I don't choreograph—you write me a piece of music, then I choreograph. Lenny did that with me in *On the Town* and *Fancy Free.*' Robbins still does that. Play the music and *then* choreograph.

"So I said, 'Will you help me?' and he says, 'Yes.' And I said, 'I'll tell you—I will write eight minutes' worth of the nine characters in the ballet. I will not connect them. I would rather do that because I can connect them however you want to connect them. The entrance music for each character I won't write. I will do that second. See if I've got the characters first.' He says, 'Gee, that's interesting. Might be a good way.'

"Going back to my very beginning, with Frank Loesser, we used to come home and have a few drinks and he would make up some funny songs, not parodies. He had a song called 'Whatever Became of Minnie?' *'Ahoy, Minnie, oh, whatever became of Minnie J. McGee—the Admiral married Minnie, I won-der if she ever did what she used to do for you and you and you and me?'* There was a tune for that, completely forgotten. I used it for the two sisters in the ballet. But the thing that I knocked Robbins out with completely was when I wrote for the Keystone Kops in the ballet. He said, 'For you to write a thing like the Second Hungarian Rhapsody—my God, for them to be running around with tambourines when they do knee drops, the audience will fall down. It's absurd!'

" 'Jerry,' I said, 'you cannot rewrite Bernstein, you cannot rewrite Stra-

* Styne refers to *It Happened One Night,* which Capra made with Gable.

vinsky, it's that or nothing. If you make *like*, it's no good. When guys make like you, it's no good. If they make an original, that's fine, but you don't *make like*. And so, since it's absurd, and since it's Keystone comedy, and since we are looking back in time, I think it is quite wild to use the *actual* Second Hungarian Rhapsody.'

"Well, that is the first time I ever saw an audience of fifteen hundred people stand up and yell, 'Bravo.' The whole audience in the middle of the thing. I never saw anything like it."

Like something out of the musical Theatre of the Absurd?

"Yes, but the word 'absurd' is *anything* you do wild. It's absurd, and in going wild, it's just going *over the edge*. Once you go over the edge, you can do *anything*. What's on the other side of the mountain? On the other side of the mountain is the something we dare not allow ourselves. It borders—it's between sanity and insanity. And you get a chance—not all the time, 'cause you don't want to do it all the time—you get a chance to go wild. But you have to be ready for the occasion. You have to know *when* to go wild."

Isn't he saying that you have to learn all the rules and *then* start breaking them?

He stands behind his desk. "*Yes*," he says after a moment.

But so many of the young people are not much interested in learning the rules, so they have nothing to break. They're starting in mid-air, so to speak. Would he not agree?

"Even to further what you just said," Jule says, having caught his breath, "which is right on the head, the people today in the arts have lost one thing. And that goes back to basic roots. They have no *tradition*, they have no *respect*, therefore they have no reference. Everything starts from *now*. Recall—the greatest writings that have lived maybe now four hundred, five hundred years, the greatest dramas, the great things—those people had a recall. Writing is recall. You recall, and then you throw it away and then you write, but you must have some reference to the world, reference to something, respect for someone—you don't have to be religious, but you have to know that it's *there*. Look, my mother died in 1947 and my father died in 1951. I suppose it's maybe every day, or every other day, that I recollect something in relationship to them, and there isn't a day that goes by that I don't tell some story about my father. Always very humorous. Some of it is very touching . . . so I am a human being.

"I have great respect for tradition. I know that Bach was marvelous. I know that Beethoven was rather a genius and Mozart was terribly talented, and I know that Ravel was something special, and I know those people, and every time I write I say, 'So-and-so would have liked that music.' I know *who* I am. I know *where* I am, all the time. But people today think they are making something new—and they are the most cliché, the most conforming group I have ever met in my life. Along comes a show called *Hair* with girl nudes, so they make a hundred nude shows! And that is a generation? Where is its originality? Now they have discovered God all over again. *Jesus Christ Superstar*. It's been going on for years. They have been singing that Biblical music since I was a kid in Chicago. Country music? My God, twenty-five years ago when I was writing pop songs, I went across the country in a car and I found out that in Texas they have got a different Hit Parade than in New York. Did *I* not write country music? Did I not write and have hits with Gene Autry at Republic Studios? Why would Republic make a $220,000 Gene Autry picture? Because they knew they would get $3,000,000 for every one, because they played it in Arizona, Texas, Arkansas, and Oklahoma. It never even came here. Later on, they heard of country music, they brought it here to the cities, there was a market for it. So all of a sudden we discover 'country music,' and that is all you will hear, country or rock music. They believe there's a big explosion, that what they have written is original, when it really isn't. Because right now we are going through a big transition in music. We are going back to the English language, with the advent of *No, No, Nanette,* with the coming back of Burt Bacharach's 'Raindrops Keep Falling on My Head'—which is a 1931 song, believe me, melodic in *texture.* So where are we? The tragedy of it all is that these kids become twenty-three or twenty-four and what can they refer to? Nudity? Therefore they have nothing to go on, so they go to nostalgia. They go to *our* time. You go to *No, No, Nanette,* and you find that sixty percent of the audience are young lions, and they love it!"

Styne is one of the few composers of his age group who is not depressed about the state of contemporary popular music.

"Why be depressed? I *love* guys like Jimmy Webb and Burt Bacharach. Listen, I discovered Burt when he was playing piano—when I was doing *Bells Are Ringing*—and I said, 'Jesus, where are you at?' Harry Nilsson, a lot of these guys, write good. Whether they can *survive,* I don't know. That is their problem, to survive. I wrote my first song in 1927—so now I am writing forty-four years, right? So I have survived forty-four years. My first hit in 1927—'Sunday.' Which I got married on. Tremendous song, sold a million copies, big hit." He sings a few bars. "My God, in 1963—from 1927 to 1963, thirty-six years—I had the number-one hit, 'People.' A whole new generation of new people. For the grandmothers 'Sunday,' for the grandchildren 'People,' and I'm still writing!

"But the thing is that I have been too hasty. In my anxiety to practice my work as Dick Rodgers and Larry Hart and Cole Porter did, I found myself doing two shows a year up until two years ago. And I have been doing a lot of bad shows, because there aren't any good books around. But I still practice my art. If you stop for a long time, no good. You have to practice. I don't care *what* you write, good, bad, rotten, write a short or long story, notes, a joke, find something, gotta write *something.* There is manuscript paper all over my house. I'll write any time. Playing golf this morning, I thought of something I should have done. This is—" he taps his forehead—"the greatest computer in the world. I teach it, and it plays back what I want it to play back. Now, I may forget what I sang to myself on the golf course, but sometime next month, next week, next year, two years, I will remember what I sang, it will come to me as I am sitting down."

The small dressing-room office is temporarily silent.

"So I have brought you up to date pretty much, haven't I?" Jule inquires.

All through his reminiscences there runs a remarkable parallel between Styne and his late friend Loesser—both the same kind of man. Both burst out of their early molds and grew and grew—and kept growing.

"We take it on," said Jule after a moment's thought. "It's called taking on challenges. You know, I never thought *The Most Happy Fella* was a great work, but, by God, I gave Frank credit for taking it on and doing it."

Styne stares at the wall for a long beat. Then he sighs. "You know, if Frank would have written with anybody, it would only have been with me. In fact, he said so once. 'You have so much for me.' And he was right. I feel that one day, even when I die, I will never have been drawn on fully. . . .

"I would say that three very important things happened to me in my life pertaining to writing. To write a song is one thing; for everybody to like it is nothing, even to get it recorded—*but* you get to meet what you think is the best. First, Robbins. To me, the directorial ability of Jerome Robbins in the musical theatre is untouchable. I think he knows more, I think he knows how to execute more, and he understands. And it isn't only me—I'm sure Lenny Bernstein would say the same; I'm sure that Sheldon Harnick and Jerry Bock would say the same.*

"And, remember, I was a vocal coach. I started out being one before I wrote songs. I think the greatest woman singer of my time is Barbra Streisand. I'll never live to hear anyone else who has so much. I love that voice so much. It hasn't been drawn on yet; it is an unending chain of events, and they will always reach and give me something new that's bewildering to me. It's very exciting to me to live to hear this thing come out of that mouth.

"And the most exciting, the greatest male singer of my time has been Frank Sinatra. There will never be anyone else who makes my music sound as well as he did, male-wise. Now, I have great respect for all the others, Tony Bennett, Harry Belafonte, and Sammy Davis, and, oh, we go all the way down the line —Tom Jones and all the others—but *Sinatra* . . .

"These three people," he murmurs, "they're *above* it. They're over the mountain a little bit, they're that very special thing, they're the Lou Gehrigs and the Babe Ruths, they're the Palmers in golf. Not just good, they are special.

"I cannot say who's better than whom in the lyric-writers, because they have all scratched the surface with me equally as great. In other times, of course, there was Sammy Cahn, then there was Frank Loesser, Leo Robin, the late Bob Hilliard, Comden and Green, Steve Sondheim—I adore Steve, a great friend, we wrote *Gypsy* together. Yip Harburg, Bob Merrill. They are all equally great in their own way, and because they are in their own way, that makes them very special people. One doesn't write like the other."

Jule Styne sits down for the first time in the two hours he has been talking this muggy afternoon. "You don't want anything like—well, advice on song-writing, or something like that?" he asks.

Isn't that what he's been giving?

"Okay. Cut." He grins.

* Both of whom worked on with Robbins *Fiddler on the Roof*, and who do agree wholeheartedly.

'Bei Mir Bist Du Schön'

(Sammy Cahn)

SAMMY CAHN'S New York abode—he still maintains a California residence—is an apartment in the East Fifties. But these days he is rarely very long at either place. He has friends in South America, in Europe, out in the Pacific, and he and his wife, Tita, spend a good deal of their time traveling. His world has expanded since the days when he played violin and told jokes with a pick-up dance band that specialized in weddings and Brooklyn bar mitzvahs. Later today he leaves with Mrs. Cahn to spend a month enjoying the Greek islands.

He has come to the door sporting an elegant flowered silk dressing gown, stylish garters holding up his socks. "Come in and let's get talking, and I'll take the phone off the hook," he promises. "What do you want to know about me that everybody hasn't already asked?" Whereupon the telephone rings, and he answers it by reflex, to tell a friend he can't discuss anything because he's too busy discussing something with somebody else. He is a garrulous man with a high-domed forehead and a tiny pencil-type mustache; his enthusiasm is cheerfully infectious.

He is also a very hard worker. He formed his first songwriting partnership back in the mid-'30s with Saul Chaplin. In California he worked extensively with Jule Styne in the World War II era and their collaboration turned out stacks of hit records. After Cahn and Styne wrote the score for *High Button Shoes* in 1947, Styne decided to make the Broadway scene his permanent beat. Cahn remained in Hollywood and began writing songs with other composers, finally teaming up with Jimmy Van Heusen. Cahn and Styne reunited, and won an Academy Award in 1954 for "Three Coins in the Fountain." Cahn and Van Heusen won one in 1957 for "All the Way," which Frank Sinatra sang in the film *The Joker Is Wild*. Two years later they won with "High Hopes," and in 1963 with "Call Me Irresponsible." Another of the Cahn-Van Heusen songs, "Love and Marriage," which Sinatra introduced in the television version of *Our Town*, won an Emmy. Cahn and his collaborators have been identified with enough Sinatra hits—songs like "Come Fly with Me," "My Kind of Town," "The Tender Trap," and "Hey, Jealous Lover"—to fill endless sides of Sinatra LPs. If Sinatra was—and is still—the King, then Cahn, Styne, and Van Heusen certainly have served him well as court composers.

Is it possible to document Sammy Cahn's long career in the short space of time before he departs for the Greek islands?

Sammy grins. "Who knows? But we'll never know unless we get started, will we?" But before he can begin, the phone rings again. His temporary presence in New York is obviously well known. He is here only for a day or so, but he draws calls as if he were the eye of a tiny show-business hurricane. This one is from a prominent night-club comic who's made his debut in the film version of *The Love Machine*—it was shown privately the night before, and he wants Sammy's honest opinion. ("Kid, *you* were great, but I have to give it to you straight—the picture is strictly dreadful. It'll be a fight, but it won't hurt you, it'll help, you'll get exposure with new audiences.") Moments later there is another call; this time it's a producer who wants to discuss a possible Broadway musical for Cahn. ("Sure, it's possible, but not probable. How can I write lyrics on a Greek island? Besides, I'm too old and thin for those out-of-town arguments.") Next there is a charity-show benefit chairwoman, a friend who desperately wants one of Sammy's celebrated satiric song parodies to be performed on the night of her affair at the Waldorf. ("Darling, I can't do it on such short notice even for you, but let me see if I can't find somebody else to run up a couple of yards of jokes for you.") And then somebody who wants Cahn to intercede for him on some matter with Sinatra. ("No way. He's retired. Listen, I'll miss Frank singing as much as you do. Probably a hell of a lot more, but you don't argue with him when he's made up his mind.")

Between these phone conversations—he finds it somehow impossible to cut himself off from the outside world by taking off the receiver—the early days of Sammy Cahn manage to emerge in sporadic bursts of total recall.

"I was born into the typical Lower-East-Side Jewish family, 1913," he says, "and I had four sisters, and for some peculiar reason my mother insisted that I would play the violin. It seemed that in her mind the girl played the piano and the man played the violin. I guess she was scared by a John Garfield movie, or something.

"I didn't like the violin, but I played it. I have a tremendous aptitude for music, and most of the credit I'm given for my lyrics results from my deep love of music. I can pick up any instrument, almost, and play it. I had a marvelous mother; she was the kind of lady you could make a deal with, which is what I loved her for. I made a deal with her—I'd play the violin until my thirteenth birthday, the fabled bar mitzvah. Sure enough, came the bar mitzvah, I played a violin solo, and that was the deal. Okay. Now, it was a typical bar mitzvah, and I had gotten all the envelopes from the relatives with the money inside, which is the way you pay for a bar mitzvah, and there was a little six-piece orchestra playing there, six guys having a good time, and at one in the morning my mother said the line which changed my whole life. She said, *'Let's go pay the orchestra.'* "

Cahn shakes his head at the memory. "*Pay* those fellows for having so much fun? I didn't comprehend it. They got thirty dollars for their night. One of them was Big Sam Weiss, who went on to play with Benny Goodman. Anyway, as we're paying them, I asked them if they did a lot of this, and they said, sure, parties, dates. And I said, 'Well, could *I* do this?' and they told me, 'Sure, if you want to.' Two years later, at age 15, I was playing with the same orchestra, down on the Lower East Side.

"Can I tell you one of the greatest thrills of my life? Years later I'm at a party where Cole Porter is. Porter, Berlin—the two single most talented men in American music. Porter, my idol. Somebody says, 'Cole Porter wants to meet you.' I said, 'Are you *kidding?*' As I turned around, he came at me, Cole Porter, on those crutches, thin and small, and I didn't know how to react to this—my idol coming up to me, I should have run to *him.* I just stood there, and he said, 'Sammy Cahn, I've always wanted to meet *you.*' I must have mumbled some kind of gibberish, like, 'You want to meet *me?*' He says, 'I've always envied you.' Envied me what? He says, 'You were born on the Lower East Side. Had I been born on the Lower East Side, I could have been a true genius.'

"You know, songwriters are highly competitive people. They don't really congregate with each other, like comics or actors. And with my feeling for Porter, oh well, to hear him say that—to *me* . . ."

Is there some mysterious reason why, consistently over the past half-century, the Lower East Side tenement neighborhoods have been the spawning ground for many of America's most successful pop-music songwriters?

"That's *any* ghetto," says Cahn. 'The ghetto is the cradle because the struggle is to get *out* of the ghetto. And in our country it comes in waves, along with the immigration. In the beginnings, the first waves, everything was Irish. The songs, the performers, comics—Harrigan and Hart, Eddie Foy, George M. Cohan, all Irish. Politicians, entertainers, writers, all Irish. Gangsters, prize fighters, all Irish. All right? Next wave into the ghetto, Jewish. Same pattern emerges. Singers, performers—Jolsen, Weber and Fields, comics, all Yiddish. Prize fighters, gangsters, Yiddish. Now it went to the Italians. Think hard—Italians. Performers—Sinatra, Vic Damone, Tony Bennett, Como. Politicians, writers, gangsters, prize fighters, all Italians, all struggling to get out of the ghetto. Now go on. The blacks are next on that ladder, the ethnic ladder, to get out. *Now* all the writers we're reading—black. Performers—I don't have to tell you about the music, the singers. The current wave is *black.* I don't say I'm Margaret Mead," concedes Cahn, "but that's how it's always seemed to me."

The orchestra with which Cahn was to play did quite well, due, he claims, in large measure to Cahn's mother. "She was a *macher* [maker]. Couldn't read or write, but she became very big with the local Democratic machine. Got us a lot of work through her connections. Then I met Saul Chaplin. Can I tell you about that?"

Cahn beams with fondness. "We're at the Henry Street Settlement House downtown, a wintry night, snowing, and I'd hired a new piano player from Brooklyn called Saul Kaplan. I was very anxious to see if he'd show up, because I'd never even met him. I'm looking down the street. There he comes, walking. He wore a black derby hat, from which emerged shocks of curly blond hair, he wore a big old raccoon coat, and he looked like King Gustav of Sweden. That was Saul Kaplan."

Cahn jumps up and grabs a small chromo-type picture from the wall; seven sober-faced young men in utilitarian-black suits, clutching their symbols of status, their instruments, as they stare at the photographer back in the East Side days of 1930. "There he is—look at him," he murmurs, pointing to the youthful piano player with his derby hat cocked jauntily to one side. "A dear man," says Cahn as he replaces the picture.

"I say this to you with deep affection, because I really love Saulie. He has very bad eyes, you know, they kind of spun in his head, and the last time he was in Hollywood, the last time I saw him driving a car, I ran up on the sidewalk with mine!" Cahn guffaws. "I went right off the road in fear! Saulie Chaplin coming at me in an *automobile?*

"I'd learned a few chords on the piano, maybe just two, so I'd already tried to write a song. Something I called 'Shake Your Head from Side to Side.' So a couple of weeks later, on a club date, Saul comes to me and asks me if I'll listen to something. I sit down while he tapped off a number on the piano. He had made an *arrangement* of my melody! And may I tell you, I've had many thrills in my life, but this has to be one of the top ones. That thrill remains. No matter how many songs I've written, the moment the orchestra leader gives the down-beat to the first *musical* interpretation, it is almost like, you know, spanking the new-born baby!

"These guys, the arrangers—they are the most fantastic people in our world. Go talk to *them*—they are the heroes of this business. Anyway, when he did this, I said to myself, 'This man belongs to me.' Saul was going to NYU, but I am indefatigable when it comes to achieving a goal, even then. I made him quit NYU—he wanted to become an accountant. So I had a great effect on his life, I hope he'll forgive me."

A somewhat rhetorical remark, considering that Chaplin has become one of the most successful producers of musical films in the past twenty years, numbering among his credits *West Side Story*, *High Society*, *The Sound of Music*, and the current *Man of La Mancha*.

"We started to write special material and take it uptown and try to peddle it around Tin Pan Alley. First it was the old De Sylva, Brown and Henderson building, where the Brass Rail restaurant is now; then it moved over to the Brill Building, on Broadway. Did you ever hear stories about that building? One day some famous songwriter had just walked out of Lindy's restaurant; he got into the elevator and he burped, right after his lunch, and he said to the elevator man, 'Sorry, something I ate,'" and the elevator man said, 'More likely something you *wrote.*'

"And there was another story they told about this songwriter. He always sat in Lindy's with his racing form, and one day there was some American Legion convention in New York, and he's sitting there reading his tip sheet, and a guy walks in, a big, burly Legion vet, and he comes up and he says, 'And where were *you* in 1917?' And the songwriter looks up and he says, 'With Mills Music!' That's the kind of thing used to go on around the business."

Again the phone interrupts. This time one of Sammy's professional acquaintances is anxious that he come to a party later this week to listen to some neophyte songwriter's material. "I will be delighted to listen to it provided he plays it for me in Greece," he counters, and hangs up to return to his saga.

"Oh boy, when I left the Lower East Side to come uptown, that was something," he remarks. "You know, at that time everything was in New York —the theatre, music, everything. So if a boy lives anywhere in the U.S., he runs to New York, right? But where does a boy who lives in New York already run away to? I went from downtown up to West 46th Street . . . and I slept on floors. I was determined. Now see, in a Jewish family, when an only son goes wrong, it's a terrible thing—a tragedy. I mean, if you have four *sons*, if two go to jail and one goes to the electric chair, well, one guy can still go on to be a lawyer or a doctor. But here I was the only son, with four sisters—and I was going to be a songwriter? Terrible. I was going bad. But I was determined. I could have been home for a nickel subway ride—that should give you an idea how long ago this was—but no. I was going to make it.

"There was a legendary outfit on West 46th Street, Beckman and Pransky; they specialized in booking acts for the Catskill Mountain hotels. They were the MCA, the William Morris of the mountains. I got a room in their offices and we started writing special material. For anybody who'd have us—at whatever price. I wrote for Dolores Reed—she became Bob Hope's wife. I wrote for Henny Youngman, Hope. And maybe sometimes we'd pick up a few bucks for writing special arrangements for the songs that performers would use in their acts. Funny how things happen. One day a door opens in the building, and out comes a guy named Lou Levy. He stops and does a double-take. 'Sammy—what are you doing here?' A childhood friend. In our East Side area he'd been considered a complete bum, a no-good. My father had a little restaurant on Madison Street, and his father had a little vegetable store around the corner. He was the neighborhood bum, and I was a little boy with a violin and not supposed to associate with him. But now we meet again in a building hallway on 46th Street. How about that for fate? Now he's become a dancer.

"Can I give you an idea how attitudes have changed? He's earning a living by blacking up his face with burnt cork and dancing with the Jimmy Lunceford orchestra, a black group. He does dances like the Lindy Hop. So we start running around together, scratching for jobs, and one day he tells us Lunceford is going into the Apollo Theatre on 125th Street, the famous Harlem vaudeville house, and Lunceford needs some special material for his orchestra, and I say, 'Hey, I'm your man,' and Saul and I quick write a number called 'Rhythm Is Our Business.' Our second published song. The first one was my immortal 'Shake Your Head from Side to Side,' published by some thief up in the Roseland Building, who stole all our royalties with a crooked contract.

"We play the number for Lunceford, and he loves it, and before we know what's happening, he's gone and recorded it for Decca Records. In those days, that was a thirty-five-cent label, lower-priced than Victor or Columbia, and getting very big. Lo and behold, the impossible comes true, a publisher named Georgie Joy sends for us, it's 1935 and we have a published song *with* a record!"

Even at that early stage of his career Sammy Cahn had definite ideas about the team's future. "I looked at the sheet-music copy and I saw 'By Sammy Cahn and Saul Kaplan.' See—up there on the wall you can still see our original billing. Kaplan—his real name. And I said, 'Saulie, Cahn and Kaplan is a dress-firm name from Seventh Avenue. You're going to change your name to *Chaplin*.' He said he wasn't going to. I insisted. He said, 'Why don't you change *your* name?' I said, 'I did—from Kahn with a K to Cahn with a C. Now it's your turn.' Okay—so we also hired a young girl that Saul had met in the mountains, a girl named Ethel Schwartz. We hired her as a secretary so Saul would stay around the office. He was a boy who liked to go home to Brooklyn. We didn't have what to eat, but we hired her! Later he married Ethel Schwartz, and they had a baby—her name is Judy, and she is now married to Hal Prince, who has done a few things around Broadway as a producer [*The Pajama Game, Cabaret, Fiddler on the Roof, Company,* and *Follies,* to list but a few], and now you have the first act of the Cahn-and-Chaplin story."

But we do not embark on the second act for a bit, because the phone is ringing again; this time it is the same comic who called earlier. He has been pondering Cahn's assessment of his performance in *The Love Machine,* and he is not happy. "I am telling you *true,*" says Cahn with fervor. "Why should I lie to you? You will come out of this picture smelling like a rose even if it is a bomb. *You* they cannot hurt. You are not responsible for what *they* did." Eventually he hangs up, after several more bursts of sincere ego-massage. "Performers!" he remarks. "They are always so insecure about what they do, and who can blame them? It is such a chancey business they're in. Where were we?"

At the days when Cahn and Chaplin were succeeding with orchestras.

"We quickly did Lunceford another piece of material called 'If I Had Rhythm in My Nursery Rhymes,' which also caught on, and then we were set with special-material-type songs. Very good training. This was the period when the big bands were really catching on in show business. Every Broadway theatre was going into stage presentations with orchestras. The first one that went into the Paramount on Times Square was the Glen Gray Casa Loma Band. Did you know that Glen Gray didn't conduct it? Some guy stood up with a violin and made like a conductor. Glen Gray played the saxophone. Their first New York appearance, they wanted a way to tell the people that the guy standing there *wasn't* Glen Gray. So it was like a forerunner of all the assignments I've had ever since, special jobs. Somebody says, 'Call Sammy Cahn, he writes good for bands,' because of 'Rhythm Is Our Business,' and I get to do the song to introduce Glen Gray. A marvelous guy, by the way.

"Glen Gray had manners, he had morals, he was a great Christian. He would not embarrass that orchestra guy standing in front of the band; he wanted it done subtly. So I wrote a thing that said, '*Once upon a time there was an aggregation that decided they would become a corporation.*'" Cahn is quoting a lyric that is nearly four decades long-gone as if he has just minted the rhymes this morning in 1971. "'*So they decided to have a vote, and they all hit a note, and that was the start of the Casa Loma Corporation. When the brass had to vote, the brass hit a note.*'" Sammy enthusiastically re-creates the entire act. "And then the brass stands up, and Glen Gray stood up, and they blew to him, and he blew a note back to them, and it slowly became evident to the Paramount audience that that was Glen Gray sitting there, see? '*Then they handed him a golden diploma . . . which made him president of the Casa Loma.*' And that was their opening song."

Very clever and slick, even by today's more sophisticated standards.

"I like that point," agrees Cahn. "I think I *am* slick. It was all those years of working for so many different talents, being in so many situations and having to shape my work to fit them. We got hired to do a show at the old Cotton Club, a night spot. The owner says, 'We got these beautiful blue costumes, what can you give us?' So we wrote him a song called 'Blue Notes' to go with the costumes.

"Anything! It was a challenge. Like, they had Sister Rosetta Tharpe there, an evangelist singer. We did her a song where she came out on a white mule. A sensation, stopped the show. Of course, the owner got sore at us. Seems the chorus girls were all quitting on him—they found out he was paying that white mule more than he was paying them!

"Then the guy books in Louis Armstrong. My God—the legendary Louis. To me, he was the absolute greatest! I'll never forget when I first met Louis—it was like the time I met Cole Porter. I'd worshipped his trumpet playing. First thing Louis said to me was, 'When were you born?' I told him, he went to a book, opened it, he says, 'You know who else was born on that day?' He had this kind of a celebrity autograph book on the days of the year—everybody signed in on the day of his birth. *I* had to sign. There I am, signing an autograph for *Louis Armstrong!* . . . We wrote him a song for the finale, brought out a little kid with a shoeshine box, we called it 'Shoe Shine Boy,' and *that* was a hit, too."

He suddenly bursts into a chorus of that song, which finishes: " '*Every nickel helps a lot.*' " And he stops. "There, that'll give you an idea how old that is—a nickel for a shoeshine!

"So, anyway, there I am writing for all the bands, and one night Saulie and I and Lou Levy are sitting up at the Apollo, and out comes an act, I think it was called Johnny, Johnny and George. Don't hold me to it—this is going back thirty years. And they sing a song called 'Bei Mir Bist Du Schön' in the original Yiddish. I don't know if you ever heard that song in its original, but you must believe me, it is funny. They're singing and dancing it, and I know you won't believe what I'm about to tell you, but that theatre is literally *pulsating*. I mean, if you could have a Geiger counter, some kind of a meter, you would find out that the theatre was actually expanding and contracting, just from the beat that song was generating that night. I turned to Lou and I said, 'Can you imagine what this song would do if they knew what they were saying?' Because I could understand the words in Yiddish. It's a boy telling a girl she's the greatest thing in the world, she's even greater to him than money—which, believe me, is the greatest tribute a Jewish boy could pay to a girl, you know?

"Tommy Dorsey calls up a day later and says he's going into the Paramount and he wants a good piece of material. I tell him about this number I'd heard in Harlem, and he thinks I'm crazy. 'You want me to do a *Yiddish* number? *Me?*' Very stubborn fellow, Tommy. You couldn't budge him. He actually threw me out of his apartment!

"Couple of nights later I go down to Ratner's, a dairy restaurant on Fourth Street and Second Avenue. *I'm* a stubborn guy too. I go into a little music store down there, and I pick up a copy of the original sheet music for this song, and again I go to Dorsey with it. And again he throws me out—with the copy in my hand!"

How did the song eventually end up such a big hit for the Andrews Sisters?

"One day I'm at home. I had a little two-room place on 57th Street, torn down now. The sheet music is on my piano, and in walk the Andrews Sisters, and they look at it and they ask, 'What's this—a Greek song?' I tell them it's Yiddish, and I play it for them. And again the total contagion of this song manifests itself—anywhere, any time, any place, the room starts to rock, and they start singing it along with me, and they ask, 'Do you mind if we record this?' I tell them, 'Be my guest. What do I care what you do with it? I am totally uninvolved, the middleman, the fellow who's doing everybody favors.' Extracurricular work —just like I've been doing *here*"— he winks—"all morning on this telephone."

Three or four days later the Andrews Sisters, who were well on their way to becoming enormously successful recording artists, were ready to record the song, in its original Yiddish version, in those same Decca studios on West 57th Street where Lunceford was under contract. "And Jack Kapp, who ran Decca, had a monitoring system that let him listen in to each studio. He turns on a button, listens in, and he hears the girls doing the song—in Yiddish. Kapp gives out a yell; what are the Andrews doing, making a race record?'"

Cahn gets up and begins pacing his pleasant living room. "I'm going to digress, because this is important, and I don't care if you quote me or not," he says soberly. "When I came into this business, there were three separate and distinct branches of American pop music. There was pop standard, in which I operated. The second was hillbilly and Western music. And the third branch was the very bottom of the ladder—race, rhythm, and blues. A race record was any record with a language—Spanish, Yiddish, there were Italian records, Polish, there was 'Cohen on the Telephone.' And the very bottom of *that* rung was blues records. Mostly black singers nobody knew, even the great ones like Bessie Smith, Ma Rainey, who sang blues like *'Go back and get it where you got it last night because you ain't going to get it here,'* and all that stuff.

"Now there's ASCAP. The American Society of Composers, Authors and Publishers, formed in 1914, one of the great organizations of the world. A performance-rights society which collects money for its members. Any place in the world that uses music for profit pays ASCAP. Don't say it's a monolithic organization—don't doctors have their AMA?

"Now, the biggest money from music came from the broadcasters. So one day they, the broadcasters, decided they were going to start their own company, Broadcast Music Inc.—BMI. And I maintain that the music we're listening to today is a direct result of that challenge, and I challenge anybody to deny what I'm saying. All the race, rhythm, and blues, the old bottom of the rung, has become the number-one music in the world today." Cahn is no longer jocular or even vaguely humorous—he is very much in earnest. "Why? Because when BMI opened up against ASCAP, they obviously couldn't ask ASCAP to defeat itself by cutting out the pop-standard field, could they? So those BMI guys went to the Western and country music composers. Well! They soon discovered that the fellows in country and Western had more cunning than they'll ever have, and they went to the next; they went down into race, the black, and now we began to hear a lot of broadcasting of all the stuff that's so strong today—the old race, rhythm, and blues of the past!"

Cahn waves an accusatory finger. "I've read about this. Any analyst will tell you about Jones, who was a disciple of Freud. He too said, what does a child want to hear when he's growing up? Does he want to go to the opera? Does he want lush music? *No*—he wants a noisy beat—*dung-dung-dung-dunga-dung!* And this is exactly what the broadcasters of America fed to the youth of America! All the old blues beats—*'Walk right in, sit right down, baby, let your mind roll on!' That* became number one in America? It sure did. And who did it? Now, who's to say what effect they've had on the manners and the morals of America? And go right ahead and quote me!"

Shaking his head angrily, he subsides on the couch.

"Okay, end of digression. Back to 'Bei Mir.' Kapp insists on a set of English words to the song before they can record it. Remember, this is 1939, ages ago. So Lou Levy leaves the copy up at my place, he wants a translation. One night I take a red pencil and under each Yiddish word I write a lyric. Now, when I write a lyric, I always start at the top. I never ever know where it is going. Jimmy Van Heusen told me later that his earlier partner, Johnny Burke,* always started at the *bottom*. He'd lay out a key idea, and then he'd write from the line backwards.

"You see, songwriting for me is a great, great adventure. I have so much fun. I've learned that if I start at the top, I will go where I need to go. It will always be there if I just stay with it. And the minute I got '*Bei Mir Bist Du Schön, please let me explain*,' that was the key to the whole song.

"I get the song finished, and here's where the drama starts. *What have we done?* We've taken another man's song and changed it, without asking permission or anything! And now, all of a sudden, it occurs to us we've done this, and somebody says, 'Hey! Now, how are we going to do this?' I look at the sheet music, it says, 'Words by Jacob Jacobs and Music by Sholom Secunda. Published by J. & J. Kamen, Roebling Street, Brooklyn, N.Y.' I had to go out to Brooklyn and find them. Now, I am not making this up to give you an anecdote. Two little men, about five feet tall, black derbies, the two of them in a little store— light blue serge suits, like Tweedledum and Tweedledee from Tel Aviv! Specialized in publishing songs from Yiddish shows. See, Yiddish composers would publish their own songs and then stand in front of the theatre when the show was playing and sell the songs to the audience afterwards. The show runs, then it closes, the songwriters were finished, they'd bring in the songs to J. & J. Kamen and sell everything for $100 or so. One of those songs was 'Bei Mir Bist Du Schön.' They'd bought it for maybe $30. That was the way it worked then. I had to explain to those two little Kamen brothers that I'd written a lyric to their song! To Jacobs' and Secunda's song. And that it was recorded already, and how could I explain to them that the thing had taken off, it's already a big hit, everybody's playing it, even Guy Lombardo is using it at the Roosevelt Grill? You can't believe what a hassle there was about royalties. By the time it's straightened out—the Kamens getting theirs, the writers getting theirs, the Warner Brothers publishing house where we're under contract getting theirs— finally, Chaplin and I, the ones who made this international hit, we get between us, for the lyric and the setting, one and a half cents a copy! Oh, I tell you, they negotiated that one out for *months*."

By now the Cahn-and-Chaplin team had found steady employment writing for films. Not the opulent Hollywood-type musicals, however; they had found a rather unique niche writing music and lyrics for two-reel shorts, out at the old Vitagraph studio in Brooklyn. "We'd signed a contract with the Warner music publishers. Herman Starr ran it, and he sent us out to Brooklyn. They cranked out shorts as if it were a sausage factory; the motto of that place was, 'We don't want it good—we want it by Thursday!' Vaudeville acts used to come out and work one, two days and make a short. We turned out instant material. Do you realize that we're the first team of songwriters that ever wrote a hit for a two-reel comedy? A song we called 'Please Be Kind.' "

---

* A longtime collaborator of Van Heusen's on "Swinging on a Star," "Imagination," "Pennies from Heaven," and literally dozens of other song hits, chiefly for Bing Crosby.

Another phone call; it is Cahn's travel agent checking on his reservations for Greece and other points. And then someone calls long-distance from California: can Sammy do some special material for a commemorative dinner? ("Baby, I would love to oblige you, but it's not only my body that's going to Greece, my head is *also* booked for the flight.")

"Where was I?" he queries.

The eventual move to California?

"Oh, yes. So now we've had this pretty good run of success, and Herman Starr, who's given us a lot of impetus, now pulls a brake on us in a kind of silly way. Because we were under contract, he never published anything of ours. A very naïve attitude. He'd say to us, 'Look, if Harry Kabibble walked in with a song, I better publish his song. *Your* songs I *got.*' Well, we went into a real rut. So Saul and I walked in and said, 'Send us to Hollywood. We're not doing anything around here; out there something could happen.'

"Starr bought that idea, we went to Hollywood, and Starr sent along some kind of note to the bosses at Warner's saying, 'Here are two songwriters, they get paid by us in the East—please use them, you got them for *nothing.*' And you know what people do with something they get for nothing? That's what they did with us. For two years. We hung around, but the only time we even got on the Warner lot itself was when I *walked* on with my old pal Jimmy Lunceford when he was there to make the picture *Blues in the Night!*'

So how did Cahn and Chaplin survive? "It got better," says Cahn. "It couldn't have been worse. Eventually I got to work for all of them—Warner, Harry Cohn, Paramount. I could tell you plenty of stories about *that,* but I won't, because I am now off to Greece."

He vanishes into the bedroom to dress and finish packing.

To call a halt at this point in his reminiscences is somewhat akin to enjoying the *hors d'oeuvres* at a gourmet restaurant and then having the chef close down the kitchen.

He emerges from the bedroom in slacks and a double-breasted blazer, very much the elegant world traveler and *bon vivant.* "It's not only *you* I'm leaving!" he soothes. "What about all those people who keep calling me and I won't be here to answer? Say, maybe you could stay here while I'm gone and answer the phone! Ask all my friends who call to carry on with my story until I get back!"

He bolts his door and walks down the hallway with his bags, headed for Greece. From behind, there comes the faint, unmistakable sound of his telephone, ringing inside the closed apartment. Sammy Cahn's friends are already missing him.

Sammy Cahn Revisited

Almost eleven months have passed since the peripatetic Mr. Cahn departed for Greece. In the interim he has been to Venezuela, several times to California, and back to Europe, thus pleasing some international airlines. Miraculously, he materializes striding down a rainy London Street and halts, crying, "Hey! We never finished! I did a two-hour lecture up at the YMHA on 92nd Street—told them all about my career. Got great notices."

Shall we continue now? No, he is off to New York in the morning.

Eventually, through a minor triumph of logistics and split-second timing, we do continue, back in New York. But now the scene has changed; Mr. Cahn is working in the opulent offices of a large cosmetic company.

The two floors the firm occupies in a huge New York tower are decorated in the avantest-garde. A lovely receptionist sits at a lavender desk, where she and it seem to float in mid-air, sans visible means of support. There are mobiles hanging everywhere. Halls are lined in soft gray furry plaster, with vivid neon tubing for illumination. Individual offices are decorated with the latest in Italian mod furniture, walls are hung with an array of wild abstracts and neo-realistic pictures; one might well be in an art gallery. Crouched over a functional electric typewriter in one of the offices is a found object, Mr. Cahn. He wears a casual sport shirt and slacks. Has he perhaps gone into the cosmetic business? Peripherally. He is working on a set of special-material lyrics which he himself will perform tomorrow afternoon at the company sales meeting in Miami. Eight solid pages of parodies to be sung to the tunes of his famous songs.

"I do this only for my friends," he says, "and I write gratis. If I were doing it for an actor to use in his act, the price would stagger you. Joey Bishop asked me would I do a take-off on *Fiddler on the Roof* for Vegas this spring. I write him a thing called 'Gambler on the Roof' and it is the biggest hit that ever happened there. Joey is thrilled and he keeps asking me what he owes me, and I say, 'Hey, I don't make my living writing special material'—although that's how I started off, remember—'I make a living writing *songs*.' If he sends me a nice gift or something, okay, but if he doesn't, I still enjoyed it. It was a kick! Excuse me, I have a line to fix here."

A smashing young secretary appears, and Cahn hands her revised lyrics for reproduction. There is discussion about his flight to Miami the following morning in the company's private jet; he will travel with the president, who is a good friend. "I'm doing this as a favor to him," he says, "but I really enjoy getting up and performing so much *I* should pay. I take all my songs and revise them for the occasion. I get up and say, 'Ladies and gentlemen, in ancient times the lyric-writer was the news media. For instance, the word "lyric" comes from the Greek word "lyre"—a man with a lyric would go from town to town singing the news. If he sang about Danny Deever getting hung in the morning, that was something that was really happening. So tonight I will go back to being the news media and tell you the story of this occasion here—with the melodies of my songs, and new lyrics.' And slowly, as I do one song after the other, it has an amazing effect on the audience. You can hear them whispering, 'Hey, he *wrote* this song . . . and did he really write *that?*' "

More interruptions—the usual fusilade of phone calls from friends and business cronies, the movers who are arranging to transport him shortly to a new East Side apartment—and eventually he returns to the subject of his songwriting. "Now. Where were we?"

Before he left for Greece long months ago, he had talked about his early partnership with Saul Chaplin, which had brought them to Hollywood in the mid–'30s. Now, what about his subsequent collaboration with Jule Styne? "Hey, did I tell you about how we wrote 'Three Coins in the Fountain'?" he demands. "Because one night I was at a party where Jule Styne and Frank Sinatra were reminiscing about it, and as I listened, I was amazed to hear how they remembered it. *I* remember it the way it happened.

"Jule and I had a great run of hits in Hollywood during the war, as you know, and then after *High Button Shoes*, which we did on Broadway, he stayed in New York—he loved the theatre. I came back to the Coast. Now it's ten years later and the phone rings. I'd been working with lots of people, but it's Sol Siegel saying Fox is going to make the first Cinemascope musical *Pink Tights,* with Frank Sinatra and Marilyn Monroe, a huge project, and Frank wants me to do it with Jule. That's why I'll always be eternally grateful to Frank, believe me. Do I want to do it? More than anything else in the world. So Jule comes out, and we're reunited, and we proceed to write what I believe is the best score Jule and I have ever written. Why do I say that? Not arrogance," he says. "It's the best score because it has not been *heard.* And, for all I know, it may contain ten hits, because anything that's unpublished is a hit. When it's published, it becomes either a hit or a flop. But till it's published, it's a hit, right?" He beams across the bright red plastic desk.

"So our score was never heard. Why not? Because the day we are supposed to go in to record it, Marilyn Monroe, our female star, runs away to Japan with Joe DiMaggio! That's on public record. Leaving everyone at the studio high and dry, and there we are, a score, cast, everything ready, no female star! Now we're just roaming around, not knowing where we were going or what to do, when Mr. Sol Siegel walked into our office. It's about 1:30, after lunch, and he said, quote, 'Could you fellows write a song called "Three Coins in the Fountain"?' unquote. I said, 'We could write you a song called "Ech!"' He said, 'I don't want a song called "Ech," I want a song called "Three Coins in the Fountain."'" I said, 'What for?' He said, 'We just finished a picture in Italy. The New York office wants to call it *We Believe in Love.* Zanuck and I hate the title, but they're adamant—and we feel that if we can get'em a song called "Three Coins in the Fountain," it may dissuade them.' I said, 'Okay, can we see the picture?' He said, 'You can't see the picture, the picture's all over the lot, they're scoring, they're dubbing, they're doing all sorts of technical things to the picture.' I said, 'Well, can I read a script?' He said, 'What—read the script? We need the song right away!' I said, 'Hey, what's this picture *about?*' He said, 'What's it about? Three girls go to Rome hoping to find love and they throw coins in a fountain.' I said, 'That's fair enough.'

"Now, you ask which comes first, the words or the music?" asks Cahn. He grins. "I'll tell you which—*the money!* Or the phone call—or the request! Which we have. I go to the typewriter and I sit down with a piece of yellow paper which is my work sheet. I look at it about two, three minutes, and I start to type. The title. '*Three coins in the fountain, Each one seeking happiness, Thrown by three hopeful lovers. Which one will the fountain bless?*' That took me two or three minutes to type. Now, as simple as it sounds, it is the result of twenty years of lyric training. And my fingers hit a cadence that comes from the title . . . da da da-da da-da, and so on. So that's already laid in for Jule. I hand this piece of paper to Mr. Styne, who looks at it. Now, I will tell you that it would take a computer the size of a universe to estimate how many different combinations of notes are available to those words. But in about half an hour, with Mr. Styne's talent working, we start to hear the first eight bars, like so." Mr. Cahn proceeds to sing them, in a soft, true voice, with a professional attack.

"And we agree that this is lush, Latin, and correct. Now, if he did not come up with something that was acceptable soon, I would have changed the lyric around, made another kind of combination. But the melody was right, and now, having agreed to that, the melody is three-quarters finished. You see, in a song, melodically, we go A—A—B—which is the bridge—and then back to

A. And we've got our A. He hands me back the paper, and I look at it, and I say, 'Jule, I don't know what else to say. I've said everything that is pertinent to this song.' And Jule says, 'How about mentioning Rome?' I say, 'That's fair.' I put the paper in, I write, *'Three hearts in the fountain, Each one longing for its home. There they lie in the fountain, Somewhere in the heart of Rome.'*

"Not bad. Swift. Easy. So I say, 'Jule, I now can guarantee you this song is finished.' And we got into a kind of dialogue, because once before we wrote a song together called 'I Fall in Love Too Easily.' I had written a sixteen-bar lyric [the customary form for years was thirty-two bars], but I wouldn't add another word to it; I said, 'That's all the song has to say!' " Again from memory, he sings the lyric of the lovely Sinatra ballad which he and Styne wrote for the young singer's repertoire many years back.

"But Jule says, 'Hey, you're not going to do one of those. We need a bridge. Give me a bridge!' So I look at the paper, I stared, and I finally typed, *'Which one will the fountain bless? Which one will the fountain bless?'* I hand it to him. He reads it aloud and asks, 'Don't you want to rhyme it?' I said, 'No, I don't want to rhyme it. That's what I want to say.' He says, 'You know, you used this line already.' I said, 'I don't care.' That is what I wanted to say. And it's getting a little edgy between us, you know? So he goes back to the piano and he's angry, and he starts to play, very flat and monotone, dum dum dum da dum da dum! Jule looks at me. I said, 'That stinks.' He says, 'You're telling me it stinks? *Of course* it stinks!' I said, 'What about trying to help it? Don't do exactly what I did.' And that's what Jule did." Cahn sings the melody with great feeling and emphasis. "I listened, and I said, 'Ah, isn't that great?' Jule goes to write it down, and he says, 'Just a moment. This bridge is only four bars.' Now, all bridges are eight bars. Eight bars, eight bars, bridge, closing, eight bars. Thirty-two bars. Why the hell was this only four bars? Now I'm floundering, because in those days songs had to be thirty-two bars. Not today. So I go back to the top of the song and I run it through, and I add, *'Three coins in the fountain, Through the ripples how they shine. Just one wish will be granted. One heart will wear a valentine. Make it mine, make it mine, make it mine!'* He said, 'You son of a bitch, we picked up the last four bars in the tag—we've got thirty-two bars!' I said, 'And you were worried?'

"It is three o'clock. The door opens and in walks Sol Siegel. He asks how we're doing. I tell him we've finished, but if he'll give us an hour we'll do it for him. He said, 'What do you mean, give you an *hour?*' I said, 'We have to learn it—we have to woodshed, we have to find what's the best key, we have to find what's the best accompaniment for it, we have to find the best way of doing it for you.' And he said, 'Are you guys crazy? Why do you have to learn it? You *wrote* it!' We simply could not make the guy understand performance.

"Understand, performance, that's the most important thing about doing a song for somebody the first time. I mean, if I walk into a room to do a song for you, I'm the most expensive singer in the world. I walk in without an orchestra, no makeup, no lights, I don't sing any song you ever heard before. It's just a little guy with a mustache and glasses. If you like what I sing, you owe me a lot of money. So we really work up to that—it's moment-of-truth time. But he was so anxious and insistent, I looked at Jule, he looked at me, and he said, 'Let's *all* hear it for the first time.' He played me an intro and I started to sing the song. I finish, and he said, 'It's marvelous—*marvelous!*' I looked at Jule—that moment is better than a kick in the head, you know? Beautiful!

"Siegel said, 'Let's do it for Zanuck!' We're all running down the hallway to Zanuck's office. He says, 'The boys have a song!' We played it again, I sang, '*Make it mine, make it mine, make it mine!*' Zanuck says 'Sensational! Listen, we have to have a record right away to send to New York. Would you make a record—for demonstration?' I said, '*Me?* You've got to see me to believe me— you can't put me on a record.' He asks, 'Who *can* we get?' I said, 'Well, Sinatra's walking around here getting a quarter of a million for *not* making a picture. Why don't we get him to do it?' He said, 'Would you ask him?'

"I go find Sinatra. I say, 'Frank, we've just written a song for Sol Siegel called "Three Coins in the Fountain" and he wants me to make the demo.' He says, 'You?' He snickers. I said, 'You're right. Would *you* do a little demo record?' I caught him in a very good mood. 'Sure, when?' I tell him if he'll come around tomorrow at two, Jule will teach him the song, not too tough, and we'll go and do it. Fine. I immediately leave Sinatra and go find Lionel Newman of the music department. I ask him is he going to have any musicians in here tomorrow. He says, 'Am I going to have musicians? It happens I'm going to have sixty men. We're scoring *Captain from Castile!*' I said, 'We've got Sinatra, we'll whip up a little orchestration, he's going to do this new song, okay?' Fine. I give him the lead sheet.

"Next day at two, Sinatra comes by. We teach him the song. And now we stroll over to the recording stage. We open the door, and there are sitting sixty musicians. And Sinatra says, 'What the fuck is this?' I said, 'Oh, they happen to be here.' He gives me the jaundiced eye and says, 'They *happen* to have an orchestration in my key?' I say, 'They happen to have an orchestration in your key.' He gave me the eye again. I said, 'However, if you would rather do it with Styne at the piano, I can have them all take five.' He says, 'Take five? It'll take them half an hour to get out of here! Let's hear the orchestration!'

"Again, that has to be the best moment for the composer and the lyric-writer . . . when the music is *heard* for the first time. Lionel Newman stood up, brought them to attention, pointed to the strings, who started to play a lush intro, and then the harpist, who began to make waterfall sounds with the harp. And then Sinatra made the record.

"And I swear to you, we were standing at the back, enjoying it, and one of the Skouras brothers—it was probably Spyros, who was the boss man at Fox—said to me, 'Let me understand you.' He then asked me one of the most naïve questions in the world. 'Sinatra's going to record this song, a record will be made of it, it will be number one? Is that correct?' I said, 'That is correct.' Anybody who asks that naïve a question deserves that naïve an answer.

"But what really makes this the most fantastic story of all is that this song does go on to be number one in the world. It won the Academy Award for Jule and me. The record Sinatra made that day was used as title music for the picture, which was a giant hit. And during all this excitement, which took place in twenty-four hours, give or take an hour, everybody forgot one vital and important element." Cahn pauses with proper dramatic effect and smiles. "Nobody made a deal with us for that song!

"People ask me what is the most I ever made on a song. Well, the most has to be 'Coins'—because long after it became a giant hit, Sol Siegel came into our office and he was very depressed. He says, 'I've just heard from the front office about a small detail—you've never signed a contract for the song.' 'Hey, that's right!' I said. 'The song is ours!' Do you know what it means to own that song a hundred percent? Incredible. He says, 'It can't be your song, Sam.' I said, 'Don't tell me it can't be mine. It can be mine, but it can't be *yours*. Let's assume that this song, for which we didn't get paid—let's say it went on to be a flop, nothing. We did the work, we did everything for nothing, nobody would have come by and said, "Hey, we owe you money." The roll of the dice came up seven, and it's our roll.' He said, 'Sammy, everything you said is correct, but we cannot perform this song in our picture, because we—Fox—don't have a deal on it.' Which is correct. They are in dire trouble.

"Well, eventually we made a deal. Fifty-percent split on the copyright, but the entire royalties remained ours. And that is the incredible story of 'Three Coins.' "

The secretary has reappeared with a shopping bag full of assorted packages —stockings for Mrs. Cahn, several flaçons of the firm's best perfumes, and Xerox copies of the lyrics for tomorrow's performance in Miami. Cahn prepares to leave, and as the secretary departs, he croons *"I adore you!"* at her (a fragment of one of his many love lyrics). The lady is obviously delighted.

"But I've always had lucky experiences with composers like that," says Cahn. "With Saul Chaplin, the words and music always seemed to come almost simultaneously. I'd start, *'This is my first affair,'* and he'd be playing a tune and give me back, *'So please be kind.'* And with Jule, he'd play you a melody. Something like, *'Time after time,'* and I'd pick it up: *'I tell myself that I'm so lucky to be loving you.'*

"Work fast. A whole melody. With Jimmy Van Heusen, the words come almost simultaneously. We got a script from Paramount, *Papa's Delicate Condition*, and I read it and the most pertinent word in the script is the word 'irresponsible.' Do you have to be a genius to come up with the title 'Call Me Irresponsible'? But then, Jimmy and I sat for hours and hours trying to figure out how to write a song that would denote the walk of a fellow who's just ever so slightly drunk—that was Jackie Gleason's character. And then we finally come up with the exact phrase." He leaps to his feet and does a slight rolling walk up and down the elegant little office. "What do you say when a drunk is walking like this? Yes, sure—that's walking *happy*, right? Which is how we got that one. We wrote a song about all the walks people can walk. Gleason sang it to his daughter. 'Walking Happy.' Later we used that as the title of a show in New York.

"Another time we're writing a picture for Sinatra called *A Hole in the Head*, and I'm walking around and I come up with the idea, *'High hopes—high apple-pie-in-the-sky hopes . . . '* ESP. Next day Van Heusen says, 'I was with Sinatra last night.' He was in charge of Sinatra from eight to five in the morning. See, I hung around Frank in the afternoon; Van Heusen was the night shift! He said, 'Frank thinks we ought to have a song for the young boy, the kid in the picture who plays his son.' 'Hey,' I said, 'I have this title, "High Hopes.' " It sounds good. So he says, 'Let me come up with a tune.' He comes back with one of those two-four tunes—very martial. *'When you're down and out, lift up your head and shout, you're going to have some high hopes!'* I didn't like it, and he knew right away it wasn't good, so he said, 'Let me try again,' and he came back the next day, and he had a spiritual. *'Sing Hallelujah, Hallelujah, and you're bound to have some high hopes!'* I didn't like that either, but I never tell a composer I don't like his melody. 'Cause that's a thing that anyone who deals with creativity knows—you never say, 'I don't like that.' There's a gentler, kinder, more graceful way.

"May I tell you that the best student of creativity, as far as *I'm* concerned, was—and is—Mr. Sam Goldwyn. Jule Styne and I wrote him a great song once. *The Kid from Brooklyn* was the picture. Goldwyn said, 'That is great. Great.' And our hearts leaped, and then he said, 'But I just feel—I just feel you guys can do better.' He said, 'Look, you see this song here—we have it right here now, nothing can destroy this song. Here it is, I love it. Great. If you cannot do better, we have this, but I know in my heart . . .' So we went away and we wrote another song, and Goldwyn said, 'That is infinitely better. Tell the truth, isn't it?' And we said, 'Yeah—it's better!' He said, 'But you know something? I feel *here*, here in my heart, you can do better than that.' Three times he did that to us! With the fourth song, I said, 'This is the best we can do!' He said, '*That's* what I want!'

"So I never say to anybody, 'I don't like it.' I say, 'Look, we have this, let's try for something else.' I said, 'Jimmy, we're writing this song from the wrong angle.' I was taking the blame. I said, 'Instead of writing this song from the angle of human beings, why don't we try it from the angle of animals?' And the minute I said it, I wanted to tear out my tongue, because I was telling the man who had written the single greatest animal song ever written!" ("Swinging on a Star," the great Bing Crosby hit, contains references to mules with long funny ears, and so forth.)

"But I know how to think on my feet. I said, 'Forget that—not animals.' I'm looking on the bungalow floor at Fox, where we're working; it's in the country-club area of L.A., and there are some ants. Ants running around. '*Insects!*' I said. 'What do you mean, insects?' he asked. I said, 'Well, you just take an ant. An ant has a sense of fulfillment when it moves from one place to another.' Jimmy looked at me and he said, 'Yeah?' The minute you say that it writes itself; I just happen to be privileged to be there. '*Just what makes the little old ant think he'll move a rubber tree plant?*' I know ants can't move rubber trees, but it has to be a rubber-tree plant, that's what makes the cadence and the syllables fall properly—and the song is home and free, and you just happen to be lucky to be there getting it written.

"Later we were asked to come out to Peter Lawford's house to meet the Kennedys. They all wanted to know did we have a song that would work for his political campaign, so I suggested 'High Hopes.' They asked if we could make a campaign song out of it, and I said, 'The question is not can I make a campaign song—the question is, do you *want* it? 'Cause if you want it to be, that's what comes first. Remember—not the words and music, the *request*. Right?' And they said, 'Try.'

"That night, going home, Van Heusen says, 'All right, big mouth, how're you going to make a campaign song out of that?' And I do not know. So we're sitting down, examining, examining. Getting absolutely nowhere. Do you know what? You *cannot* rhyme Kennedy. Try it. I defy you."

Cahn pauses, with a fine sense of drama.

"So, after hours of frustration I think of something—a trick that goes back to my old days of writing special material. I said to Jimmy, 'Why don't we spell it?' And it became, '*K-E-double-N-E-D-Y, Jack's the nation's favorite guy, Everyone wants to back Jack, Jack is on the right track, and he's got high hopes.*' The campaign song for 1960 . . ." Cahn beams. "That, for me, is great adventure!"

He grabs all his assorted belongings. "Come on, let's get going. I have thirty-seven things to do before I go to Miami tomorrow."

Our mini-safari hurries down the long gray hall with its vivid neon tubing as Cahn waves *Auf wiedersehen* to assorted young secretaries.

"But we're nowhere near finished," he insists. "I haven't told you about when Jule and I wrote 'It's Magic,' and Miss Doris Day's first screen test at Warner's." The elevator is dropping us to street level, and then Cahn is striding purposefully eastward on the crowded sidewalk. "Follow me!" he commands jovially. Tomorrow he will be wowing the assembled salesmen down in Miami, but he will be back in New York within hours after that. There are far too many people who need some of Sammy Cahn's time—and all of Sammy Cahn's talent.

"Going to tell you a secret," he announces. "I'm going to write a book about all the things that have happened to me. Got the title. It's going to be called 'Did He Write *That?*' Like it?"

Fine, but isn't he perturbed that some of it has already been bestowed on other authors, including this one?

"Hell, no!" he chortles. "I've just been auditioning it for you!"

And off he goes, walking happy.

'Tradition'

(Bock and Harnick)

$\mathbf{O}$N JUNE 17, 1972, *Fiddler on the Roof* became the longest-running musical show ever to play on Broadway—thus outlasting such previous classics as *Oklahoma!*, *South Pacific*, *My Fair Lady*, and *Hello, Dolly!* There is a wide-screen version of *Fiddler* playing all over the world. Even if it didn't exist, there are so many international productions of the musical saga of Tevye, the milkman, and his friends of the tiny Russian-Jewish village, that the show's long and happy future life is as close to guaranteed as you will ever get in show business.

The superb score for the Jerome Robbins production was written by Jerry Bock; the brilliant lyrics, which seem to be such a generic part of Joe Stein's adaptation of Sholom Aleichem's stories, are the work of Sheldon Harnick.

Both men are in their mid-forties. Even now, years after *Fiddler's* opening night, they regard the phenomenon of their work's huge acceptance with audiences everywhere with a certain amount of justifiable perplexity, "I still don't believe it," says Bock. "Sometimes I often doubt if it's all true."

He is an outspoken man, articulate and witty.

Harnick, who began his career as the writer of comedy songs, views the world (and the word) through his spectacles with much less optimism than does Bock. "Temperamentally," says Harnick, "We've always been exactly the opposite. Jerry has been the world's greatest optimist, and I've always been rather pessimistic. That's one of the things that has made us such a nicely meshing creative team. Between us, we help bring the other either down to earth, or *up* to earth.

"You really can't believe a thing like *Fiddler* and its success is going to happen when you start," says Bock. "Maybe if you're Rose Kennedy, and you nourish the ambition to have your son become President, and you move your entire life so that happens, fine. But for us, *Fiddler* was only another show— The next show. It was never designed to be a blockbuster.

"We started it down in a cellar in New Rochelle, all by ourselves," he recounts. "We're not always asked, you know. But if you're not asked to take on a project, then you have to take the bull by the horns and *do* it. If you wait for the phone to ring, then you start building a wall of self-defenses—one that eventually, you never can see over . . ."

"Somebody sent me one of the few novels that Sholom Aleichem had written, *Wandering Star*. Very wandering and diffuse it was, but I suddenly discovered in it a whole world! Remarkable. Then Joe Stein touted us onto Aleichem's short stories, 'Tevye's Daughters,' and 'The Old Country.' We ate them up! They struck such a responsive chord in both Shel and me. I'd never lived that life—I come from the Mid-West, and so does he—but as a child I'd had some of it passed down to me by my grandparents. So Shel and I decided to take off on this and write, even before we had a producer."

The early history of *Fiddler* and its creation is replete with turn-downs and negative reactions. "We were urged not to continue because it was so special," says Bock, "Some people were embarrassed to hear its open Yiddish flavor. Oh, sure, there had been shows like this years before, down on Second Avenue, in the purely Yiddish theatre, but this was the mid-'60s now, and the notion of doing such a parochially Jewish show for a catholic audience—in this case, Jewish," he grins, "struck people as very odd. They were sure that we'd run out of audiences for the show very quickly." He shakes his head with wonder. "And now it's more than eight years later. Of course, we caught a larger-than-Jewish audience very early on. We won the National Catholic Award, and audiences responded very deeply wherever it played. All over the world, Even Finland—I don't think there are more than 200 Jewish families in Helsinki! So there obviously must be something else in the show that captures them. It certainly can't be simply the Jewishness, so-called, of Tevye's story."

Eight years, hundreds of thousands of LP recordings, and stacks of fat royalty checks later, Jerry Bock and Sheldon Harnick are quite matter-of-fact about their success. Humble they are not, but neither are they arrogant. Both men are far too clear-eyed about the long and hard travail that brought them to this plateau of accomplishment. To have "made it" on the postwar Broadway scene of the '50s and '60s was a far more difficult and frustrating task than it might have been back in the lush days of the Coolidge administration, when musicals were not a luxury item with $12 tickets, but a staple item for the tired businessman.

Their partnership began in 1957, when the two teamed up to write the score for a musical called *The Body Beautiful*. The show opened on Broadway a year later, and lasted for only two short months. An inauspicious start, to be sure, but not their first professional experience. Both had been struggling separately for a long time.

Jerry Bock had never planned to compose music. "There was a piano in our house, music was always available, but I never took it seriously." He went to the University of Wisconsin intending to major in journalism. "But on an impulse one day I went into the Music School and auditioned a thing I'd written in high school. Bugle calls in the styles of various classical composers. I shudder to think of my own arrogance—it must have been terribly embarrassing for them, They said, 'Mr. Bock, you show signs of inventiveness. Are you willing to start from scratch, as a beginning music student?' I could have said no; but there it was, that moment of decision. Strictly on impulse, I said yes—when I'd had absolutely no intention before of doing it!"

Along with a fellow student, Larry Holofcener, Bock began to write songs. "After graduation, it was 'New York, here we come!' Ordinarily, we would have had our eyes blackened—but remarkably enough, there's a happy ending."

A family friend had secured the two young men an introduction to producer Max Liebman, who was at the time putting on a live weekly television revue, "Your Show of Shows," starring Sid Caesar and Imogene Coca. "He listened to our samples—four kakamamie songs—and hired us that day. Very lucky. For the next few years we worked very hard. Numbers for the chorus, and the ballet group, and for production numbers—*everything!* Three days to write, three days to stage. Seventh day, the show went out on the air—an hour—*live.* No such thing as videotape in those days; it was a new show every week!

"Later on, I found out that sort of pressure-writing was an invaluable experience for me. You go out on the road with a new show and suddenly you're faced with rewriting and replacing. I had all that accumulated experience to draw on—writing against a tight time deadline, murder, but exciting."

Bock also served an apprenticeship at a summer resort called Tamiment, in the Catskill mountains. For three summer seasons there, he and his partner wrote the equivalent of a one-act musical revue each week. "It added up to an average of two, three or four songs a week for ten weeks," he says. "Marvelous training—we got direct contact with audiences." In 1955, some of Bock's songs were in a revue called *Catch a Star* on Broadway, and he continued supplying material for Max Liebman's weekly "Your Show of Shows." Eventually, in 1956, there came a chance to do a Broadway show, an original score for *Mr. Wonderful,* which starred Sammy Davis, Jr.

Set down in order, it all seems to have happened with a steady forward thrust, but Bock today has vivid recollections of the "down" periods. Far too many of his contemporaries from the '50s have long since given up theatrical writing; he is very much aware of the rate of attrition among the talented people he knew. "From all over the country they arrive in New York, hoping to make good in show business, but most often they've ended up in advertising agencies, writing commercials, or writing arrangements for pop groups; anything where there's a living to be earned." Bock considers himself lucky to have been able to stay on the theatrical scene. "There were years when I didn't think I could stick it. Flop shows. Harnick and I worked nearly two years on *The Body Beautiful*—it closed in two months. Later, we had other flops, but I just felt I had to keep on going. My wife and my family have always been remarkably helpful and encouraging. I'm sure they'd all have preferred me to go into some more pragmatic business!"

Sheldon Harnick's years before he met Jerry Bock were also replete with adverses. His origins as a neophyte lyricist were rooted in the comic muse. "Little verse, doggerel, nonsense poetry," he says today. "Maybe it was my way of getting attention when I was in high school. I'd come under the influence of Benchley, S.J. Perelman, Thurber, Frank Sullivan. They were a constant inspiration, if that's the word, to try and write with wit, the way they did."

When the war came ("World War *II*," he grins, "and doesn't that say volumes to you about our age?"), Harnick was drafted into the Army and stationed in Georgia. There he began to do his first real writing, lyrics and sketches for soldier shows. But he was also an accomplished violin player; writing was still merely an avocation.

When the war ended, Harnick returned to college. When did the switch from music to lyrics take place?

"I was playing with a dance band," he says. "Seventeen pieces . . . Henry Brandon's orchestra at the Edgewater Beach Hotel in Chicago. Very good job. But business got worse and worse, the band got smaller and smaller. We'd broadcast five nights a week at midnight; they'd hang that mike above me and I'd have to play. Nights we played on a nation-wide hook-up, and I'd get all tied up in knots. Years afterwards, an analyst helped me to find out that I was a repressed hysteric; I didn't realize that about myself . . .

"We laid off a couple of weeks—and when I picked up the violin again, I couldn't move my fingers. Couldn't play at all! Terrified me. I went to the doctor and he diagnosed it, gave it a name which maybe he'd made up, or maybe he hadn't. He said he'd had a similar case in Vienna, and he called it *Geigerkrampf*—fiddle-cramp. Agonizing. Even though I began to come out of it, I began to realize that I couldn't make my living at this any more, so I took my savings and came to New York."

"Remarkable, when I think back on it," Harnick comments. "Years afterwards, when I'd been analyzed, my analyst said to me that I obviously possessed the quality of drive—but that in me, it expressed itself in stubborness. I'd come to New York with two major escape routes. If I couldn't make it as a lyricist, I could either be a librarian—that I knew I could do; the other thing I thought I could do was to be a guide at the United Nations.

"I just hung on. I found out that the UN only used young ladies, so that was out, and I kept on writing. How easy I was on myself," he chuckles. "I set myself the schedule of writing one song a week! . . . I got a few little things into collected revues, and people used some of my songs in night club acts, but nothing really major happened."

Among the "little things" that Harnick placed was a satiric number with which Alice Ghostley regularly stopped the show in *New Faces of 1952*, the rollicking "Boston Beguine." Harnick's friends Charlotte Rae and Arte Johnson were performing his material with great success, but usually to highly limited audiences.

"Things were very lean," he says now. I remember once a television producer, Norman Lear, came to New York to persuade me to come West and work on a new show of his out there. I was thrilled at the chance, and I desperately needed the job. But it ended up being the craziest meeting. He had one or two drinks at breakfast, and then he started saying, 'Sheldon, I'm not going to ruin your life! You have no idea what a rat-race the business I'm in is. I'm not going to spoil things for you. If you stay here in New York you'll end up doing something wonderful!'—and I kept saying to him, '*Please—corrupt me.*' "

Harnick managed to find some employment that served his talents and his lean bank account during this period of struggle, at a summer resort called Green Mansions (very much akin to Tamiment, Green Mansions was also the training-ground of lyricist Lee Adams, who has subsequently worked with Charles Strouse on the scores of *Bye, Bye Birdie* and *Applause*. Both Harnick and Adams deplore the closing of that resort).

It was also the scene of one of Harnick's most devestating flops. A musical show which he had written with Ira Wallach and composer David Baker, and which had previously had a successful try-out in the late Margo Jones' theatre in Dallas, was given a production the following summer at Green Mansions. "On a July night, 600 people in a place that should seat 400, no air conditioning, and it was stifling. By the end of the second act, we had 30 people with us."

"But failure like that is important," he says now. "Later, when Jerry and I teamed up to do *The Body Beautiful* and we saw all that work go down the drain in two months, I was prepared. I'd already had a worse experience. I'd been blooded."

It was Hal Prince, who was to produce their *Fiddler*, who took the first real chance with the as-yet unsuccessful team of Bock and Harnick. Steve Sondheim, a close personal friend who has great admiration for Harnick's work, has a vivid recollection of their first disaster. "After the newspapers came out with the bad notices, I sat there in Sardi's commiserating with them, and they were so discouraged. I said 'But it's not hopeless. For one thing, your work was heard tonight by some people who know something!' Sondheim had only recently made his debut as lyricist for the hit *West Side Story*, which Hal Prince had produced. "I'd seen Hal at the intermission of their opening and talked to him, and he'd told me that he didn't think the show was going to be a success, but he loved Bock and Harnick's music and lyrics. Just then, Hal walked into Sardi's. I introduced him to the two of them. Now I'm not making myself out to be the great brain over all this, but the point is, later on, Hal offered me the job of writing the lyrics to *Fiorello!* and I turned it down, but I suggested Bock and Harnick. And to Hal's credit, he took a chance on them.

"But then, Hal's always taken chances on unknowns, you know. He hired Dick Adler and Jerry Ross to write *Pajama Game*—they were recommended to him and George Abbott by Frank Loesser. And later Hal hired Kander and Ebb to write *Flora, The Red Menace*, with Liza Minelli—that was *her* first show, too. Kander and Ebb eventually wrote *Cabaret*, and Bock and Harnick came up with *Fiddler*. That's the terrific thing about Prince; he's willing to gamble. Not many other producers will gamble all that money on unknowns, believe me, not in this hard-nosed business."

Fiorello! was indeed a big chance for Bock and Harnick. The show was directed by George Abbott, from a book by Jerome Weidman. "We were very lucky there," says Harnick. "It was Mr. Abbott's last real success, and working with him taught us a lot, mostly about economy in writing. I'm a great believer in that—saying something well—in the least possible length. It's the secret of good lyrics . . . at least, for me."

The biography of New York's colorful Mayor LaGuardia opened in 1959, and settled down to a long and profitable run. It won the Pulitzer Prize, and was an audience-pleaser. "I had this experience twice," says Harnick. "With *Fiorello!* and with *Fiddler*. It was as though somebody was looking over my shoulder. With *Fiorello!* it was La Guardia himself. As I wrote, every so often, I would think 'No, that's not good enough. La Guardia wouldn't be happy with

that.' He's over my shoulder saying 'No, no, you've got to do better than that . . .'
The same thing happened with *Fiddler*, only that time it was the spirit of Sholom
Aleichem. I kept thinking as I wrote, 'No, no, he worked too hård on this material
for me to settle for something so easy!'"

The score of *Fiorello!* established Bock & Harnick as paid-up members of
the Broadway scene, capable of writing a lovely ballad, "Till Tomorrow," or a
bright satiric number, "Politics and Poker." The hit of the show—"Little Tin
Box," sung by a chorus of Tammany-type politicians, who happily recounted
their exploits in the area of graft and corruption, proves Bock's point about their
ability to write under pressure. It was written out of town, and put into the
show only a few days before the Broadway opening.

Fiorello! was a rare exhibit; a full-scale biography, set to music, of an actual
public figure. Not often before, or since, has such a project succeeded. And the
show was remarkable in its fidelity to the story of the man who read the funny
papers over WNYC, loved to follow fire engines when they answered alarms,
and managed to run New York not only colorfully, but efficiently.

Less than a year later, in 1960, there was another show, *Tenderloin*. "We
started working on that right after our first hit," says Harnick, "We opened in
New Haven and it was disastrous. We had an emergency meeting that night.
Mr. Abbott said, 'I had a concept for this show, and it doesn't work. Any ideas?'
And I looked at everybody in the hotel room, and I saw blank looks all around,
and I suddenly thought, 'My God, I don't have any idea what this is all about,
this whole show, except for the work I've done.' And there was a conscious
decision on my part never to let that happen again. So that the next show we
were involved in, *She Loves Me!*—there I really started involving myself with
the book, and working as closely as possible with Joe Masteroff, the book writer.
Sometimes, I'm sure, to his great irritation. Since then, both Jerry and I have
continued to work that way."

When they discuss *She Loves Me!* both Bock and Harnick refer to it with
affection. "It was the one I most enjoyed working on," says Harnick. "On the
stage, there was such a unity of idea . . . it was just beautiful."

"A very special kind of musical," says Bock, fondly.

From old Vienna and a charming *caffee-mit-schlag* romantic confectionery
to the bitter-sweet chronicle of the impoverished Tevye and the rest of the
ragged residents of Anatevka. Quite a change of scene. What caused it?

"Whenever we finish something," says Bock, "we've always wanted to do
an about-face and go somewhere else. To do something hopefully that will give
us the opportunity to break new ground, to write fresh, or to explore territory
we haven't been in before. We've never sat down to write a score and made it
a rule that we've got to come up with one or two hit songs. We concentrate on
the needs of the book. When we started on *Fiddler* that was all that mattered."

"For me," says Harnick, "the book is the basis of the musical, the thing
that makes it work. Without a good one, it's hopeless."

Some sort of alchemy was at work when Joe Stein and Bock and Harnick
prepared the show; Bock and Harnick may not have been consciously writing
hits, but the fact remains that works such as "Matchmaker, Matchmaker," "Sunrise, Sunset," and "To Life, To Life, L'Chaim!" go far beyond even the realm
of what we call "standards". The score for *Fiddler* is popular, and simultaneously
classic.

"Jerry Robbins was instrumental in that happening," says Bock. "We'd always hoped that the score would break through what appeared to be a special show, for certain people only, and begin to reach as many people as possible. That's where Jerry Robbins accomplished so much for us. He kept asking the question—as he always does—what is this show *about?* And beyond the fact that it's a family chronicle, he kept hammering away on the breakdown of tradition; on the inability of Tevye to cope with the changes that were occurring, not only in this little poor village, but the wide world as well. He guided us so that we kept that always in mind. And of course, the last song we wrote for the score really was the opening, because it was only after we had really dug into the show, and had it mostly finished, that we were able to express 'Tradition!' —the opening chorus. Which made it the signpost, really, for the whole show. That was the *circle.* Mind you, that circle was a visual concept that Robbins always had in mind, from the start."

In the past 15 years, when so much of American popular taste has favored folk-rock, electric guitars, and bubble-gum music, two Broadway show scores have achieved steady universal acceptance: *Fiddler* and *The Sound of Music* (others may argue that *Man of La Mancha* is in the same category, but that's due only to "The Impossible Dream" which has made it big with baritones).

One can understand why the sunny Rodgers and Hammerstein saga of Maria and her happy charges has sold LP's in the millions all over the world. Between Mary Martin and Julie Andrews on the wide-screen, those songs got "plugged" aplenty. But *Fiddler?*" It is hardly a "plug" score—and yet it has penetrated. One might logically expect that the lovely Bock and Harnick song "Sunrise, Sunset," in which Tevye philosophically sings of the meaning of life at his daughter's wedding, would have become *de rigeur* at Jewish weddings, along with "To Life, L'Chaim!"—a hearty drink and dance song. But when Zero Mostel did a guest-shot on the Dean Martin television show, eight years after the show's opening, his solo had to be "If I Were A Rich Man," which somehow, nobody considered ethnic. "For that universality, I believe Jerry Robbins is responsible," Bock says today.

(Earlier, in response to a question as to which of Harnick's lyrics from *Fiddler* he cherishes the most, Bock wrote ". . . I suppose I would have to pick one that was written under pressure, out of town. We were looking for a musical finish to a scene between Tevye and his wife, a song that would illustrate their very special relationship. I remember Sheldon coming into my hotel room and reading the lyric of "Do You Love Me?" He asked me what I thought of it. I could have hugged him. I think I did . . .")

Fiddler became the huge success that it is despite a rather indifferent reception at its first performance out of town. "In Detroit, for example, the critic said it was an amateur production," Bock seems fond of recalling. "And when it came to New York, we got mixed reviews,* We were a slow hit, believe me."

"God knows it's been gratifying. But along with its accumulated success— I use that for lack of a better word," Bock grins, "has come no insight as to how to do it again."

---

* The parallel with *The Sound of Music* is even more remarkable. *Music* ran for many years, and the film version is a box-office phenomenon. As the late Leland Hayward, one of its producers, was fond of saying (usually as he endorsed profit checks from the show), "I don't think I've ever seen a really *good* review for *The Sound of Music.*"

Harnick takes an even less sanguine attitude toward the huge success of the show. "I was writing to a friend of mine who was congratulating me on *Fiddler*'s longevity, and I said 'Thank you, it makes me literally feel like I'm king of the hospital.' "

Harnick is referring to the unpleasant fact that since the opening of *Fiddler* in 1964, the Broadway musical theatre has undergone a period of insanely-rising production cost, with less and less production. If it was tough to get an opening "break" back in the '50s, for young tyro talents the '70s scene is bleak. "I feel so lucky," remarks Harnick. "I feel as though in a sense I've been walking along a cliff, and I've always taken a step backwards just before part of the cliff crumbles. For instance, I got in at the end of revues—*New Faces* and a couple of others. Now there are no more revues. My first book show was George Abbott's last successful show. *Fiddler* was the last show that Robbins has done. He's capable of many more, but for some reason, he's chosen not to do them. I almost feel as though I came in and managed to make it just before the theatre dissolved. Jerry isn't as pessimistic as I am about the future of musical comedy, or of Broadway itself. I am sure there's a place for the live musical comedy— but perhaps, not any more in the style and shape it's been for the past few years."

Following *Fiddler*, Bock and Harnick attempted a completely different style of show—three short plays set to music. *The Apple Tree* was directed by Mike Nichols. "Again, something we had never done, a complete turnabout," says Bock. *The Apple Tree* was well received, and had a successful run on Broadway in 1966–67.

Bock and Harnick's next project was to occupy them for three years, and did not arrive on Broadway until the fall of 1970. *The Rothschilds*, on which they worked with author Sherman Yellen, is an adaptation of a biography of the famous banking family. The original producer of the show struggled for over two years to get backing for it. It wasn't until he brought the project to Lester Osterman, another Broadway entrepreneur, that financing could be raised. In the midst of a Nixon recession, Osterman performed that heroic task of raising most of the show's inflated costs—$850,000.

"God knows there were problems with that show," says Harnick, a year later. "It's by no means a great show. But there's a taste, a certain level of invention and creativity. And most of all, we were not trying to insult anyone's intelligence—and we did find an audience."

Happily for all concerned, *The Rothschilds* ran for more than a year on Broadway, and is breaking records on tour throughout the West Coast. But all its costs have not been recouped, almost two years later. It becomes increasingly apparent that Harnick's gloomy jest about his status as king of the hospital may be based on truth.

And so, for two craftsmen, who wish to exercise their considerable talents to enrich the American theatre (and themselves, in the process), the search for their next project goes on. They'd settle for practically anything as source material—a short-story, an old film, an original libretto written for the stage, perhaps? But so far, they've had no success.

Are they perhaps being too selective? "*No!*" says Bock. "Because when you say, 'Okay, let's do this,' you now know that you're committed to two or three years' work, without a shadow of a doubt. So it's not that you want to be careful, as much as you want to be thoroughly enthused, right or wrong, about the thing that's going to occupy all your time from that moment on. When you say *yes* it should at least be with a sense of joy and energy and enthusiasm for . . . whatever it turns out to be. I personally need to feel that I can write lots of music for this one—I'm never going to be stuck. And Sheldon's feeling is that our score will make a genuine contribution to the piece, that it will help, will inform—it will enhance it, and . . ." he hesitates, pondering the proper word, ". . . God willing, make it *soar* . . ."

And when that happy day arrives, when that piece of material crosses their threshold, when the book-writer has signed on, and the project has been launched, which will come first, the music or the lyrics?

Bock laughs. "I thought you'd never ask that. It's *both*. We can work either way—which is great. It dispenses with the horror of waiting for the other person to finish. I write out all sorts of musical ideas, and then I tape them, and send them off to Shel. He may be at the shore—I'm in the city—whatever. Then he listens and responds by telling me which piece of mine interests him for which spot in the show. With us, it's always wide open. Whoever gets an idea first passes it back to the other."

Three years of work lie ahead—that's assuming they do find a project. What will the Broadway theatre be like in say, 1974–75?

"I'm not sure," says Harnick. "I *think* the musical will survive. In what shape or form, I'm not sure. *Hair* and *Godspell*, and *The Me Nobody Knows* are all examples of new approaches; so is *Jesus Christ Superstar*. They all have a kind of life on the stage; they don't tell stories in the old accustomed way, in what McLuhan calls 'the linear concept.' My own conditioning makes me want to see a story on the stage, so that's where my preference lies. But when I went to see *Hair*, I was so astonished; here was a show which broke all the rules I'd learned about writing for the theatre—and it was successful!"

"I am not depressed by what I see," says Bock. "I try to keep an open ear, to listen to what's happening. I think, I *hope*, that the kids will eventually begin to discover the music of the '30s and '40s, and we may have a resurgence of that. It's encouraging that when I meet young writers, they all want to do their 'own thing,' but they're also going back and studying the musical forms of the past fifteen, twenty, thirty years. I don't think they're winging it on an instinctive level."

"The musical theatre will survive," says Harnick, with just the faintest hint of prayer in his aspect. "Maybe not on Broadway—the expense. But somewhere else? I was thinking recently of that Brecht expression that goes 'Where the need is greatest, then there's something that will come along.'"

So, in fifteen years, they have come a considerable distance since the days when Bock wrote instant-musical numbers for Sid Caesar and Imogene Coca, and Harnick was taking sharp satiric pot-shots at censorship and narrow-mindedness with his "Boston Beguine." Viewed in the perspective of the composers and lyricists who have come before them, Herbert, Kern, Romberg, Berlin, the Gershwins, Rodgers & Hart. Hammerstein, Arlen, Harburg, and all the others who have filled theatres, Jerry Bock and Sheldon Harnick, along with their friend Stephen Sondheim, seem to be the last of a very proud line. Or, to use their own title, a "Tradition."

"I hope that's not so," sighs Harnick.

Any words for neophytes who still plan to tackle New York?

"I once typed up a quote and put it over my desk," says Harnick. "It read

'Inspiration is the act of drawing up the chair to the writing desk.' And O'Casey, I found out, had one which read, 'Get on with the bloody job!' "

That may well be the secret of survival whether it be in Tevye's Russian *shtetl*, in Fiorello La Guardia's New York, in the Rothschilds' ghetto in Frankfurt, or on Broadway.

'Taking a Chance on Love'

(Vernon Duke)

" **. . .** **I** CAN'T GET STARTED . . .

"You can count on the fingers of one hand and perhaps on the thumb and index finger of the other the number of our theatre composers whose melodic lines and harmonies are highly individual. There is no question that Vernon Duke must be considered one of these . . ."

So writes Mr. Ira Gershwin in his book *Lyrics On Several Occasions*, and it is a bit superfluous to add that Mr. Gershwin knows whereof he speaks, especially when he speaks of Vernon Duke, née Vladimir Dukelsky. Gershwin collaborated with Duke on the songs for *Ziegfeld Follies*, from which score came "I Can't Get Started."

"We did about thirty songs for that show, of which about eleven or twelve were used. I was very proud of the stuff I did with Vernon," says Mr. Gershwin today. Among the other songs in the show were "Island in the West Indies," "Words Without Music," a beautiful "lost" ballad, and "That Moment of Moments."

"Very talented, and very quick," he continues. "He'd come in when we were working, and he'd grab me like a Russian bear—well, he was Russian, you know. 'Ira—the greatest song I ever wrote!' And he'd sit down and play it for me. I'd say ' . . . *Well* . . . I . . ." and then he'd say 'All right, I'll write *another* one!' He was very prolific, and he made the fastest piano copy I ever saw. He could do a whole verse and refrain, a good piano copy, in twenty minutes—just put the whole thing down on paper . . .

"But Duke was always arguing—with everyone. Everyone he worked with—me, Yip Harburg—he always had some supposed grievance."

Duke had worked with Harburg on the Broadway revue *Walk A Little Faster*. It was from that early Harburg-Duke collaboration that "April in Paris" emerged, to become the second of his great standards.

Bernard Herrmann, the composer-conductor, says "I could sum up Vernon Duke by saying that he really thought he *was* a Grand Duke—but there were times when he behaved like a Grand Duke's coachman. He could be very vulgar, in many ways. But I always understood him, and I never took offense. He was a gifted composer, and a gifted songwriter. A marvelous pianist; the only one who could give him any competition there was his good friend George Gershwin."

"He never really had the success that he should have had. It wasn't because he hadn't received the proper attention for his classical work. Even as a young man, he'd been singled out for praise in Europe by the leading musical authorities. But he was a very complicated man. I knew him from the time when he first came to America. I recorded his second symphony, his cello concerto, his violin concerto, many of his other works, so I understood a little of what the whole man was about. He had great success as a serious composer, he had success as a popular composer, but I suppose it was because he never really won the sweepstakes—the jackpot. Perhaps because he had very little taste in picking librettos to work on; he didn't know the difference between a good one and a bad one—but he certainly worked with good lyricists.

"In a way, I suppose with his popular music he was having his night out. But that never meant that he didn't do fine work. After all, Offenbach was the same sort of composer—both classical and popular. Lehar was always trying to write grand opera.

"Vernon in many ways was really responsible for the lack of his own success. He carried on feuds with lots of people. The one with Stravinsky is well known, and he also had one with Stokowski. I tried to get Stokowski to play one of Duke's concert works—'Ode To The Milky Way,' and Stokowski said 'I just don't like it—I'm glad *you* do.' So Duke held me responsible for Stokowski not playing it. I told Duke I'd tried, but it was no use. I tried Stokowski again. Still no use. When I saw Stokowski in London a couple of years ago, he said to me 'You know that wonderful piece you once showed me, the one about the Milky Way?' Now it's something 'wonderful'—do you see what I mean about irony?'

"I didn't see him for the last five years of his life because of something he took offense at—not of what I said—but of what my former wife said. She made him a soup he liked—but she didn't make it the way he liked it! Something as trivial as that . . .

"When he got married, I sent him a letter. I said 'Even royal dukes in Russia on their nuptial days forgive all the serfs, and release them from jail. Why don't you talk to your old friend?' he never answered. Because my wife didn't make his soup properly—or what? I never knew," says Herrmann.

Along with "I Can't Get Started" and "April in Paris," Duke had a third huge song hit, from the Broadway show *Cabin in the Sky*—the rollicking "Taking a Chance on Love."

"That was a very happy accident," recalls Arthur Lewis, the producer, whose father, Albert Lewis, produced that show in 1940. "We were having trouble with a scene change, just before opening. Ethel Waters, our star, had to have some sort of a song in one, before the curtains, while we made the change backstage. We needed something with impact. Vernon had been coming up with songs that didn't fit that need, but he came in one night with a song called 'Fooling Around With Love,' that he'd written with Ted Fetter for something else. Well, when he played us that, everybody jumped at it. There was a big legal problem involved—Fetter's lyric had to be rewritten by John LaTouche, our lyricist, and it was very difficult to iron out the problem of interpolation. Duke and LaTouche had a contract that specified nobody else's songs could be used, and here was a song written by Duke with Fetter. Finally we got it all straightened out, LaTouche changed the title to 'Taking a Chance on Love,' and on opening night, when Ethel came out and sang it, there was just no way to follow it! She sang *five* choruses—the audience wouldn't let her leave the stage. Ethel finally ad-libbed a little closing couplet—something to the effect that she didn't have any more words. A huge hit, that song—and it's always been one since that night. So ironic. If we hadn't been in a spot with some scenery, that song might still be stuck away somewhere in Vernon's trunk!"

"One of the things that gave Duke his greatest thrill," says Herrmann, "was that his show *Cabin in the Sky* ran longer in France than it did in New York. There they did a much richer and more sophisticated production—more complicated, and as he said to me, 'There, they have real choruses, who can *sing*.' But that was part of the complexity of the man," he adds. "That split personality. Up at ASCAP, he was only regarded by how well he was doing on Broadway—and all Duke was really worried about was how well he was doing up in Boston, with the symphony orchestra."

In the years that followed *Cabin in the Sky*, Duke's career as a popular songwriter had more than the customary ratio of flop to success enjoyed by his peers. He and LaTouche wrote a score for Eddie Cantor's starring vehicle, *Banjo Eyes*. The show was a hit, but closed abruptly because of Cantor's physical problems. There were to be others, such as "Sadie Thompson," which he wrote with Howard Dietz, that were less-than-hits. After the war, during which he wrote a score for the Coast Guard—in which he served—called *Tars and Spars*, Duke worked on various collected revues, and contributed songs to a pair of minor Hollywood musicals. It was while he was working in Hollywood that he met the young Bobby Short; pianist, singer, pop-song interpreter par excellence.

"I was working in a place called the Club Gala, above Sunset," says Short. "Vernon came in one night. With no urging whatsoever, he got up from his table—he was a supreme egotist—came over to the piano and sat down and played some of his songs. I sang them. He became a big fan of mine, and it was mutual. I love Vernon's music. I loved it before I was aware who'd written it."

"When I was just a kid, I heard a song that he had written for a Broadway show called *Now*, and I was immediately drawn to it. Then later on, when I was 13 or 14, I remember being attracted to 'April in Paris.' He was remarkable. His sense of harmony was something that America hadn't ever heard before in popular music—it was a whole different approach!"

"I know Vernon is well-known for putting down other composers," Short continues, "but never with me. He'd always bring me stuff by other composers, Bo Bergersen, or Bart Howard, and discuss *their* talents, not his. I learned several very obscure Gershwin songs from him—you know, he was a great admirer of Gershwin's work,*—and he came to New York one day when I moved East and brought with him twelve more obscure Gershwin songs. 'Record *these*,' he said. Never his own . . .

"I can tell you something else about Duke," says Short. "As exacting as he might have been, and as ignorant as I was about what he'd written down in his music—because I don't read notes—Vernon never took it upon himself to say 'Look, you've got those last eight bars wrong.' Never told me. I'd always find it out some other way—by hearing it played by somebody else. I know for a fact he heard me do some of his songs wrong—but he never corrected me. He left that up to me to figure it out by myself. And believe me, I've had half-baked composers with one or two songs to their credit come to me, screaming and yelling about this change, or that phrase being played wrong. Not Vernon. He and Cole Porter were alike about that . . .

"Great ladies' man. Adored eating and drinking—extremely intelligent, literate. Wrote well. Snobbish, true, and a little mean, because he never quite achieved the success he should have had, I guess. A little bitter because of that," says Short.

"You know, I never liked his song 'I Can't Get Started' until I heard him play it. That famous old Bunny Berigan record, as famous as it was, and as much fun as it was to hear, never really captured the essence of the musicality that Duke had applied to the melody of that song. Never. I then heard Vernon accompanying Hildegarde one night when she sang it, and I also have a record he made of it, playing it on the piano alone. Vernon plays it so poignantly, because it's a sad, bitter-sweet song. Very much like Cole Porter's 'Why Shouldn't I?' I sit here at night and play both of those—when I get to Vernon's 'I Can't Get Started,' people always chuckle at Ira Gershwin's lyrics, and they smile—but underneath it all, it is a very sad song that really *says*—'I can't get started with you.' "

Vernon Duke died several years ago. "Poor Duke," said Herrmann, his old friend. "Lung cancer . . . and he never smoked."

---

* When George Gershwin died, he was working with his brother on the score for a film called *The Goldwyn Follies*. At Ira Gershwin's request, Duke was brought in to complete the work Gershwin had left unfinished.

'Wish You Were Here'

(Harold Rome)

T HREE THOUSAND MILES away from his usual turf, Broadway and 45th Street, Mr. Harold Rome is walking the streets of London, smoking a new pipe, wearing a new Jermyn Street shirt, an umbrella in one hand, his fingers carefully crossed in the other. *Gone With the Wind*, with words and music by Mr. Rome, is about to take up residence in May 1972 at the venerable Drury Lane Theatre.

One block above the Strand, two short blocks west of the Old Covent Garden market, where G.B. Shaw's Professor Higgins first encountered his future flower-girl Galatea, and where lately Alfred Hitchcock has been creating bloodshed amidst the brussel-sprouts, Miss Scarlett O'Hara of Tara Plantation is about to make her stage debut. A few nights hence, the show will open on the stage of the oldest operating playhouse in the world.

"You know," confides Rome, "this isn't my first show here. A few years back they did an English production of *Fanny*. Completely miscast, I'm afraid. None of the actors could sing. As the British are so fond of saying, 'We lost a packet.' "

Born in the old South she may have been, but this Scarlett was bred in

new Tokyo. It was there, in 1969, that Messrs. Joe Layton, the Broadway di-
rector-choreographer, and Mr. Rome were asked by the Toho Corporation, a
large and very successful Japanese entertainment complex, if they would consider
creating a musical show out of Toho's four-hour-long stage version of *Gone With
the Wind*.

The Toho offer was accepted, and in the ensuing months, the Western
creative work-party labored long and hard in Tokyo to meld Layton's concept
and Rome's score to a Japanese libretto.

The show opened in Tokyo in January, 1970, and had a most successful
run of three months. "No more, no less," remarks Rome. "That's Japanese
efficiency for you. They've computerized their box-office operation to such a
point that they know exactly how large the audience will be for each production,
and the day that they have figured the current show will stop selling out, it
closes. In comes the next attraction." He smiles. "Who else could have brought
planning to such a crazy business as ours?"

Why is *Gone With the Wind* opening here in England, rather than New
York?

"We tried for a year to get a production in New York," sighs Rome. "Try
raising money in the midst of a Nixon recession sometime. A very depressing
experience—especially when you know you've got a hit property based on a
great book."

So the English production made economic sense. The Drury Lane orchestra
pit will contain 34 musicians—8 more than the customary Broadway crew. The
cast of Layton's version consists of some fifty principals and chorus, plus—
count'em—ten extras! Add the cost of scenery, costumes, orchestration, and
lighting, and this opulent attraction would cost the most penurious Broadway
producer a mininum of a breathtaking $900,000. Here in London, the show can
be produced for roughly one third of that sum. And even if the London critics
do not toss their hats in the air over Miss O'Hara's affair with Mr. Butler (so as
not to keep you in suspense, they did), all would be far from lost. The show can
run here for at least a year merely to satisfy that large audience which will troop
into London by bus and coach to pay its respects and its pounds each week.
"And for the whole summer, we can count on all those theatre-starved American
tourists who come here," says Rome.

Eventually the show will be produced in the States, but until then, it's a
long trip back to the Confederate States for Miss Scarlett, and an even longer
one for Mr. Rome. He's been following his leading lady around like a dutiful
wandering minstrel for more than three years now. For this London production,
he has written the staggering sum of twenty-one different numbers. "My lucky
number," he says. "The count I do my yoga to each morning."

Rome, a stocky, amiable gentleman, is universally known around Manhattan as "Hecky." He graduated from Yale back in the early '30s with an
architectural degree. But his blueprints were replaced by music paper very early
on. He played piano at parties, and then began to write comedy material for
summer camp shows in that legendary incubator of talent, the Catskill Mountain
borscht summer circuit of hotels and camps. At one of those camps, back in
1936, he was asked if he would consider writing a socially significant musical
revue for the International Ladies Garment Workers Union. Rome's show, which
featured a cast of talented amateurs from the union's membership, was called
(what else?) *Pins and Needles*. It was a surprise hit, and projected Mr. Dubinsky's
ILGWU into show business for several years.

Later, Rome wrote the score for a show called *Sing Out The News*, which had a rousing number called "Franklin D. Roosevelt Jones" as its show-stopper. During World War II, Rome served as a GI, and when V-J day finally sprung him from the service, he and ex-G.I.'s Arnold Auerbach and Arnold Horwitt put together a revue which was based on the subject of the returning serviceman, with a few random comments about World War II, called *Call Me Mister*. "For that show," he says today, "the timing was absolutely correct. The audience which came in and the cast of ex-soldiers onstage had undergone a shared experience. That doesn't happen very often, believe me."

In *Call Me Mister*, Betty Garrett ("one of the most talented girls I ever had the pleasure of working with") danced and sang Rome's jolly "South America, Take It Away!" Several years later, he and Auerbach tried another revue, *Bless You All*, but it was not successful. "We told the audience we loved them for having come to the theatre, instead of all the other things they could have been doing that night, but it wasn't enough."

After that show, Rome abandoned the revue. "Or vice versa," he amends, wryly. "I'm afraid it's a lost art." For more than two decades, he has been working on the scores for musical shows with books, and it cannot be said that he's a stranger to widescale subjects. When Josh Logan directed Rome's *Wish You Were Here*, the show was famous for having an actual swimming-pool on stage, as well as for Rome's title song. *Fanny*, which starred Ezio Pinza, was another broad subject. "Pinza was the most exciting, magnetic man I've ever worked with," says Rome. "And this in spite of the fact that he couldn't read music, and that he couldn't learn a new song in less than a month. I wrote a new song for him out of town, took me three days to do. A beautiful song for a father to sing to his son, "Let's Talk About Woman," and I played it for Ezio. He listened and put his arm on my shoulder and said, "My boy, that's a beautiful song, but we open in New York in four weeks, and I could never learn it in time." We had to give him his score six months before the show opened. But all I can tell you is, the first time in the theatre when I sat there during the first rehearsal and heard him sing 'Fanny,' I burst out crying."

Later, *Destry*, which starred Andy Griffith, and *I Can Get It For You Wholesale*, from which Barbra Streisand emerged, were Rome successes. "Not that I haven't had my share of flops," he says, "plus shows which I worked on for years that never saw the nervous light of an opening night in New Haven."

But this production of *Gone With The Wind* is certainly his most complex job of writing for the theatre—one whose size and scope would have (and probably did) scare off composers with less determination and stamina. "True," he admits. "Most of the show is underscored with music—exactly like a film. All of that, plus twenty-one numbers. Sometimes I think this show must have more damned music than *Gotterdammerung!*"

He walks cheerfully through the huge Drury Lane lobby, where the box-office is framed with polished brass fittings, and the walls are done in magnificently complicated woodwork. He continues up the sweeping double stairs that lead to the second floor, where there is yet a second lobby, with a skylight above. Beyond a set of mirrored glass french doors is the Drury Lane's bar (one of several) where the English conductor, Ray Cook, is rehearsing Rome's music with a full complement of musicians. "Such opulence!" grins the gentleman from New York. "Where else but here could you find a theatre with a drinking-room big enough to house thirty-four musicians?"

The orchestra is running through an arrangement of a bright, lilting ballad called "Marrying for Fun," a song in which Rhett persuades Miss Scarlett to try the pleasures of married life with him. The very rich sound of all those musicians fills the room, the sound bouncing back down from the gilded ceiling above. Rome has written this song in a strange tempo, 5/4, and the musicians are obviously not quite with it yet. But by the second run-through of the song, they begin to fall in with the finesse of dependable professionals. Rome nods, satisfied. "Amazing, isn't it? I make a few scratches on the music paper, and listen to how it comes out!"

The origin, and eventual execution of the Japanese version of *Gone With the Wind* was never simple. "After Toho had done the play, Joe Layton developed a concept of how to do the story as a musical, and then he brought me in to write the score. After that, we wanted to have an American write the book, of course. But we did not reckon with the Japanese attitude. The chap who'd done the play version, on which we based the musical, was Mr. Kikuta, the head of the Toho Corporation, and *he* wanted to do the book. Very determined fellow, Kikuta. Never came out and told us that's how it was going to be, but what he did do was make it extremely difficult for us to hire another writer. There were infinite complications in the negotiations. Finally, all this had dragged on to the pre-casting stage—and no book. So Joe laid out his entire libretto, based on his concept, and instructed Kikuta on which scenes to write, and how.

"Eventually, we got into another argument over casting Scarlett (all of this is in my book *The Scarlett Letters*), and Mr. Kikuta then disappeared. Stayed away completely. It was a question of face. So we had to take his book, have it translated into English by an American who lived in Tokyo, and then make changes and cuts, and have them *re*-translated back into Japanese."

That meticulous process applied to Rome's lyrics, as well. Written in English, they were translated, word by word, into Japanese. "Funny," he remarks, "to this very day, some of the songs are more familiar to Florence and me in Japanese than they are in English!"

As the conductor, Ray Cook, calls for a reading of the opening number of the score, *Today's the Day*, Rome pulls out a souvenir of Tokyo, a tiny Yashica camera, and begins to snap candid pictures of the occasion. "Listen to this and you'll understand Joe's concept," he says. "It's six minutes long, but from the opening chords until it's done, we've already begun the Civil War!"

Fifteen of the songs from the Tokyo production have been retained, with orchestrations by Meyer Kupferman. "Six new songs added since then," Rome says. "One of them I wrote right here in London when we arrived. Now we have a British arranger, a young boy named Keith Amos. Does absolutely lovely work."

A few moments later, Cook calls for another number, this one a big dance number called "A Time For Love." "I borrowed the lead-in verse from Ecclesiastes," explains Rome. "It becomes slightly sardonic in this context, because it's a song for Belle Watling, and her 'ladies of pleasure.' "

The song is strong, the chords loud and brassy, laced throughout with a throbbing beat-beat-beat, very nearly bump-and-grind music, that serves as counterpoint to the sensuous melody. In the final chorus, the arrangement builds to a strident eight-bar climax which fills the room and echoes throughout the Drury Lane.

"A very big finish, but it had to be added since Tokyo," says Rome. "A real applause-bumper. Nothing like that there. In Japan, audiences never applaud a song, it's strictly against custom. So all our numbers just sort of tailed off into the dialogue of the next scene. Well, that's dandy for Japan, but not for England. The English love to applaud, so we've had to go back and re-do all the songs, add climax chords, big tags and finishes. And don't think *that* hasn't been a lot of work, with this size score."

Cook annnounces the customary tea-break, and his musicians rise and begin heading, lemming-like, towards the nearest source of supply. "You know," murmurs one bearded British violinist to another as they leave the room, "there's some very nice writing here." Which, in British terms, is praise.

The task of transferring Margaret Mitchell's mammoth Civil War romance to the screen was a long-term endeavor which consumed years of the late David O. Selznick's time and money (it was generally referred to as "David's folly"), the talents of a long roster of top-priced screenwriters and several directors, a famous talent-hunt for Scarlett O'Hara, and a mammoth amount of shooting time, even by the most opulent of Hollywood standards. Selznick's road-show film ran for almost four hours; the Japanese play version equally as long. But this new version has had to be trimmed down to fit the eighty-foot wide Drury Lane proscenium opening. The Layton-Rome version, with a revised libretto by Horton Foote ("he had to take the Japanese version and restore it to the Southern idiom, bringing it all back home"), can only play for two-hours-plus of the British audience's time. Surely this has been a difficult job of compression—something akin to inscribing the Lord's Prayer on the head of a pin—and then reducing that inscription to the size of the pin's *point*.

"It's all in Joe's concept, thank God," says Rome. "He's broken down that vast story into segments—each of the two acts has four of them—and within those segments, the numbers maintain a story-progression. I've never written a song for a song's sake, it always has to do more. This next number they're going to rehearse is a lullaby called "Blueberry Eyes." It's sung by Mammy when Scarlett is first an infant. From the beginning of the song, through two choruses, Joe has Scarlett growing from a baby, whose mother has no time for her, but whose father adores her, right up to the age of six."

Downstairs, on the huge Drury Lane stage, stagehands are beginning to set up some of the physical production. Audiences will be given their money's worth with this one; they'll see Tara, the city of Atlanta will burn with amazing reality, there will be riverboats, and shops and farms, and an actual train will bring the wounded home from the front. All through rehearsals, Layton will be rehearsing his actors with actual scenery and props. "A big luxury, believe me," comments Rome. "In New York or out of town, the actors and the director never get to *see* the scenery until the first dress rehearsal. The way costs are, nobody can afford to pay the stagehands before that. That's why our dress rehearsals in America are such shambles. You know, the theatre gets tougher and tougher. Everybody keeps saying there'll always be a musical theatre in New York—New York needs it. Trouble is, no matter how much New York needs it, nobody makes it easier for us!"

Rome stands in back of the Royal Circle (British for mezzanine) and surveys the many technicians working down below.

"I'm very relaxed about this show," he murmurs. "Have you noticed? I tiptoe around here, the most unobtrusive composer and lyricist I've ever been. I've worked with Joe long enough now to know that if there's something wrong, he invariably finds it out before I even tell him. So I let him go on—it's his baby now. I've got myself a fine conductor, beautiful arrangements, a great orchestra . . . and if they weren't, at this stage, what the hell could I do about it? So I relax."

Rome's "relaxing" takes the shape of selective shopping in the many London shops between his home in Chelsea and the Covent Garden area. He compulsively acquires new shoes, Havana cigars, shirts, ties and tweeds. "Could be my way of releasing tension," he admits. "Or maybe I'm subconsciously rewarding myself for all the work I've put in on this project."

Rome's final score consists of twenty-one songs and a huge amount of underscoring, arranged by the talented Trude Rittmann ("My good right hand," he calls her). But to arrive at that stage, he has composed and written his own lyrics for over forty songs. "Wrote a lot and threw a lot out. But my theory is, you write it first and worry about it after. If you hesitate at the beginning, if you spend your time worrying if it's going to be any good, then you'll write nothing, and you'll end up with nothing. Rome's rule is *Do it*. "You know, this creative writing is such an ephemeral thing, anyway," he muses. "Anything you do to stop it up front is liable to kill it. The only way I know to be creative is to let it go, and not to worry about how good it is. If it doesn't work, what have you lost? You've gained experience, you've learned something. I've *always* written double what I needed for a show. But even when I make mistakes—and I have a pretty good average in that department—I always learn. Take that song you heard this morning, "Marrying for Love." I wrote it five times. Did a verse in 4/4 time, then I began to think maybe the whole song might be more interesting in 5/4. So I wrote it again in that tempo. Now I've got myself two versions. Luckily, I brought the second one along from New York. When I first gave Harve Presnell the 4/4 version, it seemed a little slack. So I dragged out the second version for him to try. Amazing! The song came to life. But what would have happened if I'd edited myself back there at the beginning—said 'This isn't going to be any good'—we'd have had a dull song, and deserved it."

Rome, who graduated from Yale in the lowest depths of the Depression, is one of the last of the 1930s and '40s breed of American show composers who has remained active. "I have to keep writing songs—I certainly don't make any money selling my paintings," he once remarked wryly. Of that once flourishing upper-echelon of composers and lyricists—Rodgers & Hart, Hammerstein, Porter, Berlin, Dietz & Schwartz, Vernon Duke, Frank Loesser, E.Y. Harburg and Harold Arlen—who so richly endowed the American musical theatre with their collective largesse, only a handful still function. And Rome's position is even more unique in that, as did Loesser, Berlin, and Porter (all of them departed now), he writes his own lyrics.

Which makes it even more lonely. "I don't even have a collaborator to go to the mat with," he grins. "I have to be my own critic, all the time. That's why I can't allow myself to be depressed going in. Hell, if I ever stopped to consider all the pitfalls that lie ahead of me when I first start writing a song, I'd be stopped dead after the first chord."

Measured in terms of output, Rome's career in the past two decades has been sporadic. In addition to his musical shows, he contributed songs to *Michael Todd's Peep Show*, and had one big commerical song hit, "All of a Sudden My Heart Sings" ("my one out-and-out commercial, knocked it off in no time"). Out of his score for *I Can Get It For You Wholesale* came the song "Miss Marmelstein," which is notable as being the Broadway number that blasted young Barbra Streisand into orbit. "She's got something like dynamite. I'll never forget when we were casting—we had her come back and audition five times because we'd been sitting in that theatre for a month, listening to people, and it got a little dull. Not when *she* sang. She'd always come around in some ratty kind of fur coat she'd bought at a rummage sale, and when she opened up her mouth— pow! Finally we told her she had the job, and she jumped up and down and said, 'Goody! Now I can get a telephone!' "

His ratio then is roughly one production for three shows attempted. "Why anybody is a songwriter anyway, I don't understand. Especially today. It's no profession for a self-respecting man . . . the improvisers and the performers have taken it all over. The only consolation for me is that all these young ones cannot write a *show*, where you have to know where you are going. I go up each year to a class in songwriting that Lehman Engel the conductor runs, and the kids put on a program of their songs. You listen, and you think, *'yes, pretty good'*—and then you suddenly realize that these aren't songs—they're music and lyrics. Putting words together and then adding music doesn't make a song. Songs have to have a point of view, a reason for being, a something inside . . . and all these things I hear rarely have that . . ."

"I wasn't always this relaxed around my shows," he continues. "In my early days, I'd be very eager to tell the director, or the actors, or anybody, just what I thought. I used to be known as the Madman of Broadway. Yelled at everybody—blew my top. But all these people working on this show are so good; Layton, Trude Rittman, the cast. All there is for me now is to sit back and enjoy. Believe me," he adds, grinning, "it doesn't always happen like this. This is rare, very rare."

Theatrical people are by nature more superstitious than civilians, and Rome mutters, as if to ward off imminent disaster, "I'm just waiting for the shit to hit the fan. You know, in Tokyo, the guy who played Rhett Butler, our lead, broke his leg. Why is everything going so well here? Last time it was like this, it was *Call Me Mister*. A very happy show. Everything went so well from the day we thought of doing it right down to the first night in Philly. Smash! Came back to New York—opened—still no trouble. Amazing. It wasn't until the second year of our run that something terrible finally happened," he chuckles. "We looked down one night and saw our first pair of empty orchestra seats!"

In a few days *Gone With The Wind* will have its gala premiere. Mr. Rome's pre-opening night jitters about something going wrong will prove to be un- founded; the show will be received by the London critics with high praise, and become another solidly established Drury Lane success. Miss Scarlett O'Hara will be in residence at the Drury Lane for a good long time to come.

Mr. Rome, his pipes and his shirts and his tweeds all packed, will return to Manhattan, and begin to look around for his next project. He is far from the sort of gent who plans to spend his golden years sitting in the living-room browsing through his scrapbooks, or serving as curator to his vast and valuable collection of African sculpture. Don't call him in the morning; he'll be sitting at his piano, as he has been since 1936, up at Green Mountains in the Catskills, working on a song. Or two.

"There's nothing like a really good show," he says, simply. "A really good musical moves you and stirs you the way nothing else can. It's a very rare baby these days, but it's a great experience. And I hope, as weak as the theatre is, there'll still be a place for it . . ."

In the words of the Drury Lane audience, hear hear!

'On a Clear Day You Can See Forever'

(Burton Lane)

FROM HIS EARLIEST years on, Burton Lane's considerable musical talent earned him the billing of "my-son-the-genius-prodigy." Even today, he thinks back on that period with obvious distaste. "I had a very pushy father," he sighs. "Even now, the aches go through me, and the pains come when I remember. Whenever my father saw a piano, he'd say to me, 'Go over and play.' It was so painful for me—and to this day, when people ask, 'Will you play?,' my first reaction is 'no.' "

Lane is a composer's composer. In show business, his gifts are well recognized. But the general public hardly knows him as the man who wrote "How Are Things in Glocca Morra?," "On a Clear Day You Can See Forever," "Old Devil Moon," and a raft of other hits. Lane is a modest, retiring sort, whose anonymity does not seem to bother him very much. At 60, he is tall, trim, and retains a good deal of that youthful manner that he must have possessed back in 1929 when, at the senior age of seventeen, he got his first job as a staff writer at the Remick Music Company in Manhattan. "Gershwin had been there a long time, but I felt very good because his starting salary was $15.00, and *I* got $17.50! As an advance against royalties. Of course," Lane laughs, "there never *were* any royalties."

"But George was already a big star. He and Ira were very good friends of mine; they treated me like their protege. I had tremendous admiration for everything George did. He had a show that was running then called *Funny Face*. At that time, there were two marvelous pianists in the theatre orchestra, Ohman and Arden—they did two-piano arrangements of his music in the pit. I did a *one*-piano arrangement of what *they* were doing . . . I remember playing it for George. It had a lot of staccato chords . . . ' '*S'Wonderful!*—ba-ba-ba-*ba*-ba-*ba!*—like that—and I started it too fast. I was so worried that I'd lose control of my right hand, but I didn't. When I got through, George grabbed my hand. He said 'Make a fist,' and I was like steel. He said, 'I couldn't do that when *I* was your age. I don't think I could even do it right now.' Oh, he was great . . .' "

Since the days of his first job at Remick's, Lane has written songs with several top-rank lyricists. In his early years in Hollywood, he and young Frank Loesser worked for a long spell at Paramount. Later, he and E.Y. Harburg wrote the brilliant score for *Finian's Rainbow*. His last Broadway work was *On A Clear Day*, in collaboration with Alan Jay Lerner, and he has also supplied melodies for the words of Ira Gershwin, Harold Adamson, and Harry Warren's ex-partner, Al Dubin. ("That was a strange collaboration," he says, "for a show with Olsen & Johnson called *Laffing Room Only*. Out of it came a song called 'Feuding and Fighting.' Five or six years after the show, Dorothy Shay did the song on the radio and it became a big hit. All of a sudden, music publishers I'd never met before started calling me up and asking me if I'd like to play golf.")

The regular rediscovery of Lane's abilities is traceable to the fact that there are long periods of silence in his career. Not out of choice, but because Lane is known as a man who will not rush to the piano and start composing at the drop of a producer's advance check. "I guess I should have done more," he admits, "but I've never had a permanent partner. George and Ira; Dick Rodgers and Larry Hart; DeSylva, Brown and Henderson; teams. When you're a team, you somehow get to think together, and you develop a judgment about properties. So I wouldn't have had to rely so much on my own judgment," Lane grins, "which is often faulty."

At fifteen, when his classmates were playing stickball, Lane signed his first contract, to provide songs for Shubert musicals. "My father was in the real-estate business, and he was putting up a building in Brooklyn, a very tall apartment house. I'd already met and played some things for Harold Stern, the Shuberts' musical director. One morning at two A.M. our phone rang. We never got phone calls at that hour—I remember my father trembling. He thought maybe one of the girders had collapsed and killed somebody! But it was Stern asking if my father would bring me down tomorrow morning at the same time —two A.M.! Apparently that was when the Shuberts usually did their business."

Nothing immediate came of the Shubert contract, but Lane did turn out a collection of melodies for one of J.J. Shubert's productions, *The Greenwich Village Follies*. "I hadn't yet learned how to write the piano parts down, so their musical director sat with me at the piano and took down all my tunes . . ."

"Fade out. Two years later, 1929. I'd written two songs for *Three's A Crowd*, an intimate revue with Libby Holman, Clifton Webb, and Fred Allen—a marvelous opportunity for me. I was in Philadelphia with the show, and I had a call from my father. The Shuberts had opened a new show in Newark with Chic Sale—I think it was called *Hello, Paris*, and he'd gone to see it—strictly on a hunch. The music had been written by the same guy who'd taken down my piano parts. They were *my* songs! My father recognized them. He ran over to

Brooklyn, where another Shubert show had just opened, and again, most of that score was mine! Turned out there were four Shubert shows that had my music—that that musical director—it wasn't Stern, but another fellow, had taken my tunes and put his name on them!

My father immediately brought the matter up with the Shuberts—I'd had a contract where I was supposed to get $24 a week for each show where they used my music. They refused to honor the contract. My father had a lawyer send a letter, threatening suit. Would you believe, in that one week, they closed *all four* shows? They wouldn't pay me the $100 per week!"

Already becoming aware of the pitfalls that were waiting to engorge a talented Candide from Brooklyn, young Lane refused to be discouraged. ("My God, I was so naive!" he laughs. "I wrote a song with Edgar Leslie called 'Under Vesuvius Skies.' I didn't even know where Vesuvius *was!* A couple of months later it erupted, and that's how I found out.") Not only were two of his songs, with lyrics by Howard Dietz, in *Three's a Crowd*, but he and another youngster, Harold Adamson, contributed a song to the third edition of *The Little Show* and material for an Earl Carroll show, *Vanities*. "We also had a couple of songs in *Singing the Blues*, a straight play with songs. I had at one time music in four shows playing on Broadway, around 1931. Must have been earning a total of forty-eight dollars and sixty cents for all of it. Those were very tough times, you realize."

And they were to become even tougher. Eventually, as did most of the creative people who'd been frostbitten by the icy winds of economic disaster that whistled down 45th Street, past darkened theatres, Lane and Adamson went out to California. "1922 . . . a six week gamble to see whether we could end up with some of our songs in pictures. We were ready to take anything. Harold stayed there*—he's been in California ever since—and I stayed on for twenty-one years."

"Just before we left, I had written my first ballad. Up to then, the publishers thought of me as a rhythm-writer, jingle-songs and that sort of thing. But Harold added a lyric to my ballad, and we took it out West with us. We went to a party one night and we ran into Allen Rivkin, a writer who was working at Metro on a big Joan Crawford picture to be called *Dancing Lady*. He said they were having trouble getting songs for the picture, so we sat right down and played him some of ours. He loved that ballad we'd written. Called us out to Metro the next day. He had us play it for David Selznick, the producer of the picture. He flipped. Then we went to Joan Crawford, and *she* loved it. And then we went right up to L.B. Mayer himself! After he said *he* loved it—we must have played our stuff at least fifty times more that day—practically every executive and producer in the studio auditioned us! They ended up buying three songs from us. The ballad was called 'Everything I Have Is Yours,' and Fred Astaire did it in the picture. It was *his* first picture, too. That was our first big success."

Lane did more work at Metro, and eventually was hired to work at Paramount. "I kind of wandered from studio to studio. Then I was looking for a lyricist and I ran into young Frank Loesser. Even then, Frank was a fantastic talent."

---

* Adamson, who worked on Hasty Pudding shows while at Harvard, is an extremely gifted lyricist who has since supplied lyrics to the work of many other composers: Jimmy McHugh, Hoagy Carmichael, Duke Ellington and others. He and Mack Gordon wrote the lyric to Vincent Youmans' "Time on My Hands."

Loesser and Lane were responsible for several hit songs, including 'The Lady's in Love With You', but their partnership ended when Loesser's draft board sent him greetings from Uncle Sam in 1942.

"After that, it got tough again," he says. "Musical films were bombing at the box-office, and producers were avoiding them like a disease. For composers, things were very very lean. I couldn't get a job. I figured I'd better do something, so I organized a dance orchestra, invested what was left of my money. On the evening of our first job, I came down with the flu. Disaster. There I was, floundering around, flat broke. Then, out of the blue, I got a call from Alex Aarons, a dear friend of mine in New York. He'd done a lot of shows with the Gershwins. He wanted to know if I'd do a show back East with Yip Harburg. *Would* I? I borrowed money, went to New York, and started to work."

Lane and Harburg were no strangers to each other's work. "Ira Gershwin had introduced me to him back in 1929. They were friends from their college days. Yip had written "Brother, Can You Spare a Dime?," and we'd done a few songs together, but nothing much had happened to them. Yip's another loner, like me. He's worked with lots of marvelous composers, but he's never really tied himself permanently to any one. He's always wanted to try new things with different talents. The results are usually fascinating."

Harburg and Lane wrote the score for a show called *Hold Onto Your Hats*. After a good deal of preliminary jockeying back and forth, based mostly on the difficulties of raising capital in those days, they reached the starting gate with a major star, the legendary Al Jolson.

"What a plot!" sighs Lane. "The character Al played was a radio entertainer, a guy who's known as 'The Lone Rider.' Somehow, he gets sent out West to do away with some outlaws. An actor, who's faced with a real-life situation. Can you imagine trying to get away with a plot like that today?"

In the score were three fine songs. "Don't Let It Get You Down," "There's a Great Day Coming, Manana," and "The World Is in My Arms." "They seemed to register with the audiences," Lane says, "and the show got good reviews, but with my customary luck and timing, we opened up in the midst of the fight between ASCAP and the new firm, Broadcast Music, Inc. (BMI), and since the networks, who owned BMI, were blacking out all ASCAP songs, we never got any of ours played until long after the show closed."

Providing Mr. Jolson with new songs wasn't an easy experience either. "We knew going in that Al always relied on his old standards; it was traditional for him to say to the audience 'You ain't heard nothing yet!' and then forget the show, come down front, and do all his old favorites. Yip and I knew that *no* new song was ever going to sound as good as Jolson's 'Mammy,' or 'Swanee,' or 'California, Here I Come!'. So we wrote a thing for him to open up the show with —in which he interpolated a lot of those old hits. A smash opening. But Al had the bit in his teeth. He'd get down to the second act, and at 10:45 P.M., he'd come down front, forget the show, and stand there and do all his *other* standards as well! So very little happened to what Yip and I had written, believe me."

Lane remained in New York to write songs for the Olsen & Johnson show, *Laffing Room Only*, and then returned to Hollywood, again to work at Metro, where the wartime musical boom had begun. "Most of the time," he admits, "I hated what I did in Hollywood. Oh, once in a while I'd get an assignment that I really liked, or I was writing for talent that I respected; Mickey Rooney and Judy Garland, for instance. Ralph Freed and I did songs for *Babes on Broadway*. One of them was a smash hit—'How About You?'—and I guess there were others, but I usually found it very difficult to get myself inspired by what I had to do. Most of my own work I just didn't like. How I used to admire guys like Harry Warren! No matter what piece of junk he was working on, whatever picture, with those meaningless plots and ridiculous subjects—backstage, Argentina, whatever—Harry would always come up with some wonderful tunes. That's when I began to learn something about myself, and my own work; That its quality would rise and fall, depending on how much *I* liked what I was working on."

The war was almost over when Lane began to work with his friend Harburg again, in Hollywood. Harburg and Fred Saidy had written an original musical comedy book for eventual production on Broadway. It was, as any old theatre hand will testify, the most difficult sort of work to attempt—a fantasy about a displaced leprechaun who finds himself in the Deep South—and the story was replete with social satire. It was to be *Finian's Rainbow*, which most critics consider to be one of the best musical comedies of our times. The show has been written about and discussed many times since. Is Lane bored with the subject of its creation?

"Of course not!" he chortles. "You can never be bored with that kind of a success. I remember once talking to Dick Rodgers; I was complimenting him on something he'd written, and then I added, 'But you must be bored hearing this,' and Dick said *'Don't stop!'*

"Oh, *Finian's* was a hell of a challenge," he says. "Perhaps that's why it ended up being so good. I sweated like mad. We wrote and rewrote, and we auditioned the material all over Hollywood—it was a marvelous way to get the feel of what we'd done.

"You know, I've known Yip since I was seven, so there is almost a father-son thing in our relationship. And when I write songs with him, I don't think there's a more satisfying creative experience in anything I've ever done, before or since. More than anyone else I've ever worked with, Yip makes my tunes come to life. I mean, he has a tremendous *ear*—catches every nuance that's in a tune—fits it with lyrics that are right, and it's a joy. He makes *me* like my own tunes better. "I had never done anything as challenging as that show," he says, emphatically, "and I didn't know whether I could make it. And this isn't false modesty or anything, but I can only judge things by how well they've stood up *after* you've written them." He thinks for a moment. "I don't think I'm embarrassed by anything in that score."

Finian's Rainbow opened in New York in January, 1947, and was an immediate thundering smash hit. "We didn't have any stars, either," recalls Lane. "Ella Logan sold about four dollars' worth of tickets in advance—nobody really knew who she was." A quarter of a century later, the Harburg-Lane score does much more than stand up. It's nearly as perfect as any producer could hope for; the show is constantly performed each summer, and never fails to enchant an audience. Not only are the ballads superb—"How Are Things in Glocca Morra?," "Old Devil Moon," "Look to the Rainbow," and "If This Isn't Love" come very close to perfection—but there are also the classic satiric songs. "The Begat," "Something Sort of Grandish," and "When the Idle Poor Become the Idle Rich," which retain their finely honed edge and stand up like rocks on a shore. "Who else," remarked a critic, "but Harburg would have dared to write a song about a sexy leprechaun ('When I'm Not Near the Girl I Love, I Love the Girl I'm Near')?"

Lane readily admits that his own compulsive tendency to question the essential quality of the material he has been offered is the reason he did so little writing for Broadway after *Finian's*.

"It bothers me, of course," he confesses. "I have always felt I could do a show a year standing on my ear, *if* I could find things that I liked. Even though I'm willing to work on something where we'll eventually compromise, you still have to find something first where it's *worth* compromising. Remember, on *Finian's*, we had a great book. It's when you don't have that that you're in terrible trouble from the start. In the old days, before Broadway musicals began to have good books, it was completely different. When I first knew the Gershwins, I'd ask them, 'What are your plans; what are you doing after this show?' And George would say 'Well, we have a show with Fred Astaire to do,' or a show with this one or that one. George and Ira would only know that they were doing something to star Fred. They wouldn't know what the hell the book was going to be. Usually they'd have merely the first draft of the first act, and an outline of the second —and they'd go into rehearsal! George would have seven or eight tunes, and Ira would have written the lyrics to them. Think about *Funny Face*, a show where they threw out the whole book while they were on the road, and wrote a whole new book before they came into New York!

"But those were different days. You had Fred and Adele Astaire, or Victor Moore and Bill Gaxton, Lou Holtz, Jolson, Marilyn Miller, Jack Donahue; *stars.* Shows were built around personalities; that was the whole business then. But after all those stars were grabbed up by the movie business the emphasis in New York had to shift onto the material. It led eventually to the shows of Rodgers and Hammerstein. A whole new kind of a musical, where the book was major.

"I've always attacked my own work because that's the way I learned to be about what I wrote when I was a kid. Then I had to ask myself, how can talented people get involved with terrible shows? Even the Gershwins, they had flops; *Let 'Em Eat Cake*, and *Pardon My English*. Lovely, lovely songs, and terrible books. I'd ask myself '*How* can people who've been around so long do shows with terrible books?' I mean, when you do a funny show, you know what the jokes are—when they're funny, you *know*—when they're not, you know that too. So you have to know when a story line makes sense to you and when it doesn't. I'm not saying that every show can be a hit, or has to be a hit. What I am saying is, how can it be so many of them that flopped were really embar- rassing? Top people, too. How does a Jerome Kern do a *Very Warm For May*, or an Irving Berlin do a *Miss Liberty*? How is it possible for people with that kind of experience not to know ahead of time when it's lousy?

"My theory," says Lane, answering his own hypothetical question, "is that they're all too polite to tell the truth. You get snagged into it. You're sitting around with people you respect, and you lie. Robert E. Sherwood, Moss Hart, Irving Berlin, they do a *Miss Liberty* and it's a disaster! But nobody ever says, 'Irving, that's a bad tune,' or, 'Moss, that scene is rotten; Bob, it needs work.' That would be like slapping them in the face. Ira Gershwin, Arthur Schwartz, Nunnally Johnson, George S Kaufman; they get together and do a *Park Avenue*. Disaster." He grimaces.*

"Professionals should have some judgment and taste," Lane says. "I think

---

* Mr. Lane makes a point which not only applies to Broadway but to films as well. With production costs constantly escalating, producers have come to rely more and more on established creative names as "insurance" on their investments. More often than not, such protection rarely does more than to assure a large advance sale of tickets, and is no protection against an inevitable disaster. (*Breakfast at Tiffany's, Dear World;* to cite two disasters an Broadway.)

I have, and I'm honest enough to say what I think. I don't know any other way to work. I've always told people I work with what I think. I started two shows with Dorothy Fields and I ended up resigning from both of them. A very tough thing to do, believe me, but I had to do it. Dorothy and I are still friends. But I often wonder, why did I have to grow up thinking this way? Most writers don't. It's so damned tough to be selective, and to say 'no' to so many things until you get something that makes some kind of sense!" he concludes, with more than a touch of sadness.

Lane returned to Hollywood after *Finian's* where he exercised his deeply-ingrained selectivity for a long time. In 1953 with Ira Gershwin he did a score for a bright Metro musical called *Give a Girl a Break*, from which came a somewhat mocking little song called "Applause, Applause." Then, at the behest of Arthur Freed, he teamed up with Alan Jay Lerner to write a score for *Royal Wedding*.

"Alan is an entirely different sort of fellow from Yip," he says. "If he wants you to do something with him, he can be so winning that it's very difficult to refuse. That first picture we did together was *his* first, and I think we turned out a good score. Judy Garland was originally supposed to do it with Fred Astaire, but she was having her emotional problems then, so Jane Powell ended up playing the girl. I guess people remember it mostly for Alan's lyric 'How Could You Believe Me When I Said I Loved You When You Know I've Been a Liar All My Life,' " Lane remarks. "A somewhat autobiographical title, I was to discover."

Again, there followed a long period of inactivity on Lane's part. "Nothing much worked," he says. He moved back to New York, read Libretti, and waited for something to turn up in which he could have confidence. In 1964 he went back to work with Lerner, writing the score for Lerner's book, *On a Clear Day You Can See Forever*. On Broadway, the show was a vehicle for the very talented Barbara Harris. When it reached the screen, it starred Barbra Streisand.

"That show was a painful creative experience," he says. "Two years to write five songs! Alan came and went; I never knew when or where. For me, his book never worked properly. And when that's the case, you can't get a project off the ground, ever! Think back to any musical show that's successful. You're in the theatre. When a song begins, before you ever even meet the song—if the book is right, you're already liking that song! You're already with it! You're not sitting back, waiting for the numbers, and saying, 'All right, *show* me.' You're loving the show, you're loving what's happening with the characters—those people up on the stage. You're with it, you're just *riding* with it! And all that is *built in* by your book. You'll even tolerate four or five terrible songs, because things are going so well you don't stop to analyze, you're just enjoying.

But with *Clear Day*, it was a book that never could work. What was done to it in rewriting was never enough. And the things that were wrong with that book when we opened were wrong with it on the day that Alan came up and read it to me for the first time!"

Lane's analysis of the deficiencies of Lerner's tale of a girl gifted with ESP were largely echoed by the critics. But the strength of the score will enable it to survive. In an era when Broadway musicals no longer serve as the incubator of popular music hits, the driving excitement of "Come Back to Me," and the broad sweep of the title song "On a Clear Day" seemed to strike very responsive chords, not only with the audiences but with performers. There is hardly a male singer with any sort of a voice who hasn't recorded one or both of the two songs. Since *Clear Day*, the sad fact is that few, if any Broadway shows have come up with such "standards" in their LP cast recordings.

"Despite all our problems, I consider Lerner a very gifted guy," says Lane. "Just recently, we've started discussing the possibility of doing something together, even though when he first brought me his *Lolita* (an abortive failure two seasons back), I had to tell him it was an impossible idea. What could I do but be honest?

"Oh well, Alan's had his share of failures lately, but he has so much ability that people will go along with him because they know that somewhere, somehow, that talent which enabled him to do such great things as *My Fair Lady* and *Gigi* will reassert itself. Maybe it'll happen with us, maybe it won't." He smiles ruefully, "Provided Alan can stand me and my self-criticism.

"I suppose it would have been easier if I'd ever been the permanent half of a partnership," Lane says, in summing up his predicament. "It's when your're a Cole Porter, or a Berlin, or you do what Frank Loesser did—go it alone, and you do it all, music *and* lyrics—oh, it's so much easier. Look at Steve Sondheim today. He does his 'Company' and 'Follies' all by himself. Tremendously talented, a marvelous lyricist. I guess it's harder in one way—the burden's all on yourself—but it's also easier. You have only yourself to please.

"You know another wonderful thing about Steve? He knows the value of the old classic show business forms. Take that vaudeville number that he uses in the opening of the second act of *Company*. All of that stuff has worked for years with audiences, and he's found a way to adapt it to our current idiom . . . and how it works!

"Jerry Herman did it with *Hello, Dolly*—the number is pure vaudeville. So is *Mame*. Banjos plunking, music building, changes of tempo. Anyone who's ever had any vaudeville experience knows that when you want to stop the show musically, there are certain things you do with the beat, and stop-time. When you get the right song to go with those tricks, it's an unbeatable combination!"

There's a fine piano in Burton Lane's study, on Central Park West, with piles of music paper stacked on top. Like any other composer with as much talent as he's demonstrated since those days back in the '20s when his father insisted that he play, the jovial Lane usually writes something every day. At this particular moment, his unfinished tunes have no specific home, so he's waiting until one appears. Show business is a peculiar game of optimistic roulette. Any day now, a musical comedy book may turn up in Lane's mail, one that will pass his hypercritical standards, and start him working. He's accustomed to waiting. There were eighteen years between *Finian's Rainbow* and the next; *On a Clear Day*.

And while we wait—is it presumptuous to open up his "trunk," take out some of the new tunes, sit down to his piano, and play?

"Years ago, the Gershwins invited me to a party one night," he says. "I got there, and George hadn't come downstairs yet, nor had Ira. And Arthur and Frankie—George's brother and sister—got me to the piano and I was playing. After a while some girl came up behind me and put her hands over my eyes and said 'Guess who this is?' She thought I was George!

"I've always felt very good about that . . ." says Mr. Lane.

'Put On a Happy Face'

(Lee Adams)

BREAKING INTO the Broadway turf as a professional lyricist for a musical comedy usually involves a.) talent; b.) endless self-confidence and patience; and c.) willingness to write, audition, and rewrite for anybody you can find who'll listen to your stuff. You can short-cut them all by having a rich aunt in Boonton, New Jersey, who's willing to provide most of the backing for your first production, but that's usually only a one-shot venture. After your cousins have had your aunt committed, you're left with a simple choice. Is it Broadway, or should you go after gainful employment?

In the past twenty years or so, it's become even more sparse around 45th Street. Getting your lyrics onto a stage, and having them sung past next Saturday, can only be compared to Eliza crossing the ice . . . in August. As fast as she makes it to the next floe, it melts.

Lee Adams, a modest man in his mid-'40s, is an authority on the stamina quotient it takes to hop and skip across those vanishing ice-floes. He wears very conservative clothes, keeps regular work-hours, and would easily be taken for a Fairfield County executive type, rather than for what he earns a very good weekly living at—the writing of lyrics for Broadway shows. He and his partner, Charles

Strouse, provided the score for the long-run hit *Applause!* But for twelve lean years, the pair struggled to establish themselves as professional songwriters. "From 1949 to 1960," Adams says, with feeling. "That is how long it took before we got our first real break, with *Bye, Bye, Birdie!* Luckily, neither Charlie nor myself were married at the time. The only reason I didn't actually starve was that he lived at home—and we could eat there. Twelve years his parents subsidized us with food!"

Adams grew up in Mansfield, Ohio, a town not noted for its population of songwriters. What got him started with a yellow pad and a pencil and the desire to rhyme a couplet?

"Cole Porter," he says. "I was kicked right in the head at college when I heard the record of *Kiss Me Kate.* Heard that score and I said, '*That* is what I want to do.' I was a journalism major at Ohio State—got my M.A. at Columbia. But from the time I heard Porter's lyrics, I knew that was my ambition. I never realized how long it took Porter to get to that plateau. All I knew was that score was—and still is, for me—just about the best ever. Others I've heard are great, but I think Porter is the top guy. Genius. Could write everything—the most sophisticated songs, and also a 'Don't Fence Me In.' "

"While I was still at Ohio State, I'd written a college show called *Howdy Stranger.* Then I came to New York. Met Strouse. I showed him my stuff. I thought it was really high class writing. He played it all over, sang it. 'Well,' he said to me, 'it's really impossibly bad.' "

Adams laughs. "Here was this young kid, five years younger than I! 'What do you mean?' I yelled. Well, he *told* me what he meant. Explained what was bad. Ripped it to shreds . . . and then I got really pissed off. Slammed out . . . But later, I got to thinking about it, and I thought, 'There's an *honest* guy. Maybe he's right. Maybe I'm not quite Cole Porter yet!' So we began working together."

The Adams-Strouse collaboration faced an even rougher future than that of most neophyte teams. "Tougher, because we never aimed at pop songwriting," says Adams. "We always tried to write for the theatre. We don't know to this day how to write a pop hit. But that was by design. We found out early that a lot of people don't make it in the theatre because they come in and try to write a show and they have no theatrical background—they have only songwriting experience. That's simply not enough. You cannot just sit down and write a bunch of unrelated songs for a show—or drag stuff out of your trunk and say 'Here, let's try this song in that spot.' You have to stay *around* the theatre, you have to learn what works on stage, and what doesn't. Very, very hard. I suppose the only thing that kept me hanging in there for twelve long years was *liking* to do it—and gradually learning how to write for the theatre. Because, believe me," Adams says, "that is a very slow, painful process."

In the early '50s, Adams and Strouse were fortunate enough to make it to one ice-floe—the Borscht circuit summer camp—before that talent incubator vanished. "Charlie got a job at Green Mansions as a rehearsal pianist," he says, "and the following summer he took me along. We were up there for three summers—and that's where we really began to learn to write. Great training—you see, we had to write a show for each Saturday night—a full scale revue. They had a set designer, a costumer, a full orchestra—a marvelous operation. They'd do plays on Wednesday nights, ballet on another, opera excerpts—and Saturdays, the original revue. A whole company of actors and writers. Sheldon Harnick worked up there before we did—so did Harold Rome. Do you know who was in our company with us? Don Adams and Carol Burnett. Everybody was learning. We got $250 for the summer, and all the sour cream we could eat!

"Charlie and I did all sorts of scratch jobs in between. For years, we worked for club acts, writing special material for them. *There's* a swell job," he says, sardonically. "If you get paid, you're lucky. A lot of actors still owe us money from fifteen years ago. It's incredibly tough to write special material, but you learn your craft that way.

"I had all sorts of other odd jobs to keep myself going. Once, Mel Brooks, who was an old friend, was producing a show for Polly Bergen on television. He made me an offer: If I'd work two weeks for free, and they thought I was good and liked what I did, then he could get me on for a couple hundred dollars a week. How could I say no? I figured it was a big chance. So I went to work for the two weeks. Mel's a funny guy, and we're good friends. Later we did a show called *All American*—not a hit, but we've still remained friends . . .

"At the end of the second week, Mel said, 'You've been very good. I think it's all right. I'm going in to the regular weekly meeting and I think I can get you on.' He went into the production office, and I waited outside. In a little while, Mel came out with a funny look on his face. I said, 'Mel, I know—you tried . . . ' He said, 'No—*I'm* fired!'

"Oh, I had some funny jobs," continues Adams, who can look back on his early struggles with the same sense of humor that has obviously sustained him ever since. "One of my friends at ABC created a job for me. I would come in there to the news department on Saturdays and Sundays—he knew I was broke and starving. He gave me $15 a day to do traffic and weather reports. I had a little form and I would type up these reports and they'd put them on the air in the newscasts. I'd come bursting into the studio and hand them to the announcer, and he thought I was coming from some special weather and traffic center newsroom, right? Well, I was getting weather reports from the telephone weather service—which *anybody* could do by dialing it—and I was making up the traffic reports! I was supposed to call the AAA, but their line was always busy! After a while, I knew exactly what the metropolitan traffic would be like at certain times, and I'd make them up. We got away with that for almost six months.

"Charlie and I have never had any song hits—not really hits. Up at Green Mansions we wrote a song called 'Once Upon a Time.' It's become a good standard for us. We had it in a show up there. Don Adams was in the show—he met his wife while she was up there, and that became their song. Don used to say to us, 'That's a great song, fellows. *Someday*, that's going to be a big hit!' Marvelous guy. Then he was making $80 for the summer. 'Someday, that's going to make it!' he insisted. The years went by, and then we had our second Broadway show—*All American*—and we put that song into the score. By now, Don was working with Perry Como, on television. We met him on the street one day. He said, 'I see you put my song in the show. It's going to be a hit!' Well, nothing happened to the show, or the song, because the show lasted a big four months. But Don began to badger Perry Como to hear our song. He kept after him. He finally got Como to hear it, and record it. And after the Como record, the other singers began to sing it. It became a big standard . . . and it was Don who made it for us. Now, when we see him, he says, 'You see? I told you so!' "

Adams and Strouse continued their precarious journey; the revue as an entertainment form was rapidly disappearing. "Some of our things were done at the Pittsburgh Playhouse—that's the theatre where Charlie Gaynor had done so many shows. It's where the original production of his *Lend an Ear* began. We had things in Ben Bagley's *Shoestring Revue* and material in a revue called *Catch a Star*. We sold material to a producer in London; he was doing the last of those English revues that used to be such a staple of the theatre there. All of that is finished now," Adams sighs. "Matter of fact, I don't know where a writer would start today in the theatre. Off-*off*-Broadway, maybe—wherever that is. Only Carol Burnett does revue material on television. Fifteen years back, there were all sorts of different shows where young people could get started. Gone today, all gone. For guys from our age on up, there's really no more pop song business, either. All the young kids today write their own stuff, perform it, and they all have their own publishing firms. It's a whole different scene."

Bye, Bye Birdie, in 1960, was Adams and Strouse's first real break. "I was working on a magazine called *Pageant*", says Adams, "as a copy editor. I'd get to the office every morning around six or seven. The editor would come down the hall around nine and he'd be so impressed—I'd be in there writing. What I was doing were the lyrics to *Birdie*, which was a hit. A big fluke, you know— a complete 'sleeper.' We opened with about seventeen dollars in the box-office. It was everybody's first show. The producer, Ed Padula, Gower Champion the director—his first book musical. Dick Van Dyke, our star, had been in a revue for a couple of months, but it was *his* first musical show; all of us made it with *Birdie*. And I guess it was just in time for us," he adds, "because I don't see anybody around today on Broadway who'd be willing to take chances like *that* any more . . . unless it's Hal Prince, perhaps, who's the only producer left who'll gamble on relatively unknown talent.

"*Birdie* was marvelous for us. Our song 'Put on a Happy Face' became a standard. Not just a hit, a hit is a song that shows up in the Top Ten on the charts, but a standard is one that goes on for a long time, being played and sung over and over again. 'Put on a Happy Face' was used as the theme-music of *The Hollywood Palace* on television for six years—that's a big help, believe me. That constant performance adds up; at the end of each year, ASCAP sends you a check based on your performances. It can get you over lean years . . ." Which were still ahead.

The next Adams-Strouse score for *All American* was a flop, but by now the team was sufficiently established to continue following the precarious Broadway path. They worked on another musical, *Superman*—also a flop—and they wrote the score for *Golden Boy*, which had a successful run, with Sammy Davis Jr. playing the lead in the adaptation of Clifford Odets' play. And then, several years ago, they went to work on *Applause*, which was to star Lauren Bacall. It was based on the film *All About Eve*, and it had a long and profitable stand at the Palace on Times Square.

"It's a really difficult job, working on a book musical." says Adams. "First of all, you have all those different talents coming together, each one with his own ego-problems, and they all have to be subordinated to one thing—the show, and what's good for it. If all those chemistries don't make a proper blend, you're in terrible trouble.

"Very little of what we write ever ends up in a 'trunk.' So much of what we write has to be part of the character we're writing for. When I work on a musical, I end up very much involved with the book writers; on *Applause* it was Betty Comden and Adolph Green. We have to weave our stuff into the fabric of the show. We wrote songs for that show right up to the opening. Four of the best songs we wrote aren't even in the show. They didn't work. One of them is *my* absolute favorite—it was a song for the actors, in which they expressed their own attitudes toward their careers. It went:

> 'We trade our lives for just some good reviews,
> We're 'Smash' in *New York Times*, 'Terrific' *Daily News*,
> We do our show, and what does it all mean?
> We're grateful when we get 'Just swell,' *Cue Magazine*,
> The words we love are not from our lover,
> But words some stranger writes,
> Fond caresses from newspaper presses,
> Will warm you on winter nights,
> So hold me close, and whisper soft to me,
> 'Perfection,' CBS—'Just lovely,' NBC . . .

"It said everything I could think of about that rueful world of the actor—everyone loved it. But whenever we did it in the show, it stopped the forward motion of the book. We tried it in several places. No use. Ron Field, the director, finally called a meeting, and he said, 'Do I have to say it?' We knew. It came out . . .

"But that's something you never know ahead of time. It's part of writing for the theatre. You write a whole batch of songs and see which of them works with your audience. Of course," he adds, a trifle edgily, "there's another thing that bugs me. You open a show with ten, twelve songs, the critics come in and see it once, and then write reviews. I ask you, how is it physically or intellectually possible for *anybody*, even a composer, to hear that many new songs at once, and instantly judge which one is good, and which one is bad? But hell, that's one of the gauntlets you run that go with with the territory.

"My trouble is," he admits ruefully, "I don't know any other way to earn a living. Writing lyrics is a very strange thing to get into," he says. "First of all, it's being what every writer is, which is masochistic. But it's even worse than that. It's getting your kicks out of miniaturization. I think it was Oscar Hammerstein who said that it's the same sort of psyche that leads a man to want to engrave The Lord's Prayer on the head of a pin. It's that sweating-down process, that distillation, that drives most writers up the wall. Certain people like that paring-down. Me? I'd be petrified by the immense sweep of a novel—such a frightening project to contemplate. But to work within the confines of a lyric—to get an idea, and be able to capture it in 32 bars . . . that's a kick. Very challenging, very tough. And I'm hooked."

'Oh, How We Danced'

(Saul Chaplin)

SAUL CHAPLIN is generally considered to be one of the most adept men around. He's a real "pro," and that is a word not lightly bestowed by his peer group. He was and still is a successful songwriter, but, unlike his ex-partner Sammy Cahn, who continues to ply his crafts strictly as lyricist, Chaplin early on became a skillful music arranger, a musical director, a composer of film scores, and then an associate producer of many film musicals.

"When Sammy and I got to Hollywood," he muses, "it was 1939, and the absolute wrongest time to go out there, because they weren't making musicals. Did he also tell you that they wouldn't even let us *on* the Warner lot, where we were supposed to be under contract?"

In the ensuing three decades Chaplin's career has traveled a considerable distance upward. His varied talents have been put to use on such memorable musical films as *Cover Girl, The Jolson Story, On the Town, Seven Brides for Seven Brothers,* and *High Society.* For his musical direction of *An American in Paris* he received an Oscar in 1951, another in 1954 for *Seven Brides,* a third in 1961 for *West Side Story.* And add to the list his awards for his work on *The Sound of Music.*

We are in Chaplin's Belgravia hotel room; the desk is covered with work schedules and masses of paper that are architectural notes for his current production. Making a large-budget film such as *La Mancha* is an intensely complicated venture; Chaplin is responsible for all of the intricacies.

It's no accident that he's worked with the best—Jerome Kern, Ira Gershwin, Mercer, Cole Porter (he's done four Porter film musicals, more than any other music man); and with the superstars—Garland, Sinatra, Bing Crosby, Gene Kelly, Julie Andrews. "For heaven's sake, don't leave out Ann Miller!" chortles Chaplin. "That's my real distinction! I have done more films with Ann Miller than anyone alive! The entire time I worked at Columbia, from 1940 to 1949, it was always Ann Miller. My life from 1940 to 1959 was Ann Miller, because when she moved to Metro, I did too! There I was working with her on *Kiss Me, Kate* and *On the Town* and all those big-budget Metro musicals. Believe me, I am the world's foremost authority on Ann Miller!"

Where was the first Hollywood break?

"Sammy and I got to do a picture at Republic, a thing called *Rookies on Parade*. The producer didn't want songwriters, he wanted a story. Our agent told him, 'Don't worry—these two guys write *anything!*' We'd never written anything in our lives like that, but we *were* authorities on vaudeville acts because of our Brooklyn Vitagraph days, so we sat down and rewrote half a dozen routines that we remembered, put them together with the cockamamy story about a songwriter—who can even remember what it was? If you look at the credits of *Rookies on Parade* today—although I cannot imagine why you ever would— you will see, 'Original story and songs by Sammy Cahn and Saul Chaplin.'

"Then we got to meet Harry Cohn, who ran Columbia. Oh, I know the book's been written about Cohn, but think about his early background. He'd been a frustrated songwriter, then a song-plugger. And we came in with a lot of hits behind us. Sammy is a very brash guy now, but in those days he was even brasher. He was Harry Cohn's kind of guy. We were invited to play at a party, and Harry was singing along with the songs that I knew *he* knew, old songs, and he told Morris Stoloff, who was the head of his music department, who also loved us, to hire us. Cohn was starting to make all those cheap musicals—*mostly* with Ann Miller!" he adds.

And Cohn, with his shrewd nose for a bargain, no doubt got Cahn and Chaplin at a very low price?

"That," says Chaplin succinctly, "goes with the territory. Eventually Sammy decided to write with Jule Styne—I suppose Jule has filled you in on that next period—but I stayed on. I had a wife and a baby and I needed a steady job. Eight or nine years I was there, running all over the Columbia lot. The music department had four or five people on staff—we did everything. One week it would be a couple of songs for a quickie musical, the next week it would be arrangements and choral work on one of Cohn's big musicals, like *The Jolson Story* or *Cover Girl*. That is where I really learned the movie business. Later on, when I got to Metro, I couldn't believe that I was only working on one project, sometimes for months at a time. *One* picture—such luxury!"

One of those frantic Columbia sessions produced an inadvertent smash-hit song for Chaplin, an all-time "standard"—"The Anniversary Song," which Al Jolson (or, rather, Jolson's *voice*, since it was Larry Parks who played the title role) introduced in *The Jolson Story*.

"The idea came from Sidney Buchman, the producer. He felt Parks, as

Jolie, needed something at the scene where his parents had come from the East for their anniversary party. A little throwaway thing, just for the background to the dialogue. We were at lunch, and Jolie said he knew a tune that would fit— an old semi-classical Russian waltz written by a man named Ivanovici. He hummed it, and it sounded great. So they said, 'What about lyrics?' and I said—remember, I did *everything* over there—'I'll knock out a lyric so we can use it.' I went back to my office, and I swear it can't be more than forty-five minutes later I called Buchman and told him I had a lyric. Jolson recorded it and it came out beautifully. So they decided to make more out of it, to show Parks actually singing it at the party. I said, 'If that's the case, let me rewrite the lyric. This isn't the best I can do, it's almost off the top of my head.' I must tell you," says Chaplin with candor, "there are still parts of that lyric that embarrass me. Things like, '*we vowed our true love, the word wasn't said.*' Nobody says 'true love.' It's terrible. But Buchman refused. He said, 'You're going to rewrite it into a failure; it sounds fine now.'

"Jolson had had the idea for the first line of the song, so, as he had music. Which was all right by me, because, as it turned out, he got us a marvelous royalty deal from the publishers. I thought he was crazy at the time—there hadn't been a waltz hit for maybe twenty years! But Jolie made it into a hit. 1947 . . . it's been a hit for twenty-five years, can you believe it?" Chaplin shakes his head in honest perplexity. "Something exists even in that sloppy lyric. It's another 'Happy Birthday.' You cannot go to a wedding or to a ballroom or a club where somebody's going to have an anniversary party without the orchestra going into that song."

The meeting of a good song with a great performer made the electrical connection, the right chemical formula for a hit. Other songwriters have remarked that the greatest song in the world sung by the wrong person won't "work"—that is, move into the Top Ten.

"And vice versa," agrees Chaplin. "The wrong song done by the *best* person won't 'work' either. It has to be a meeting of both."

If "Anniversary Song" is unique, then so is the entire *Jolson Story* saga. Once one of show business' biggest stars, Jolson had come upon a dismal stretch after World War II. Well-to-do financially, Al was out of work. Afternoons at the race track did nothing to assuage his battered ego; after years of stardom, he was a has-been. Sidney Skolsky, the columnist, decided that Jolson's life story would make a marvelous film. But practically all of the major studios—including Warner Brothers, where, ironically, Jolson had starred in *The Jazz Singer*— turned Skolsky down flat. Jolson was too old. Who had any use for a faded singer? It was Sidney Buchman who became interested in the possibilities and brought the idea to Harry Cohn, who eventually agreed to make the film at Columbia. *The Jolson Story* was an immense financial success; the irony deepens when it is recalled that Jolson's voice, circa 1947, when he was recording the music tracks for Larry Parks to perform to, is now considered by critics to have been at its period of absolute perfection.

"Cohn went for the Jolson project *again* because he was an old song-plugger," explains Chaplin. "When Cohn was peddling songs in his early days, Jolson was the guy you got the top plug from. If he sang your song, it was bound to make a noise with the public. And here was Cohn, in the '40s, hiring the guy he'd once been struggling to see. It must have been a big kick for him.

"I was assigned to that picture months before they started," he recalls. "I worked very hard on it. Knocked my brains out. They had dug up a lady in Pasadena who was a Jolson record collector. I sat in an office, and part of every day I used to listen to her old Jolson records, to get familiar with them. The day of the first recording session, Jolie did 'April Showers' first, and, strangely enough, he had forgotten *how* he used to do it! But when you first heard Jolson, you were never aware of things like that because he was such a thrilling performer that you were . . . in awe. So he finished the recording, and everybody cheered and yelled, 'Great, Al!' *I* knew he had left out the talking part, the *recitative* in the second chorus. He said, 'What about *you?* Don't you like it?' I said, 'It's good, but it's not like the record I remember.' He said, 'Well, you know, it's not easy to do this sort of thing.' I said, 'Al, I'm not saying it's easy, but it isn't what I think it should be.' This got us into a whole big argument. And he pulled this famous Jolson thing on me. He took out the big roll of bills that he carried. He said, 'I made *this* in show business; show me yours!' So I said something that you can't quote, and I walked out. Went home. I was angry too!"

Chaplin smiles. "Al was famous for that sort of arrogance. Eventually I came back, and he'd done it wrong again! But I persisted, and finally we got Al to do it right, and I must say it was better. After that, I was teaching *him* how he used to do his own songs! I have a record of Jolson doing 'Who Paid the Rent for Mrs. Rip Van Winkle (While Rip Van Winkle Was Away)?' in his old-time Low Dutch accent from forty years before. Never used in the picture, sadly."

"Oh, Al was an incredible performer. It was a privilege to get to work with him. I've been so fortunate in that respect—Jolson, Judy Garland, Frank Sinatra. And the songwriters! Take the great Jerome Kern—before the Jolson picture I'd worked on *Cover Girl*, which he wrote with Ira Gershwin, for Rita Hayworth and Gene Kelly, in 1940.

"Kern was a very strict man about changes, you know. Don't let anybody tell you the Hollywood people pushed *him* around. He was not to be used up, or kicked around, or moved, or budged, or in any way maneuvered by anybody. He had a very strong personality, and everyone conformed to what *Kern* wanted. Ask Ira Gershwin what it was like to get Kern to change one note in a song to fit an extra word in the lyric that Ira had written.

"There was one sequence in *Cover Girl*—a comedy bit for Gene Kelly and Phil Silvers, something on the back of a truck when they're entertaining the soldiers. They couldn't think who should write it. I'd known Phil for years, so I said I'd take a crack at it. I took a song of Kern's that was to be in the picture called *Put Me to the Test*. Ira Gershwin had written a patter chorus, and I extended it and added some quote comedy unquote material. It was funny in those days . . . I guess. Right for Phil and Gene. I needed a couple of extra lines for it, and now I must tell you a marvelous scene. I'd explained to Ira I needed a couple of lines, and he told me to come over to his house. I went there, and sitting around were E. Y. Harburg, Marc Connelly, Leo Robin, Arthur Schwartz, and the late Oscar Levant. I spoke to Ira, and Ira said to the group, 'Listen, don't leave—we need two lines for this thing.' So I played it. Well, the joke lines started coming from all these talented guys so fast you could not believe it! Harburg had literally dozens of them! There were so many coming from them all, it became a contest of their own prowess instead of what I needed!"

Who ended up supplying the two needed joke lines?

"Ira, of course." Chaplin grins. "A marvelous man.

"Anyway, I finished the thing, Phil and Gene recorded it, and suddenly Morris Stoloff said, 'Listen, you have to let Kern hear it. He doesn't know anything about this.' You can imagine with what trepidation I faced *that* hurdle. We got Kern to come to the studio, and we put on the sound track we'd recorded. He listened to the comedy material and he didn't crack a smile, and I thought, 'Well, that's the end of *that*, and it hasn't even been shot yet.' When it was over, he said, 'Well, if it works, keep it in. If not, throw it out.' And he left. It worked, thankfully. Oh yes, it worked quite well.

"Later, I did a picture with Ira at Metro called *Give a Girl a Break*," says Chaplin, "and I must tell you what I've been doing lately with him. I've been going through all his brother George's unpublished manuscripts, books, note-books, and out of them, as a result, there's a piece coming out called 'Two Waltzes in C,' which Ira edited and I arranged for the piano. Both were written in 1931 for *Pardon My English* and were cut out. Lovely waltzes for that period. Oh, this has been an incredible experience!" He beams with undisguised joy. "I've found the beginnings of *Rhapsody in Blue*, the changes in *Concerto in F!* And besides, there's a kind of a blues piece that George wrote in 1916, in two keys, where the right hand's in one key and the left hand's in the other. It's just marvelous!" He shakes his head with wonder. "He was seventeen, eighteen years old! Incredible! Now it's just a matter of Ira releasing it."

Now to the post-Columbia period. What about the four Cole Porter films which Chaplin worked on—*High Society, Les Girls, Kiss Me, Kate,* and *Can-Can?*

"Well," says Chaplin, softly, "this is something I really cherish. The fact that I had a little something to do with shaping Cole's scores of *High Society* and *Les Girls*. We had a marvelous time on *High Society*. I was by that time working as associate producer to Sol Siegel. Porter was supposed to write the songs, and they sent me to New York to see him. I was in such awe of him, because all my life, although I've written music, I've also written lyrics, as you know. And Porter did both—to a fare-thee-well!

"First we had an evening meeting. He said, 'I want to play you a song.' He played a song for me which was a nice song but wasn't right for that particular spot in the picture. But I can't tell that to Cole Porter, can I? I mean—how am I going to tell *him* he's done anything wrong? So I said, 'A nice song. I like it. Good.' He played it again. I said, 'It's nice. Yes, it's fine.' Cole said, 'Come here.' And he was limping very badly then, you know, and used canes. He took me over to the sofa, and he said, 'Look. We are going to work together. Now, I can tell you didn't like that song, for whatever reason I don't know yet. *You* have to tell me what the reason is, because if I agree that your reason is right, I'll rewrite the song. If I don't, we'll use the song. But let's start out honestly from the beginning.'

"Do you know something?" Chaplin says fervently. "I never got that from anybody before or since! And from then on we had the most marvelous time. He was sick; he wasn't playing very well. He'd written part of a song called 'I Love You, Samantha,' which is one of my favorite songs. And he couldn't really play it. I got exasperated and I said, 'Cole, for God's sake, do you have it *written down* someplace? I can't tell what you're doing!' He only had eight bars. I played the eight bars. I said, 'Finish it, my God—it's marvelous!' That was the kind of relationship we developed. I remember later I unearthed that song 'Well, Did You Evah!' from one of his old shows, *DuBarry Was a Lady*, and Cole wrote a new set of lyrics, although I'm proud to say I had a word or two in there, with his approval, of course.

"You remember that number 'Now You Has Jazz'? Such a completely untypical Porter number. It was sung by Bing Crosby and Louis Armstrong at what was meant to be the Newport Jazz Festival. Well, Cole, in his typical thorough way, got Fred Astaire to take him to a few jazz places. Except, you don't get to learn jazz that way." Chaplin smiles. "But he tried; he wrote a first chorus of the song. If you listen to it, it's really a very straight verse and chorus. I wrote part of the rest of it, and then I got Bing and Louis down onto the sound stage and we batted it out in about four days—just playing around with it, so to speak, and then I'd go home at night and organize it, and write whatever needed to be written. That's how it eventually emerged on the screen."

Wouldn't that be considered by anyone else as a collaborative effort?

"No, not at all," says Chaplin. "I was only doing a job. The song was all Cole's—just embellished. *High Society* had a lovely score—'You're Sensational,' 'True Love'—lovely. There were other good Porter songs, a pretty one called 'Ça, C'est l'Amour,' which was in *Les Girls* . . . very nice. Got lost. The crazy thing is, I have songs of Cole's that they didn't even know existed after he died. You see, our relationship evolved into this; he'd write songs for a picture and I'd say, 'Cole, let me make a copy of it and think about it.' He would play it, and I'd take it down, and I would have the only copy. We'd later discuss whether it worked or not—and then I'd give it back to him and he'd either rewrite it or not. As a result, I ended up with four or five songs of his that nobody knew about.

"Four times at bat with Cole Porter," Chaplin muses, staring through the hotel-room window at the wet London streets below. "Who could ask for a better experience?"

Should we return to the performers?

After Jolson, the one who springs first to mind has to be Judy Garland.

"To start with, I've got to tell you that Judy Garland and Julie Andrews have one thing in common which is unique. They learn music like a vacuum cleaner. The minute you played it for them, it came right back again. When it first happens, you're left with your mouth open because you can't believe it. Which may not sound like much, but the most tedious part of producing musicals is teaching people new music. You want to get them started so you can have more time for polishing and for acquiring style. Now, with Judy—I wrote an arrangement of Harold Arlen and Ted Koehler's 'Get Happy' for her in *Summer Stock*. Her record of it was a big smash hit. It's a very complicated arrangement. Judy heard it three times, but never sang it. Then she got sick. Two weeks later she came in, rehearsed it *once*, and recorded it in about four 'takes.'

"Great humor. Bright, and fun to be with—when she was there. Judy may have been the most fun to work with of anybody—no, I suddenly think of Gene Kelly and Phil Silvers, they were lots of fun, too. But Judy was funny, she was cooperative. She was late for every single appointment. I mean, so late that sometimes it became annoying. Until she got there—and then, after she'd arrived, you forgot the whole thing. I remember doing a picture with her here in England, in 1963. We had an appointment to rehearse at eleven in the morning. She came in at seven fifteen that night . . . and didn't think anything was wrong with that, you know!" He thinks back for a long silent moment. "Judy had lots of suggestions, and if you didn't take them, fine," he says. "If you did, great. Absolutely no temperament about things like that. When it came to recordings, it was the same kind of thing. She was a very good critic of herself. Toward the end,"— he shakes his head slightly—"she got . . . Well, even then it would be hard to say she was less critical. She wasn't singing so well, and I have a feeling she knew it. But I also have a feeling she knew she couldn't do anything about it.

"But that aptitude of hers for learning was remarkable. It was the same with dancing. Judy would learn routines *immediately*. That is the kind of talent that girl had.

"The crazy thing is, to have worked with her and then Julie Andrews, who is like that, too. In a way, Julie is . . ." He hesitates. "I was going to say Julie is a better musician, but I'm not sure that's true. Both of them have the same past, you know. Not exactly, but similar. Vaudeville parents, broken homes. Not that it means anything, but I suppose it adds to the personality. In both *Sound of Music* and *Star* Julie learned the music very quickly, she had valid suggestions, and, more than just that, she had a viewpoint on a song, the same as Judy. You don't just sing a song, you know. In most cases, songs in a film are scenes.

"You've been mentioning a lot of my credits. I'm proud of them, of course," admits Chaplin, "but what I'm really prouder of is that starting way back with, I guess, *High Society*, the people in my films were never just *singing*. They're always part of a scene. I don't care about great vocal power; I care that they have the right dramatic *feel* for the character—more important. The days when songs were only songs left us with Nelson Eddy and Jeanette MacDonald. At that time the important thing was to rear back and sing; they used to scream in each other's faces. Not now. Not for me, anyhow. Every time I've done a musical, I have long discussions with the director as to the *intent* of the song. What are we trying to *prove*? And if we start at *this* point, where should we be at the end of the song—where have we progressed? If we haven't progressed, the song doesn't belong in the picture. Because, unless it's something special, such an unintegrated song will fall out, be cut, when we find out the picture's too long. That's generally what happens.

"The best example of songs progressing a picture is in a film I worked on that absolutely would not work without its songs: *Seven Brides for Seven Brothers*.* Very quickly—the seven brothers are very despondent; they haven't got girls. Howard Keel walks in and says, 'You're so depressed, why don't we go out and *get* the girls?' He sings a song called 'Sobbin' Women.' By the end of the thing he's got them so roused up that they all ride off and kidnap the women! Now, if you remove that song, the scene won't make any sense. The song did it, made the transition for us. That, to me, is the perfect example of the integration of a song in a film."

Jule Styne has remarked that the three authentic geniuses he's been privileged to work with were Streisand ("Her I've never worked with," says Chaplin), Frank Sinatra, and Jerome Robbins.

"Well, Frank I first met way back in the days when he was singing with Tommy Dorsey's band. Cahn-and-Chaplin days. The interesting thing about Sinatra is that the world-famous Sinatra, personality-wise, is no different from the one we knew back in '37, '38. A marvelous musician, knows exactly what he wants. Also knows exactly what he wants to hear. Rehearses as little as possible. Frank's big expression is 'I don't want to over-rehearse.' But he's always been

* The score was written by Johnny Mercer and Gene DePaul. The film itself is widely considered to be one of the best original musicals ever produced.

that way. Great ear—learns music very quickly. He'll also take suggestions—depending, certainly, on who is giving them. I've never had any kind of trouble with Frank. But what Frank will also do is to make up endings. He'll say, 'How about doing this?' and try something on you. Very easy to work with—*if* you can get him to rehearse. The problem," Chaplin sums up, "is to *get* him there in the first place.

"As for Jerry Robbins, I worked with him on *West Side Story* and I've always said, all my life since I've known him—and I go back to those days when he was doing *On the Town* with Betty Comden and Adolph Green; I worked on the film version—that the only person I've ever met that I'm *positive* is a genius is Jerome Robbins. If you know him, you cannot come to any other conclusion. I know Lenny Bernstein very well, I know a lot of others. They're enormously talented, true, but Robbins is a genius. That's it. As a genius, it makes him very difficult to work with, and if you're willing to put up with that, fine."

Does it then follow that the results justify the difficulties?

"The results are incredible," Chaplin says without hesitation. "I've worked with Jack Cole, with Michael Kidd—marvelous choreographers. But even they admit Robbins is something else. He is something *apart.*"

The film version of *West Side Story* was a huge success, both financially and artistically, a landmark musical film. And yet it was far from an easy film to make; throughout its production a steady stream of stories concerning frictions and arguments emanated from behind the sound-stage doors.

"So many things went wrong with that picture while we were doing it, I cannot begin to tell you," admits Chaplin now. "It was the hardest picture to make, *ever.* You read my list of credits. The difficulties on all of them *put together* wouldn't compare with the problems we had on *West Side Story.* Toward the end, you know, there was only Bob Wise [the producer-director] and myself left. We had an expression, 'We're chipping away at it.' We figured there was some sort of a jinx hanging over us. Rita Moreno was talking to me one day on the set, and she said, 'I have to do the next scene out of breath; I better run around the set.' She runs around the set, sprains her ankle, and is out for a month! Another time, we're about to start a big dance sequence—our lead dancer comes down with mononucleosis! We're dubbing* the picture, we finally get a perfect take . . . and find that some idiot in the booth has accidentally rubbed out the entire tape! You cannot begin to believe the things we went through!"

Was there any sense, on the part of the creative people involved, that a filmic masterpiece was being fashioned?

He shakes his head and sighs, with remembered *angst.* "All we cared about was getting it finished. We had absolutely no idea that it was as great a picture as it was. And I must also tell you," he adds, "that I saw it several years ago, for the first time since I'd done it originally, and I think it's good. But there are things that I would still change! Things that we didn't get to do *right.*"

There followed the mammoth success of *The Sound of Music,* which Robert Wise also produced and directed, again in close collaboration with Chaplin.

"Never that difficult," says Chaplin. "It was fun to do, because Julie is fun. We took that to the same theatre in Minneapolis where we'd previewed *West*

---

* The addition of voice tracks, music tracks, sound effects, synchronized to the photographed film. The process entails "mixing," by an engineer, of perhaps half-a-dozen tracks into a balanced whole. "Dubbing" is where a film can be made . . . or broken.

Side Story. When the opinion cards came in, they were insane—such ecstatic cards! So we knew we had a hit, and we were delighted. But we had no idea that it was going to become what it has become."

The "what" Chaplin refers to is a box-office gross for *The Sound of Music* which has been toted up past $120,000,000 *so far*. "The next release date is 1974," he says with a certain amount of awe, "when it goes back into the theatres . . . for more profit."

Not bad for a musical which, from its original opening on Broadway until now, has never received what could be called "hit" notices.

After *The Sound of Music*, Wise and Chaplin did the film biography of the late Gertrude Lawrence, again starring Julie Andrews. *Star* was a box-office failure. Is there a post-mortem?

"My personal feeling is that it came out at a time when suddenly the generation gap opened up and the movie audiences no longer wanted to see this kind of musical. They wanted *Easy Rider*. Remember, after *Sound of Music, all* the musical films bombed, including the big ones—*Paint Your Wagon, Hello, Dolly!, Goodbye, Mr. Chips*. By the way, *Star* didn't lose anywhere near the money that those others lost. As far as I'm concerned, if we gave Fox one picture that's made as much for them as *Sound of Music* did and they lose maybe $12,000,000 on another, they shouldn't really complain, should they?

"Another thing, I think," he muses, "is that audiences did not want to see Julie in this sort of role. They simply did not want her playing a real person."

In other words, the public prefers the lady as their private image of Mary Poppins?

"And as Maria, the ex-nun. Not as Gertrude Lawrence—and they told us so in no uncertain terms, when they stayed away from *Star*."

So where does the film musical go from this point? Does Chaplin consider that the musical era has faded out?

"Not by a long shot," he says. "But nobody ever again in our lifetime is going to spend $20,000,000 to do a musical. There's no necessity for it, anyway; for proof of that look at *Fiddler on the Roof* and *Cabaret*.

"Hey, listen!" he says, "have I said anything that makes sense?"

If there is an award for understatement, Saul Chaplin has just collected it, along with all the other kudos he's received, since his arrival in Hollywood in the days when the only way he and Sammy Cahn could get onto the Warner lot was to sneak on with their old pal Jimmy Lunceford.

In those long-gone days the film business was full of people who made musicals. In 1972 Saul Chaplin seems to be one of the last survivors. Is he practicing a dying art?

"Oh, no!" he promises. "The audiences are there."

'Brother, Can You Spare a Dime?'

(E.Y. Harburg)

IF YOU'VE BEEN fortunate enough to listen to E. Y. Harburg sing his own lyrics and discuss the hows and whys of such classics as "Brother, Can You Spare a Dime?," "Over the Rainbow," "How Are Things in Glocca Morra?," and "April in Paris," either in the YMHA auditorium in Manhattan, or on various television shows, you won't need to be reminded of the electric excitement and the amazing nostalgic warmth that he communicates. He lights up the stage and the tube with a high-voltage rating of near-incandescence.

"Yip," as he has been known ever since the days when he and Ira Gershwin sat next to each other in classes at City College, is a stocky, vigorous gentleman who shows little physical evidence of becoming seventy-five at his next birthday. Since the bleak days of 1932, when he wrote "Brother, Can You Spare a Dime?," he has been turning out top-rate songs with a variety of our best composers— Harold Arlen, Jerome Kern, Vernon Duke, Arthur Schwartz, Burton Lane, Earl Robinson. He's also a complete man of the theatre, having often developed his own story ideas into musical comedies (he and Fred Saidy were co-authors of *Finian's Rainbow*), and during his Hollywood tour of duty he added to Metro's yearly profit figures by producing a batch of profitable film musicals.

There may not be any valid course in lyric-writing available to the tyro—in fact (as Lee Adams, another wordsmith of considerable talent, has remarked), it's more than likely that along with playwriting, or any other creative work with words, songwriting is a craft that is simply unteachable. Harburg is blunt on the subject. "We never knew anything about schools," he says, rocking back and forth on the porch of his comfortable summer home on Martha's Vineyard. "We just got up and wrote, that's all. Like Topsy—kind of growed. Nowadays there are so many different courses in the universities. I personally think it's a lot of nonsense. The bright kids get lost in a welter of formulas, clichés. Not that I don't say you must have some analytical basis and some awareness, but I think that in every age there are only a few people born with talent. You *can't* make 'em."

What follows, then, in Yip's own words, is a compound of his own life story, a goodly helping of pragmatic know-how, and a sparkling of philosophy. A short course, perhaps, but long in content.

Yip—you're on.

"How did I start? I wrote all the parodies of the day. Name every old song, and I had a parody for it. That gave you status—there was no other way. No money. You were a slum kid and you had no identity. And suddenly you could hear a bleacher full of little gangsters singing *your* song . . . That's how it started.

"I come from a rough area, right there on the East Side—the East River, with all the derelicts, docks, lots of sailors and gangs. There wasn't any such thing as an East River Drive down there. This was before World War I. Italian gangs on Mulberry Street—we used to play them in baseball. I was on the Tompkins Square Park team; we won the New York State championship. And then there were the Irish, a little further up on 14th Street. Plenty of gang fights. Those of us who were a little more sensitive and didn't care for that so much were directing ourselves to the settlement houses, like the Henry Street Settlement. Wonderful places. They took the kids under their wing. They had wonderful social directors. They had clubs, athletic clubs, literary clubs. I belonged to a literary dramatic club. We were putting on plays, and that excited me.

"The public schools were better then, too. I went to P.S. 64, on Avenue B and Ninth Street. Great teachers—they were aware of the poverty conditions of the kids they were teaching. I had an English teacher—his name comes back to me as though it was yesterday: Ed Gillesper. I'd write something for the school newspaper, or a composition, and he'd read it and see something funny in it, and say, 'Harburg, come up here and read it to the class.' I'd read, and there would be twenty-odd kids laughing out loud, and, by God, that was really something. I'd tell myself, 'I want to repeat *this* experience!'

"We'd do shows at the settlement house, or in school, and I'd usually get parts. I found I had the ability to act and to write my own stuff. Scrounging around for costumes, putting on shows—it was great. We were poor, always out in the street with our furniture, and never knowing if the next rent would be paid. But I had an exciting time. More fun than I ever had in Hollywood. It was real. If you wanted to play a basketball game, you had to make the equipment yourself. No basketball, no bat or ball—you made everything, improvised.

"Luckily, there was City College, which was free. And attached to it was Townsend Harris, a high school that crammed a four-year course into three. I went there, and earned money at night lighting street lamps. In those days they'd employ kids for $3.06 a week to go around at night and turn on the lamps. I was twelve. They gave me a three or four-mile route. I'd put the lights on when dusk set in, and then I had to get up at three or four in the morning and go out and turn 'em off! Earned enough for food and whatever else I needed. Worked my way through college, too. All kinds of jobs. God, you worked every minute of the day!

"In high school I worked on the newspaper. Began writing things with more sophistication—light verse. By that time I'd begun to know about W. S. Gilbert. When I got to City College, I began to send in stuff I'd written to 'The Conning Tower,' a column Franklin P. Adams ran in the old *World*, a hell of a good paper. Verses. You see, at that time everyone was writing light verse— sonnets, acrostics, things like that. Dorothy Parker, Deems Taylor, Edna St. Vincent Millay, George Kaufman, Marc Connelly, you name them. They'd write that sort of thing, and had a lot of fun doing it. When Adams accepted things of mine and I saw my name in his column, along with Marc Connelly's or Dorothy Parker's—well, it gave me such a lift I felt I could conquer anything! Not financially, of course. I never got paid until I started sending verse to some of the magazines—*Judge* and *Life* and so on. Then I'd get $10 checks, $15 checks. Which meant a great deal.

"My classmate at college was Ira Gershwin. We sat next to each other— G, H, you see. We began collaborating on a column for the City College news-paper. Yip and Gersh. He was always interested in light verse, too. He introduced me to a lot of things that I'd not had access to. The Gershwins weren't poor— they had restaurants. George was a kid then, just a snip of a kid, and Ira sort of sloughed him off because George didn't care too much about education and had dropped out of school. I remember once going up to the Gershwins' to hear the Victrola—that was a very new thing, Victrola records. That was the first time I heard W. S. Gilbert's lyrics set to Sullivan's music. Up to that time I thought he was simply a poet! Ira played *Pinafore* for me, and I had my eyes opened. I was starry-eyed for days. I couldn't sleep at night. It was that music —and the satire that came out with all the emotion that I never dreamed of before when I read the thing cold in print!

"Ira dropped out in sophomore year. I suppose I should have taken a B.A. degree, but I didn't. I went on to a B.S. I took all the damned hard courses like integral calculus. Nothing like the so-called 'crap courses.'

"When I got out of college, I didn't pursue poetry. That was work for a dilettante—nobody made a living at that. That's for fun, that's a sideline, you don't earn money that way, I used to think. Money is made by the sweat of your brow. This is the old Puritan ethic that we're brought up with. You've got to do something real nasty, dirty, get calluses—you don't just sit and write. Because you couldn't live on $10 checks for poetry, could you?

"So I went into the electrical-supply business with a college classmate. I don't know why he wanted me as a partner. Maybe it was because by that time I was something of a local celebrity with my poems. For the next few years we made a lot of money and I hated it. I hated every moment of it. I'd signed a contract saying I wasn't going to spend any time except on the business—the guys who put up the money for the business probably figured I'd go off and neglect it.

"But the economy saved me. The capitalists saved me in 1929, just as we were worth, oh, about a quarter of a million dollars. Bang! The whole thing blew up. I was left with a pencil, and finally had to write for a living. As I told Studs Terkel once, what was the Depression for most people was for me a life-saver!

"I called up my friend Ira. By that time he and George had a lot of shows and had become big names in the business. Ira introduced me to Jay Gorney, and we began writing songs. I was penniless—in fact, I owed a lot of money. And one of the first songs I wrote with Jay was 'Brother, Can You Spare a Dime?' for a show called *Americana* that J. P. McEvoy was producing.

"McEvoy was a satirist. He was writing this show, which was to be about the Forgotten Man. Roosevelt had just made that phrase popular. McEvoy wrote the book, and I did the lyrics. I started writing with Vincent Youmans, but he left. Then I worked with three or four other composers,* because we had to get it done in a short time. But the show turned out to be very good. I think it was the first time ballet dancing was used in a Broadway revue; we had the Charles Weidman dancers, with Doris Humphrey.

"It was a terrible period. You couldn't walk along the street without crying, without seeing people standing in breadlines, so miserable. Brokers and people who'd been wealthy, begging. 'Can you spare a dime?' . . . that was for a cup of coffee. That's what the big thing was, a dime could keep you alive for a few days.

"When Jay played me the tune he had, I thought of that phrase 'Can you spare a dime?' It kept running through my mind as I was walking the streets. And by putting the word 'brother' to the line, I got started on it.

"But I thought that lyric out very carefully. I didn't make it a maudlin lyric of a guy begging. I made it into a commentary. That may sound rhetorical, but it's true. It was about the fellow who works, the fellow who builds, who makes the railroads and the houses—and he's left empty-handed. How come? How did this happen? Didn't I fight the wars, didn't I bear the gun, didn't I plow the earth? In other words, the fellow who produces is the fellow who's left empty-handed at the end.

"I think that lyric lives because it doesn't tackle the thing in a maudlin way. It's not a hand-out lyric, like a lot of the old English ballads; they're lachrymose, almost begging. This is a man proud of what he's done, but bewildered that this country with its dream could do this to him. I think a lyric first of all hits you emotionally, directly. And this did it because of the music, and because the fellow wasn't being petty, or small, or complaining."

(Jay Gorney says, "Several years later, when I'd come back from Hollywood, Lee Shubert sent for me and said, 'Good to see you, Gorney. What I wanted to ask you is, do you have another song like "Mister, Will You Give Me Ten Cents?" ' But his brother J. J. never shared Lee's enthusiasm. Whenever anyone mentioned the song, he'd say '*I* don't like it. It's too sordid!')

"I kept on writing after that; you could say I was launched. Gorney and I wrote songs for an Earl Carroll *Vanities*. At that time Carroll specialized in selling his beautiful girls. He used a novelty gimmick: 'Through these portals pass the most beautiful girls in the world!' When I first saw these most beautiful girls rehearsing, I realized the effect of theatrical showmanship. Carroll's girls were really ugly—dogs—but on the stage, made up, in costume, with lighting and special effects, he could sell them to the audience. People *believed* that slogan of his!

"I did two shows with him—one a *Vanities*, the other a *Sketchbook*—and

* One of whom was the young Harold Arlen. *Americana* opened October 5, 1932.

then in 1932 I did a revue with Bea Lillie and Bobby Clark called *Walk a Little Faster*, and some songs for Willie Howard and Bob Hope—Hope's first Broadway show, a revue called *Ballyhoo*. That's when I discovered that I could write comedy songs. That really titillated me the most—the comedy, the satirical idea—because with that sort of song I felt more at home. After all, my earliest education at that was from Gilbert and Sullivan.

"Gorney had gone off to work in Hollywood with Lew Brown, and I was by now working steadily with Harold Arlen and with the late Vernon Duke.

"Billy Rose was doing a play by Ben Hecht and Charles MacArthur, *The Great Magoo*, and he called and said, 'We need a song here for a guy who's a Coney Island barker. A very cynical guy who falls in love and finds that the world is not all Coney Island—not papier-mâché and lights and that sort of gaudy stuff. But it's got to be a love song.' Well, I tried to think of a cynical love story, something that this kind of a guy would sing. But I could never really be cynical. I could see life in all its totality, its reality. In a song I wrote for another show at that time, I wrote that it's fun to be fooled. That was a love song also. But I doubt that I can ever say 'I love you' head-on—it's not the way I think. For me, the task is never to say the thing directly, and yet to say it—to think in a curve, so to speak. In 'Fun To Be Fooled' I was saying life is all being fooled, we are all being fooled by it, but while it's happening it's a lot of fun. *I* think it's a lot of fun. I think it's a lovely excursion, and I'm glad I got a ticket for this short cruise, and that's all.

"So when it came to the other song, it was an extension of that same idea. I called it 'It's Only a Paper Moon.' The idea there was that the guy says to the girl the moon is made of paper, it's hanging over a cardboard tree, but there's a saving grace called love. Without it, life is all a honky-tonk parade. In other words, it's not make-believe as long as someone believes in it. *The Great Magoo* was a failure, but that song became a big hit.

"So was 'April in Paris,' which I wrote with Vernon Duke.* That lyric has a very special quality. First of all, I think it captures Paris in a way that only French people have been able to do. And then, it's not about simply being in love in Paris but about *wanting* to be in love anywhere. Again, I tried to avoid the cliché. This is a person who has never been in love, never wanted to be in love. He goes to Paris and, for the first time, experiences wanting to be in love with somebody. He wants to run to somebody. Paris has opened him up for the first time.

"I met Vernon Duke through George Gershwin. After Gorney went to California, I started writing with various composers, and I began to realize different types of songs that existed. It was fine for me because it allowed me to learn my own abilities. Vernon had just come over from Europe. He was a Russian—his real name was Vladimir Dukelsky—and he was very far advanced in his music. Very serious composer. As Dukelsky, his symphonic works were performed in concert halls. In Europe he'd worked with Diaghilev, writing

---

* Harburg had written, with Duke, "What Is There to Say?" and "I Like the Likes of You" for the *Ziegfeld Follies of 1934*, before *Life Begins at 8:40*, which opened in the fall of 1934. "April in Paris" was born of theatrical necessity. The producer had ordered a set which represented a Parisian scene, and instructed Harburg to write a song that would go with it. Never having been abroad, Harburg went to a travel agent and accumulated brochures about Paris. From them he crafted the lyric.

ballets, and he was very avant-garde for this period, the mid-'30s. George Gershwin was very impressed with Duke's music. I suppose you could say he learned a lot from Vernon.

"I liked Vernon's facility. He was fast and very sophisticated, almost too sophisticated for Broadway. *Walk a Little Faster* had some very smart stuff in it. In fact, that's when I bounced out of the bread-and-butter stage into sophistication. My light-verse background popped up to reinforce me, and I could write much easier with Vernon than I could with some of the others. It was light, and airy, and very smart.

"Vernon brought with him all of that Noel Coward/Diaghilev/Paris/Russia background. He was a global guy with an ability to articulate the English language that was very interesting. A whole new world for me. He could drive you crazy, and he could also open up a new vista. Maybe it was a little bit chi-chi and decorative, but with my pumpernickel background and his orchid tunes we made a wonderful marriage. Maybe we were a strange mixture. We didn't compromise with each other. I applied the everyday down-deep things that concerned humanity to his sense of style and grace, and I think it gave our songs an almost classic feeling, along with some humor. We came together at a certain point, and for a while it was fine. He satisfied my sense of light verse and the need for sophistication.

"Later I felt that his music lacked the essential theatricalism and the histrionics that writing for shows demanded—the drama, the emotions. So gradually I gravitated more and more to Harold Arlen.

"Ira Gershwin and I collaborated with Harold on a score for *Life Begins at 8:40.* That was when I first got to know Harold as a craftsman. There were Ira and I working together again—a nice nostalgic thing. We wrote "Fun To Be Fooled" and "You're a Builder Upper" and "Let's Take a Walk Around the Block," and it was truly a joyous collaboration, a very happy few months. Ira would come in with one idea, I'd come in with an idea, Harold would come in with a tune. Lovely.

"After *Life Begins at 8:40,* Harold went out to California to write music for movies with Ted Koehler, with whom he'd written 'Stormy Weather.' Carl Laemmle, who ran Universal Pictures, came to New York and took a shine to my work, and gave me a contract to come out to his studio and do musicals there. After Harold's contract was up and mine at Universal had run out, there was an opening at Warner Brothers, and we were teamed up again to do some pictures there. And from then on, we've worked together, on and off.*

"Things began to get very tough around Hollywood. I got an idea for a book show, *Hooray for What?*, that would be a satire against war, and Howard Lindsay and Russel Crouse wrote it. Harold and I did the score, and Ed Wynn played the lead, and it was very successful. Ed played an inventor who'd come up with a gas that would end wars. That story would be much more pertinent now than it was in 1937, I'm sure. We had great notices and ran a year, which

---

* Harburg and Arlen wrote the scores for an Al Jolson picture, *The Singing Kid,* and for *Gold Diggers of 1937* before they returned to New York with the musical comedy *Hooray for What?* In 1936 their comedy song "The Song of the Woodman," was one of Bert Lahr's great moments in *The Show Is On,* possibly presaging what was to come when they wrote the score for *The Wizard of Oz,* in which Lahr played the Cowardly Lion.

in those days was a very good run. I've often thought it should be done again, now.

"When Harold and I started writing the score for *The Wizard of Oz,* we weren't thinking in terms of classics. We were just doing work, earning a living and liking what we were doing, trying for a hit song or two. We never thought of posterity. We were very excited about the film, we loved it. For the first time we'd gotten something that we both felt had the feeling of being fun. It was a chance to express ourselves in terms we'd never been offered before. I loved the idea of having the freedom to do lyrics that were not just songs but *scenes.* That was our own idea, to take some of the book and do some of the scenes in complete verse, such as the scenes in Munchkin Land. It gave me wider scope. Not just thirty-two-bar songs, but what would amount to the acting out of entire scenes, dialogue in verse and set to Harold's modern music. All of that had to be thought out by us and then brought in and shown to the director so he could see what we were getting at. Things like the three Lullaby girls, and the three tough kids who represented the Lollipop Guild. And the Coroner, who came to avow that the Witch was dead, sincerely dead. All of that was thought up by us, it wasn't in the book. Even a thing like 'Over the Rainbow'—there was no such thing as a rainbow mentioned in the book.*

"When we brought in the song, all we were thinking about was a little girl who was in trouble with her folks, in conflict with them, at an age when she wanted to run away, and knowing that somewhere, someplace, there was a colorful land that wasn't this arid flat plain of Kansas. She remembered a little verse from her childhood that mentioned a colorful place where bluebirds fly. The only thing she'd probably ever seen that was colorful was the rainbow. And that gave them the idea of doing the whole first part of the picture—when she's in Kansas—in sepia, black-and-white. And then when she got to Munchkin Land, the fairyland place, it became colorful. This whole new country was rainbow country.

"When you write music and lyrics, you have to think of all those things. You think of what's going to happen on screen or on stage—the action, what you can do pictorially—so that you really direct the lyric toward the pragmatic medium. If you can do that, it's working in showmanship terms, to work with your lyrics and music as a director would work, and as a book-writer would, and still have that song written in such a way that it could step out of the histrionic medium and plot—which it accelerates—and be made to flourish and blossom. In other words, if the song can be taken out of the picture and still have a life of its own, be a popular hit, then you have accomplished the real premise of songwriting. This is a pretty hard thing to do.

"Of course, when you get a man like Harold Arlen working with you, it's easier. Later on I found out that Burton Lane could function with me, too, but

---

* In discussing the Arlen melody for "Over the Rainbow" a few months ago, Harburg told an audience at the YMHA how his collaborator found the melody for the bridge of the song. Arlen had his first strain, but was searching for the central line (*"Someday I'll wish upon a star . . ."*).

"Harold," said Harburg, "you know that whistle you use when you call your dog into the house? Try that."

Arlen had been in the habit of whistling a distinctive trill without being aware of it. The notes to his whistle are embodied in the bridge of the song.

in a different way. And George Gershwin always was tremendous at this sort of thing.

"What made 'Over the Rainbow' such a success? Well, hindsight always furnishes you with a lot of material for analysis. First, we had the luck to have a good picture. Many great tunes and fine songs have been lost and have faded away in the framework of shows that didn't stand up. Harold and I have had some beautiful songs in shows that just didn't make it. And then we had a book based on a classic. *Wizard of Oz* was known to so many people. And then, of course, there was Judy Garland. She found an identity with all the young children. One of the great voices of the century, one of the great entertainers. She had an emotional quality that very, very few voices ever had. The whole world seemed to have an empathy with her, not only because of the way she sang that song but because her own life was the epitome of it. This girl who was so loved, and who had everything in the world that she'd reached out for, was the unhappiest. She could own everything that she reached for, and yet couldn't touch the thing, somehow, that her soul wanted. I think people must have felt the condition of her spirit. Her whole life, almost like a Dostoevsky novel, seemed to fit this beautiful little child's song that had color and gaiety and beauty and hope . . . and yet she was so hopeless. That must have had a lot to do with the song bringing into everybody's life almost the sadness of being a human being.

"You're talking about a big giant of a composer writing a hell of a great tune . . . and I happened to take a hitchhike on his coattails.

"Show business is a strange thing. Right after we did the score to *The Wizard of Oz*, Harold and I went through a period where we didn't get too much work. Metro called us back to work on a song for Groucho Marx which he did in *At the Circus*—it was 'Lydia, the Tattooed Lady.' Then Harold went off to write with Johnny Mercer on some other films—he felt he needed a change, and so did I—so I teamed up with Burt Lane on the score of *Hold On to Your Hats*, which Al Jolson starred in on the stage. Burt and I wrote what I've always thought was a very fine score. The show had a respectable run, but Al got itchy to leave for Florida—he missed his horse-racing—and he closed up the show. Al was that kind of a guy.

"Then I went back to Metro, this time as a producer-writer. I worked on the film version of *Meet the People*, and Harold and I wrote songs for the film of the Broadway hit *Cabin in the Sky*; we did 'Happiness Is Just a Thing Called Joe' and 'Life's Full of Consequences.'

"Whenever the studio needed a song for a musical, they'd get hold of me and I'd get hold of Burt Lane. We did one for Frank Sinatra. I think it's the first that was ever written for him to do in a picture—'Poor You.'

"I was always very involved in politics, very politically oriented. I gave it a lot of time. I gave up jobs whenever there was something to fight for that I thought was right. In 1944 I spent a lot of time writing material to help get Franklin Roosevelt re-elected. I wrote a song with Earl Robinson called 'The Free and Equal Blues.' We did that on a national radio show, four networks— all the big names of show business, and then, for ten minutes at the end, Roosevelt himself.

"Harold and I got together again, this time on the score for *Bloomer Girl*. That was also a political subject. It dealt with the rights of women and Negroes—all tied up, indivisible. It had a Civil War background, and the story had to do with runaway slaves and Mrs. Bloomer's fight for recognition of woman's equality.

"There were so many new issues coming up with Roosevelt in those years, and we were trying to deal with the inherent fear of change—to show that whenever a new idea or a new change in society arises, there'll always be a majority that will fight you, that will call you a dirty radical or a Red. Or a Christian. I love Bernard Shaw's *Androcles and the Lion*, because Shaw took such delight in showing how, when Christianity arose, the Romans considered the Christians such radicals, so dangerous, that they had to be thrown to the lions.

"Eventually, in time, they had to get around to me. I was blacklisted. I didn't mind. I think I'm a rebel by birth. I contest anything that is unjust, that causes suffering for humanity. My feeling about that is so great that I don't think I could live with myself if I weren't honest.

"I had trouble all the time at Metro, with executives. They'd call me in and say, 'Now look, we want a show here that has no messages. Messages are for Western Union. We like your stuff, but you're inclined to be too much on the barricades. Let's get down to the entertainment.' Sam Katz, Arthur Freed . . . they were always worried about me. But I always felt my power. They had to have me. If they wanted funny songs, there weren't too many around that could do them. If they wanted songs with some kind of class and quality—well, there weren't too many guys around like Larry Hart and the Gershwins. There were just a few of us, maybe five or six. I figured, hell, if they wanted me, they'd have to endure my politics.

"My wife thinks it was because I was liked—and she maintains I have a certain spell-binding charm, with men especially. Now that I look back on those days, I think she may be right. They were all frightened of my ideas, but they all liked me. All of them, even Louis Mayer. Maybe it was some sort of chemistry. I was never a wheeler-dealer, never a businessman *per se,* and they always thought I was a pretty poetic sort of guy and not a conspirator. They couldn't connect me with conspiratorial things, somehow. They always thought of me as living in a fairyland world of leprechauns and rainbows . . . therefore, I couldn't *really* throw a bomb. And I'd also always laugh at their fears. I'd joke with them, I'd kid them, I'd quote George Bernard Shaw. But in the end it wasn't so sunny—I was blacklisted.

"But then, I had the theatre. I could run back to Broadway. I went back with *Finian's Rainbow* in 1947. I'd had the idea for the story and had written it with Fred Saidy, after doing a lot of research. Not only all the Irish folk songs and the background, but I went down to Kentucky and went into the mountains, long before that became popular, to immerse myself in the folk music and the colorful speech they use.

"I really loved *Finian's Rainbow*. I was so wrapped up in it. The whole thing had come to me as two separate ideas which somehow worked together. I'd wanted to do a show about a fellow who turns black, down South; and I'd always loved the idea about a leprechaun with a pot of gold. And when Saidy and I had written it all—bang, it was there. It was right. No rewrites. Just the way I'd always wanted it to be.

"Burton Lane and I worked on that score in Hollywood. Burt had a gaiety and a bounce, and he bubbled. He was really very much akin to George Gershwin in his lighter vein. He struck a very responsive chord in me because his music gave me the chance to do the kind of light, airy, humorous-satiric things that I've always loved to do.* He has zest, life—he has verve. He has upbeat in all of his music.

"Another thing about Burt is that he's very, very concerned about getting the right thing for you, and he's very critical of himself. Burt will never fight you for a tune. He's always changing, and he's always saying, 'Is this right, or isn't it?' He always wants to try and get something better. But that's true of any good writer, isn't it? The writer who isn't a hack is always afraid of what he's written. Never gets incensed, always feels that criticism is valid. Never knowing, and never sure. It's the hack who's always sure of what he's written.

"From *Finian* came 'How Are Things in Glocca Morra?' I had a situation where there was the father who'd left Ireland for America, and brought his daughter to the South. I wanted to write a song that would indicate how she wanted to get him back to Ireland. I'd done a lot of research in Irish poetry and, for some reason, had become imbued with the sound of those two names, Glocca and Morra. Why, I don't know. Probably because they sounded romantic, mysterious, Gaelic. Also because Glocca seemed like a lucky name—in fact, in German the word is *Gluck*. Lucky tomorrow . . . that's how it seemed to me.

"I told Burt to write an Irish tune, but to make it his *own* Irish tune. I didn't want to box him in; I wanted him to roam free, not restrict him. Well, he wrote five or six tunes, but none was right. Neither of us liked them. I'd given him one line—'*There's a glen in Glocca Morra*'—and finally he came up with one we both liked. I said, 'Burt, you know the Irish always add a little bit,' so we did that too. I was influenced by old Irish writing; I added '*Killybeg, Kildare . . .* ' And then we found the notion of a lark singing somewhere off, and the girl saying, '*That's the same skylark music we have in Ireland, it must be an Irish bird, a Glocca Morra bird.*' And out of *that* came the idea that she would ask the bird, 'How are things in Glocca Morra?' Out of the title came the cue, the sound of the bird singing, and then the verse of the song. It's what I've always tried to do, to get away from the direct approach and find another way of getting into the material, one that would be stage writing, where the song was actually a scene. That kind of songwriting is really dramaturgy.

"Burt did a great job on that show. He used the archaic spiritual things, and instead of saying, 'On that great day,' which was a typical spiritual phrase, I just twisted it into a political comment by making it 'Great *come-and-get-it* day.' Then there was another song which had more of a Negro feeling to it, 'That Old Devil Moon.' We had written another ballad before this called 'We Only Pass This Way One Time.' Harold Arlen came over to my house one night and heard what Burt and I had written, all of it, and said he thought that was the only weak song in the show. So I had Burt play him a tune he'd been fooling around with—it was to be 'Old Devil Moon,' though it had another lyric; we'd written it for a movie, but never used it. Harold said, 'How can you equate these two? The one is champion stuff, and the other is lightweight!' That decided me; I tossed out the first song and the lyric to the other, and started looking for an idea, something that had to do with witchcraft, something eerie, with overtones of voodoo. Eventually it became 'Old Devil Moon.' Strangely con-

* "Who else but Harburg," demanded a critic, "would have dared write a lyric about a sexy leprechaun?" ("When I'm Not Near The Girl I Love, I Love the Girl I'm Near")

structed. It doesn't have a verse, and it isn't the ordinary thirty-two-bar song at all, but it became very popular. That's what made it a great song—it was original.

"I think I've been very lucky to work with men who were really original craftsmen. Men like Arlen, who are not satisfied with merely turning out tunes. Always trying. Burton Lane is certainly the same, as far as that is concerned. Vernon Duke was also dissatisfied with the ordinary. Sammy Fain* was, I would say, more on the common denominator, but he had a great sense of lovely melody which also seems to be part of me, too. I like a completely outgoing melodic phrase such as Kern wrote, although it was harder for me to write to the Kern sweetness and light.† But there's some specific hangover in me that makes me love that kind of melody. . . . And the thing is that what I like to do is to test myself in almost every direction. I don't like to stay in one spot. I like to try a new tangent, to explore. That's why I'll never be a great golfer, because I've got to keep changing my game. I could be a hell of a golfer, but I can't stick to one thing! I say, 'No, there must be something else!' It's a kind of necessity for variety.

"I've always attacked everything with the same amateurish fear that I had at the beginning—of not knowing where it's going to come from . . . will it come? I know that if I sit down the pen will flow somewhere and the words will come, but I've always had great concern and trepidation that I don't know if I'm going to do this, I don't know where it's going to come from. Maybe it's some form of perfectionism—you're afraid you won't get the very top of yourself.

"Gershwin didn't have that problem. Gershwin just sat down and was sure of himself. George was an originator. George's music almost needed no lyrics; he understood the theatre so well that he could make a humorous scene laughable and funny and titillating with just his music alone. Right off the bat. He had that real genius and affinity for the stage. You hear his songs, they can't be anyone else's. You listen to another songwriter, the melody might be anyone's. But I know a Gershwin tune, I know a Cole Porter tune, I know a Jerome Kern tune, I know a Harold Arlen tune. They're not imitators. They have their own hallmark, they're uniquely their own.

"Writing with different composers is always a different psychological experience. Each one has his own approach to creation. To know their idiosyncrasies and to be able to get the best out of each one is fascinating. Each composer brings out a different aspect in your work. Duke, with his very sophisticated music for that time, the late '30s and '40s, demanded a certain kind of lyric. Vernon's particular personality also required that you talk to him in a certain way, that your criticism and objections be registered in a diplomatic way that would neither reject nor demolish him.

"Lots of times the composer will give you a whole tune, and if he's sensitive to your lyrical quality—for example, Harold Arlen is very sensitive to what will fit his melody—and you give him a title or a first line, and if he doesn't agree, he'll tell you. But it's the way he tells you, and how you respond . . . and what

---

* Harburg collaborated with Sammy Fain on the score for *Flahooley*, a Broadway musical, in 1951.

† Harburg wrote with Jerome Kern in 1945, when the assignment was the score for *Can't Help Singing*, a musical film which starred Deanna Durbin. "More and More," "Can't Help Singing," and "Californi-ay" were among the songs they provided for her.

your coefficient of acceptability is toward criticism. That is what your relationships with all these men depend on.

"It's diplomacy, it's psychology, it's a lot of psychiatry—it's knowing the person you're dealing with, and the sensitivities of the two of you. Some writers can't collaborate—they are at each other's throats all the time, hostile to one another because of that constant rejection that has to go on in your day-to-day work. Writing and creating is nothing more than a series of those rejections, or, rather, criticisms. And the man who knows that, the *good* writer, always feels that criticism is valid.

"As far as lyric-writing is concerned, I've always found that my fellow workers agree it's terribly hard. Nerve-racking, brain-racking. Oh, it's easy if you want to rush out crummy verse, such as the stuff they're writing today. I could do ten of those a day—one an hour. But I couldn't do something for a show or a film in less than two weeks. When you're rhyming, and looking for imagery, those lines don't come easy. They take a lot of digging. Harold will write a tune, and it may go all over the place musically, and then you've got to fit that tune.* Very touchy work. As I said before, I doubt if I'll ever be able to say 'I love you' head-on. It's my curved thinking, I guess.

"Nowadays a kid gets a guitar, he goes out and he knows he can make it. Three chords and one sentence repeated over and over again, and there you are. What's terrible is that the broadcasters put out nothing but that stuff. No more Rodgers, no more Gershwin, no more Arlen or Kern. I try to listen, and I think most of what I hear is written very naïvely and crudely, without real form, real taste. Of course, here and there you see glimmers of some kind of really good talent, but it's usually lost in the noise and the raucousness. I can't distinguish one song from another.

"The really good fellows don't have much of a chance these days. The businessmen get hold of record companies, they hire a bunch of kids to form bands, they get the records out of them, and they blanket the radio with sheer volume. Music today is money, that's all. It's rhythm, it's hypnosis, it's a good deal of hysteria and a lot of complaint. The words spell out the terror of the age in which the young are growing up. If you want to look at it as a social phenomenon, fine. It is. It belongs to today, but it won't belong to tomorrow. Good music and good lyrics should belong to all time.

"I think my generation grew up with an entirely different attitude. The world had its problems then, and just as many drab and terrible things, too—but there was a certain hope. A dream. A goal. Measurements of grace that we all looked up to and had ambitions someday to reach. Everybody, every immigrant family that came to this country, was aware of education, aware of getting somewhere, moving forward. I was aware. I knew what my father was going through in his sweatshop down there on the Lower East Side. I always had the hope that someday he would be liberated from that. That was part of my whole chemistry, my nervous system. To get somewhere, to move forward . . . Whereas today the emphasis seems to be all on escape: 'It's a rotten world, get away from it, the hell with it!'

"We've reached an era of abundance, I guess. Ours was an era of scarcity,

---

* Arlen and Harburg collaborated again on the score for the show *Jamaica*, which starred Lena Horne in 1957. Their latest song, written on the occasion of Dr. Martin Luther King's tragic death, is called "Silent Spring."

and we had our eyes set on satisfying some of our hungers. But when you reach an era like this one, with abundance everywhere—and when that abundance isn't distributed properly, so that only a few grab it and so many are left in poverty and in slums—then the immorality of the situation shows.

"But I've always been aware of the idiocy of the whole establishment and the system. That's what titillated me into using satire. I've always thought that the way to educate, to teach, the way to live without being miserable, even though you're surrounded by misery, was to laugh at the things that made you miserable. For me, satire has become a weapon . . . the way Swift used it in his prose, Gilbert in his verses, Shaw in his drama. I am stirred, and my juices start flowing more when I can tackle a problem that has profundity, depth, and real danger . . . by destroying it with laughter."

'Everything's Coming Up Roses'

(Stephen Sondheim)

STEPHEN SONDHEIM arrived on the Broadway scene as the lyricist for Leonard Bernstein's score for *West Side Story*, in 1957, when he was a mere twenty-six. In the years since then, the ranks of Broadway's working composers and lyricists have thinned down with the regularity of the passing of Foreign Legionnaires in the last reel of *Beau Geste*. But Sondheim can well say (to quote one of the songs from his score for *Follies*), *"I'm still here."*

Sondheim fields all the accolades that come his way with an offhand candor that is refreshing in a business so dominated by ego hang-ups. If you sit with him in his New York home, surrounded by his vast collection of antique puzzle games, amusement-parlor novelties, and an authentic nickel-grabbing Las Vegas slot machine, he is quick to point out that he has always had considerable assistance from others.

"There were three major influences on me, lyric-wise," he says. "The first being Oscar Hammerstein, who really taught me everything. He was articulate, tough, and, I think, almost never wrong—quite a different man than the public imagined. He was a totally urbane man, yet he *believed* 'Oh, What a Beautiful Morning!'

"The point is that in Oscar's work the thought is always what counts. Which is why rhyming is not up his alley. I mean, he rhymed perfectly marvelous rhymes, he was impeccable, and every now and then he'd even do trick rhymes. But, you know, trick rhyming is parlor games. You can take any group of your intelligent or even vaguely literate friends, or even your unintelligent and illiterate friends, and ask them to rhyme 'mouth'—they can all do it, it doesn't take anything.

"The main thing Oscar taught me was that clarity of thought was what counted. It's *what* you say first, and *how* you say it second. When I started out writing love songs I would write about stars and trees and dreams and moonlight, the usual songwriter's vocabulary. That's fine if you believe it, but I didn't. Oscar said, 'Say what *you* feel, not what other songwriters feel.'

"Oscar also stressed the opening of a show: 'The first lyric the audience hears, the first song, is what really makes or breaks a show. If you start with the right opening, you can ride for forty-five minutes on the telephone book. On the other hand, if you start off with a wrong one, it's an uphill fight all the way.' "

Sondheim's course of training with Oscar Hammerstein included not only writing and submitting his work to that talented gentleman for criticism, but also an invaluable course of study as a general office boy and handyman around the Rodgers-and-Hammerstein productions of *Allegro* ("I was seventeen at the time, and he said I could now learn what the real *geshrei** of the theatre— what people really went through—was all about"), *South Pacific,* and *The King and I.*

The second major influence on Sondheim's emerging talents was Burt Shevelove, who, with Larry Gelbart, wrote the book of *Forum.* "I didn't even know there was another way to write songs until I met Burt, who said, 'But not all songs have a beginning, a middle, and an end, and develop like little one-act plays,' which is the way Oscar wrote, and the way he taught. Burt then said, 'Haven't you ever heard a song by somebody named Cole Porter?' I was about twenty, and it had never occurred to me, even though I knew every Cole Porter song in the book, to see what Porter could do with other forms of lyrics . . . say, his 'list' songs, like 'Let's Do It' or 'You're the Top.'

"I got to be good friends with Burt; we've talked ever since, endlessly, and one of the things he taught me was that the best art always seems effortless—maybe not true of something like Picasso's *Guernica,* but true of lyric-writing, I think. Burt advised me, 'Never sacrifice smoothness for cleverness. Better dull than clumsy.' I agree. An awful lot of lyrics suffer from the lyric-writer having a really clever, sharp idea which he can't fit into the music, so it sits there clumsily and the actor is stuck with singing it. The net result is that it doesn't land with the audience. It has to be smooth if you are going to make the point.

"I happen to love style, and even when I read I'm more taken by style than I am by content. At least, I tell myself I am. But people point out to me that I'm more interested in content than I pretend to be, so it's arguable. I work essentially from tone. I appreciate tone first, always, in any kind of writing, be it songwriting or other."

The third of the Sondheim influences is librettist and playwright Arthur Laurents, with whom Sondheim has worked on four Broadway shows—*West*

* Loosely translated as "yelling."

Side Story, the Ethel Merman hit show *Gypsy, Anyone Can Whistle*, and *Do I Hear a Waltz?*, on which Sondheim collaborated with Richard Rodgers.

"Arthur taught me mostly about playwriting—the major thing was sub-text. That's a big Actors' Studio word. It refers to what's going on underneath a scene. A shallow scene is what exists only in the words, whereas if there's a tension or a counterpoint underneath, it gives the actor something to play. Look, we're sitting here and having this nice conversation, you're asking me questions and I'm answering them, and it's not very interesting to watch. But supposing you came here and what you really have in your mind is to kill me. Even though it never comes out in your words, now, as a scene, it gives the actor something to *play*, instead of just sitting there. Very important lesson for me.

'For instance, in *Gypsy* we—Jule Styne and I—had a song for Ethel Merman called 'Some People.' Rose is singing a song about how she's got to get out of this place, but in fact what she's trying to do is to con her father out of $88. It's not only a statement about how small-town life is stifling her and she wants to get to the city and the bright lights and the glamour and success—it's really that she's determined to get that plaque on her father's wall that represents the money to do it with—which, in fact, she steals! But that gives Merman something to play, and it's more interesting, much more than having her come out and address herself to the audience and just sing it flat out. Now she's playing something . . . sub-textual.

"I can give you an example of that from *Follies*. Dorothy Collins has what seems to be a ballad called 'In Buddy's Eyes.' She sings it to the guy who jilted her thirty years ago, and she's angry at him still for having loused up her life. So she's singing this sweet-ass song about how her husband makes her so happy, and just having him there at home is all that counts, and he's a wonderful guy. But what she's doing is trying to get the other man's goat. So Dorothy sings the whole song with a sub-text of anger. She could kill him, but it's a very sweet, pretty ballad; and she's lying through her teeth. She's doing it to get a knife into his groin, and the fact that it doesn't work is even more frustrating. But the point is, it's a *scene*, rather than a pretty ballad. That's the kind of thing that Arthur taught me. It's the kind of thing that Oscar did use occasionally, but that wasn't essentially what he was about as a dramatic songwriter.

"Arthur is the collaborator with whom I've worked the closest. He's taught me a great deal about matching diction with ideas, and about continuity of content. He also is terrific on titles, as any good bookwriter-collaborator had better be if he works with me, because I steal from them all the time. 'Some People,' the one I told you about, is one of Arthur's; so is 'I Feel Pretty,' from *West Side Story*, and 'Something's Coming,' from the same show.

"I can give you another example of what he taught me in *West Side Story*. You remember when Maria sings 'I Have a Love.' Anita is singing 'A Boy Like That' at the same time; the tension is that she doesn't know her lover has just killed her brother. We do; she doesn't. That makes the song have something. All Maria is trying to do is to get Anita not to tell. She sings, '*I have a wonderful love*'—she could sing that straight out, but it wouldn't be a very interesting idea. But it *is* interesting when she's using it to calm down a girl who's about to spill the beans and screw up her life. And that song functions; at the end of it, Anita is on Maria's side—and, remember, at the beginning she was against her. So there's something for Anita to play, too."

The question inevitably comes to mind: What with writing his songs for such sub-textual scenes, songs which have to be so tightly molded to fit his characters, with lyrical ideas that must fit his own firm standards of style and content and yet succeed with the audience, does it bother Sondheim that so few of the songs in his shows have become popular hits?

"No!" he says firmly. "You don't get hits out of the theatre any more except on very rare occasions. Everything in the past ten years or so has been rock, anyway, with exceptions like *Hello, Dolly!* Very rare exception. But the business of writing songs to become hits has never bothered me because I really don't know what makes a hit, do you?

"And I have to tell you," adds Sondheim, "that it's a great relief not to worry about it any more. When Jule Styne and I wrote *Gypsy,* Jule was appalled when in 'Small World' I wrote a line that said, '*Funny, I'm a woman with children.*' He said, 'Well, that means no man can sing the song.' I said, 'Jule, if I make the song general, then it's got no texture for the show at all. We've *got* a general song. 'You'll Never Get Away from Me,' that's general. 'Everything's Coming Up Roses,' general. But here's this lady, she's trying to con the guy into handling her vaudeville act—it's a con song. It's got to be terribly personalized.' Well, I changed the lyric for the printed music, the sheet music, so that a man could sing the song. But nowadays nobody has to worry about that sort of thing.

"I used to worry, and tell myself, 'I should be thinking about making this into a hit.' I had a chance, I suppose, to make a hit song out of *Forum,* because 'Lovely' is a very pretty, easily hummable tune, and those were the days, back in 1962, when you were still occasionally listening to easily hummable tunes. But it's a comic show, and I can't have a straight song in a comic show, so I had to write '*I'm lovely, all I am is lovely, lovely is the one thing I can do.*' Well, Eydie Gorme is just not going to sing a song that says '*Lovely is the one thing I can do,*' is she? So I screwed myself out of a possible hit." He shrugs.

"But so what? When you come down to that choice, I'll make it every single time. You make an awful lot more money out of a show that *runs* than out of a possible hit single song. Perhaps not if you have a *Hello, Dolly . . .* but essentially, if you really want to equate it financially, better the show should be a hit.

"As a matter of fact," he says, "the only two show albums that have sold at all in the past five years have been *Hair* and *No, No, Nanette.* So you must regard them as freaks. Albums don't sell any more—the hit songs today are created by pop groups, for groups. When this era passes, then maybe everybody, including me, will have to give some thought again to the business of getting hits out of shows." He hesitates. "If there's still a musical theatre running."

Sondheim readily acknowledges how fortunate he was to have arrived on the Broadway scene when he did. "Nowadays the terrible thing is that the young people don't get a chance to be heard. And therefore they get discouraged, and they say 'Screw it,' and they start writing stuff for movies, or they try to start a rock group. It's awful. A terrible shame—nobody gets a chance to learn what he's doing.

"On the other hand, my era, that of the middle '50s, was just as tough. Even after I'd done the lyrics for *West Side Story* with Lenny Bernstein and I was supposed to do the music for *Gypsy,* Ethel Merman wouldn't allow it because I hadn't done any music for the theatre before. She didn't want to take a chance because she had just done a show with new composers and had gotten burned. Thank God for Hal Prince—he's the only producer around who's consistently taken chances with unknown composers and lyricists."

To have achieved the difficult status of being his own composer—that lonely plateau on which only Irving Berlin, Cole Porter, Harold Rome, Sir Noel Coward, and Frank Loesser have successfully functioned in the past—was far from easy for the relatively young Sondheim. Even though in the past he has written with Leonard Bernstein, Jule Styne, and Richard Rodgers, he has no intention of returning to the collaborative art. "Each time I did, it was for a very specific reason," he says. "The first time, on *West Side Story*, it was because I needed a job. I met Lenny and he liked my work, but I definitely did *not* want to write just words. I had been trained mainly as a composer, in school. But I spoke to Oscar Hammerstein about it and he said, 'Do it. The experience will be wonderful.' "

So were the results of that Bernstein-Sondheim-Laurents collaboration. "Lenny is astonishing," says Sondheim. "For me, the basic principal of art is economy—make the most out of the least. And Lenny is economy, all economy. He works things out. Things relate. We'd meet and talk about each song for the show—weeks of talk." He grins. "By now you must realize how much I enjoy talking. . . . Then we'd separate to work, and meet later to see how our ideas coincided. Some of the songs were set to tunes he'd already written; others, such as 'A Boy Like That,' I'd write and bring to him, and he'd immediately set them to music. And if you look at those words on paper, and then remember the tune Lenny wrote for them . . . it's astonishing, his invention, his facility!"

One of the songs he wrote that he is least fond of (and most fond of citing as that) is "I Feel Pretty." "To this day," Sondheim told another interviewer, "it embarrasses me. I mean, Maria would simply not say, 'It's alarming how charming I feel!' " On another occasion Sondheim told an audience at the YMHA, "On one level, I suppose, lyric-writing is an elegant form of puzzle, and I am a great puzzle fan. There's a great deal of joy for me in the sweat involved in the working out of lyrics, but it can lead to bloodlessness, and I've often been capable of writing bloodless lyrics. There are a number of them in *West Side Story*."

When it came to the production of *Gypsy*, which was to star Miss Merman, Sondheim was again frustrated. "After Ethel put the kibosh on my doing it, I decided to bow out as a lyricist. Arthur Laurents insisted that I stay. So again I went to talk to Oscar, and I said, 'If I do this, I'm going to be trapped as a lyricist,' and Oscar said, 'It's only six months out of your life.' And, you know, he was right. *Gypsy* was written in three months, from beginning to rehearsal. We sat down on an October day, Jule Styne and I, and we were in rehearsal at the beginning of February!"

On both shows Jerome Robbins was the director and choreographer. "Genius," says Sondheim, "is not a word I toss around a lot, but for me it means an endless fountain of ideas, and that describes Jerry. He never stops having ideas, ever. About everything."*

---

* The brilliance of Robbins as an overall man of the theatre was to be demonstrated during the out-of-town tryout of Sondheim's next show, his first as both composer and lyricist, *A Funny Thing Happened on the Way to the Forum*. "We opened out of town, and it was a disaster, the critics hated it," Sondheim says today. "Usually, when you have a show that's in such trouble, you can sense what's wrong and why it's not working when you stand in the back of the theatre. In this case, we were totally baffled. Finally, we got to Washington, and we called in Jerome Robbins, whose first comment was, 'Everything's fine, but *please* change the opening number. You've got to tell the audience what the evening is about.' Well, of course the trouble was up front. The opening song was a

The musical score which Sondheim wrote with Jule Styne for *Gypsy* is strong, astringent, and completely successful in the context of the show—the story of how Rose promotes her daughter into stardom as a burlesque stripper in the late '30s. It is generally considered to be Jule Styne's very best work for the theatre. (Styne unhesitatingly agrees.)

"Julie's melodic fertility is extraordinary," says Sondheim. "Julie throws it away. He's profligate with it—he's too impatient. If Lenny Bernstein makes the most out of the least, then the opposite is true of Jule. He's the least economical composer I know. He plays you something and you say, 'That's not quite right —perhaps if you did something after that opening strain . . . ' Jule says, 'I'll write something else.' And he writes a whole new piece. It's certainly not laziness. I guess he's so talented that if he writes enough melodies, he assumes one of them will be good." Sondheim shrugs. "That's very tough for me to adjust to," he says, "because of my insistence on economy."

When *Gypsy* had its first run-through on the bare Winter Garden stage, sans scenery, costumes, or props, a full house of professional New York theatre people stood up and cheered. Those who were fortunate enough to have been invited to that performance will never forget the electricity generated by Laurents' book, the score, and Miss Merman's performance, all masterfully directed by Robbins.

"Probably the most exciting afternoon of my life," Sondheim says, thirteen years later. "Funny thing about *Gypsy*. It was a hit—ran for two years, but no longer. I think it was because the show was essentially unpleasant. Tells you something about people and how they behave that you don't want to hear. Same thing is true of *Company* and *Follies*—they tell you things you don't want to hear. And when you run down the list of hits, *smash* hits, in musical theatre over the last twenty years, every single one of them has one thing in common: they tell you a story you *want* to hear.*

"Of course, the major revolution that's taken place in the last decade isn't in music, it's in lyrics. And the fact that lyrics of the last five years have, quote, something to say, unquote. That's the big revolution of rock—*Superstar*, *Godspell*, and *Hair*. They're forcing the public to *listen*. I had a fascinating experience with this revival of *Forum*—the songs got laughs this time, and they never got laughs in 1962. That's because the audience is *listening* to the lyrics, which they never did a decade ago. You see, if *Forum* has a flaw, it's a huge one, and that is that the score I wrote and the libretto that Burt Shevelove and Larry Gelbart wrote don't go together. The libretto is truly low comedy—literate and polished, but very low comedy. Very traditional. Plautus invented it two thousand years ago, and if he were alive today, he'd be making a fortune still. But my score for the show was essentially intellectual—it doesn't mesh with that low vaudeville comedy."

perfectly charming song that preceded a not-charming evening of low comedy. That's what led to 'Comedy Tonight.' I can remember the last matinee in Washington when we played to fifty people—that's how disastrous the show was. We put in the new opening at the first New York preview, and it was cheers and laughter the entire evening at the exact same lines that audiences had received in complete silence throughout the show four days earlier in Washington! That's, again, the difference an opening can make. Of course," he adds, "it's also an advantage to have one that's staged by Jerry Robbins!"

* If one considers *The Sound of Music*, *Hello, Dolly!* and *Fiddler on the Roof*, Mr. Sondheim's point is irrefutable.

Since *Gypsy*, Sondheim has worked on only one show solely as lyricist—he collaborated with Richard Rodgers on the score for *Do I Hear a Waltz?* "Right after Oscar died, Dick asked me if I would be his partner, and I said, 'I really want to do my own music. I'm very flattered. Thank you. If a project should come up that excited both of us, I'd be honored to work with you.' Which I meant." (To another interviewer Sondheim added, "I knew I could learn from Rodgers, and *anything* you can learn to make songwriting a little less tortuous is invaluable.")

Future projects? It's certain that Sondheim intends to remain with the musical theatre, to write and compose for it as long as there's anybody left who'll buy a pair of seats for his shows. He may not be quite as sentimental about the theatre as was his late mentor, Oscar Hammerstein. ("What Oscar liked to do," he says, "was to stand in the back and glow with the audience's applause. He loved the theatre. He always talked about quitting it and writing poetry, but in fact he was so much in love with the theatre that he couldn't.") But Sondheim is quite clear about his own need to write for a live audience in this highly mechanized and electronic age. "Somebody told me once that the essential difference between theatre and movies is that theatre always acknowledges the existence of the audience. That's a simple but very profound statement, you know. A movie doesn't know you're alive; theatre does."

There have been wide differences of opinion about Sondheim's two later efforts, *Company*, which is based on George Furth's book, and *Follies*, which has a libretto by James Goldman. Sondheim's detractors accuse him of writing coldly, sans emotion. He has also been widely criticized for having perpetrated an anti-marriage tract in *Company*. ("And that I do not understand," he told an interviewer, "because it's the most *pro*-marriage show in the world. It says, very clearly, that to be emotionally committed to somebody is very difficult, but to be alone is impossible. To commit is to live—and *not* to commit is to be dead. Every marriage on that stage has its problems, but every one is a good marriage.")

Follies, too, has attracted acid criticisms. There are those who consider that it breaks exciting new ground in the musical comedy; others were unmoved by the story of the reunion of beautiful showgirls on the stage of a theatre where they triumphed years ago. With Sondheim's latest efforts, there seems to be no middle ground; you pay your money and you take your choice of either hating what's been done or finding it stimulating. The important fact, however, is that you pay your money. Sondheim's newest, *A Little Night Music*, is a hit; not only with the critics and with those of his peers who awarded it the Tony for Best Musical of 1972–3, but also (and most importantly) with audiences.

. . . Mr. Hammerstein would be pleased as well.

'Guys and Dolls'

(Frank Loesser)

HE ALWAYS COULD write songs," says his good friend and coworker, genial Abe Burrows. "They burst out of him! How, or why, or where? I don't know how you can ask that. What makes any artist, even a Van Gogh or whoever? When he first was writing lyrics with Hoagy Carmichael, like 'Two Sleepy People' or 'Small Fry,' he had some fascinating things. And all the way along from there, the stuff was pouring out of him. It was always there. He read a lot, he asked questions a lot, he knew a lot. He was fascinated with words, the way I am. He lived with dictionaries. *Not* rhyming dictionaries. A terribly literate guy. Loved words—and loved to toy with them. And he used to work very hard. Always."

Burrows stares out of the window of his New York apartment. "I think," he says finally, "I've been a very lucky guy. Had the good luck to work with the two best lyric-writers of all time. Frank and Cole Porter. So I'm spoiled.

"Frank was always an intricate guy. Before he ever did a Broadway show, we were friends, and he used to help me. When I wrote a lot of my parodies, I didn't care where it was, I'd play 'em any time. Out in Hollywood, lots of times we were at a party and I'd be loaded. One night I ad-libbed 'The Girl with the Three Blue Eyes,' completely as it is. First time Frank and I met, I was doing it and another song of mine, 'I Am Strolling Down Memory Lane Without a Single Thing to Remember.' There I was, ribbing his whole profession. Next morning I had completely forgotten what I'd sung. I see Frank a couple of days later—he hands me a piece of paper with all my lyrics written down for me. That's how he'd responded. That's the kind of a guy he was."

It was on the night of January 22, 1936, that there opened on Broadway a revue called *The Illustrators' Show*. Its subsequent run was brief; in a matter of days the show folded and its scenery was carried off to Cain's Warehouse, the Potter's Field of flop shows. The world of show business would little note nor long remember that flop, but it must be considered a historic event. In its score was a song called "A Waltz Was Born in Vienna," written by Frederick Loewe (who was later to write *My Fair Lady* with Alan Jay Lerner), and also, the first professionally performed lyric by Frank Loesser. In collaboration with Irving Actman, young Loesser, aged twenty-six, contributed to the proceedings the words to a number called "Bang—the Bell Rang!"

Such is the humble beginning of Loesser's remarkable career as a professional songwriter, one that ended, shockingly too soon, when he succumbed to lung cancer in 1969.

Measured quantitatively against the large output of some of his more prolific contemporaries, the volume of what he left behind is, alas, small. But apply the yardsticks of quality, of execution, of brilliance of idea, and it's an entirely different horse race. In that sweepstakes Loesser moves ahead of the field and stays there. In the argot of the Broadway types he so deftly portrayed in *Guys and Dolls*, Loesser has class, he has style, he has that extra-special something that is blue-ribbon all the way.

In all his prolific years of writing lyrics for Hollywood films from 1937 on, Loesser always had a clear idea of where he was headed. "From that first day he was signed up at Paramount, Frank was going," says Burton Lane, who did many songs with Loesser there. "He kept on saying to me, 'Why should Irving Berlin be the only guy who owns his own publishing house—and writes all his own songs?' "

After his World War II hitch in the Army, during which he wrote both words and music for "The Ballad of Rodger Young" and "Praise the Lord and Pass the Ammunition," Loesser came back to New York in 1948 to work on *Where's Charley?* for Ray Bolger. "You know," says Jule Styne with deep affection for an old friend and collaborator, "here's a fellow with hardly any musical education, and he took it on and wrote some marvelous songs. But he had a *right* to write his own music. Certain fellows, who shall be nameless, haven't. But Loesser had; he could write his own music. He told me, 'Listen, after I write with you and Arthur Schwartz and Hoagy Carmichael, and this one and that one, by God, I have got to learn something, if I'm smart. You boys showed me how it goes.' "

And it went. After *Where's Charley?* there followed *Guys and Dolls* in 1950; *The Most Happy Fella*, for which he wrote his own libretto, adapted from Sidney Howard's play *They Knew What They Wanted*, in 1956; and *Greenwillow* in 1960. His last hit show was the brilliant *How to Succeed in Business Without Really Trying*. All of them have musical scores which must be considered permanent eighteen-karat jewels in the American treasury.

And Loesser also achieved the second goal he had mentioned to Burton Lane back in the early Paramount days. He set up his own publishing house, Frank Music, not only to publish his own works but also to nurture and develop the talents of others. His discovery of the tyro talents Richard Adler and the late Jerry Ross led to his sending them over to George Abbott. When the two young men wrote *The Pajama Game* and *Damn Yankees*, their work was published by Frank Music. Loesser, with his business acumen, might well fit Alexander Woollcott's description of his friend Harpo Marx: "A genius . . . with a fine sense of double-entry bookkeeping."

Even though he was the son of a classical music teacher, and the younger brother of Arthur Loesser, a highly accomplished pianist and major music critic, he never formally studied music. "I didn't have the patience to concentrate," he was to say later. He had attended Townsend Harris High School in Manhattan (an early incubator for high-IQ'd youth), but he dropped out of City College in his teens—"I wasn't in the mood to learn."

There followed a series of dead-end pursuits, assorted jobs which led nowhere. At eighteen he served a brief stint as city editor for a New Rochelle, N.Y., newspaper. According to his brother Arthur, he first displayed his talent as a lyricist one night when he was assigned to cover a Lions Club dinner. "He obliged an officer by supplying couplets celebrating the exploits of all the club members. Such lines as '*Secretary Albert Vincent, Read the minutes—right this instant*,' got him started on his eventual career with words."

On his days off, Loesser wrote acts for various performers on the Keith vaudeville circuit. "Somehow you had to find a way of getting a job," he was to remark years later. "The Depression was here, and I even got one job checking the food and service in a string of restaurants. I was paid seventy-five cents each to eat eight or ten meals a day. At least I was eating, which a lot of people weren't. You had to keep alert all the time. I suppose that's where this tremendous energy of mine originated."

Loesser's first published song was written in 1931, in collaboration with William Schuman, who is now president emeritus of Juilliard and of Lincoln Center. It was called "In Love With a Memory of You." "I gave Frank his first flop," says Schuman, "and, really, the only song flop he ever had. You can't be condescending about musical genius. He was one of the greatest songwriters the United States ever produced."

It's almost impossible to find somebody who'll take the negative side of that debate—if it can be considered one. Even such a stern critic as Stephen Sondheim is on record as saying, several years back, "Any man who has the nerve to set the line '*Some irresponsible dress manufacturer*' the way Frank did in *How to Succeed* deserves a medal."

Loesser and Actman were brought to Hollywood in 1936, but their stay at Universal Studios was brief. Soon the young lyricist was again job-hunting. But now he was unemployed in Hollywood; in that town, such status is akin to that of an Untouchable in far-off India.

"I had been in Hollywood about a year, and had an option coming up on my contract," says Burton Lane. "My agent brought two young writers around. One wrote music; the other was Frank Loesser, who did lyrics. I looked at his things; they were just great. Superb. I went to the front office at Paramount and told them I'd flipped. I called Frank, told him to go right down and they'd listen to him. A guy named Lew Gensler was head of the music department then, a former songwriter himself. *He* flipped over the stuff, too. While they were making their corporate mind up whether to sign him on, I had a call from Frank. He wanted to know what I was doing. Could I come over, he wanted to show me some of his work that I hadn't heard. He lived on Sunset Boulevard. I had to walk about two hundred steps down from the street to get to his little apartment.

"I'd been there about five or ten minutes when Lynn, his first wife, asked me if I'd like to have dinner with them. I said no, I'd already eaten. She opened a can of beans—one can for the *both* of them—and an apple, which she sliced for their dessert. They were absolutely broke.

"Anyway, Paramount came through with the contract. A ten-week deal for starters. So I told Frank he could use my office any time. I came in the day after he'd signed, and I'll never forget this—there was one guy measuring him for shirts and shorts, another guy measuring him for suits—the works! The day after he'd signed that contract, everything was going to be made to order!"

Loesser and Lane shortly thereafter turned out their first hit song; it was one which Bob Hope and Shirley Ross were to perform in a Paramount B-picture musical comedy, and it was called "The Lady's in Love with You."

"From then on, we were assigned to everything," says Lane. He himself was not to return to Paramount until three decades later, as the composer of the Broadway hit show *On a Clear Day You Can See Forever*. But today he winces at the recollection. "I did one picture with Frank—it is the most embarrassing thing, it's shown on TV all the time. I wish they'd burn the goddam negative! *Spawn of the North*, with George Raft—we wrote everything in it. I don't remember the titles—I must be subconsciously blocking them out. Oh yes, one of them was 'I Like Hump-Backed Salmon.' I didn't even know what a hump-backed salmon *was!* Maybe Frank made it up.

"He was a very difficult guy even then. Very secretive. He'd sit across the room from me, and I'd say, 'Well, what are you thinking about?' He wouldn't tell me. He'd keep it to himself. And then I'd see him smile. I'd say, 'All right, Frank, what is it? Don't keep it to yourself; let *me* know the goodies, too!' And suddenly he'd jump up, and he had it all written out, a complete lyric. I'd put it on my piano, and he'd want me to sing it right away. Hell, I hadn't even seen the lyric yet! And if I'd stumble, he'd yell. 'God damn it, can't you *read?*' Here I was, trying to think of what I'm doing, and reading his handwriting, which was terrible, and I've never seen the lyric before, and he's yelling at me!

"An amazing guy," muses Lane. "Another time one of the B-picture producers picked one of Frank's lyrics and called me in and asked me to set it to a tune. 'We like this lyric, but we gotta have it set by this afternoon.' That's how they worked—always pressure. I said, 'Okay, if you need it that badly, it can't be so important. I'll just knock something out for it.' Went back to my office, and I guess it took me five minutes to write that melody. The title of what Frank had written was 'Says My Heart.' *'Fall in love, fall in love, says my heart.'* Lovely lyric, bright idea. Five minutes was all it took—big hit! Oh, he was a fantastic talent."

Loesser was already demonstrating his remarkable versatility with the *éclat* of a seasoned pro who'd been at it for years. When Dorothy Lamour crooned "The Moon of Manakoora" in *The Hurricane*, it was a Loesser lyric; Bob Hope and Shirley Ross introduced "Two Sleepy People"; and Bing Crosby made a hit out of his "Small Fry." These last two hits were done with Hoagy Carmichael.

Working with Frederick Hollander, a diminutive German who had written songs for Marlene Dietrich in their homeland and had followed the lady to Hollywood, Loesser turned out a score for *Destry Rides Again,* including the durable "See What the Boys in the Back Room Will Have."

At the behest of composer Jule Styne, who had signed on as a fieldhand at Republic Pictures, a deal was arranged whereby Paramount loaned Loesser to Republic for a low-budget Judy Canova musical. Cy Feuer—who with Ernie Martin was to be responsible, ten years later, for bringing Loesser to New York to write *Where's Charley?*—was at that time the head of the music department at the tiny Republic studio.

"Oh, when Frank heard about being loaned out to Republic, he blew up. He had a powerful temper, anyway. He's the only guy I ever saw who would make his point by jumping with both feet off the ground! While yelling," grins Feuer.

"He came to me and he said, 'How can you *do* this to me? Here I am, just working my way up, I'm getting to work with some really good composers—and you pull me back into this thing!' And I had to *schmeichel* [sweet-talk] him and talk him into doing it. He had to do the job—it was part of his contract—but he didn't like the idea one bit. Finally he came over, and he went to work with Jule, and they gave us a hell of a good score for *Sis Hopkins.** Their songs were fine, the lyrics bright and clever. Something very special for a place like Republic, believe me. By the time it was done, Frank was very pleased with the job; he went back to Paramount and arranged to borrow Jule—from Republic! There they did a picture called *Sweater Girl.* They had two songs that were hits right out of the box. One of them was 'The Liberty Magazine Song'—'I Said Yes, She Said No'—a big novelty. And the second was a big ballad called 'I Don't Want to Walk Without You, Baby!'

"That's where Frank demonstrated his marvelous instinct for picking out tunes," says Feuer, a cheerful, energetic man whose latest success is the musical film *Cabaret.* "When Jule played Frank that tune, it had another lyric, but Frank insisted that they buy out the other lyricist. 'I can make a hit out of that tune with *another* lyric,' he told Jule. And he was absolutely right!"

The songs that Loesser wrote in those pre-World War II Hollywood years are remarkable for their strength. The ordinary idea, the shortcut, the triumph of technique to cover the absence of an idea—none of that for Loesser. He was on the prowl for a brighter notion, a stronger line. Certainly he could turn out an "I've Got Spurs That Jingle, Jangle, Jingle"—that was part of the job. For Betty Hutton he could write dynamite material—"Poppa, Don't Preach to Me" and "He Says Murder, He Says." And he was already coming up with such gems as "I'd Like to Get You on a Slow Boat to China."

But listen to his ballads—the haunting "Sand in My Shoes" (which he did with the late Victor Schertzinger) or "Spring Will Be a Little Late This Year," "Let's Get Lost," "I Wish I Didn't Love You So," or "What Are You Doing New Year's Eve?" They reveal the deep strain of romanticism that underpinned his later work.

"He really worked from his gut," says Abe Burrows. "He was an incurable romantic. Once, in giving me a big compliment, Frank looked at me when I came up with some ideas, and he says, 'You got so much talent. Why can't you

* See an earlier chapter for Jule Styne's recollections of this collaboration.

save it for romance? Why do you waste it on *comedy?*' 'Cause he himself knew
he could write the big comedy songs, but what he wanted was to *reach* the
audience, get into them."

With Arthur Schwartz, Loesser did the lyrics for *Thank Your Lucky Stars*
at Warner Brothers, which treated audiences to Miss Bette Davis chanting his
wry "They're Either Too Young or Too Old"—and then his draft board sent him
greetings. Shortly thereafter he became Private Frank Loesser, part of a Special
Services unit.

"You should've seen him!" chuckles Burrows. "He was proud of being in
the Army, but he insisted on having his private's uniform *tailored!* He was the
sharpest buck private you ever saw—he had a uniform that a general would have
given his four stars for! And he really hit his stride in the Amy. That's when he
started writing his own music."

The first of Loesser's solo jobs was to become an enormous wartime success;
based on the exploits of a heroic service chaplain, it was the rousing "Praise the
Lord and Pass the Ammunition."

During his Army years the talented private became a powerful one-man
propaganda weapon. He turned out dozens' of songs for service shows; "First
Class Private Mary Brown" for recruiting WACs; and another wartime smash
hit, "The Ballad of Rodger Young." For the foot-soldier he did "What Do You
Do in the Infantry? You March, You March, You March!"

"He always excited me," says Cy Feuer. "His turn of mind would always
have a sort of a curve. And the way he used to sit and pick at the piano, and
these inventive things that would come out *musically,* that fascinated me too."

By this time the war had ended and Loesser, Feuer, and Ernie Martin
were all back in civilian clothes. Feuer and Martin, with no previous experience
at producing on Broadway, were struggling to make a musical-comedy version
of Brandon Thomas's classic *Charley's Aunt.* (The two producers now share an
executive office, and there are times when their enthusiastic conversation over-
laps.)

"It was tough going," says Feuer. "But I was so *sold* on Frank. I got hold
of Ernie one day and I said, 'Look, we've got to go with Frank!' Which Ernie
agreed to. So we originally planned on having Frank team up with Harold Arlen.
Fine. But something came up and Arlen had to bow out—a problem in his
schedule. And there was Frank without a composer. So Frank said, 'Why don't
I do it myself?' We were enthusiastic, but then we had to sell him to the Bolgers.
[Bolger was the prospective star of the show.] Not easy, because who the hell
was Frank? What had he written? He had some good lyric credits, sure, but,
frankly, not much music. Well, finally the Bolgers agreed; they were fascinated
with Frank himself, who was kind of fun—socially, he was a real charmer—and
they agreed to take a chance on him."

Ernie Martin adds, "At the beginning, Rodgers and Hammerstein were
instrumental in getting the thing off the ground. See, we'd never raised any
money for a show before—who the hell were *we?*—and we were struggling.
But they knew Frank's work, and when we brought over the stuff he was writing,
Dick and Oscar bought two units in the show as an investment. They had absolute
faith in Frank; and they also said we could tell people that they'd become
backers—which was a hell of a big boost, believe me. And of course Frank went
ahead and did a fantastic score. I think what he wrote for *Charley* is one of his
outstanding things even now."

Where's Charley? is endowed with the lovely ballad "My Darling, My Darling" and a raft of other brilliant songs—"Make a Miracle," "The New Ashmolean Marching Society," and the rollicking "Once in Love with Amy," the show-stopper which Ray Bolger sang and danced, enchanting Broadway audiences.

'Everything new, everything a fresh concept, musically and lyrically," says Feuer. "He was just a natural show-writer. As a matter of fact, Frank never came to life fully until that show. It was his natural medium!"

Martin picks up. "It didn't make much of a splash at the beginning, we didn't get great notices at all. But there were telegrams from all the other composers—Rodgers, Hammerstein, Cole Porter—congratulating him on his brilliant work. Cole was always so starry-eyed about other people's work. With Loesser, he used to sit there and say, 'How can he have thought of a thing like that?'

"After a while, while we were still limping along, Arthur Schwartz wrote a piece in the *New York Times* Sunday section saying that Frank was the greatest undiscovered composer in America. Wrote it completely on his own, spontaneously. It was quoted. Then people started to pay attention to what was in that show. But that's the sort of thing other composers felt about Frank."

"Everything he did was totally fresh," enthuses Feuer, "even the things we had to cut out of the show. I remember one delightful thing he'd written— it was called 'Strolling in the Park.' For Jack's father, who was this elegant gent but didn't have a nickel. It's written like an English hunting song, with two French horns carrying the tune—two down-and-outers."

"Oh, Frank was a unique fellow," Feuer states with obvious feeling. "A great companion for fellows. Never drove a car. Didn't know how to drive. Never learned how."

Martin tunes in. "Strictly a city boy. Loved to quote Nunnally Johnson, who said that if he had a place with green grass, he'd pave it."

Feuer chuckles. "Once he said to me, 'Cy, there's something about the country—working there—it's very bad. There's something about the chlorophyll that keeps me from writing!'"

"He had strange work habits, you know," continues Martin. "He'd get up at four thirty or five A.M., have a martini, and go to work between five and eight in the morning. He wasn't a boozer, he merely oiled himself up. Then, after he wrote, he'd go to sleep, get up later, work some more. Napped again during the day, for maybe three or four hours. He knew that I was an early riser; sometimes he'd call me up on the telephone in the morning, six A.M., and the voice would say, 'Are you up?' and I'd say, 'Yeah.' And he'd start to whistle something he'd just written—on the phone!"

"Frank never stopped thinking about his things," says Feuer. "How to improve them—always working to make them better."

"But," interrupts Martin, "paranoid about people. Wouldn't sit in a restaurant unless his back was to the wall. I never knew what that was all about. Hated to make commitments. He'd make a date to go out to dinner. 'Okay, Frank, when?' Two weeks from next Tuesday. He'd say, 'Call me next week.' Call him next week—'How about it?' He'd say, 'Check in next Tuesday.' Tuesday you call—'What time?' 'Oh, call me at four this afternoon.' In other words, he was unable to make a definite commitment. Several of our shows, he didn't agree to do them until after they got on the stage! He never said, 'Okay, I'll write *Guys and Dolls.*' Never. One day he hands us four songs, and now we knew he was doing it!'"

"Do you realize we never signed an actual contract with him until after the show was playing on Broadway?" exclaims Feuer.

"There's something else about *Guys and Dolls*—it shows how brilliant Frank's instincts were," says Martin. "The first book that we had done, by Jo Swerling, wasn't right. We wrestled with it for weeks, but it didn't capture the Runyon quality at all. So we finally brought in Abe Burrows to rewrite it, based on a different concept and a new story line—the business of the wager, Sky betting all the horse-players their souls. But by this time Frank had written an entire score . . . to the *original* wrong book! Then Abe rewrote the book to suit Frank's score, keeping all of Frank's songs! In other words, Frank's instincts on it were so right that Burrows actually fashioned the new book from song to song, created scenes about the songs that Frank had already written!"

"Frank came in with that wonderful trio, the 'Fugue for Tinhorns,' " recalls Feuer. "We had no spot in the show for it. He said, 'This *feels* right to me for this property.' Three horse-players singing about the morning's selections. But it had nothing to do with the plot, nothing to do with the book. So we had it, a great piece of material, and we're struggling to find a spot for it. And then Ernie finally said, 'If you've got no place to put it, why don't you stick it up front, as a genre piece? Where it's not about anything, but it opens the show and sets the whole thing going.' Which is where it went, and did exactly what Frank thought it would do."

("When you're dealing with songwriters," says Abe Burrows, "I think you're dealing with the most intuitive kind of guys. None of them can explain where the hell their stuff is coming from. They're all a little nuts—and it comes out. See, everybody forgets that the purest example of abstract art in our world is music. Music gives you all of those things, love, hate, anger, fear, all of it in abstract form. So I had those songs of Frank's to go by, but then we'd sit and we'd look hard for song spots. Some of them came out of the dialogue. And one day we were in Philly and we were stuck for a song, and I had a line of dialogue, 'The oldest established permanent floating crap game in New York.' And I said, 'Gee, Frank, it lays out, like a lyric, you know?' And I took that out, and Frank made a song from it.")

"Tell him about the ice-cream cone," says Martin, chuckling.

Feuer does. "Frank wrote 'The Oldest Established Permanent Floating Crap Game' over a weekend. And it was now going to be put into the show. Everybody was supposed to sing it. The people had learned the song. We were onstage, and Michael Kidd, the choreographer, was there, and we were ready to stage it. We hadn't done a thing yet. We had the guys going through the number, and they're mumbling. We were just fashioning the introduction—you know, where the music hits a chord, and it's 'There's Hot Horse Harry—ba ba *ba!*—Big Red from Philadelphia—ba ba! And Mike says, 'All right, fellas, just run through the number once, and we'll try to pick who does which line,' and so-and-so. And they start singing it for the first time. Suddenly, from the back of the empty theatre, down the aisle comes Loesser, and yells, '*Hold it! Stop!*' And he is yelling, 'That is the worst goddam thing I have ever heard!'—plus a lot of four-letter words, all about a bunch of guys who've never seen this number before!

"Everyone was terrified. Mike Kidd, who's very level-headed, says, 'Look,

Frank, we're just starting.' And Frank says, 'You shut up!' And I said, 'Frank, for Christ's sake, we're just getting *started.*' And he says, 'You're Hitler!' He said to me, '*Hitler!* And you're working for me! *I'm* the author—you're working for *me!*' And the guys on the stage don't know what's happening, and he turns around and he says to the conductor, 'Take it from the top! I want to hear the best goddam singing possible—I want to hear this full out!'

"The conductor says, 'Okay, boys, from the top,' and they're all standing rigid on the stage, and they start to sing what they only learned yesterday. They bellow it out. Now they're singing their hearts out! Really singing! And Frank backs up the aisle, they're singing—and he's headed out."

Martin continues. "I could see he was going out of the theatre, so I followed him. He went into a little ice-cream store that used to be on the corner there, bought an ice-cream cone, took it, and he walked to his hotel, eating it."

"You know what it was?" asks Feuer. "It was *pay attention to the music,* that's all."

("It was because he worked so much from pure feeling," says Burrows. "You see, Frank always thought of himself as conscious of everything he was doing, and completely in charge.")

"What a temper," muses Martin. "What about hitting Isobel Bigley in the schnozzle? She was doing this song he'd written called 'I'll Know.' We're rehearsing it. You know that lyric, '*I'll know when my love comes along*'—nobody can really sing that; she always broke somewhere in the middle of that range. She could never do it, who the hell could? We're rehearsing it, and again she breaks. Frank walks up and he gets up on the conductor's podium—a little box they have there—and he hits her, *boing!* right smack on the nose! So she starts to cry. Now he drops on his knees—he doesn't realize what he's done, but it's done."

"Yelling, 'Forgive me!' " follows Feuer, doubled up with laughter.

"He sent her a bracelet that must have cost a thousand bucks," says Martin. "Such apologies! Of course, from then on she had him buffaloed, because whatever she wanted was not good enough—she'd get it."

"The only guy I ever saw punch a soprano in the nose."

Martin: "Took a swing at *me* once, too! It was in his house in California. We were in the living room having an argument about some clause or other. His agent was sitting in the middle, between us. I don't remember what it was about—something unreasonable Frank was insisting on. *Not* his billing. He used to say, 'I don't care about billing my name—leave it off! *My songs* are my billing!' There we are, arguing and wrangling, and suddenly I say, 'Fellas, *look!*' There's Frank's agent—a little guy—and he's fallen fast asleep on the sofa between us! I don't know why, but Frank got sore at this, and he gets up to give me a belt across the coffee table. We're both the same size, him standing and me sitting, and he really swung!"

"Missed Ernie, but went all the way around!" chuckles Feuer.

If *Where's Charley?* had taken a few weeks to catch on with the audience, there wasn't a moment's hesitation about the success, in 1950, of *Guys and Dolls.* From the second the curtain rose on the three Runyon characters singing "*I got the horse right here!*" until the finale with the cast singing the title song, Loesser had the audience in his back pocket.

"Do you know what the great thing about him and his lyrics was?" asked Feuer. "Do you realize that he was the master of the one-syllable word? Look at that couplet—'*When a bum buys wine that a bum can't afford, it's a cinch that the bum—is under the thumb—of some little broad!*' All but three are actually one-syllable words. Who else would have been able to do that?"

Guys and Dolls is generally conceded to be one of the four or five best American musical comedies. That chancey word "classic" can safely be applied to the saga of Sky Masterson, Nathan Detroit, Miss Adelaide, and all the rest. Burrows' libretto melds perfectly with Loesser's songs. ("He worked so *intuitively*," says Burrows. "He would say to me, 'For the next three or four minutes the stage should be filled with a big choral sound.' He didn't know why, he just felt it. Then he'd make it happen.")

Every one of Loesser's songs was a happening. The chorus girls and Miss Adelaide doing "A Bushel and a Peck" and "Take Back Your Mink," the rousing "Sit Down, You're Rocking the Boat," the duet "Sue Me," the brilliant lyrics to "Miss Adelaide's Lament."

> *The female remaining single, just in the legal sense,*
> *Shows a neurotic tendency—see note.*
>   [Looks at note]
> *Chronic, organic syndromes—toxic or hypertense*
> *Involving the eye, the ear, the nose and the throat.*
> *In other words, just from wondering whether*
> *The wedding is on or off,*
> *A person . . . can develop a cough.*

As Loesser himself put it, his songs are his billing. But it was always the ballads—"I'll Know," "I've Never Been in Love Before," "If I Were a Bell"— that were his special pride and joy.

"I remember," says Feuer, "he always used to say to Abe—this was when he'd be jumping up and down with both feet to make the point—'I'm-in-the-*romance business!*' And he was always frustrated by the fact that so many of the actors we used couldn't sing. I mean, take Sam Levene, our Nathan Detroit. You have no idea what a problem it was to get him to come in on the same note each night. He was tone deaf. Night after night, it was anybody's guess where he'd hit the cue note on 'Sue Me!' And since Frank had a good voice himself and he could sing well—maybe that's why he'd get so angry when the actors would sing the songs differently from what he heard.

"We once had a hell of a fight with Frank about his ballads in the second act of *Guys and Dolls*. George S. Kaufman, our director, was with us, and he kind of acted as a mediator. Frank was saying to me, 'When are we going to have a reprise?' He wanted the ballads plugged in the second act. I told him we weren't going to do that arbitrarily; it would spoil the flow of our show. He's yelling about how every composer gets to reprise his ballads—that's what makes them into hits. I'm telling him I don't care if it's customary, it's wrong for this show. 'Where are they going to hear my songs?' he yells. 'What the hell do you think I'm in this for?' We went on arguing like that, and then finally George Kaufman said, 'Wait a minute, fellas. I'll tell you what. Frank, I'll agree to reprise your ballads in the second act—if you allow us to reprise some of the first-act *jokes* in the second act!' "

For the next three years Loesser worked by himself on a project based on Sidney Howard's hit play *They Knew What They Wanted*. "This time he wanted to try it all himself, as a kind of exercise," Burrows remarks. "This was the one he really got his gun off with—he was proud of it. He had a right—it was a helluva show."

This time Loesser would not only write music and lyrics on a grand scale but he would do his own libretto. Howard's play was set in the Napa Valley and dealt with the bitter-sweet love story of a prosperous Italian-American grape grower who takes himself a mail-order bride. Loesser told an interviewer, with his customary directness, "I figured, take out all this political talk, the labor talk, and the religious talk. Get rid of all that stuff, and you have a good love story."

When he had completed his version and called it *The Most Happy Fella*, the work fell between two stools—somewhere between a grand-scale musical and a minor-scale grand opera. Contrary to established Broadway custom, the program for *The Most Happy Fella* did not list the individual songs Loesser had written; and he insisted that his work be billed as "A Musical."

Burrows went down to Philadelphia for the première performance. "Frank asked me to come down and take a look," he wrote in the *New York Times* after Loesser's death. "This time he was flying solo. Music, lyrics, libretto. Pretty nervous about it, too. And so was I, for him. The show was remarkable. New kind of musical? Opera? Whatever it was, it was something special."

To perform his music as he wished it to sound, Loesser had cast as his lead an ex-Metropolitan Opera baritone, the late Robert Weede. The part of his mail-order bride was played and sung by lovely Jo Sullivan.* The new show was filled with more than thirty separate musical numbers—choral passages, arias, duets, trios, quartets. There are, indeed, so many and varied pieces of complex music in his score that it must be described with one of his own titles, "*Abbondanza!*"—abundance.

"I came out of the theatre in great excitement, dashed up to Frank, and began chattering away about the marvelous funny stuff," continues Burrows. "All those songs like 'Standing on the Corner, Watching All the Girls Go By,' 'Big D!' Suddenly, he cut me off angrily. 'The hell with those! We know I can do that sort of stuff! *Tell me where I made you cry!*' Always searching. He went out and tried something different the next time, too."

Loesser's next venture was an adaptation of B. J. Chute's gentle novel *Greenwillow*, a delicate fantasy set in a totally imaginary bucolic world. In that show the Loesser propensity for romantic balladry was given wide range. His "Never Will I Marry" is an as yet undiscovered treasure; so are "Summertime Love" and "Walking Away Whistling."

But the show was not to repeat the huge success of his three previous works. Perhaps the words of one critic, Walter Kerr, help to explain its failure. "Folklore may just be the one dish that can't be cooked to order."

---

* "Leo McCarey, the director, was once talking to the late Bobby Dolan," remembers Johnny Mercer, "and he asked Dolan, 'By the way, what's been happening to that guy who wrote 'Two Sleepy People'?" Loesser had been very much around Paramount when McCarey was there.

"'Oh, Frank?' said Bobby. 'He's in New York.' Loesser was preparing *The Most Happy Fella* at that time. Bobby said 'Loesser's writing the lyrics and doing the music, he's also written the adaptation, he's publishing the score with his own firm, and he's also going to co-produce the show.'

"So McCarey thought a second, and then he asked, 'Does he get the girl?'

"Funny thing about that is, Frank *did* get the girl. He married his leading lady, Jo Sullivan."

"A very complicated guy," comments Martin. "He'd begun to concentrate on building up his own publishing house. By then he'd married Jo Sullivan and they had a daughter; she was about five. You know, if you haven't gathered it already, Frank was a damned good businessman, and his firm was flourishing. Once we were out in California with him and he was telling us how he was going to leave behind this great estate. Copyrights, copyrights, that's all he could talk about. And we said, 'Yeah, you know who's going to get it all, Frank? Susie's going to marry some pimple-faced little guy whom you're going to hate! And *he's* going to be the guy who'll wind up with all your dough!' Well, he took care of that as soon as possible, believe me, because the next child they had was a boy!"

"Do you realize that Frank was an expert cabinetmaker?" asks Feuer. "He had a basement workshop in his house, fitted out with all sorts of tools, and he could turn out some of the most beautiful, complicated furniture you ever saw."

"But always a New York kind of guy. Street boy," says Martin. "In California he had this house with a tennis court—the net was always down. He never went outdoors. One day he said to me, 'Let's go sit in the sun.' Which in itself was a remarkable thing. I said, 'Okay,' and he said, 'Wait a minute.' He went upstairs and he came down again in a little pair of blue swimming pants. And he had left on his garters and his socks and his shoes. We went out there and we sat in the sun for about five minutes, and that was enough! But later on he became more of a family man and he did a lot of cute things. Bought a house out in Westhampton, near us. One day he arrived at my house. He had bought a boat which was a raft kind of thing with an awning; and he had a little orchestra kind of thing. He and the kids were all playing. And he came sailing up like a Southern riverboat captain. Little jokes like that. . . . We gave a Fourth of July party once, and Frank came dressed like Uncle Sam—in a red, white, and blue outfit! . . . And then he got interested in bird-watching. He loved gadgets. He built a one-way mirror into a window—had birdhouses outside, and he'd sit there watching: 'Wait a minute, wait a minute; there's a Baltimore Oriole!' "

The winning combination of Burrows, Loesser, and Feuer and Martin reunited in 1962 to produce another smash success, *How to Succeed in Business Without Really Trying.* Once again the dimension of Loesser's virtuosity remains dazzling. The cutting edge of Burrows' satire, working together with the score, does a masterful job of puncturing more of our most precious American shibboleths about the Horatio Alger world-of-commerce success story. But, as always, it wasn't the comedy numbers that Loesser looked for; he was digging down for romance.

"Before I wrote a line of libretto," says Burrows, "we had figured out eight song spots, and then we'd kick it around. Then he came in with the ballad 'I Believe in You.' And I said, 'Frank, it would be great if the guy sings it to *himself*—in the mirror.' And I figured he'd hit me that time! Thank God, it stayed a love song, which it was. But that was how we worked; it was kind of a back-and-forth that grew between us."

Out of that back-and-forth were to come such brilliant musical-comedy numbers as "Dear Old Ivy," "The Company Way," and the rousing choral hymn to American mediocrity, "The Brotherhood of Man."

"When it came to 'A Secretary Is Not a Toy,' Frank said we could never make it work," recalls Feuer. "It was written for Rudy Vallee to sing. Vallee wanted to sing it in another tempo, and he was rehearsing, and finally Frank got sore and we had another one of those big blow-ups! I got them into the office and I tried to reason it out with both of them. I told Rudy that Frank had written this score, that he had it in his head the way it should be done, and that Rudy should respect that and do the song the way Frank had conceived it. Well, Rudy said, 'You don't understand. I'm an *interpreter* of songs.' And he starts giving me a list of all his hits, the songs he's helped make in his time. And while he's talking, I see Frank is ready to hurl himself at Rudy's throat! So I kept hold of Frank—I wasn't trying to arbitrate this, but to let off all the steam and get everything back on the tracks. Frank is now yelling, and I'm saying to him, 'Take it *easy*, Frank.' And I'm telling Rudy, 'Frank must have his way with every goddam piece of material he's written for this show—that's fundamental, and that's the way it's going to be!' And we all left the office. Frank went and put on his coat and hat and quit the show. Left.

"We called for him, and when we reached his house, we get the word that Frank says he's finished, he's not coming back, he's out of it—we can go ahead any way we want. I asked to speak to him, and they said, 'He won't speak to you.'

"Then I receive a telegram, two pages long, in which he said he was deeply disappointed in me, I'd let him down, I'd finked out on the whole thing, and he went on, after all the years that we've known each other, and the friendship, and everything. You know what Frank wanted me to do? I hadn't punched Rudy Vallee in the nose—and I'd also prevented *him* from punching Rudy in the nose! Even though I'd told Vallee that he'd have to do it Frank's way, Frank wouldn't buy that. He wanted the guy floored for saying his piece!

"So I sent back a wire ignoring his wire. What the hell am I going to answer? That I'm sorry I didn't punch Rudy? Sent the wire and I prevailed on him to return. And back he came—smiling, sort of sheepishly, and went back to work."

"It was another ice-cream-cone incident, just like in Philly," observes Martin. "Frank used to burst. It was kind of like a volcano."

Martin pauses for a moment and chuckles, then nudges Feuer. "Remember that night in England?"

"Sure! We could talk about Frank for eleven years!" says Feuer.

"He never stopped thinking about things!" Martin continues. "We were opening *Guys and Dolls* in England, in Bristol. We're in this dreadful little English hotel, and Frank and I are sharing the room; we'd registered at night, so we hadn't seen where the hotel was located. About three in the morning we hear a terrific WHOO!—one of those big ship whistles—and the whole hotel shook! We wake up, run to the window, pull up the blind—and there's a porthole outside! *A ship!* The damned hotel is sitting by the side of some canal!

"So I finally get back to sleep again, and about an hour later Frank is shaking my shoulder. He can't sleep any more. He's up and in his bathrobe, and he's been pacing around the room. I see cigarettes everywhere—you know, he was a chain-smoker. He doesn't want me to be asleep because now he has something on his mind. He says, 'Listen, we can open it in *Detroit!*' And he starts ad-libbing to me a whole black version of *Guys and Dolls!* We should do the thing with a cast of blacks. Four in the morning, and he's already up and away with a whole new goddam concept!"

"Oh, the cigarettes," says Feuer sadly. "You know, Frank literally smoked himself to death. Jo, his wife, was always after him to give it up. When we went down to Philly with *How to Succeed,* he would rent a piano and put it in the suite—a small baby grand for him to work on. And he was having cigarettes smuggled in. He'd say, 'Bring me a pack of Camels, but don't let Jo see.' Three packs a day. With cigarettes Frank was like a junkie or an alkie.

"Calls me one day. I should come down to the suite. I go down. 'You won't believe this!' he tells me. 'What are the odds against *this?*' He points at the piano, and the piano is all white, covered with white dust. 'Look!' he says. '*Look!*' A piece of the ceiling above the piano has broken, and dust has fallen down all over the piano. 'What are the odds against this?' he yells. 'In this whole fucking hotel—*look* what happened!' He lifts up the piano lid. 'Jo comes in,' he says, 'cleans off the piano—and finds my carton of Camels inside the piano!' "

"His work on *How to Succeed* was brilliant, musically and lyrically," says Burrows, up in his Central Park West apartment as the dusk is falling. "A tough, abrasive score. The satire was savage and funny. He and I got a Pulitzer Prize for that one. But a week later, when we met at lunch to search out a new project, he was once more hunting for romance and tears. I respected him for that. That big talent had to be respected.

"You know, Frank was always after *me* to write songs. We'd done one once—on the old *Duffy's Tavern* radio show. It was called 'Leave Us Face It, We're in Love.' Shirley Booth sang it.

"We had a tremendous feeling for each other. Though he was only about six months older than I, he always treated me like an older brother. We fit together, kind of. We talked the same way, you know. Matter of fact, when we did *Guys and Dolls,* it was strange—Cy Feuer and I went to the same high school, so did Mike Kidd, and Frank had grown up in the same way we had. We all talked the same language, even.

"So different from Cole Porter. See, Cole I was also close to, but in a different way. A very serious musician, worked like a dog. I remember lots of times seeing Cole at three in the morning, working on a song. But you know how Billy Rose described Cole—he said he was a 'toff.' The last of the great toffs. Cole always had that terrible physical pain—suffered like hell—but he's the only guy I ever worked with who opening night would come to the show. I mean, he'd sit down there. Come right down the aisle, take a seat in about the fifth row, and sit and enjoy it hugely. 'Beautiful!' he would say. 'Lovely!' Liked everything. The rest of us all sick from nervousness. Not Cole. I know Cole would have moments when he'd get disgusted, but I don't think he ever had the agony of spirit that Loesser had—that constant striving . . . and extension . . . and dissatisfaction.

"See, Frank always minded that his really big songs were 'Two Sleepy People' or 'Standing on the Corner,' comedy stuff like 'Miss Adelaide's Lament.' Remember his 'Baby, It's Cold Outside'? An absolutely brilliant piece of comedy material. I always was sore at him for selling it to Metro for an Esther Williams picture. That thing was much too good for where it went—it belonged in a Broadway show! But what Frank wanted was the hits to be his romantic songs.

"That's what I mean when I say we were so alike in our approach. We always saw that *curve.* You know, when I go out on lectures, people always stand up afterwards when they ask questions, and the first question is always, 'Mr. Burrows, haven't you ever wanted to write something serious?'

"And I always answer the same. I say, 'But everything I do is serious. It just comes *out* funny.' Which is true. And Frank was the same way." Burrows stares out the window as the lights begin to come on through Central Park. "That's about all I can say."

"I visited Frank the day before he died, up at the hospital," says Martin softly. "I knew Frank was dying—he was sitting cross-legged on the bed with just his pajama bottoms on, looking like a cadaver. There was this breathing-machine going next to him . . . and Frank was smoking a cigarette."

"Abe loved him very much," says Cy Feuer. "All of us did. In fact, I must tell you, when Frank died I couldn't get used to the idea that he wasn't there any more."

The office is silent, the only sounds are the traffic moving past on Park Avenue.

"I couldn't either," says Ernie Martin. "I still can't."

'Always'

(Irving Berlin)

IRVING BERLIN. Where does one begin to write about this American phenomenon?

In December, 1972, Mr. Irving Berlin presented his upright piano to the Smithsonian Institution in Washington D.C. where future generations of Americans will be able to stare at the set of piano keys on which, for nearly six decades, were fashioned hundreds of popular songs.

The Smithsonian may have the Berlin machine tool, but the vast output of the "little man with the melodies in his head" will always belong to anyone who can hum, whistle or sing.

Apart from newspaper stories and other publicity pieces, there is very little in print about him. In 1925 Alexander Woollcott composed an effusive biographical paean about America's most successful songwriter; and a quarter-century later a somewhat simplified story of his achievements, obviously intended for a juvenile audience, appeared. But since then nothing, not even a filmed biography.

"This is a paradox of Irving's character," comments Abel Green of *Variety*, a longtime friend of the little man with the melodies in his head. "He was normally one of the most inaccessible people in show business. But when he made a picture or did a Broadway show, he, usually reticent, became an open sesame to disc jockeys and the press. Nobody knew the value of publicity better than he. He'd give away hours of marvelous material in order to get coverage for his picture, or his show, and his songs. But as far as an autobiography is concerned—well, today he probably figures, 'What's there to plug now?' "

A. L. Berman, Berlin's lawyer for many years, was more explicit. "Irving doesn't like to talk much for publication, especially about himself," he cautioned.

But in any book about popular American songwriting, how could Irving Berlin possibly go unrepresented?

Some months later Mr. Berlin consented to talk, albeit from his end of the telephone.

"All right, all right, tell me, what is this thing of yours all about?" demanded the familiar high voice. "If it's a collection of gags about the music business, don't bother talking to me—I'm no comedian."

When the book's intention was explained to him, he was unimpressed.

"You're wasting your time," he scoffed. "Nobody ever wants a songwriter to *talk*—all people want to hear is his music! Besides, who cares any more? There's a whole new public out there, and they don't even know people like me are still around. Don't you read the papers? We're antiques, museum pieces. Today it's all kids!"

But if that was so, how could he explain the growing wave of nostalgia that seemed to be engulfing audiences of all ages? Even the "kids" are turning more and more toward the roots of today's music, trying to identify the sources, to enjoy the old "museum pieces."

"Never mind the sales talk," said Mr. Berlin. "Who've you been to see?" And added, with a chuckle, "Most of us songwriters are terrible liars, anyway."

He was supplied with a list of some of the men and women who had consented to discuss their careers.

What had they discussed?

After some twenty-odd interviews, a rather omnibus question to answer. Perhaps the spine of what had been discussed was that evanescent X factor, that electric connection between a songwriter and his audience that turns his song into a hit.

"Oh, good," chuckled Berlin. "Go ahead, let *me* in on the secret. I'd love to have it!"

Hadn't Mr. Berlin been born with it?

"Stop selling me," he answered. "You still haven't told me what anybody said. Tell me *one*. And give me his formula."

The name of a major songwriter was raised, one who had said that when he writes, the song must please *him* first—and then if his own taste is lucky enough to coincide with the public's, he has a popular song.

Berlin burst into laughter. "He told you that, did he?" he chortled. "All right, I'll tell you what I think about that. *I* write a song to please the *public*— and if the public doesn't like it in New Haven,* *I change it!*"

Might he be quoted?

---

* For many years the town in which musical shows first try out—the arena where the men are separated from the boys.

"Why the hell do you think I just told it to you?" demanded Mr. B.

("You should be very pleased," remarked Abel Green when this remark was reported to him. "That's more than anybody's gotten out of Berlin for years—and, come to think of it, it's as valid a wrap-up of his secret as he's ever given *anybody*.")

Some months back Mr. Berlin was housecleaning in his office files. Tucked away in a musty drawer, he unearthed the printed menu for a stag dinner which was held in New York almost six decades ago. The exact year remains cloaked in vagueness. But when Mr. Berlin had the menu photocopied and sent to certain of his contemporaries, he placed the time at "a year or so before we organized ASCAP" (the American Society of Composers, Authors and Publishers, established in 1914).

The cover sheet of the menu, in ornate steel-gravure typography, heralds:

BEEFSTEAKDINNER
UNITED SONGWRITERS OF AMERICA
(For Tonight Only)   (In Name Only)   (By Tolerance Only)
E. RAY GOETZ, *Chairman*
BERT GRANT   JAMES V. MONACO
JOS. McCARTHY   EDGAR LESLIE*
KEEN'S CHOP HOUSE
107 West 44th Street
New York

On the second page is the dinner menu. The next page contains an ode, obviously written for this occasion, by Irving Berlin. Still in his twenties, he had already achieved considerable success as a songwriter. What songs were played and sung that night, what was the small talk, all are lost to us. But Mr. Berlin's words remain.

THE POPULAR SONG

Born just to live for a short space of time,
Often without any reason or rhyme,
Hated by highbrows who call it a crime:
Loved by the masses who buy it;... †

* Goetz wrote such songs as "For Me and My Gal" and "Yaaka Hula, Hickey Dula." Grant wrote "Arrah Go On, I'm Gonna Go Back to Oregon." Monaco composed, among other hits, "Row, Row, Row," "You Made Me Love You," and "What Do You Want to Make Those Eyes at Me For?" Leslie's name can be found on such hits as "He'd Have to Get Under (to Fix Up His Automobile)," "Oh, What a Pal Was Mary," "Among My Souvenirs," and he collaborated with Goetz on "For Me and My Gal."

As for the United Songwriters of America, its president was Stanley Murphy ("Put On Your Old Gray Bonnet," "Be My Little Baby Bumble Bee"). Vice-president: L. Wolfe Gilbert ("Waiting for the Robert E. Lee"). Secretary: George W. Meyer ("Mandy, Make Up Your Mind"). And treasurer: Theodore Morse ("Hail, Hail, the Gang's All Here" and "Dear Old Girl").

Pragmatic words from one so young—and yet, oddly wistful. A rude form of true poetry, unsophisticated, easily assimilated, hard to forget. And typical of Berlin.

For this is what Irving Berlin is. An American bard, a *minnesinger* to the man on the street. Born in 1888, Irving Berlin arrived on the American scene in time for the invention of the talking machine, the radio, the motion picture, and television, and we are the luckier for it.

If Berlin is the one authentic genius of twentieth-century popular song, what is it that makes him so?

It isn't the sheer volume of his work (although a book compiled in 1966, a songography which lists all of his songs since 1907, as well as their recordings, runs to an amazing 170 pages). It isn't the rich and dazzling variety of his output—rags, fox-trots, comedy songs, topical numbers dealing with fads of the day, love songs and ballads—for other composers, such as Gershwin and Kern and Rodgers and Hammerstein, have proved equally versatile.

But consider: Berlin is both composer *and* lyricist. Very few of his American contemporaries managed that incredible feat. Consider, also, that Berlin has been his own publisher and promoter. And, in most cases, the producer of his own shows. With no formal schooling, little or no musical education, and nobody to help him get started but himself.

So we cannot indulge in vague generalities about "genius." In trying to discover what makes Berlin the composer he has been, one must deal in specifics, and hope that they will provide us with some random insights that, when put together, will show the shape and depth of his intricate character.

"What impresses me most about Irving Berlin is that his inner ear is tremendous," says Robert Russell Bennett, the dean of American orchestrators. "Irving can't express himself; he has to go to the piano. Bobby Dolan used to do a little imitation of Irving running his fingers over the piano before he started to play. It was really comical, because Irving couldn't play a scale, an arpeggio—nothing. He had no piano technique at all. Now *inside*, he hears it. I remember in particular when we were together and he was doing a song for

Fred Astaire and Ginger Rogers in the picture *Carefree*. It's called 'Change Partners.' He came to a spot in this where he played a plain diminished chord, and he turned to me helplessly and said, 'Is that the right chord?' 'Well,' I said, 'I don't think it's the chord you hear, somehow or other.' He said, 'No, that's not it. You play me a chord there.' I played him one. He said, 'No, that's not it.' I played another. 'That's it!' he said.

"He couldn't put his fingers on it, but he *knew* which one it should be. Fantastic.

"But I say the great people come into this world without any clothing at all, just naked geniuses of some kind, and out it comes. They may not be able to express it. They don't even speak your language. They just sit there, and they bring you something, and that's all there is to say about it."

Bennett's description of the arrival of geniuses sans clothing may, in the case of Berlin, be only a minor exaggeration. For Izzy Baline, who was born on May 11, 1888, was the son of Moses Baline, of Temun, in Siberian Russia, and one of a family of ten. Whatever clothes Israel wore were minimal. The Balines were poor, very poor. The father was a cantor who sang in a small *shul*—until the czar's soldiers began their pogroms. The Balines fled to America, the promised Land, in 1892. For the next four years Cantor Baline struggled to support his family. When Izzy was eight, his father died.

In the battle for day-to-day survival, everyone in that emigrant family had to pitch in, and Izzy was shortly out on the streets selling newspapers. An incident will serve to measure the strength of his determination, even at such a tender age. One afternoon, walking by the East River docks, he was inadvertently struck by a large crane and knocked into the river. When he was fished out by passers-by and saved from drowning, still tightly clasped in Izzy's small fist were the five or six coppers he had earned that day from his newspapers.

When survival is paramount, who has time for school? The life around the small boy was more of an education. He passed by and peered inside the doors of the many Lower East Side saloons; there waiters served drinks and sang the popular songs of the day. Something inside him must have responded intuitively to that music. But when he proposed to his mother that he take a job singing in one of those places, she objected strongly. Holy music in a synagogue? Yes, fine, that had been his late father's high calling. But vulgar ragtime, cheap music in a low barroom? No, no!

By the time he was fourteen he had run away from home; it was his way of reducing the family overhead. He joined a street singer named Blind Sol, who wandered from bar to bar, singing for coins from the customers. With Izzy as his seeing-eye boy and assistant, Blind Sol made the rounds—and Izzy absorbed more of the music of the day. His voice was high-pitched and quavering; soon it became known around the streets. Then it was merely a matter of time before he found himself a job as a song-plugger for Harry Von Tilzer, a famous composer of the day. In the balcony of Tony Pastor's Music Hall, in Union Square, young Izzy stood up and bravely sang out Von Tilzer's latest songs to the crowd.

So Berlin's piano playing is rudimentary? Certainly. He is self-taught. Whatever he learned, he picked up not at Juilliard but at barroom pianos, where indulgent owners allowed him to explore the keys of their uprights during slack periods.

The next stage of his upward journey took place in Pelham's Café, on the Bowery, run by "Nigger Mike" Salter. There, in 1906, young Izzy was employed as a singing waiter; at last he was one with all those others he'd heard through the swinging doors. He'd arrived. Nigger Mike's was not a typical lowdown Bowery joint. It attracted a large drop-in clientele from uptown, a high-class crowd fascinated by the atmosphere and the music and the Bowery "types."

And where did the first Berlin song come from? The most inventive screenwriter could not have dreamed up a more improbable set of circumstances. Nearby, at another Bowery joint called Callahan's, there was a piano player named Al Piantadosi. (Later, he was to be co-author of "Goodbye Broadway, Hello France.") In partnership with "Jerry-the-Waiter," Al had delivered himself of a ditty called "My Mariucci Taka de Steamboat." Said song had been played and sung into a popular hit, and Nigger Mike got very annoyed at the publicity accruing to his rival. He instructed his singing waiter, Izzy, to run up a song that would publicize *his* joint. Collaborating with Nick Nicholson, another house employee, Izzy, who had already regaled the patrons with improvised parodies of current song hits, went to work to construct one of his own.

In his 1925 biography of Berlin, Alexander Woollcott gives the following account of what took place thereupon:

> This masterpiece was wrought with great groanings and infinite travail of the spirit. Its rhymes, which filled the young lyricist with the warm glow of authorship, were achieved day by day and committed nervously to stray bits of paper. Much of it had to be doctored by Nick, with considerable experimenting at the piano and a consequent displeasure felt by the patrons at Nigger Mike's, who would express their feelings by hurling the damp beer cloths at the singer's head. Truly, it might be said that Berlin's first song was wrought while he dodged the clouts of his enraged neighbors.

Neither Berlin nor Nicholson knew enough about music to write their masterpiece down; it was finally committed to paper by a man named Fiddler John, cobbler by day, violin player by night. The name of this first masterpiece? "Marie, from Sunny Italy." Royalties accruing to the writers? Seventy-five cents. And on the title page the publisher printed, "Words by I. Berlin." At which point our young songwriter decided that Israel was no longer suitable to such an elegant Americanization of his last name. He went the whole distance. He cast off the Izzy and became henceforth Irving Berlin.*

"Marie" made a small stir, but as yet there was no sign of the musical career that was to follow. However, it was at this time that Berlin first displayed his intuitive feel for *le beau geste*. One evening a party of upper-class "swells" appeared at Nigger Mike's, among them royalty, one Prince Louis of Battenberg. Manhattan café society was showing the Prince the town. So impressed was the titled gentleman's party by Irving's singing that, upon leaving the Bowery café, the Prince proffered a five-dollar bill as a tip.

Five dollars, in 1907, was a solid piece of security. That fin backed by

---

* But never lost his sense of humor about it. Many years later he wrote the score for *Call Me Madam*, to star Ethel Merman. Bill McCaffrey, who represents Art Carney, received a call from Berlin, who was most anxious to hire Carney. "Bill" said Berlin "I'll tell you what—if you get Carney for us, from now on you can call me Izzy Baline!"

Uncle Sam's good gold could support one thin waiter for a week. Nevertheless, young Berlin airily waved aside the Prince's *pourboire*. It had been his pleasure to sing for nobility; let that be its own reward.

A young newspaperman was witness to this incident; he hurried uptown to his office desk and wrote down the story. When it appeared in the paper, I. Berlin's name was properly spelled. The reporter was named Herbert Bayard Swope. In time, both he and Berlin would be famous, Berlin making headlines, Swope reporting them as one of New York's most important editors.

In 1908 three more songs from Berlin, one of his own, two with collaborators. Still not much of a stir. A year later, now graduated to a place called Jimmy Kelly's, he came up with the first manifestation of his ability to cash in on current events. A passing vaudevillian asked Berlin if he could write some "special material" for his act, something to do with affairs of the day. Berlin picked on Dorando, an Italian long-distance runner who had come to America to race, and who was defeated by Johnny Longboat in the 1908 Olympic marathon. He set to work and composed a set of verses in Italian dialect, in which an Italian day laborer explains what took place at that great event.

"I remember it from when I was a kid; it was a great song," said Irving Caesar. "You see, in those days you could deal in stereotypes, like this Italian day laborer who'd bet his hard-earned money on his countryman. You could have a little fun, and nobody's feelings got hurt." To illustrate his point, Mr. Caesar then sang "Dorando" from memory, some sixty-three years *ex post facto*.

> *Dorando! Dorando!*
> *He run-a run-a run-a, run like anything.*
> *One-a two-a hundred times around da ring.*
> *"Please-a," I cry, "Nun-ga stop!"*
> *Just then Dorando, he's-a drop!*
> *Good-bye poor old barber shop.*
> *It's no fun to lose the mon'.*
> *When da sun-of-a-gun no run,*
> *Dorando, he's good-a for not'!*

The vaudevillian who had commissioned the song from Berlin for $25 never reappeared to claim it, nor to pay the fee. Unwilling to discard his work, Berlin made his way uptown to a song-publishing house in what was beginning to be known as Tin Pan Alley.

In the offices of Watterson and Snyder he demonstrated his lyric. Watterson was sufficiently impressed to purchase it on the spot. As an afterthought, he inquired of the young man who had just run through it, *a cappella*, "You have a tune for it, don't you?"

Even though he did not, Berlin maintained that he had. And having sold the song, he hastily repaired to another office in the same firm, where, with the help of an amiable piano player, he improvised a tune and managed to get it written down on a lead sheet so that it could be played, published, and subsequently sung . . . and remembered by young Irving Caesar.

The topical scene, the passing parade, was to serve the young songwriter as an unending source of material through the years; in fact, in the year following "Dorando" he came up with a song which drew on the current public craze for the classic "Spring Song" of Mendelssohn. "That Mesmerizing Mendelssohn Tune" was to be the first of a long series of popular hits that would draw attention to fads and fancies of the day.

But the first big authentic Berlin hit was a song with a somewhat more universal theme. It bore a title which couldn't possibly miss with at least fifty percent of the public. Consider this from 1909, dear Ms's of Women's Lib: "My Wife's Gone to the Country (Hooray, Hooray!)." Berlin's co-author on lyrics was George Whiting. According to legend, the writing of this song led to the breakup of Whiting's own marriage.*

By now Berlin was established, and firmly under contract to Watterson and Snyder. Throughout 1909 and 1910 he collaborated on songs with Ted Snyder, but also turned out works that were completely his own. In the *Ziegfeld Follies of 1910*, one of the major showcases on Broadway, he provided Fannie Brice with the first of his major theatre numbers, "The Dance of the Grizzly Bear." For May Irwin, another leading performer, he wrote "That Opera Rag," and by the end of the year he was already treading the boards as a full-fledged performer. In a show produced by the Shuberts, entitled *Up and Down Broadway*, out came Messrs. Berlin and Snyder, fashionably attired in collegiate sweaters and brandishing tennis racquets. What those costumes had to do with their songs, "Sweet Italian Love" and "That Beautiful Rag," only the Shuberts knew.

Young Berlin was now a bit more familiar with the piano, although, in the words of Mr. Woollcott back in 1925:

> Like most men who play only by ear, Berlin is a slave of one key. Since he always plays helplessly in F Sharp, he has had to have a piano especially constructed with a sliding keyboard, so that when he wants to adventure in another key, he can manage it by moving a lever and rattling away on the more familiar keys.

Berlin has continued to use that piano through the years. He refers to it as "my Buick."

Somewhat rapturously warming to his subject, Woollcott continued:

> To the man who has written more than any one man's share of the songs this land has liked, the hieroglyphics of written music are still a trifle baffling. That incongruity is more striking to those of us who spent all our youth in the rough and ready company of textbooks. It might not be amiss for the likes of us to remember from time to time that a not unsuccessful poet named Homer was, in all probability, unable to read and unable to write.

· It was with exactly that sort of ingenuity and inventiveness that young Berlin was fueling his forward thrust through the fiercely competitive Tin Pan Alley scene. Everything that his sharp eyes saw or his ears heard, in the cafés, on Manhattan streets, in theatre lobbies, or in the newspapers, was to be raw material for his output. It was to be a lifelong work pattern.

In those early years he was finding his way. In time to come he would develop a fine sense of the right subject at the right time, be it war, love, peace, patriotism, or a Presidential candidate. But in 1911 he was still unselective. In the space of one year he turned out some *forty*-odd songs, alone

---

* Some years later, in an effort to atone for his musical sins, Whiting contritely wrote a song called "My Blue Heaven," which celebrated the joys of coming home at night to the little woman . . . her smiling face, the fireplace, etc.

or in collaboration. He went off on all sorts of gambits. For the shopgirl it was "How Do You Do It, Mabel, on Twenty Dollars a Week?" For assorted ethnic groups there were "Business Is Business, Rosey Cohen," "That Kazatsky Dance," as well as "When You Kiss an Italian Girl." For the Irish, "Molly, O!, Oh Molly," and then "Sombrero Land." Not to forget "Dat's-a My Gal," as well as "Yankee Love" and "Italian Love." Gone, most of them, and happily forgotten.

But in that same year, in the *Ziegfeld Follies of 1911* he had placed four songs. With Vincent Bryan he wrote "Woodman, Woodman, Spare That Tree," which was sung by the great Bert Williams, the reigning black comic star. Another of Berlin's solo ventures, "Everybody's Doing It (Doing What? Turkey Trot)," was a popular success. And out in vaudeville an equally youthful Eddie Cantor, also an upwardly mobile youngster from the Lower East Side, was touring theatres and singing Berlin's "That Ragtime Violin."

Getting a new song placed with a performer for "plugging" was the important aspect of the business. In years to come, there would be talking pictures, radio, phonographs, television, and in a matter of hours a song could be heard everywhere. But in this live-entertainment era the "plug"* was primarily the performer, be he a singing waiter or someone in the legitimate theatre or vaudeville. The newly developed phonograph record helped disseminate songs, but sheet music was still the true indication of a song's popularity. When people bought it, that meant they had heard some performer do a song and wanted it for their own pianos.

Stars were plugging Berlin's output, people were humming and whistling his songs, and sheet music with his name on it was selling nicely, but in that year of 1911 his real triumph was to be a song which he introduced himself at a Friars Club Frolic.

The Friars, a theatrical club, enjoyed it, but nobody in the audience that night can be reported to have gone wild about the new song. When Berlin next offered it to the management of a new Broadway production called *Folies Bergère*, he was turned down. The myopic management subsequently folded the show. Perseverance being a Berlin trademark, he allowed the song to be used by the performers at the far less prestigious Columbia Burlesque. It was also "placed" with vaudevillians, among them young Al Jolson, who was touring with Lew

---

* Harry Ruby, who, like so many of his fellow songwriters, began his career as a "plugger" for the Gus Edwards Music Company, described his earliest activities. "I knew how to play the piano, and that's how I got the job. Twenty-five bucks a week. It was a very nice job—only seven days a week, eleven in the morning until one in the morning. Here's what a plugger had to do. Every one of the publishing companies would have four, five, maybe even ten little offices with pianos. The vaudeville actors, the café performers, and the singing waiters would come in, and we'd demonstrate whatever songs the company was plugging. This was from eleven in the morning until six. At six at night you got into the subway and went home to the Bronx to have your supper—then you came back. Five cents each way—which was a lot cheaper than the sixty cents that a downtown restaurant would charge. Then you met a singer someplace in a café and demonstrated a song. Then you went to the nickelodeons with the illustrated slides— the projectionist up in the booth threw the slides on the screen, while you were downstairs at the piano, playing the song and singing it with the audience. That's till eleven. *Now* you make the cafés and rathskellers! . . . That's the way songs were made, back in the 1912–13s."

Dockstader's Minstrels. Out in Chicago, Emma Carus, a variety star, made it part of her act.

Considering the relaxed tempo of the day, and the size of the audiences which heard "Alexander's Ragtime Band"—for that is the song Miss Carus was plugging—its eventual success was amazingly immediate. And the word "hit" cannot begin to describe its impact. "Alexander's Ragtime Band" has to be considered the keystone work of a whole new trend in American music. Those infectious lyrics which announced the arrival of jazz were not only spread across our entire continent, but were rapidly exported across the Atlantic, to let all of Europe in on what was happening.

Berlin's output over the twelve months of 1912 was as prodigious as that of the prior year, but a certain amount of variation had begun to creep into his subject matter. His favorite theme—American ragtime—was duly celebrated with "Ragtime Soldier Man," "Ragtime Jockey Man," "That Mysterious Rag," and "Ragtime Mocking Bird," to name but a few. Current events, however, were moving into the fore. There was "Keep Away from the Fellow Who Owns an Automobile" and "I Was Aviating Around." The vast area that lies below the Mason-and-Dixon line, which all native New York songwriters used to call "de Souf," was saluted with "When That Midnight Choo-Choo Leaves for Alabam —All Aboard, All Aboard!" Berlin tried his hand successfully with comedy, in "In My Harem," and with that marvelously wry lover's complaint, "All Night Long She Calls Me Snooky Ookums."

There was yet another song, one which has since become a permanent part of the repertoire of Yale's Whiffenpoofs. It is a peculiar work, amiably chauvinistic in its simple-minded way, called "Those Pullman Porters on Parade." (The song was written in collaboration with Maurice Abrahams, who also wrote "Ragtime Cowboy Joe" and was to be the husband of the great vaudeville star Belle Baker. Contractual clauses kept Berlin's output exclusively at Watterson and Snyder, so you will not find Berlin's name on this song issued by another publisher, but you will find the credit "Ren G. May." With this clever anagram he left his mark. "Ren G. May" is an anagram for Germany.)

In 1913 the very successful composer fell in love with a beautiful young girl named Dorothy Goetz, the sister of E. Ray Goetz, the songwriter. The couple were married and went off to Cuba on their honeymoon. Upon their return to New York, the bride suddenly became ill and, within a very short time, died. Shocked into despair, Berlin was able to express himself in only one fashion; he wrote a haunting and heart-felt ballad, "When I Lost You."

For the first time Berlin was drawing on his own emotions, rather than commenting on fads. It would not be the last time; when the public responded to the simple lines of "When I Lost You," it was teaching Berlin a valuable lesson. Simplicity + honesty + truth = hit. He was to employ that formula for the next half-century.

A year or so later Berlin went to London to embark upon a triumphant vaudeville tour, singing his own songs to the English audiences. The legend goes that the young American songwriter was so stimulated by the sights and sounds of London that he sat up until four A.M. in his hotel room on that first night of his stay, and dashed off a song called "That International Rag." He sang it the next night at his opening performance. The event was properly celebrated by the press—Berlin had already developed his knack for gaining publicity—

and the song went on to become, as its author had predicted in his lyric, an international smash.*

In December 1914, at the ripe old age of twenty-six, Berlin did his first complete score for a Broadway show. For this solo venture, which starred Vernon and Irene Castle and was called *Watch Your Step*, the composer wrote no less than twenty numbers. One of those 1914 efforts has shown remarkable staying power; it is an intricate duet in which the lead melody, a very clear line, is sung to a patter-lyric counterpoint. Singers like Bing Crosby obviously enjoy singing it as much as their audiences enjoy listening to it; it's called "Play a Simple Melody."†

Another song in *Watch Your Step* was called "We'll Settle Down in a One-Horse Town." It may serve to illustrate how much slower in 1914 was the process of exploiting popular songs, as compared to our high-speed electronic era. In conversation last year Ira Gershwin fell to discussing the simpler era in which he had grown up. "We lived in a brownstone down on the Lower East Side, above a doctor," he recalled. "And I noticed a man walking down the street—I was looking out the window on Second Avenue—and he was whistling 'Then We'll Settle Down, Dear, in a One-Horse Town, Dear.' I said, 'He's from *uptown!*' Because I had seen that show—it was Irving Berlin's first complete show. I went with George, and we sat in the second balcony at the New Amsterdam. And it took a *year*—this was 1915—before that song came downtown. He was whistling it—that meant there was somebody else on the East Side who knew that song. Oh, it was a different world, entirely. In those days, if a song did become popular—one like, say, 'How're You Gonna Keep 'Em Down on the Farm?'—it was good for three or four years."

The years prior to the U.S. entry into World War I were extremely busy ones for Berlin. Not only did he continue to turn out popular songs and dance

* Woollcott reported that on Berlin's trip to London, "He hailed a cab at Victoria Station to drive to his hotel. The wisp of a newsboy who opened the cab door for him on the odd chance of getting a penny for that unsolicited attention is probably wondering to this day . . . why the mad young American that day gave him a sovereign for his pains. Ever afterwards he made a special point of opening cab doors for people who looked as if they had come from America, but the miracle never happened again. Like Dr. Jekyll, he had been working with an unknown ingredient. He had, as it happened, been whistling 'Alexander's Ragtime Band.' "

† Thirty-six years later Berlin was to write the score for the Broadway show *Call Me Madam*. According to George Abbott, who directed the show, he mentioned to Berlin during the out-of-town tryout that he felt the need for a second-act duet for their star, Ethel Merman, to sing with the juvenile lead, Russell Nype. "Something catchy, like 'Play a Simple Melody,' " suggested Abbott. "I've always loved that song," At the same time, he conceded that such an intricate counterpoint duet was as difficult to create as anything he could think of.

Berlin disappeared into his hotel room, and went straight to his upright piano. The following day Russel Crouse, co-author of the book, came bleary-eyed into a rewrite conference. Crouse explained that he had the room below Berlin's and he'd been kept up all night by the tinkling of Berlin's piano. "But don't worry," he said, between yawns. "What kept me awake sounds awfully good."

Berlin emerged shortly with a completed duet, the scheme of which was exactly what Abbott had suggested. The song was "You're Just in Love (I Hear Singing and There's No One There)," and, as performed by Miss Merman and Mr. Nype, it promptly became the second-act show-stopper of everyone's fondest dreams.

numbers by the armful, but he now had made the legitimate theatre his stamping (or should it be stomping?) ground. In 1915 another Charles B. Dillingham show, *Stop! Look! Listen!*, starred Gaby Deslys, and had its audiences humming "I Love a Piano" and "The Girl on the Magazine Cover." The following year Berlin and the other reigning composer of the day, Victor Herbert, jointly contributed the score to a revue called *The Century Girl*, which starred Elsie Janis and Van and Schenck. In 1917 there were two shows—one with George M. Cohan called *The Cohan Revue of 1918*, and another called *Dance and Grow Thin*.

But by 1918 we were fully engaged in the war that would end all wars. And of all the men drafted to serve in Uncle Sam's fighting forces, who could have been less likely doughboy material than a thirty-year-old songwriter whose prior skirmishes had been fought not with hostile enemies but with critics and audiences, far from No-Man's-Land, in theatres and cafés?

What Berlin's draft board did not know, when it pulled his number from the glass bowl and sent him off for induction, was that the Army wasn't gaining another fighting man; it was enlisting what was to be the most powerful one-man entertainment force ever to don khaki.

Arriving at Camp Upton, then known as Yaphank, the new draftee proceeded to defy Army protocol—which from time immemorial has suggested that a doughboy should keep his bowels open and his mouth shut. Listen to old friend Harry Ruby, who was also on the scene:

"I can tell you how *Yip, Yip, Yaphank* started. It's amazing. I tell these stories and people think I'm making it up. I don't have to make 'em up—they're too good the way they *happened!*

"Berlin gets into the Army at Upton, and now he's getting up with all the other soldiers, five A.M.! Irving had never before gone to bed before two or three in the morning. He would work until two, three, and then sleep, and get up around ten. All of a sudden, he's getting up with the birds at five, and he's going out of his mind!

"This is not for him, believe me. So he has to get an angle. Some sort of an angle so he won't have to get up. He goes to see General Bell. Now, you have to know that this is 1918 and Berlin is already a famous man. He asks to see the General, and he gets in, and the General says, 'Yes, Berlin, what is it?' And Berlin says, 'I have an idea and I wonder what you think of it.' 'Go ahead,' says the General. 'General,' says Berlin, 'do you know how many people are in this Army who are from show business? The camp is full of them. Fine actors, vaudeville headliners like Dan Healey, acrobats, singers—you never saw anything like it. Why don't we do a show with all these people? We could even play it on Broadway in one of the theatres—boost morale, help recruiting, everything!'

"Well, the General thinks that's a fine idea, and he's all for it, and he wants to know how they'll do it, and Berlin says he'll write it. 'But here's the thing, General,' he says. 'I write at night. Sometimes I work all night when I get an idea. And I couldn't do that if I had to get up in the morning at five, you understand.' 'Why, you don't have to get up at five,' says the General. 'You just forget about all that. *You write this show.*'

"Berlin sends for me. I was working for his firm, Watterson, Berlin and Snyder—by that time he was a full partner. They called me in and said, 'Irving Berlin wants you to be his pianist. He wants you to go out to Upton and live there and work for him.' It was a big thrill for me, I can tell you.

"You see, he always had a piano player to take down his melodies—at one time he had four of them working for him, just to take down his songs. He'd come up to me in the morning while I was out there at Yaphank with him, and he'd say, 'Harry, got a pencil and some music paper?' and I'd say sure, and he'd say, 'Take this down,' and sing me a melody—some song that's become a classic now. I'd take it all down for him, and I'd ask him, 'When the hell did you write *that?*' and he'd say, 'Oh, I was up all night. Do you like it?' And I'd say it was great, and I'd play it back for him to hear what he'd dictated—and he'd listen, and he'd say, 'You got one chord wrong in there.' And he'd be right—he couldn't *play* the chord, but he could *hear* it all right!*

"I tell you, it's hard for me to put down on paper this man's talent in words. Writing about him is almost impossible. I wrote Berlin once and I said, 'The only word I can find to express your talent is *uncanny.*' And I still think so. No education, no schooling. No music. Sure, his fingers know how to play the piano, and he's self-taught—but he learned on the *black keys!*

"Here's my big regret, schmuck that I was—why didn't I hang on to those lead sheets I was taking down for him? Today I wouldn't part with them for half a million bucks. 'Oh, How I Hate to Get Up in the Morning,' 'Poor Little Me, I'm on KP,' 'You Can Always Find a Little Sunshine in the YMCA.' He even wrote 'Mandy' out there, and put it in the show for a minstrel number. I took 'em all down, wrote harmonies for his chords, gave them to the arranger who was doing the orchestral parts, and then I forgot about 'em—can you believe it? Even Irving's 'God Bless America.' I did the original lead sheet. Of course, that wasn't in the show. He took it out, and for twenty years it stayed in his trunk.

"As a matter of fact, I'm partly responsible for 'God Bless America' being taken out of *Yip, Yip, Yaphank,*" admitted Ruby, smiling mischievously. "See, there were so many patriotic songs coming out everywhere at that time. It was 1918, and every songwriter was pouring them out. He'd already written several patriotic numbers for the show, and then, when he brought in 'God Bless America,' I took it down for him, and I said, 'Geez, *another* one?' And I guess Irving took me seriously. He put it away.†

* An echo of Robert Russell Bennett's comment.

† I was once a first-hand witness to this highly tuned inner sonar system of Berlin's. In the pre-Christmas season of 1942 Berlin was on tour with his second soldier show, *This Is the Army.* Earlier that year he had written the score for the picture *Holiday Inn,* and among the songs was the famous Bing Crosby number "White Christmas." When the Academy Awards were handed out, an Oscar went to Berlin for this lovely ballad.

With Christmas 1942 approaching, with GIs being shipped out to bases overseas, there began to be reports of a strange phenomenon. Armed Forces Radio Service was receiving requests from servicemen all over the world for "White Christmas." Something imbedded in the words to that song seemed to spark a spontaneous expression of their homesickness in this, the first winter of our global war.

At the request of the news servces, Berlin held a press conference in Cincinnati. The reporters wished to know if Berlin thought that his "White Christmas" was on its way to becoming the classic song of this war, much as "Oh, How I Hate to Get Up in the Morning" had registered with the doughboys of 1918.

That, said Berlin, was not up to him to decide. He was, of course, pleased and touched that our fighting men responded to his ballad, but as for posterity, well, only posterity ruled on such questions.

One of the newsmen present asked if Berlin would oblige those assembled by singing "White Christmas." Berlin obliged. He sat down at his upright piano—his most

"Twenty years go by. I'm in Hollywood now, writing movie scores with my partner Bert Kalmar, and it's 1938. Out of the blue, I get this wire from Berlin—all it said was: BE SURE TO LISTEN TO KATE SMITH TONIGHT ON THE RADIO. I said to my wife Eileen, 'What's this all about?' And she said, 'I don't know, but you know Irving. There must be a reason.' So that night we tune in Kate's program, and on the air she introduces a song by Irving Berlin—'God Bless America'! And the audience in the studio goes crazy. And Eileen says, 'That's the same song you transcribed for him—no wonder he wanted you to listen!'

"You see, he'd figured, by 1938, with all the trouble in Europe and those dictatorships—Hitler and Mussolini—that the mood of the country was changing, and that we could use a little patriotism. He was so right. As I said before, his sense of what the people will want is uncanny.

"Oh, sure, Irving can be tough. A very tough businessman. But underneath, he's a warm human being. He wrote me a couple of months ago and said, 'Of all the songs I've written, "God Bless America" is the closest one to my heart.' You know he's turned over all the royalties to the Girl Scouts of America—and I think he said that to date they've received over $350,000 from that song.

"And do you know what he did just the other day? He bound up in leather all the sheet music from *Yip, Yip, Yaphank* and sent it out here to me . . . so I'd finally have all those numbers I transcribed for him in 1918 at Camp Upton."

The war ended, and Berlin hurried back to civilian life, the music business, and Broadway.

His first venture was the *Ziegfeld Follies of 1919* and the cast included Eddie Cantor, Bert Williams, Van and Schenck, and that delightful young dancing star Marilyn Miller. "Mandy" was demobilized from the Army and restaged as a splashy minstrel-show number in which Miss Miller re-created that great

basic piece of luggage—and proceeded, in his small voice, to sing.

In the film *Holiday Inn,* Crosby sings the song in a sun-drenched California background. The verse to the song describes the Beverly Hills scenery, cum orange trees and palms.

As Berlin sang this verse, several of the newsmen glanced at each other in almost imperceptible reaction to the words. Beverly Hills, orange trees, L.A.? For GIs in foxholes? It didn't quite work, did it?

But when Berlin finished his verse and got into the chorus, the universal sentiment of the song filled that small hotel room. When he finished, on that cold December night in Cincinnati, his audience broke into spontaneous applause.

A few moments later, when the last reporter had gone off to file his story, Berlin made directly for the telephone and called New York to speak to his professional manager, Saul Bourne.

"I want you to cut the verse out of the sheet music of 'White Christmas,' " he instructed "From now on, that song goes without a verse. That's an order."

Which may serve to explain why you can hear that verse when Bing Crosby launches into "White Christmas" on the Late Show. But on the official sheet music of the song, which since 1942 has sold millions of copies, you will not find it.

When I reminded Mr. Berlin of this incident almost thirty years later, it caused him to laugh. "Sure, I cut the verse," he said. "You know what happened? The music jobbers who handled sheet music all over the country wrote in and complained like hell—they figured we were cheating them out of a verse!"

star George Primrose. Eddie Cantor scored with Berlin's "You'd Be Surprised," and Bert Williams had a number which Berlin wrote with Rennold Wolf, a wry comment on the oncoming Prohibition era which prophetically warned "You Cannot Make Your Shimmy Shake on Tea."

Ziegfeld, who specialized in filling his stage with parades of beautiful girls, asked Berlin to furnish this production with some sort of musical number to accompany the sedate parade of "long-stemmed American beauties." Berlin obliged by quickly writing another song. Half a century later that simple statement of his is still standard entrance music for displays of femininity in our society. Can one imagine a fashion show, or a beauty parade, being held without "A Pretty Girl Is Like a Melody" being played in the background?

Then came the building of the Music Box Theatre.

Fifty years later, in 1971, Berlin recalled how that theatre had come to be, in an interview with Mel Gussow of the *New York Times*.

He said that in 1919 Sam Harris, the producer (and an old friend from the Lower East Side), said to him, "I may build a theatre." Berlin responded, "If you ever do, I have a great name for it—The Music Box."

A year later Harris said to him, "I bought a hundred feet of the Astor property on 45th Street. You're my partner."

Berlin went to the motion-picture producer Joseph M. Schenck—they had been friends since the days when Schenck had been a clerk in a drugstore while Berlin was a singing waiter on the Bowery—and said, "Joe, I'm in trouble."

"Who's the girl?"

"Not a girl, a theatre."

Said Schenck, "Why do you want me?"

Said Berlin, "You're my partner."

Schenck put up half of Berlin's half, and the theatre was built as an elegant, intimate musical house. "It stinks from class," Berlin remembers Sam Bernard, the comedian, as having commented. On September 22, 1921, the Music Box opened with the first edition of *Irving Berlin's Music Box Revue*, starring William Collier, Florence Moore, and Irving Berlin.

After the opening, reported Berlin, "Sam [Harris] and I were in a room at the Hotel Astor. Very frightened men. We spent more money than we should have on the theatre [$930,000, in 1920 dollars]. But the notices were ecstatic. The show-stopper was 'Say It with Music,' which became the theme song of the show and of the theatre."

The Music Box proved to be a lucrative investment except during the Depression, but he and Harris stubbornly held on, and soon *Of Thee I Sing* bailed them out.

The second edition of *The Music Box Revue* offered another lovely Berlin ballad, "Lady of the Evening," and a double-time rousing finale, "Pack Up Your Sins and Go to the Devil." These were opulent, lavish shows, where audiences which paid $5.50 per ticket were treated to talented casts in spectacular production numbers. When, in the third *Music Box Revue*, young Grace Moore sang "An Orange Grove in California," the audience was sprayed with orange scent. It was in that same edition that a Harvard graduate turned drama critic and humorist, Robert C. Benchley, made his stage debut. His "act" was a monologue of his own creation called "The Treasurer's Report," a deathless parody on those fumbling speeches delivered at annual meetings by ineffectual clubman types.

"Bob had done it first at a little show that was put on by members of the

Algonquin Round Table, most of whom were friends of ours," recalled Donald Ogden Stewart, Benchley's close friend and fellow humorist. "There had been a recent production on Broadway called *Chauve Souris*, so we called ours *No Siree!* That should give you a general idea of the level of the humor.

"Irving Berlin and Sam Harris came to see the show, and they insisted that Benchley do it professionally. They offered him such a large salary that he finally agreed, and from then on, Benchley had himself another career, as an actor. That was in September 1923. In November I had a birthday party up at Neysa McMein's studio, which she and Dorothy Parker gave me, and Irving Berlin showed up. He brought a bottle or two of champagne along, under his coat, to celebrate. (This was during Prohibition, remember.)

"While we all sat around, celebrating and drinking the champagne, Irving went to the piano and kept on playing the first part of a song he had written. It was called 'What'll I Do?' But he hadn't been able to finish it. He played the part he had over and over, and we all liked it—but the best part of the evening was that after Irving had had enough of his champagne, he was finally able to finish the song that night. So you might say everybody got a present out of that birthday!"

"What'll I Do?" went into the *Music Box Revue* promptly thereafter, and became another Berlin standard. It should also be noted that it was the first of a series of love songs that Berlin wrote for a young lady with whom he had recently fallen in love. She was Ellin Mackay, the beautiful and talented daughter of Clarence Mackay, a wealthy businessman.

The story of their romance could easily have been derived from a current operetta. Mackay bitterly opposed any union between his socialite daughter and a man whom he had to consider a *parvenu* of the most obvious sort—an upstart Russian immigrant's son who had written and sung his way out of the East Side slums and the Bowery cafés to a certain notoriety as a songwriter, whose clubs weren't Union League and Piping Rock, but Lindy's Restaurant and the Friars, and whose wealth was *nouveau* to the last dollar.*

In the fourth *Music Box Revue* another of Berlin's love songs to Ellin Mackay was interpolated after the show's official opening—the ballad "All Alone." The courtship of Miss Mackay, despite all the obstacles which her father was able to place in its path, persevered. Berlin wrote a third love song to his lady, this time calling it "Remember." Never has the anguish of love been so publicly celebrated. All of America (as well as large sections of Great Britain) was serenading Miss Mackay by proxy, along with Berlin.

When Miss Mackay defied parental disapproval and married Berlin, he made her a wedding present of—what else could a songwriter bestow upon his beloved?—a new love song: "Always." A magnanimous gesture not only toward the new Mrs. Berlin but also toward the American populace, which happily played it on the piano, sang it, and cranked it up on the parlor phonograph.†

* During the darkest days of the Depression, Berlin would be able to salvage his father-in-law's fortunes with a loan of one million dollars in cash, thereby adding the perfect O. Henry ironic twist to the third act of the story.

† In the *Dramatists Guild Quarterly*, 1967, there appeared a note. "Here is Irving Berlin's 'Always' as it might have been written by Lorenz Hart. Its authorship in the 1920's is a mystery, although Mr. Berlin advises: 'I've known about this parody. Many

It may have been the euphoria of happily wedded bliss that underscored the writing of Berlin's subsequent hit, "Blue Skies," but its public introduction in December 1926 perhaps has less to do with inspiration than with a certain amount of desperation.

Belle Baker, the vaudeville star, had been signed by Florenz Ziegfeld to star in a Broadway musical called *Betsy*. "How my mother came to do that number is a saga in itself," recalled Herbert Baker, a film and TV comedy writer, lately responsible for the *Flip Wilson Show*.

"*Betsy* had a score by Richard Rodgers and Lorenz Hart, who were even then very clever and accomplished men with a raft of hits to their credit, but when they did this score, they'd concentrated on songs that would fit into the book—what there was of it. But as my mother said—and she said it a lot, believe me—there wasn't a 'Belle Baker song' in the score. By that, she meant something which she could really belt out to her audience. Remember, in those days microphones didn't exist. A performer sang—and my mother wanted something she could *sing*.

"*Betsy* tried out in Boston, and it did fairly well, but it wasn't anywhere near a hit. The night before Belle opened on Broadway, she was brooding because she felt she was missing that one big song, so she picked up the phone and she called Irving Berlin.

"She'd introduced a lot of Berlin songs before. You have to understand that my mother, who'd broken into show business when she was only nine, had become one of the most important 'plugs' that a songwriter could have. Berlin had given her such fantastic successes as 'Russian Lullaby' and 'Remember' and 'Always' and even comedy material—'Cohen Owes Me Ninety-seven Dollars.' So you can readily understand how much faith she placed in the man.

"She said, 'Irving, I'm opening in this show tomorrow night, and there isn't a Belle Baker song in the score, and I'm so miserable—what can I do?'

"Berlin said, 'Belle, I'll be very honest with you. All I have is a song in

years ago, the late Buddy De Sylva, who I think wrote it, sang it to me.'

> *I'll be loving you*
> *Always*
> *Both in very big, and*
> *Small ways.*
> *With a love as grand*
> *As Paul Whiteman's band*
> *And 'twill weigh as much as*
> *Paul weighs,*
> *Always.*
> *In saloons and drab*
> *Hallways*
> *You are what I'll grab*
> *Always.*
> *See how I dispense*
> *Rhymes that are immense,*
> *But do they make sense?*
> *Not always.*

my trunk. I've often thought it would be great for you, but I never got around to finishing it.'

"She said, 'Irving, please come over here. Maury* is here. We'll feed you, and he'll help—because even something half finished by you is better than what I've got now, which is nothing!'

"Berlin agreed to come over, and my mother sent me off to bed.

"Now, try to imagine what it's like to be six years old, and trying to get to sleep, and constantly being awakened by the sound of four hands on the piano in the living room. My father was playing along with Berlin—playing, over and over again, the first eight bars of 'Blue Skies.' That's all Berlin had. Da, da—da-da-da-*da!* Da da da *di* da—da da *da!* Over and over it went, that same refrain, pounded out on the piano from our living room. He couldn't get the middle eight. The first time I went out to complain I couldn't sleep, I remember my mother saying, 'Sweetheart, darling, I know it's annoying, but *try* to get to sleep.'

"The second time I went out, my father turned around from the piano— he was ordinarily a very gentle man—and he said, 'Get out of here or I'll kill you.'

"I remember Berlin turning around from the piano and looking at me, and then saying, 'Say, Herbie's getting fat, isn't he?' and my mother saying, 'Never mind him, Irving, *get back to the song!*'

"Finally, I did doze off, and I must have slept until about six in the morning, and then I was awakened by shouting from the living room, and this I remember distinctly—I heard the two men playing the middle eight-bar bridge of 'Blue Skies.'

Berlin had finally gotten the strain he wanted, and he'd also written the lyric to go with it. It had taken all night, but he had the middle eight bars he needed.†

"It's now about seven in the morning, and the show is due to open that night. My mother gets on the phone and calls Florenz Ziegfeld. She wakes him up and she tells him that Irving Berlin has been up all night working on a song for her, and it's finished, and it's great, and she wants to sing it tonight, and if she can't sing it tonight, she doesn't want to open in the show.

"You have to realize that there was a big problem here. *Two.* Rodgers and Hart. They had a contract with Ziegfeld that stipulated specifically that there would be no interpolations of songs by other composers in this show. So Ziegfeld said, 'Belle, you can do it—but, for God's sake, don't tell Rodgers or Hart.'

"I went to the opening that night. I was up in the balcony. At about eleven my mother came out and she sang 'Blue Skies' for the first time. The audience went crazy. They really had been starved all night for her to do one like that.

---

* The close friendship of Berlin and Maurice Abrahams, Herbert's father, dated back to 1908, when the two had written a song called "Queenie, My Own." Abrahams was a first-rate man of music who often accompanied his wife onstage and rehearsed her orchestral accompaniments when she toured.

† Some years later in an interview about writing songs, Noel Coward said, "Watch that middle eight! There's a theme to the melody, always, a main theme. Well, those middle eight bars put it over, they're the solid core. I say—watch that middle eight. The best exponent of that is Berlin, Irving. That chap is the grandest of the middle-eight boys."

Would you believe that the audience made her sing that song over and over again, twenty-four times? And that on the twenty-third reprise she forgot the lyrics? Berlin stood up—he was sitting down in the front row—and he threw her the words—and they finished the next chorus singing together!

"*Betsy* got fair notices, and it ran for a while. But 'Blue Skies' became a terrific hit . . . and Rodgers and Hart didn't speak to my mother for the next twelve years."

Al Jolson sang "Blue Skies" in *The Jazz Singer*, the first talking picture with music that the Warner Brothers made with their new Vitaphone process, in 1927. In succeeding years the musical film was to become Berlin's widest-ranging and most successful plug, but for the first few years of sound's infant existence he sat back and allowed others to experiment with the noisy brat.

True, in 1928 he dabbled with "theme songs"—to a Vilma Banky epic called *The Awakening* he contributed "Marie." Later it was to be adopted by Tommy Dorsey as *his* song—at a somewhat more rapid beat than Miss Banky's. When America's Sweetheart, Mary Pickford, tried her first "talkie," *Coquette*, it was with a Berlin tune of the same name for Mary's personal security blanket. In contrast, when Lupe Velez starred in *Lady of the Pavements*, her theme song had nothing to do with sidewalks; instead Berlin had Miss Velez ask (somewhat rhetorically), "Where Is the Song of Songs for Me?"

The following year Berlin provided Harry (Yeth-thir!) Richman with one of that singer's biggest hits, the title song to an all-talking, all-singing, all-lisping film, *Puttin' on the Ritz*. And in 1930 he wrote a score for his old friend Al Jolson's follow-up film to *The Jazz Singer*, a little number called (what else?) "Mammy." The film was not to be noted for advancing either Berlin's or Jolson's career, but it did contain Jolie's most autobiographical lyric, "Let Me Sing and I'm Happy."

This was far from Berlin's most fruitful period.* "Irving had a very happy marriage, but he wasn't producing much musically," comments Abel Green. "There were the usual Broadway wise-guys around who said he'd gone society, but that wasn't true at all. He was still going to Lindy's every day and seeing the boys there, but nothing much was coming out. Maybe it was just a dry spell. It can happen to anybody, even to as talented a man as Irving."

Whatever the cause of his temporary slow-down, there is no problem in pinpointing the time when Berlin's creative oil well began to gush again. It was 1932, the very depth of the Depression. A dire period for the populace, but for Berlin a vintage year. In that one year, not only did he write "Say It Isn't So" and "How Deep Is the Ocean (How High Is the Sky)?"—two of his most effective torch songs—but he also did the score for a sharp-edged, satiric Broadway musical, *Face the Music*, in which were the lilting "Soft Lights and Sweet Music" as well as a gay chin-up song which attempted to cheer a depressed world, "Let's Have Another Cup of Coffee."

---

* Ever since the early days when he wrote "Alexander's Ragtime Band," the popular Broadway legend about Berlin had it that his enormous output was not solely his but that he was assisted by "a little colored boy," whom he kept hidden. It was about this time, when Berlin was producing far less than usual, that a Lindy wag stopped him on the street to ask, "What's the matter, Irving, has the little colored boy been sick?" "No," snapped Berlin. "He's dead."

Face the Music proved to be simply a warm-up session for what was to come in 1933—the brilliant revue *As Thousands Cheer*, at the Music Box, which amply demonstrated that the old master was back at the top of his form.

"I'll never forget when I was a kid, just out of Princeton, and acting in *She Loves Me Not*," said Joshua Logan. "It was in the summertime, when they opened the theatre doors to cool the house off—no air-conditioning in those days. And I could look onto the stage of the Music Box next door to us and watch *As Thousands Cheer*. He had a great opening chorus—it was a topical show, based on all the headlines of the day.

"Now, having given the audience 'Heat Wave' and 'Supper Time' and a batch of other marvelous songs, he came up with a finale. Not 'Easter Parade,' which ended the first act—and which anyone else would have cheerfully reprised and let it go at that—but he had the chorus come out at the end of the show with lyrics to the effect that '*We can't bring the curtain down until we've sung you the hit song.*' And *that's* where he introduced 'Not for All the Rice in China'—in the very closing minutes of the show. What a way to bring down a curtain!"

With that triumph behind him, Berlin was prepared to do labors for the musical films—on his own terms. The Hollywood studios plied him with offers. Once again he was "hot." What would Berlin deign to do? He chose the hard way, as usual. He crafted an entirely original score for the brightest pair of dancing stars who ever hoofed across the screen, Fred Astaire and Ginger Rogers.

In his first film, *Top Hat*, he provided them with the title song, with "Cheek to Cheek," "Isn't This a Lovely Day (to Be Caught in the Rain)?," "No Strings," and "The Piccolino." The following year he replenished RKO's coffers with another shower of box-office takings when he did the score for the next Astaire-and-Rogers film, *Follow the Fleet*, again with a ship's roster of Hit Parade numbers.

"Nobody can sell you better than a great agent," says Abel Green. "That's why the biggest talents need agents. But Irving is the greatest agent in the world. He can sell himself like Fort Knox. It's amazing how he sold himself, especially to all those so-called Hollywood moguls. Toughies like Sam Goldwyn, Darryl Zanuck, Louis B. Mayer—he had the Indian sign on all of them. His attitude was, 'So you want to use my songs? You're lucky to have them! You could have been stuck with some junk; instead, you're getting the *best!*' "

In the light of the '30s and '40s in Hollywood, such an attitude cannot be considered arrogance. Berlin was merely countering their stupidities with his own self-confidence. Producers had never been known for their humility, and when it came to the question of supplying music to their new toy, the film musical, more often than not they exhibited abysmal ignorance. "Everyone in this town," complained Alfred Newman, one of Hollywood's leading musical directors, "has two businesses—his own, and music."

Someone, then, had to stand firm on questions of talent and taste. Too many of his fellows were being pushed around by know-nothings. Not Berlin. He had long since earned the right to put the Beverly Hills nabobs in their places, and he did so. The late Robert Emmett Dolan, a long-time friend who was later to produce Berlin's musical *White Christmas* for Paramount, liked to tell of the time when a producer for a rival studio stopped Berlin at lunch to inquire what Berlin would charge to let one, only one, of his songs be included in the man's current film. Berlin shrugged him off. "You couldn't afford it," he said.

Underlying everything he did was a basic desire to go first-cabin in all departments. "Irving has always had a special respect for quality," says Abel Green affectionately. "He's seen through the fakery and the dross, and goes directly for the best."

So for the next few years out West he called the tunes—and they were his own. Not only did he score high marks for *On the Avenue* at Fox, and for *Carefree*, his third Astaire-and-Rogers musical, but then he came up with his canniest formula. For Darryl Zanuck he created a mammoth project, *Alexander's Ragtime Band*, in which the screen echoed to the strains of nearly thirty Berlin "oldies," as well as three new songs. Thus he became the first composer to demonstrate that incredible nostalgic value of popular music of the past. One of his own titles says it—"An Old Fashioned Song Always Is New." In later years, golden hits from the Berlin catalog were to grace the sound tracks of *Holiday Inn, Blue Skies, White Christmas,* and *There's No Business Like Show Business.* If there was ever such an item as "insurance"—a guarantee of a film's eventual success at the box office—then for years fortunate producers could buy it with a package of Berlin "standards."

But Hollywood was never home to Berlin. It was always a nice place to visit, or in which to work and then hum all the way to the bank . . . a New York bank. The California sun could be shining, but he was dreaming of a Broadway Christmas. He returned to the theatre with another smash musical-comedy score, this time *Louisiana Purchase*, produced by his fellow songwriter, the late B. G. De Sylva. Later, when De Sylva became head of Paramount, he lured Berlin back to the Coast to make the film version of his own show. And the following year there was the film *Holiday Inn* for Bing Crosby and Fred Astaire, a musical which celebrated each holiday of the year with a different Berlin song.

When World War II exploded on the American scene, Berlin was fifty-three years old. Far too old to be drafted again, he promptly reversed the process. He drafted the entire U.S. Army.

Within a brief space of weeks, in the spring of 1942, Berlin, with his astonishing sense of producing the perfectly right attraction for the perfectly right audience at the perfectly right time, had devised the idea of a new soldier show, an updated *Yip, Yip, Yaphank.* Its purpose would be to boost morale, both on the home front and in Army camps and hospitals. Profits from ticket sales (eventually they would total a staggering $10,000,000) would accrue to Army Emergency Relief, a service charity.

His idea was enthusiastically backed by Major General Irving Phillipson of the 2nd Service Command, on Governor's Island, and endorsed by General George Marshall. With the Commanding General of the Army as his quondam executive producer, and the entire resources of the Pentagon to draw upon, there was only one thing left for Berlin to do. Just as he had done a quarter-century before, he moved out to old Yaphank—now Upton. He brought to the camp some clean linen, music paper, and his battered upright piano, and started writing a show at top speed.

For once the much maligned Army classification system did its job. From all over the country it produced some three hundred servicemen. GIs now, they had formerly been actors, dancers, singers, stagehands, electricians, set designers, musicians, arrangers, box-office men, even press agents. In the detachment were such talents as Burl Ives, Gary Merrill, Henry Jones, Anthony Ross, dance director Robert Sidney, comics Julie Oshins and Hank Henry and James MacColl.

Working on the directorial side were Ezra Stone, the former "Henry Aldrich" of radio, and Joshua Logan.

As anybody will corroborate who was fortunate enough to secure an opening-night ticket to the Broadway Theatre on July 4, 1942, or to any performance thereafter, *This Is the Army* was a blockbuster of a GI show. It had comedy, a fine score, and an abundance of that indefinable ingredient called showmanship, Berlin-style.

Chauvinist, in retrospect perhaps oversimplistic, and certainly drenched in sentiment, *This Is the Army* remains a supreme expression of superb musical-comedy agitprop. Consider its ingredients. A brisk theme song, "This Is the Army, Mr. Jones." Solid comedy, "The Army's Made a Man Out of Me" and a burlesque, "Ladies of the Chorus." Two lilting ballads, "I'm Getting Tired So I Can Sleep" and—after a fond take-off on that service club on 44th Street—"I Lost My Heart at the Stage Door Canteen." A topical song about the Russian winter, and a great dance number about black GIs. Fraternal salutes to other branches of the service, "American Eagles" and "How About a Cheer for the Navy?" Then, splashed across the wide stage, a military minstrel show, topped off by Berlin's famous old standard "Mandy."

But it was near eleven P.M., in the next-to-closing slot, that Berlin personally provided his own show-stopper. The curtains parted to reveal a cadre of middle-aged men, somewhat gray but still expert at close-order drill—members of the original cast of *Yip, Yip, Yaphank*. When they had finished their routine, then came roll call. "Berlin?" bellowed the drill sergeant. No answer.

"Ber-*lin!*"

"Here!" replied a piping voice, and the spotlight picked up the interior of a GI pup tent. There, seated meekly on his cot, unhappily blinking in his 1918 OD's, was ex-doughboy Berlin, re-creating *his* performance of 1918.

As he rose and came downstage, audiences greeted him with rolling breakers of applause that drowned out the first few words of the verse of his famous old song, and on into two choruses of "Oh, How I Hate to Get Up in the Morning." The resultant ovation sounded like Niagara Falls.

A master stroke of showmanship, a rare compound of nostalgia, patriotism, and superb schmaltz. Certainly it worked. Who else has been so successful in learning to play the keys of his country's emotions? "I don't want to write a nation's laws," goes the old truism. "Just let me write its songs."

By the summer of 1943 the film version of the show was completed out in California, the first musical film ever to star a future senator from California, George Murphy, as well as the state's future governor, Ronald Reagan.

But when the picture reached the movie houses in 1943, Berlin and his soldier troupe weren't around to count the huge grosses. They had long since departed for other theatres overseas. For the next year and a half the *TITA* unit was to entertain GIs and sailors and marines in every fighting front.

"After I staged *This Is the Army*," said director Joshua Logan, "I went off to Officers Candidate School and Intelligence School. I went into the Paratroops, and then I went overseas with an outfit called the 50th Troop Carrier Wing, and we were stationed way up north in a little town in England. I went down to London for the weekend, and I ran into Berlin. He said, 'Are you here? Great! I want you to direct a new thing we're putting into the overseas touring version of the show.' You see, everywhere he went with his show, he kept writing material for various areas—England, Italy, North Africa, the Pacific. Now he had some sort of a new sketch about the WACs—pretty raw, but perfect for the troops. It hadn't yet been put into the show.

"I told him that I couldn't leave my outfit. My general would never let me go; he had a group of men he'd trained, and he wouldn't let anybody out for anything—it would throw the whole unit out of kilter. Berlin nodded and said, 'Oh, that's all right, Josh, I'll get you, I'll get you.'

"So Berlin called General Dwight Eisenhower. And Eisenhower, believe it or not, spoke to General Hap Arnold, who commanded the Air Force! They both requested me, and it went down through channels until it got to *my* general. When the request came down to him, he took a look at it, and then he said, 'Nope.'

"That didn't stop Berlin. He went to the *Navy*. I don't exactly know who, but the top admiral, I'm sure, and that went down through channels again until it got to my general, and again my general said, 'Nope.' I knew all about this; I'd heard.

"Finally, Berlin picked up the telephone and put in a call to my general, *direct*. My general picked up the phone and the voice said, 'General, this is Irving Berlin.'

"The general was so excited, he practically dropped the telephone. Berlin got right to the point. He said, 'General, could I have Logan?'"

"And my general said, 'Yes, *sir!*' "

And then the war was over.

General Motors, U.S. Steel, Du Pont . . . all the major monoliths of American industry rapidly converted to peacetime. Berlin put his 1918 uniform back into mothballs, this time (as one of his martial songs so hopefully put it) for the last time, came back to Broadway and Lindy's and home, reinstalled his upright in his office, and looked around for something new to do.

She—for the next project was to be about a sharp-eyed female—showed up as the result of a set of ironic circumstances. The lady who was in on *Annie Get Your Gun* from its earliest moment of conception is Dorothy Fields, a lyricist of the first rank, and co-author, with her late brother Herbert, of the show's libretto.

"During the war," she remembers, "my late husband did volunteer work down at Penn Station, for Travelers' Aid, from midnight to seven A.M. And one of the ladies told him one night about a kid who'd just come in, a young soldier. Very drunk, he'd been to Coney Island and had kewpie dolls and lamps and every piece of junk you could possibly win. How come? Across his chest he had a row of sharpshooter's medals.

"And as if out of the sky, from Heaven, comes this idea. Because my brother and I had a commitment to write another show for Mike Todd. Annie Oakley —the *sharpshooter!* With Ethel Merman to play her! So the next day we went to see Mike, to try the idea out on him. And he said, 'Merman? That old——! She'll never work again!'

"We asked him if he'd do it anyway, and he said he wouldn't touch it. So Herbert said to me, 'Okay, we're going to go to somebody else.' Now, there happened to be a meeting at ASCAP after our meeting with Todd, and the first person I saw when I came in was Oscar Hammerstein. He and Dick Rodgers were producing shows then as well as writing them. I said, 'Ockie, what do you think of Ethel Merman as Annie Oakley?' He said, 'We'll do it.' That's all! And then he said, 'Talk to Dick after the meeting.' I talked to Dick, and Dick said the same thing—'We'll do it.'

"Then they both said, 'But can you get up to see Ethel?' She'd just gone to the hospital to have a child, by Caesarean, and she was feeling awful. I had a hell of a time getting into the hospital, but I did, and I went over to her bed and I leaned down and said, 'Merm, what would you think of yourself as Annie Oakley?'

"She looked up from her hospital bed, and blinked, and said, 'I'll do it.' It was as simple as that.

"We wrote the book right away; writing the book was a dream. It's the one show out of all the shows I've done that went so beautifully. Only one thing in the second act—a scene which took place in the old Brevoort Hotel—we later rewrote so many times that it got to be an inside joke with all of us. Whenever somebody said to somebody else, 'What are you going to do tonight?' the answer was, 'Rewrite the Brevoort!'

"Dick and Oscar had gotten in touch with Jerome Kern in Hollywood, and he'd agreed to write the music. I would have done the lyrics. Jerry came to New York. And then he dropped dead—on a street. Unknown. That was the worst week of my life. The worst week of everybody's life. Horrible . . .

"After the funeral, we were all sitting at a restaurant, and we started discussing whom we could get who could possibly replace somebody as gifted as Kern. And Dick finally said, 'Well, I know somebody, but it means that Dorothy can't do the lyrics.' I said, 'I have enough to do with the book. I don't care, who is it?' And he said, 'Irving.' Well, we all thought that was fabulous. We went back to their offices and we called Berlin, and he said, 'Well, I don't know whether I'd want to do a show that isn't "Irving Berlin's whatsoever." '

"So Herbert and I said, 'Irving, sorry, but this is our idea, our play, and it can't be "Irving Berlin's Annie Oakley." ' He said, 'Let me think about it over the weekend. And if I decide that I want to relinquish the billing that I've always had, then we'll talk about it.' He wouldn't read the first act we'd written—he wouldn't let that influence him. Monday he called up and said, 'Yes, I'd like to take a look at it.' He read the first act, and read the outline of the second act. And do you know that in the twelve days after he agreed to do the show, he wrote *five* songs? One of them being 'There's No Business Like Show Business'!"

"After I became involved in the show," said Joshua Logan, "I'd see Berlin every other day. Sometimes while he wrote the score he'd go away to Atlantic City or up to his farm in the Catskills, to work on his lyrics or a second chorus, or to write a new song.

"One day he played us 'Show Business,' and, naturally, we all thought it was simply marvelous. We figured that Buffalo Bill, our leading male character, would sing it, and then Merman, as Annie, would reprise it.

"Berlin was very proud of it. You know, when Irving sings a song in that tiny voice—there's a famous crack somebody once made: 'You have to hug him to hear him.'* But when he sings right into your face, he's *reading* you, studying you every second for your reactions.

"A couple of days later Berlin came in and he sang us a new song we'd been waiting for, 'Who Do You Love, I Hope?' It was for the two young juveniles

---

* The legend attributes this crack to the late comic Joe Frisco.

in the show. We all raved about it. Then Berlin said, 'Oh, by the way, I have the second chorus of 'No Business Like Show Business.' And he sang it, and we said. 'Well, that takes care of *that*, too.' That about wrapped things up, and we were on our way.

"Berlin asked me if I'd drop around to his office that afternoon. He was going to play the score for Hugh Martin, and he wanted me around because he said I organized things and 'excited them.' He didn't have to ask me. I could be around Berlin for the rest of my life. I love to see him work. To me, *he* genuinely represents the excitement of show business.

"Hugh Martin is a pretty respectable composer in his own right—'The Trolley Song' and 'The Boy Next Door,' among others that he did with Ralph Blane—and Martin was very excited by what Berlin played him. Berlin finished the score, but he left out 'There's No Business Like Show Business.'

"I said 'Irving, what's the matter? You left out the finale!'

"He shook his head and said, 'Oh, well, I didn't like the way you all reacted this morning. It didn't register.'

"I protested, 'But we were all so excited to hear your new song. We all reacted that way because we'd already heard "Show Business" and this was its second chorus.'

"He went on shaking his head. 'Yes, but it's a great second chorus, and if you didn't really like it, I'm certain I don't want it in the show.'

"It wasn't petulance. He meant it. I was astounded. I asked him what he'd done with the lead sheet, and he shrugged and said he'd put it away in his files somewhere, and I said, 'Irving! Get it out of those files and sing it for Hugh!' He argued with me, but I kept on insisting, until finally he gave in and went out to his secretary and asked her to dig it out of the files, and do you believe this—*they couldn't find it?*

"They searched and they hunted, arguing back and forth all the while, rummaging through his whole office. Eventually, thank heaven, they came up with his original lead sheet. There wasn't even a copy. Can you imagine—for a good ten or fifteen minutes there, 'Show Business,' that show-stopper, that standard, an absolute classic of popular music, was missing!

"I remember during that preparatory period we'd have meetings where we'd all of us check in and see how we were getting along. I was beginning to wonder why we didn't have two songs for Annie and Frank, our two leading characters. They sang 'They Say That Falling in Love Is Wonderful' in the first act, which was a beautiful song for Merman and Ray Middleton, but in the second act there really was no song that they sang together.

"It was about two or three days before we were actually going into rehearsal. We were all up at Oscar Hammerstein's house on 63rd Street. Berlin was way over on the other side of the room, Oscar and I were on this side, and there were also Lucinda Ballard, our costume designer, Jo Mielziner, our set designer, Helen Tamiris, our choreographer, Dorothy and Herbert Fields, everybody. I said to Oscar in a very low voice, 'Oscar, I'm worried we haven't got enough songs, we need another one for Ethel and Ray.' And he said, just as softly, 'Well, where would it be?' 'I don't know, but I think it should be on Governor's Island, just before the shooting contest in the second act.' He said, 'Listen, Josh, don't bother Irving with that now. Don't bring it up. It'll worry him, and he won't be able to finish his work; so you keep quiet about it—we'll bring it up when the time is right.'

"And just then Berlin, who had suddenly appeared behind Oscar's shoulder, leaned over the two of us and asked, 'Another song?'

"How he knew it, I do not know. Maybe he simply smelled it in the air.

"He said, 'Just a minute, please, everybody quiet. A discussion has just come up about a new song. They think there's got to be one for Annie and Frank. Let's have a conference right now. If I'm going to write a song, I have to know what *kind* of a song.'

"So there was some discussion—everybody pitched in. Finally Berlin said, 'The only thing that I can possibly think is that if it's before a shooting contest, it has to be some sort of a challenge song. Okay, challenge song. Right?'

"At this point we were all exhausted, and we started to leave. My wife Nedda and I left Oscar's house and we took a cab. Let's see, we were up on 63rd Street, and at this time we were living down at the Lombardy, that's on 56th Street, near Park. As I was unlocking our door at the Lombardy, I heard the telephone ring, and I ran inside to get the phone.

"And Berlin, on the other end, said, 'Hello, Josh—this is Irving. What do you think of this?' And then he sang the whole damned first chorus of 'Anything You Can Do, I Can Do Better'!

"Most amazing thing I ever experienced in my whole life! It couldn't have been more than, at most, fifteen minutes from the time he'd first heard about it to the time he had me on the phone. He'd written the song—the entire first chorus. It was done like that."

Annie Get Your Gun opened on Broadway in 1946 and was a smash hit. Everything worked; the book meshed brilliantly with Berlin's songs. At one point in the first act he performed a musical feat still unduplicated by other composers. Frank, the hero, sings "The Girl That I Marry," which explains his preference in potential brides. Annie answers, without so much as a scene between the two songs, "You Can't Get a Man with a Gun." Two hit songs, back to back. And in addition to the previously celebrated "Show Business" finale and his challenge song, "Anything You Can Do," Berlin provided his cast with "Doin' What Comes Naturally," "I Got Lost in His Arms," the Merman-Middleton duet "They Say That Falling in Love Is Wonderful," a lively song called "I've Got the Sun in the Morning," and the masculine chorus "My Defenses Are Down." All hits, all out of one score. It's a record that still stands. When, in 1966, *Annie* was given a triumphant revival at the New York State Theatre, with Miss Merman again in the lead, Berlin went back to his upright and somewhat gratuitously tossed off still another song for the show, a bit of icing for the cake—a duet called "An Old Fashioned Wedding."

Berlin filled his next years with a steady parade of entertainments—original musical comedies for Broadway and large-scale film musicals.

After the films *Blue Skies* and *Easter Parade,* he came back to Broadway with a libretto written by the late Robert E. Sherwood, one which dealt with erecting the Statue of Liberty in New York harbor. *Miss Liberty* held her torch aloft for most of one season, but it was one of the very few times when American history plus Berlin haven't equaled success.

A year later he returned to the lists with another reliable formula—satire on the current scene—and this time it worked. *Call Me Madam,* with a book by Lindsay and Crouse, featured Ethel Merman as a character loosely drawn from Perle Mesta, the famous Washington, D.C. hostess—in Berlin's words, "The Hostess with the Mostes' on the Ball."

In 1953 Darryl Zanuck produced a successful film version of *Call Me Madam*, with Merman re-creating Mrs. Sally Adams in Technicolor. A year later Berlin conceived two more large-scale entertainments. There was *White Christmas*, at Paramount, in which Bing Crosby and Danny Kaye sang and danced through a full menu of Berlin standards—including "Mandy," produced, for the first time, as an all-*white* minstrel show. Back at Fox, with Zanuck, there was *There's No Business Like Show Business*, with Ethel Merman and the late Marilyn Monroe. That lady's version of a new Berlin song, "After You Get What You Want, You Don't Want It," induced such high temperatures that it melted the Canadian snowscape: north of the border, censors excised it from the film.

Even though that film contained a choice assortment of Berlin standards, dating back to "Alexander's Ragtime Band" and ranging forward through "Lazy" and "Heat Wave" and his old Depression-era ditty "Let's Have Another Cup of Coffee," the story was definitely *not* Berlin's own biography set to music.

Berlin remains the only major American composer whose career was never adapted by the Hollywood studios into an omnibus musical. Abel Green offers an interesting footnote about Berlin's reluctance to be portrayed by another star. "I think," he says, "if Irving ever had a hero, it was Jerome Kern. Do you remember when Hollywood was making all those musical biographies of composers? Cary Grant played Cole Porter, and Robert Alda was George Gershwin, and so on. I used to review them all for *Variety*. Metro had just finished making *Till the Clouds Roll By*, which was supposed to be the life of Jerry Kern. I mentioned to Irving that they were going to screen the picture for me. 'That's one I'd like to see,' he said. So we went up to the Metro office, and when the picture was finished, Irving shook his head. 'Jerry would revolve in his grave,' was all he said."

One more Broadway musical score was to be pounded out on the ancient upright "Buick." In 1962 the late Leland Hayward produced *Mr. President*, with another satiric book by Lindsay and Crouse. If the music and lyrics weren't exactly as overpowering a parade of knockout hits as *Annie's*, they were still first-drawer Berlin. His song "Don't Be Afraid of Romance" floated melodically through the contemporary world of rock-and-roll dissonance to find popularity with record-buyers who still cherish melody. That show and the triumphant revival of *Annie* in 1966 are the latest full-scale Berlin works to have brightened the Broadway scene.

During the mid-'60s Metro-Goldwyn-Mayer announced an Arthur Freed musical project, to be based upon some twenty-odd Berlin "evergreens," and to be called *Say It with Music*. In the lush postwar years such a project would have had exhibitors all over the country rubbing their hands together in greedy anticipation. But the economics of 1968, Hollywood-style, were light-years removed from the old damn-the-cost era. Opulence, nostalgia, spectacle—and Julie Andrews, a reigning star. It might have worked. "But there were three complete changes in the Metro administration while the script was being written," recalls George Axelrod, who wrote the last draft. "And by the time the project was ready to be shot, the studio was practically broke. Too bad; it was a good idea. We'd taken all the problems attendant on making such a big film musical and turned them into the story itself."

Perhaps some enterprising producer will devise a less costly way of re-creating the best of Berlin for contemporary film audiences. But until that happens, all those Berlin classics, on records, tapes, and sheet music, whistled and hummed and sung and danced to for most of the twentieth century, will no doubt survive.

In 1955, half a century after Berlin began writing, *Variety*, the bible of show business, celebrated its first fifty years, and to make that event official, the weekly published a thick Golden Anniversary issue. Inside, on a double-page spread, an advertisement from the Irving Berlin Music Corporation made a jovial comment on the occasion. On a double-page spread appeared the number 50. Imbedded in each numeral were a vast number of Berlin titles, with no comment save the titles themselves. Fifty years' worth of *his* history . . .

The words of his friend Jerome Kern, in a letter to Woollcott back in 1925, say it all. "I once delivered myself of a nifty," wrote Kern. "It was at a dinner in London, and I was asked what, in my opinion, were the chief characteristics of the American nation. I replied that the average United States citizen was perfectly epitomized in Irving Berlin's music. He doesn't attempt to stuff the public's ears with pseudo-original ultra-modernism, but he honestly absorbs the vibrations emanating from the people, manners and life of his time, and in turn, gives these impressions back to the world—simplified, clarified, glorified. In short, what I really want to say, my dear Woollcott, is that Irving Berlin has *no* place in American music, *HE IS AMERICAN MUSIC.*"

And what about Mr. Berlin in 1972?

He is something of a recluse. He spends a great deal of his time at the Berlin farm in the Catskills, or in his Beekman Place home in New York City. He has a small circle of very close friends with whom he keeps in touch by phone. On the occasion of his eighty-second birthday, when one of his friends inquired about his state of mind, he said, "You know, from the neck up, I could do another Broadway show. From the neck down, I'm not so sure."

How does he fill his hours? He has developed another talent: he paints. His friends are regular recipients of Berlin oils, which are naïve in style, often humorous, and completely charming.

"There's a current story about Irving that I think is darling," said Robert Russell Bennett. "You know, Irving has a little granddaughter who's in school, and she had to write a paper. She wrote 'An Afternoon with My Grandfather.' The teacher asked her, 'Who *is* your grandfather?' And she, drawing herself up to her full height, which isn't much, said, 'Irving Berlin is my grandfather.'

"And he said, 'Irving Berlin? What does *he* do?'

"And Irving's granddaughter said, 'He *paints!*' "

Coda

Fifteen-odd years have whizzed past since the days when the late Bernard Herrmann, a major composer and conductor, somewhat gloomily predicted to me that the future of American popular music would probably relegate the works of Messrs. Gershwin, Berlin, Kern, Rodgers & Hart, Porter, et al., to the status of *leider*. In those dark days of over-amplified rock, back in 1972, such a vision of Bernie's seemed quite probable, and it was not easy to imagine quite clearly a world in which, as in Ray Bradbury's *Farenheit 451*, gallant individuals would tomorrow stroll from person to person, humming, singing, and chanting songs such as the eighteen extra Noel Coward choruses of Porter's "Let's Do It," Larry Hart's verse to "Ship Without A Sail" say, or the Styne-Sondheim song "Little Lamb," which was cut from "Gypsy," etc., in an effort to keep our treasures alive for generations to come.

But it hasn't turned out that way.

In fact, there is good news. Very good news.

Open up your ears, and you're bound to hear it.

On this warm and lovely day in May, 1986 (appropriately it is Mr. Irving Berlin's 98th birthday, and God bless *him*, as well as America), the works of the wonderful coterie of songwriting talents whose careers are celebrated in this book are thriving. We may, alas, have lost their physical presence—far too many of them have departed–but to cite the words of the late Abe Burrows, "They done it!" Daily, hourly, we are surrounded with the visible and aural evidence of their accomplishments. Gresham's Law—bad music drives out good—seems to have been rewritten.

Consider. On Broadway, in the past decade or so, which is where it all began, we have had a steady series of revivals. *Sweet Charity*, with its terrific Dorothy Fields' lyrics, set to Cy Coleman's marvelous music, just opened to raves and is doing excellent business. Down the street, there is that long-running perennial, *42nd Street*. And even the late Harry Warren, who petulantly re-minded me of his constant anonymity over all those years he was turning out hits with Messrs. Dubin, Mack Gordon and Johnny Mercer, would be pleased to know that his Broadway melodies are being played and sung tonight and every night all over the world, eight performances a week. Mr. Sondheim's *Sweeney Todd* has now been added to the permanent list of productions uptown at Lincoln Center, in the opera, yet! Plans are in the making for a major revival at the New York State Theatre this coming season for *South Pacific*. Down at the Kennedy Center, there will shortly be a revival of *Carousel*. The late great Yul Brynner broke box-office records everywhere with *The King and I*, and Anthony Quinn is doing the same with *Zorba*.

Let us also call the roll of some of the other musical successes of the past decade on Broadway: the works of the great Duke Ellington, as brought to us in *Sophisticated Ladies;* Mr. Fats Waller's catalogue of songs, brought so bril-liantly back to permanent life in *Ain't Misbehavin'*. *Sugar Babies*, with Mickey Rooney and Ann Miller celebrating the songs of Jimmy McHugh and his friends, has been selling out everywhere for the past four or five seasons. There's also *Eubie, Bubbling Brown Sugar*, and *One Mo' Time*, to commemorate black pop music. And we must not overlook the constantly rewarding yearly collection of musical comedy revivals by Kern, Youmans, Friml, Porter, DeSylva, Brown and Henderson, et al., mounted each year at the Goodspeed Opera House in Had-dam, Connecticut. And we are being treated each season to more and more "concert" versions of light opera by Victor Herbert, Hammerstein, Harbach and all the rest, and to vest-pocket "revivals" of hitherto lost or buried-away librettos, and scores of '20s and '30s musicals. The archeology of American popular music is a thriving process, thank goodness.

True, we may have lost dear Ira Gershwin, but it's also very clear, his and George's songs are here to stay, so long as there's an Ella Fitzgerald, a Lena Horne or a Sara Vaughn to chant or croon them to us. Harold Arlen has departed, but he's not the man who got away, not when a Liza Minelli or a Peggy Lee or a Margaret Whiting is standing up there reminding us of his wonderful melodies. Mr. Mercer may have crossed his moon river in style, but we've got Mel Torme, Blossom Dearie, and Sylvia Simms who will continue to accentuate the positive and eliminate the negative, night after night, so obviously Mr. Mercer was doing something right, wasn't he?

Be of good cheer. After years of being ignored by the major recording companies, Tony Bennett is back with his original parent, Columbia Records, and is also performing on the stage of Radio City Music Hall. In years when any other singer might be chanting "The September Song," Frank Sinatra, the Chair-man of the Board, is still selling out any and every time he chooses to sing Cole

Porter or Rodgers and Hart. He, and other great singers such as Rosemary Clooney, Cleo Laine, and all the others cited above, are, like Porter's best French champagne, so good for the brain!

Night after night, it gets better for our side. Miss Barbra Streisand has returned to the scene of her former triumphs, American musical comedy, and has delivered herself a million seller record with great arrangements by Peter Matz which features great songs by our greatest composers and lyricists. She's not only back atop the sales charts, but she has made a liar out of all those cynics who insisted that while Steve Sondheim is a tasteful genius, he doesn't know how to write "commercial" hits. On Miss S.'s latest million-odd-seller are Mr. Sondheim's "Send In The Clowns," an easy choice, perhaps, but how about taking "The Ladies Who Lunch" from *Company* and "Pretty Women" from *Sweeney Todd* and turning them into a *double* hit?

Oh yes, and let us not overlook the "cross-overs" the remarkable phenomena of performers moving from one field of success to achieve it in another. Take, for example, country-and-western star Willie Nelson, who's been selling zillions of records all over the landscape with an unlikely (only in retrospect) choice of material, Irving Berlin's 1926 hit, "Blue Skies." And he's been digging out similar classic ballads ever since.

And how about Miss Linda Ronstadt, who left rock-and-roll behind to join forces with the late, great Nelson Riddle, and to create a smash formula–not one LP but two–on which she has brought us lovely versions of Styne and Cahn, Berlin, Gershwin, and the rest, and once again proved wrong those pessimistic characters who've been singing the blues for all those years, and warning us that the so-called golden age of America's popular music was dead, dead, dead, buried deep amidst a sea of cacaphony from deafening 32-track arrangements, perpetrated by an army equipped with boom-boxes.

And there was that Dutch chap, Taco, three years back, who decided to call back "Puttin' On The Ritz" in the style of the roaring '20s, and re-created that sound. Smash. Woody Herman out touring somewhere tonight. Benny Goodman playing retrospective concerts. Smash. Jo Sullivan Loesser doing a one-woman performance of her late husband Frank's great catalogue. Smash. The revival of Lerner and Loewe's *Brigadoon* at Lincoln Center this past winter. Sold out. Bobby Short, playing and singing at the Carlyle tonight. Try to get in, but be warned, it won't be easy. Steve Ross, who's been touring the great hotels of the world, with his program of tasteful songs from practically everyone you can think of. Booked far in advance, as is Michael Feinstein, who specializes in Gershwin. Want to drop by the Oak Room of the Algonquin tonight to hear Julie Wilson do her remarkable one-hour tribute to Irving Berlin, with Billy Roy's expert assistance at the piano? Call ahead; reservations are a must.

In other words, it's a pleasure to report—as he would have been the first to applaud it—that Bernie Herrmann's crystal ball was clouded. Very very clouded. What's obviously happened is that the pendulum of American taste has swung backwards, away from cacaphony and rock, and we are returning, thank heaven—our blue heaven—to the era of the well-made song. The giants I celebrated in this book, and their songs—*our* songs—have become an integral part of our lives, and so long as we have LP's, cassettes, compact discs, or whatever sound systems the Japanese wizards are concocting for us, they're going to remain giants.

A sweeping statement? I don't think so. Try imagining Easter without Mr.

Berlin's parade, Christmas without his annual blanket of white, a pretty girl without his melody, stepping out without his white tie and tails, or dancing without her cheek to your cheek. Impossible. And the same applies for life without the night and day of Cole Porter, or a world without *Porgy and Bess*, or anything by Jerome Kern, or Rodgers and Hammerstein and/or Hart. And which generation is growing up without travelling over Mr. Arlen's rainbow, to the wonderful words of the late, great "Yip" Harburg (who told us he'd whittled his wit, and whipped his rhymes, for a small obit in The New York Times)?

We shall cherish them all, and continue to be exhilarated by their works.

Leave it to Mr. Berlin, as always, to find the precise words with which to describe the state of things (remember, he said it with music for almost sixty years). He has one particular ballad which cautions us to remember . . . "An Old Fashioned Song Always Is New."

Believe it.

It doesn't pay to argue with Irving Berlin.

And now that we've got the good news out, let's sit back and compile a list of the songwriters and lyricists who belong in the *next* volume.

Shall we sit down beside the piano and meet and talk with Jerry Herman, John Kander, and Fred Ebb, and . . .

You name them, we'll get to them.

—May 12, 1986